The Energy Syndrome

The Energy Syndrome

**Comparing National
Responses to the
Energy Crisis**

Edited by
Leon N. Lindberg
The University of Wisconsin-Madison

Lexington Books
D.C. Heath and Company
Lexington, Massachusetts
Toronto

Library of Congress Cataloging in Publication Data

Main entry under title:
    The Energy syndrome.

    Includes index.
    1. Energy policy—Addresses, essays, lectures. 2. Petroleum industry and trade—Addresses, essays, lectures. I. Lindberg, Leon N.
    HD9502.A2E552   333.7   76-6772
    ISBN 0-669-00662-9

Published simultaneously in Canada.

Printed in the United States of America.

International Standard Book Number: 0-669-00662-9

Library of Congress Catalog Card Number: 76-6772

Contents

Foreword

This volume is devoted to a cross-national comparison of national policy responses to the energy crisis and their implications for society. It is neither the first study of the impact of the oil shortage on the international system, nor is it likely to be the last! Dozens of books and hundreds of articles—some of them significant in scope and intellectual content—have dealt with a variety of aspects of the subject. Many make recommendations on how to handle or come to terms with the new situation. Such universal concern on the part of policymakers, journalists, and scholars was, of course, prompted by the joint action of OPEC, which, in 1973, suddenly revealed to the public how dependent industrial society is on cheap oil provided by a handful of developing countries. In fact, however, the oil embargo and the four-fold increase in price which followed, were only the dramatic events revealing a broader and more fundamental set of issues that involved the life styles and value systems of a civilization based on continuing growth and increased consumption. Awareness that the world's resources are finite came slowly. Deep-seated patterns of behavior and well-established national and international institutions had to change; but reforms were envisaged with reluctance. Turmoil in the universities in the late 1960s was only one symptom of the painful transition to the post-industrial era. In spite of early warnings, a slumbering and complacent Western world awoke with a start in October 1973. The problems had become tangible. Indeed, they required urgent attention. Among the analysts there were, as usual, the prophets of doom and the eternal optimists. The case was made for the oil-rich or for the oil-poor, for the East or for the West. Economists and strategists, political scientists and technicians all had their word to say; thus, literature on the subject has on the whole been partisan, sectoral, regional, or national.

The contribution of the present study lies in the fact that the authors have deliberately chosen a global and interdisciplinary approach. They have attempted, on the one hand, to include in their purview technical, social, economic, and institutional considerations; on the other hand, they have not adopted the vantage point of any of the main actors while looking at the implications of the crisis for each one of them. The goal was ambitious; if it has been only partly attained the effort will have been worthwhile.

As a point of historical interest it should be mentioned that this study originated at two successive meetings: the first held in 1972 under the auspices of the Maison des sciences de l'homme and the Tavistock Institute and hosted by Electricité de France at Bréau-sans-Nappe, and the second organized by the European Centre of the Carnegie Endowment, at La Mainaz, France, in the Spring of 1973—both before the outbreak of the crisis. Work was continued under the auspices of the newly established Centre for Research on International Organizations in Geneva by a small coordinating group consisting of Leon

x

Lindberg, Hasan Ozbekhan, Ignacy Sachs and Jean Siotis. Research and meetings were made possible by a grant from the European Cultural Foundation in the Netherlands, to which the Centre wishes to express its profound gratitude. Material help and assistance have also been forthcoming from the Maison des Sciences de l'homme, the University of Wisconsin and the Electricité de France. The latter institution not only made a major substantive contribution through its director of studies, M. Louis Puiseux and his colleagues, but also hosted the international working sessions in its very pleasant Conference Centre at Bréau-sans-Nappe. The atmosphere created there by the staff was favorable to the development of a real team spirit which characterized the work of the group.

It is unlikely that the project would have got under way had it not been for the drive and imagination of Leon Lindberg; without his patience and persever-ance as responsible editor, the book would certainly not have seen the light of day. The Centre is also greatly indebted to the authors of each of the case studies that appear in this volume. Not only have they devoted their time unstintingly to the preparation of this volume, but they all readily accepted the general pattern proposed by the coordinating group. The final product bene-fitted considerably from comments and suggestions made by participants at the two meetings held at Bréau-sans-Nappe, namely: Hayward R. Alker, Jacques Auger, Göran Bäckstrand, A. Barrière, Etienne Bauer, R. De Bauw, Francis Bonnet, Irwin Bupp, B. Cabanal, Jean-Paul Ceron, Jean-Paul Chauvet, Pierre Daures, Jean-Claude Derian, István Dobozi, Joseph El Zoghbi, David Fischer, John Friend, Alain Frigère, John Goormaghtigh, Jean-Charles Hourcade, Siri Kalnins (Mrs.), William Kapp, Yannis Katsaouinis, Didier Kauffmann, Robert Keith, Serge Kolm, Leon N. Lindberg, Mans Lönnroth, Jean-Marie Martin, Horst Meixner, Klaus Meyer-Abich, Francisco Miéres, François Moisan, Hasan Oz-bekhan, John de B. Pollard, Louis Puiseux, Albert Robin, Philippe Roqueplo, Ignacy Sachs, Zdziaslaw Sadowski, Francisco Sagasti, T.L. Sankar, Dominique Saumon, Jean Siotis, J. de Smit, John Steinhart, A.J. Surrey, and Robert Villeneuve.

All those connected with this venture will, I am sure, have benefitted from the common experience; we trust that readers will find their own experience rewarding as well.

Geneva, November 15, 1976 *John Goormaghtigh*
Director, Centre for Research
on International Institutions

Editor's Preface

The general thesis of this book is that there are important obstacles standing in the way of the efforts of industrial societies to respond to the short- and long-term implications of rising energy prices and the prospects of eventual depletion of some energy resources. National policies are characterized by what we term *the energy syndrome*—a group of symptoms that occur together and that describe a pathology or system malfunction. These symptoms include: production and consumption practices that require steady increases in energy supply; public policies that are dominated by the perspectives of energy producers and that are almost exclusively oriented to meeting exogenously determined demands for energy; and an interacting set of political, institutional, and structural obstacles that constrain the search for alternative policies.

This *syndrome* represents a complex of lags and rigidities that frustrates the supposed rationalizing capacities of planners, of market mechanisms, or of incremental pluralistic decision processes. In the absence of a more optimal response, national policies seem locked in an energy policy trajectory that promises economic instability, political centralization and conflict, and heightened international tensions. If these policy lags and structural rigidities are to be overcome, they must be made explicit objects of policy, and this presupposes systematic understanding of their nature and dynamics. This book represents an effort to contribute to such an understanding.

The authors and I have chosen quite self-consciously not to assume a posture of value neutrality. The analysis is premised on a conceptualization of the role of the public policy analyst that assumes the necessity of going beyond the interests and perceptions of the actors involved. Our own evaluative framework is made explicit in the introductory chapter. It guides our judgments of national policy experiences, and animates our search for explanatory factors and for proposals for policy intervention. On the other hand, the descriptions and empirical analyses will, we think, stand on their own merits.

In addition to the authors and those others listed in the Foreword, I want personally to acknowledge the help of a number of friends and colleagues who commented in detail on various versions of my introductory and concluding chapters. Special thanks go to Hugh Heclo, Ernst B. Haas, Andrew Martin, Theodore Marmor, Peter Katzenstein, Robert Alford, John Woolley, Martha Caldwell, Jeff Hammarlund, Lawrence Scheinman, Alberta Sbragia, David Tarr, Matthew Holden, Bernard C. Cohen, Lawrence Krause, Denis Hayes, Michael Leavitt, Joy Dunkerley, and John Steinhart.

Beatrice R. Lindberg translated the French chapter into English and toiled long hours to produce some harmonization among the diverse literary styles of contributors from seven different nationalities. To her we all express our admiration and gratitude.

Washington, D.C.   *Leon N. Lindberg*
January 1, 1977

The Energy Syndrome

1

The Energy Crisis: A Political Economy Perspective

Leon N. Lindberg

The energy crisis reached the front pages of the world press during the Arab oil boycott of 1973-74 when oil prices quadrupled and supplies were threatened. However, it had been in the making for a long time. After the Second World War, industrialized and industrializing countries alike developed patterns of energy consumption that, as we can now see, led directly to the present situation in which political and economic stability are threatened by overreliance on vulnerable and increasingly costly energy supplies. This evolution was rooted in a common set of assumptions about the desirability of economic growth, the virtues of a "liberal" international trade system, the future availability and price of energy, and associated patterns of consumption and resource use. In other words, the energy crisis must be seen not as a random external impingement upon an otherwise rational policy world, but as the unanticipated outcome of deliberate decisions and nondecisions of public and private actors and of the routine functioning of economic and political institutions.

This book examines in some detail the shape energy policies have taken over time in seven different countries: Britain, Canada, France, Hungary, India, Sweden, and the United States. It has four principle objectives:

1. To provide a comparative view of how and why strikingly similar patterns of energy consumption and supply developed in the postwar period;
2. To describe the typical problem perceptions, governmental policies, patterns of private-public sector relationships, and organizational forms and routines that developed in all these countries during this period;
3. To analyze the extent to which these consumption and supply patterns, policies and perceptions, and structures and processes have fostered or impeded the development of new energy policies more suited to the changing conditions ushered in by the oil embargo, the OPEC price actions, and the subsequent rapid escalation of the price of all forms of energy;
4. To provide a framework for the evaluation of the likely future consequences of the present trajectory of national energy policies and to suggest in what ways lessons of relevance for the design of alternative policies and institutional arrangements might be extracted from a comparative analysis of the policy experience of these seven countries.

Our focus in this book on national energy policy and policy making does not imply a denial that energy is basically an international problem for which

1

the optimal solution is international. Indeed, this volume is the first product of a three-year program of research undertaken by a group of scholars and planners from more than a dozen countries whose basic assumption is that the energy crisis reflects a fundamental restructuring of the international political economy that will require new international rules and regimes, as well as income and resource transfers.

But whether this transition to a new international order will be managed successfully depends on the actions and inactions of governments. The energy crisis as we now know it is a pattern of international petroleum interdependence, which has developed over the past several decades, and oligopolistic control over prices and production by a relatively small number of oil producing countries. What the energy crisis *becomes* will depend above all on the future policy responses to that situation by decisionmakers in nations that are heavy users of energy, especially net petroleum importers.

The case studies gathered together here not only tell us a great deal about the past. They will also provide the base for a *tentative* estimate of how policymakers are likely to respond in the future and of how constrained those responses will be. Our projections will be tentative because these complex matters depend on a great many contingent factors (technological developments, price movements, overall political and economic conditions, the political cohesion of OPEC, and so forth) and because our analyses must be based on the *past trajectory* of energy policies. We cannot avoid basing our conjectures about the most likely future on some kind of extrapolation and understanding of the past. The natural objections that can be mounted against this procedure can be softened in three ways.

First, we have reviewed the evolution of policy over thirty years, which is a substantial period of time. These years have seen several critical changes in both the environment of policy and in relevant technologies. The continuities across such changes are most revealing, especially the ways in which the direction of energy policies did not change even with the stimuli of 1973-74. Second, we have examined the experience of nations with very different energy resource endowments, varying degrees of import dependency, different levels of economic development, different types of political and economic systems, and contrasting elite ideologies and values. To the extent that particular factors appear systematically as causes or consequences in nations as different as these, we will be more confident of their explanatory (and predictive) powers. Finally, we have rooted our analyses in general propositions drawn from political and organizational theories of the determinants of public policy outcomes. Hence, we can claim to provide the basis for a systematic comparison of the dynamics of energy policy choices with choices in other policy areas of like internal and external characteristics. Once again, our confidence in our findings and forecasts will be enhanced to the extent that our conclusions about factors inhibiting change and making for policy continuity are founded in such theories and in interpolicy comparisons.

The remainder of this chapter will introduce the reader to certain common perspectives on energy policy analysis and evaluation that underlie the book as a whole. It will provide a necessary background for the seven case studies of energy policy making in different nations and for the effort in the concluding comparative chapters to generalize about present and future policies, their structural determinants, and strategies for policy and institutional reform. This chapter first spells out what we take to be the contours of energy policy as a problem area: How shall we define *energy policy* and *energy crisis*? What makes a *rational* evaluation of energy policy options particularly difficult for the policymaker and policy analyst alike? What policy criteria appear to dominate policy making? What criteria do we feel are ultimately most important? On the basis of these criteria, this chapter then outlines a scenario of the medium-term future that is a plausible and imaginable extrapolation of past and present trends in national energy policies. This outline will serve to specify in some detail what we consider to be the stakes of energy policy and to explain why the chief thrust of the analyses to follow is essentially critical. Finally, this chapter describes the specific questions in common that the authors of each of the case studies were asked to address as well as the "quasi-experimental" research design that provides the basis for the comparative analysis that concludes the book.

Energy Crisis and Energy Policy

The term *energy crisis* is used variously and loosely, and not surprisingly, a good deal of confusion has been created about what *crisis* actually means, what is in crisis, and whether there is one crisis or many. What problem(s) is policy supposed to address? Is the problem the scarcity of supply or the vulnerability of supply? Or is it the rising cost of energy resources as an important cause of the worldwide inflation and recession of 1974-76? Or is the crisis defined by an "excessive" demand for energy, or by widespread habits of energy waste? Is it a crisis of international interdependence with ominous implications for increased military and economic conflict? Should the crisis be understood as a "crisis of capitalism," or of industrial society more generally? Of course, it may be all of these things, and that is why energy policy is distinctively problematic as a policy area.

Definitions of the crisis and of energy policy objectives also depend on the temporal and national perspective of the policymaker (or the policy analyst). These perspectives change over time as perceptions of issues and uncertainties evolve. Thus, for decisionmakers in Japan and Western Europe, the energy crisis in 1973-74 was preeminently the interruption of oil supplies from the Middle East, which created real shortages and revealed a crucial strategic vulnerability. It has since become primarily a problem of higher oil prices and the resulting economic recession. For the United States, the energy crisis has been primarily a problem of foreign policy, involving Israel, relations with Western Europe, the future of NATO, detente, and so forth, but it is fast becoming a problem of supply vulnerability as the United States is more and more dependent on imported oil in spite of the boycott of 1973-74 and in spite of Project Independence. The U.S. recession seems due more to restrictive fiscal and monetary policies than to energy prices. Indeed, the increase in prices was seen by many Europeans as a net advantage to the United States, not only from the point of view of the American-owned oil companies, but also because of its impact on the American competitive position relative to Western Europe and Japan.

A similar confusion surrounds the concept of *energy policy*. The chapters that follow will confirm that most policymakers and policy analysts have traditionally defined energy policy as having to do with government and industry activities relative to the several stages (prospecting, mining, refining, transforming, transporting, marketing, and research and development) of the *supply* of the various forms of energy (coal, natural gas, petroleum, electricity) needed for individual and collective consumption and for industrial production. Increasingly, however, the boundaries of energy policy are expanding to include:

The environmental and safety effects of producing and consuming energy;

The capital requirements of various energy options and the complex interrelationships among economic growth, energy consumption, and income and wealth distribution;

The implications of various energy supply technologies for the structure of economic and political power within nations;

The implications of existing and proposed patterns of energy production and consumption for national power and security, for international conflict, and for the future evolution of an increasingly interdependent global political and economic system.

How one defines what is problematic about energy and how one evaluates the performance of the policy process with regard to energy depends, of course, on the level of conceptualization chosen. In principle at least, most policymakers and policy analysts would subscribe to some notion of "rationality" as a measure of policy performance. What is generally meant by rationality can be summarized as follows: Competing interests and values are balanced or integrated; alternative outcomes are analyzed and evaluated systematically to take account of uncertainty. New information relevant to the underlying definition of the problem is integrated into explicit causal inferences, which then become the basis for changes in policy.[1]

Developing a "rational" public policy towards *energy supply* narrowly conceived is probably seldom achieved by most nations for a variety of technological, political, and bureaucratic reasons. But it is not too difficult to achieve fairly widespread agreement among the politically relevant actors on what policy *criteria* should be applied. This observation seems to be a fair reading of the policy record that is presented in the case studies that follow, but this record also makes clear that no such consensus is possible when the policy boundaries expand. Not only do we find that policy and institutional responses that appear to be adaptive to the needs of guaranteeing some given level of energy supply may have adverse consequences for the environment, for economic welfare, or for the distribution of power nationally and internationally; more fundamentally, such policies and the institutional arrangements and public-private power networks they imply may actively obstruct the development of energy policies rooted in criteria of environmental quality, economic welfare and equality, and the overall structure of the political economy. Thus, policies that are "rational" (in Steinbrunner's terms) from one perspective may be profoundly "irrational" from another.

Evaluating Energy Policy

One possible conclusion from the foregoing is that it is not at all surprising that collectivities as complex as modern nations cannot meet criteria for policy coherence and rationality in an issue area like energy. Energy is both too sweeping (lifestyles, development styles) and too circumscribed (growth, profits, jobs requiring that energy needs be met) to become an explicit object of policy in its own right. Truly "coherent" policies may exist in the idealized world of the policy analyst, but not in the real world of competing values and interests, imperfect information, and constrained governmental power. Organizational survival, short-run crisis management, limited consensus on *some* policy among multiple disagreeing actors, the "art of the possible" are all more suitable and viable policy performance criteria than elusive "higher-level" conceptions of analytically rational policy processes or policy outcomes.

Such a position would be sensible, realistic and above all, reassuring, but this is not the evaluative posture that underlies this volume. The following chapters will show that supply-side criteria and definitions of the problem have so far dominated agenda setting and the substance of policy. This situation reflects, among other things, the political power of a relatively small number of corporations and agencies sharing an immediate financial interest in or intellectually committed to maintaining or expanding energy consumption. The ability to define the criteria on the basis of which policy options are generated and evaluated is a critical element in the politics of energy policy. But we feel that the present dominant criteria and the political coalitions responsible for them are too narrow and unidimensional to provide the basis for a desirable or politically viable long-term policy towards energy.

Two rationales underlie this view. First, it is important to affirm that energy is one of the foundations of the modern industrial state. Economic growth and economic stability depend critically on the availability of energy. No resource can be exploited without energy. All forms of energy production are capital intensive and require an infrastructure of production, transmission, and consumption that heavily influences overall economic structures. The relative price of energy is a strong determinant of which types of agricultural production will be economically viable, of the pattern of industrial development and the direction of innovation in production technology, of land use, residential patterns and urban forms, and of the spatial distribution of jobs. The more energy intensive an economy becomes, the more difficult it will be to change the energy consumption pattern without long lags and major social and political dislocations. Energy is thus a critical planning variable in economic development. The control of energy supply—production, information, rate of exploitation, research, and development—is an immensely powerful lever of influence over the pattern of production, employment, allocation, and income and wealth distribution.

Secondly, the production and consumption of energy involves an intricate pattern of international flows of resources (petroleum, natural gas, coal, uranium) and associated flows of technology, information, money, arms, and trade. These flows imply complex and changing patterns of international interdependence.[2] Nations that are net importers of energy find themselves increasingly vulnerable to the actions of producers (embargoes, price uncertainties, investments of oil revenues). Since energy enters into every sector of production as a vital input, a substantial reduction or disruption in its availability not only threatens to paralyze large sectors of the economy and to transform the routines of industrial societies, but also makes them extremely vulnerable militarily. Exporting countries gain new sources of power and control and also develop a new stake in the economic life, relative prosperity, and the trading relationships of net importing countries. All are locked into an increasingly sensitive network of exchange with a very high potential for conflict and malfunction. An ever broader range of the policies of any given nation are affected by those of other nations and in ever more decisive ways.

The normal response of national policymakers to such vulnerability is to seek to regain autonomous control by decreasing the scope of interdependence. But this approach can be costly, if not impossible, and efforts in this direction may prove to be counterproductive, for interdependence develops precisely because of issues that lie beyond the control of any one nation and require a common or negotiated response. According to Nazli Choucri, the policy paradox of energy interdependence is that

... any effective allocation of authority cannot be done unilaterally. Yet any successful coordination of behavior can only be undertaken in the belief that it enhances national autonomy. Only through the pursuit of autonomy is coordination possible politically, and only through coordination can disputes over control be resolved.[3]

Policymakers in energy-importing and -exporting countries alike are thus confronted with the problem of developing "a harmonious basis for the joint management of an asymmetrical economic interdependence." This solution will require operational rules of behavior to accommodate divergent assessments of the situation, competing national objectives, and the mounting redistributive claims of the countries in the developing world.

For these reasons, we believe that evaluating energy policies and policy making from a broader political economy standpoint is imperative. This view implies that our criteria should derive from some overall conception of a desirable strategy of economic and political development at both national and international levels. Consequently, we will treat energy policy choices as indivisible from choices and preferences involving overall economic activity and distribution, the structure of the political economy itself, the uses of national power, and the direction of change in the international system.

The implications of such a perspective on energy policy will be brought out in the scenario to be presented below. There we make explicit what appear to us to be the principal consequences of the present supply-dominated national energy policies when evaluated in such broad political economy and structural terms. It may be called a "worst-case" scenario. But we feel that the analyses of national policy that we have made indicate that the dynamics described *are* the presently dominant ones in the global system. We do not claim that the policies that impel us in these directions cannot be changed, or that they *must* have the consequences to be spelled out below. What we present is a conjecture and not a prediction. It is, in the words of Bertrand de Jouvenel, an "intellectual construction of a likely future."[4] It describes "those descendants of the present state" that now seem "plausible and imaginable" and spells out relevant causal relations and intervening triggering facts. Such a construction is "art" and not science and should be evaluated in terms of its ability to stimulate inquiry and debate. Its chief purpose will be to define what is at stake in energy policy as we see it.

The argument presented here seeks to evaluate the implications of three trends that seem central to the established energy policies of most countries. These trends are (1) the increasing cost of energy and its likely impact on general economic activity; (2) the economic and political centralization that is implied in most proposed energy systems; and (3) the potential for international conflict that is inherent in the prevailing pattern of national energy policies.

The policy analysis stance we have adopted does not identify the energy problem with decisionmakers' perceptions of that problem. It goes without saying that an understanding of how policy elites perceive problems is central to an understanding of why they do what they do, but our focus is as much on the problems policymakers cause for others as on the problems they themselves face.

Energy as a Policy Problem

It seems clear that the failure of energy policies (as well as economic policy or social policy) to meet public expectations of them is not due so much to insufficient decisional or technological capacities as to disagreements about the criteria whereby policies are made and judged, to uncertainty, and to the multiplication of interested constituencies. In the terms employed by modern decision and organizational theorists seeking to understand apparent tendencies toward policy failure or "overload" in modern industrial societies, energy policy shares in quintessential degree three characteristics of an ideal type "complex and interactive policy problem."

1. *Many values are affected by any decision or policy, and there are increasingly complicated tradeoff relations among the values.* "Supposedly external factors seem integral to the prospects of any particular policy just as any given policy imposes externalities vitally affecting other areas."[5] Because of increasing differentiation and reciprocal interdependence among sectors of modern society and because multiple value systems operate within each sector, the boundaries of public policy problems have an increased tendency to expand. Integrating values is also becoming more difficult because the earlier cultural homogeneity, that spanned most sectors and was based on the norms of industrial and commercial life, no longer exists.[6] Policymakers must cope with increasingly difficult political problems in achieving consensus or value integration. As Hugh Heclo puts it:

As policy boundaries expand, government bureaucracies cannot mandate the cooperation required for effective programs. They must depend more and more on a mutual "sense of the situation" among government authorities, private groups, and individual citizens—an ability to see the connections among things, expenditure and taxes, benefits and costs, personal claims and social side effects.[7]

It would be hard to imagine an area of public policy more subject to these dimensions of complexity than energy. Energy transitions (wood and wind to coal, coal to petroleum, petroleum to ?) have always been concomitants of profound societal transformations,[8] but governments have rarely been called upon to deal explicitly with energy policy at this level. Today a complex of political, social, and technological trends makes such a radical expansion of policy boundaries inevitable, and the externalities and tradeoffs that confront the policymaker have proliferated. Postwar energy shortages led to the policy objective of expanding coal supply. This objective was subsequently extended to incorporate petroleum and nuclear energy as the potential of these resources became obvious, and tradeoffs emerged between sustaining a domestic coal industry and speeding an oil-based growth, which implied reliance on overseas sources. Nations then attempted to develop coordinated fuel supply policies covering research and development allocations, pricing policies, and the like. With the 1973 boycott the policy boundary was suddenly expanded again to *energy*—a concept implicitly incorporating demand and international and security dimensions and leading to a new and complex set of tradeoffs. The economic crisis that ensued rapidly forced upon one and all the realization that energy policy has profound implications for price, employment, and economic growth policy. Awareness of higher prices, impending shortages and continued international vulnerability now begin to highlight the extent to which energy policy is inseparable from development policy writ large and from the evolution of economic and political structures, cultures, lifestyles, the human and the natural environment at national and international levels.

2. *Policy making is carried out under conditions of increasing uncertainty that make difficult evaluating the available alternatives or even knowing whether all the possible alternatives have been taken into account.* Policymakers in firms, governments, and other organizations see the possibilities inherent in an advancing technology for "altering the world around them or augmenting their role in it" and are led to intervene on an increasing scale in socioeconomic systems. Policy interdependence and value uncertainty impel them in the same direction. However, they do not possess adequate causal knowledge about the behavior of these systems or their interactions with the ecosystem; nor can they accurately gauge the impact of their own interventions.[9]

Uncertainty is clearly an important factor in error and miscalculation in energy policy. Nations have erred repeatedly in estimating supplies, forecasting consumption, costs, the rates and impacts of technological innovation, and the intentions of other countries. Uncertainty has led them to a "normal" state of reactive policy making in response to surprise or crisis. This uncertainty is rooted in the distribution of natural resources; in the state of our knowledge about these resources; in the control of this knowledge; in the uncharted terrain of potential alternative technologies; in our limited knowledge about the health, environmental, and security implications of these technologies; in the poorly understood relationship between energy and economic growth; in the incredibly complex interactions between energy and political power, both domestic and international; and in the political conflicts spawned by the growing awareness of the awesome stakes of energy policy. The impact of uncertainty is especially pernicious in view of the very long lead times and massive amounts of capital required by most energy infrastructure investments. Governments invariably must act on the basis of incomplete and probably erroneous information, and once decisions are taken they are very difficult to reverse.

Uncertainties have been rife with regard to existing energy supplies. What are the "known" reserves? What is "estimated" to exist? What is the discovery rate? What new finds can be anticipated in as yet unexplored regions? What prices are "necessary" to encourage exploration and technological innovation? What will secondary and tertiary recovery or productivity innovations yield, and at what cost? What credence can be given to estimates of resources, almost all of which depend upon information provided by private companies or producer countries?

Estimating the growth and composition of future demand has been equally difficult. Regression techniques based on historical relationships have proven grossly unreliable. The relationship between GNP and energy consumption varies widely. Little is known about energy elasticities of demand or about the efficiency gains that could actually be realized by regulatory policies or by one or another form of incentive or disincentive.

Technological options with regard to nonfossil fuels present a host of severe uncertainties and have given rise to intensely contradictory expert opinion. Uncertainty reaches a peak when establishing grounds for determining the validity or credibility of information becomes nearly impossible. We are acutely aware that knowledge and information are rarely neutral or separable from vested interests or established orthodoxies. Nowhere is this more the case than with nuclear energy. Massive investments and perhaps irreversible decisions have been made before technological problems have been solved and cost implications assessed. Furthermore, surprisingly little is known about health hazards, accident incidence, the likelihood of terrorism, the consequences of proliferation, the techniques for waste disposal, or the political and institutional requirements of a nuclear economy. We lack the information and systematic understanding to compare the feasibility, desirability, and relative costs of a nuclear versus a coal versus a solar future, and yet policymakers everywhere act resolutely (which perhaps they must) as if these were calculations based on reliable knowledge.

3. *The power to determine policy decisions and affect outcomes is increasingly dispersed among separate individual actors and ever more complex organizational units.*[10] This characteristic is one consequence of policy interdependence, value uncertainty, the application of technology, and the scope and scale of governmental intervention. But it may also be brought about independently through institutional changes or processes of political mobilization that expand the political arena to actors who were previously excluded from or inactive in policy making. Because this clearly complicates the policymaker's task, it is not surprising that great effort is made to limit participation and mobilization. This political dimension of complexity is particularly striking in the energy field, where the crisis was triggered by the emergence of a new actor, OPEC, and where national policies are increasingly challenged by newly mobilized environmental groups or by citizens opposed to the installation of nuclear reactors in their area.

Coherent policy is difficult to achieve when the actors involved are numerous and the organizations complex and when they are likely to differ on what the problem is, what weight should be given to different values, and how major uncertainties should be resolved. In all countries, energy policies involve a bargaining and exchange process among a multitude of actors that is orchestrated in some fashion by complex governmental bureaucracies that are themselves a congeries of more or less loosely articulated agencies with a variety of tasks and definitions of the situation. Government acts simultaneously (or different agencies do) as consumer, producer, broker, regulator, and promoter. In so doing, various state agencies form more or less stable alliances with "outside" industrial, professional, or special interest groups that lead them to different policy positions.

A "Worst Case" Scenario

Three trends characterizing the energy policies of most countries have already been mentioned: rising energy prices and their negative effects on growth and employment, energy systems that imply and require economic and political centralization, and national policies that exacerbate international conflicts. Here these trends are projected forward in a scenario that places special emphasis on structural factors and forces making for lags and rigidities in the capacities of economic and political systems to respond optimally to changes in the price and availability of energy supplies.[a] It is a "worst-case" scenario because it focuses on what is likely to happen if these lags and rigidities are as important as we postulate them to be. Hopefully, the confident assumptions of most economists and energy analysts with regard to the rationalizing capacities of the market and political decisionmakers will be borne out. We are inclined to be skeptical that this will be the case *unless* the lags and rigidities themselves are made explicit objects of policy. What these lags and rigidities are and how they constrain policy response will be analyzed in detail in Chapter 9, and Chapter 10 will examine some policy strategies for dealing with them. The likely consequences of a failure to address them directly is suggested by what follows below.

Energy Consumption and Economic Activity

The general contours of the debate over the relationship between economic growth and energy consumption are well known. There is no denying that there

---

[a]A much more elaborate and fully documented version of a similar scenario was published in December 1976 by the Center for the Study of International Institutions (Geneva) and the Institute for Environmental Studies (University of Wisconsin). It consists of separate chapters on Energy Supply, Energy Demand, International Conflict, Production and Capital Allocation, and The Capitalist State and Energy Policy. See Jeffrey R. Hammarlund and Leon N. Lindberg (eds.), *The Political Economy of Energy Policy: A Projection for Capitalist Society*, Report 70, Institute for Environmental Studies, University of Wisconsin-Madison, December 1976.

has been a historical correlation between rates of growth in GNP and rates of growth in energy consumption:

The higher a nation's income or output is on the current international scale, the higher, in general, is its level of energy consumption; as its GNP rises over time, so does its energy consumption—in close, even if not proportionate, conformity.[11]

On the other hand, as the following chapters will confirm, the relationship is not a constant or rigid one. The energy inputs associated with a given rate of economic growth vary over time and from one country to another, thereby reflecting differences in level of economic development, varying "industry mixes," trends in thermal efficiency, shifts among energy sources, and different national or regional lifestyles (including the spatial organization of human activities). Countries with comparable living standards and GNP per capita can vary dramatically in their levels of energy consumption.[12]

The debate has been over the issue of whether or not and by what means any given country can decide to cut back its energy inputs and still maintain economic growth and full employment. Most official government policy and virtually all energy producers defend the proposition that the relationship between economic growth and energy consumption is, within unspecified bounds, a causal one and that if we want to sustain economic growth, we must assure continued and rising levels of energy use. The contrary proposition holds that the relationship is not necessarily causal and that with proper governmental policy (e.g., conservation, urban planning, industrial development) energy use can be held stable or even decreased without adversely affecting either growth or employment.[13]

The rapid rise in energy prices since 1973 and the prospect that these levels will be maintained and even increase suggest a third proposition: Economic growth, welfare, and employment will be adversely affected *unless* countries cut their marginal intensities of energy consumption so as to limit the cost impact of energy on production and consumption. Most economists will reject this proposition on its face. Some will argue that only a radical reduction or complete cutoff of energy supplies could have this effect—that the cost of energy is too small a proportion of total economic output for even major price increases to have any lasting effect.[14] Others will stress that major changes in relative factor prices will cause manufacturers and consumers to conserve energy and to shift to cheaper factors of production or, if necessary, to change the final composition of production and consumption. Still others will emphasize that efficiency has been improved in the past by technological innovation and that there is no reason not to expect this trend to continue.[15] But evidence is accumulating that casts doubt on these assumptions. Surely there has been little sign in recent years to suggest either that market forces have operated to reduce significantly the reliance of economic output on fixed inputs of energy or that government policy is systematically oriented to conservation and demand management. Quite the contrary. Hence there is sufficient reason to fear that an energy policy developed in terms of energy supply criteria may profoundly exacerbate those forces leading the industrial economies and the world in general into a new period of chronic economic instability.

The 1974-76 experience is a case in point, but the message can easily be misread. The quadrupling of oil prices did have a severe impact on employment and economic activity almost everywhere. Most governments reacted to the inflationary effects of this supply-side shock with deflationary policies that reduced the level of total demand and increased unemployment. On the other hand, by 1976 a general recovery had begun: Inflation rates were down and growth had resumed. The industrial economies apparently had adapted to and absorbed the cost increases. But at what cost—and to whom? A glance at Table 1-1 will show that the burden of domestic adjustment was borne by those who had lost their jobs, primarily blue-collar workers and other groups at the lower end of the income scale. Unemployment rates increased dramatically in 1975 and although other economic indicators swung upward in 1976, there was every prospect that unemployment rates would remain at very high levels into the late 1970s.[16] Furthermore, in 1975-76 almost every capitalist country began to experience both a fiscal crisis, as public expenditures strained the willingness to tax or be taxed, and at least the harbingers of a capital shortage unless there is an increase in investment relative to consumption. As a consequence, the political forces calling for a reduction in public expenditures—notably on welfare services—were strengthened, which further exacerbated the negative distributional effects.[17]

The industrialized nations made a remarkable recovery in their international accounts as well. The enormous balance-of-payments deficits of 1974 were replaced by a slight surplus in 1975. What had happened, however, was that the burden had shifted to the energy-poor developing nations, such that by 1975 their deficit relative to OPEC countries was approaching $45 billion. Their commodity exports were the big losers in the worldwide recession of 1974-76, and they are much less able to absorb the higher oil import bill without severe internal disruption.[18] Industrialized countries, especially the stronger among them (notably the United States and West Germany), were able to overcome oil-based deficits by increased exports of technology and manufactured goods, especially to oil-producing states.[19] But once again there were losers. First, a substantial portion of the offset was in the form of arms, which add to the political and military instability of the Middle East and do not contribute to the industrial capacity of these countries or to the well-being of their populations. Second, to the extent that these exports were increased at the expense of other countries' exports or potential exports, the burden of adjustment once again was merely shifted from the strongest to the weakest countries.

Table 1-1
Unemployment Rates, 1973-1976

	Unemployment Rates			
	1973	1974	1975	1976[a]
Canada	5.6	5.4	7.1	8.0
France	2.3	2.9	5.0	5.9
Great Britain	2.7	2.7	4.4	6.1
Sweden	2.5	2.0	1.6	2.2
United States	4.9	5.6	8.5	8.8
West Germany	1.2	2.6	4.7	5.9
Japan	1.3	1.4	1.9	–

Source: German Federal Ministry of Economics, Release of March 12, 1976.

[a]The 1976 figures are for the month of January.

Furthermore, the recovery may be more apparent and short term than real and sustained. Economists are not uniformly confident that the 1976 upswing is not just a phase in a more sharply oscillating business cycle. The inflation-recession episode of the 1971-1976 period began before oil prices went up. We do not fully understand its dynamics. To the extent that it reflects supply-side rigidities of energy, food, materials, and labor, demand deflation will be inadequate as a technique of economic policy. And the very manner in which the initial oil price shocks were "absorbed" (as well as the way in which energy policy tends to be defined) seems likely to intensify these pressures toward rigidity in the medium and long term. Labor may not continue to accept the major burden of adjustment and may initiate a pattern of catch-up wage demands that sets off a wage-push inflation. Efforts to decrease public welfare expenditures simultaneously with increasing income inequalities are likely to intensify political conflict and induce a general loss of legitimacy, at least in the advanced capitalist democracies. Developing countries will become more and more dependent and vulnerable and their potential as a source of international economic and political instability will escalate.

We cannot present here a full defense of the proposition that economic growth, welfare, and employment will suffer increasingly unless countries limit their demand for energy. But we can take note of four basic arguments upon which such a defense would rest.

1. *The real price of energy will continue to go up, as will the prices of other raw materials.* The prospect that industrialized countries will continue to be dependent on imports of petroleum should be sufficient to keep oil prices high. All the more so because even at the 1976 price of $11 to $13 a barrel for Middle Eastern crude oil, imported petroleum was a bargain compared with most alternative fuels. New sources of natural gas in the United States (e.g., from coal

conversion, methane, geo-pressured zones, shale, tar sands) will require at least a fourfold increase over the regulated price prevailing in 1975-76.[20] Price estimates for oil from conversion of coal or from shale and tar sands are in the $16 to $26 a barrel range, and the cost curve is rising.[21] The cost for electricity from conventional nuclear reactors will also increase sharply. Such reactors have already increased in price by two and a half times over the past few years due to construction and design problems and to the increasing cost of uranium. Coal-fired plants are also escalating in price.[22] The breeder reactor will probably be more expensive, perhaps by a factor of two or more, compared with LWR plants. The situation with regard to other raw materials is much the same due to the need to move to more remote locations or less concentrated ores and due to rising inputs of energy required for extraction.

Earl Cook observes:

[T]he history of economic exploitation of non-renewable resources over the past 200 years is, in general, one of decreasing costs and increasing reserves. However, the direct energy or work costs of recovery have been rising, slowly for a long while, then more rapidly as the number of tons of ore required to produce a ton of refined metal has started to rise more steeply with decreasing ore grade. The seeming paradox of decreasing total costs and increasing work costs is explained by a long record of decreasing real costs of energy used to extract and process most renewable resources. Now that energy resources themselves are beginning to cost more in work, now that the efficiencies in energy conversion appear to be nearing limits dictated by the strength of materials and the laws of thermodynamics, and now that the work costs of recovery, at least for some resources, are moving up the steeper parts of exponential curves, the nature of the limits to exploitation of nonrenewable resources is beginning to be recognized.[23]

2. *There is good reason to question the assumption of so many economists and policymakers that the consumption of a particular kind of energy will decline smoothly as its price goes up.* And if technological limitations and scarcity of materials were to combine with structural rigidities in markets and political-administrative processes to hold energy consumption on a rising curve, inflationary (and recessionary) forces will be continuously fed on the supply side. We have already pointed to the pervasiveness of the supply orientation among energy policy criteria. Our discussion of the complexity of the energy policy problem suggests how difficult it will be for public policymakers to broaden these criteria effectively.

The market behavior of decisionmakers in profit- or performance-oriented firms and corporations may be more price sensitive. Indeed, one would expect some industrial sectors to make what savings they can within the constraints of their existing investments in plant and stock. However, most producers and distributors of energy have a strong interest in expanding supplies. And as the chapters that follow amply demonstrate, they loom large in the energy policy-making process. Indications of a general trend toward a declining productivity of energy mean that increasing amounts of energy will be required to extract and refine given amounts of minerals and metals. The strong trend toward increased demand for electric power means that increasing amounts of primary fuels will be required to accomplish the same amount of work since electricity generation efficiencies are close to their limits. Trends in agriculture, transportation, and industrial production all point in the same direction. Barry Commoner describes the situation in the United States, but much of what he says is applicable to most industrialized countries:

> In agriculture . . . [the declining productivity of energy] has come about through the substitution of fuels and energy-intensive chemicals for solar energy. As a result, although farm output has increased in the last thirty years, the amount of energy used to produce it has increased faster. . . . In transportation, the modes that are low in energy productivity (trucks, private cars, and airlines) have increasingly displaced those with relatively high productivities (railroad freight and passenger traffic; trolley cars). . . . [T]he amount of transportation (and therefore the amount of energy) needed to accomplish the task of moving food from the farm to the city has increased sharply as small-scale operations have given way to large, geographically concentrated ones. . . . These changes exemplify a centralizing tendency that has made the production system more dependent on transportation. . . .
>
> The petrochemical industry exemplifies the trend toward reduced energy productivity. It not only takes a large share of the nation's energy, but uses it at a very low efficiency. . . . [W]ith a curious and pernicious precision, almost every product which the petrochemical industry has displaced has been particularly efficient in its use of energy.
>
> Thus, out of the enormous post-war changes in the production system, there has emerged a dominant industrial complex founded on the intensive use of conventional sources of energy . . . both as fuel and as raw material. . . .This energy/chemical complex—petroleum and natural gas; coal mining; nuclear fuel production; transportation; and a large part of the chemical industry—dominates the U.S. production system. . . . It is the most dynamic, economically powerful sector of industry, and—if nothing is changed—it is likely to determine the future behavior of the entire production system.[24]

A reversal of such trends will not only take time, but will make extraordinary demands on the capacity of political authorities for planning and coordination and for the mobilization of public support.

3. *Guaranteeing supplies of energy (and other nonrenewable materials) sufficient to preserve the existing structure of production and consumption will require vast infusions of capital.* This action can adversely affect the functioning of the political economies of advanced states in at least three ways: direct impacts on economic efficiency, exacerbation of a capital shortage, and increased pressures to reduce public expenditure for welfare benefits and public services. These issues are in dispute among economists and political scientists, and the available evidence is mixed. Nevertheless, there are persuasive arguments in favor of each point, and recent economic and political performance offers little justification for complacency.

Burkhard Strumpel has argued:

The frontier of economic growth has shifted from natural resources to human resources. While growth in the production and processing of primary materials and production of "through-put"—intensive goods encounters increasing barriers, manpower has become more abundant, both quantitatively due to high and rising rates of labor force participation . . . as well as increasing educational attainment and job experience. In order to achieve growth we must change our factor input and utilization so as to make more intensive use of amply available (human) resources while husbanding scarce (physical) resources.[25]

The trend toward rising productivity in the primary and secondary sectors is slowing down and may eventually reverse itself because of the internalization of social and environmental costs, and because past productivity increases depended on declining energy and materials prices. A strategy that tries to use technology to overcome natural and environmental limitations on the development of the manufacturing sector will most likely, in Strumpel's view:

. . . entail rising marginal costs, more inflation, and less economic growth;
forego the chances for full employment;
ignore current trends in changing needs and tastes as well as the longer-term market signals (declining profits, capacity utilization and investment in the manufacturing sector).[26]

This general position also finds support in theories that chart a progression in industrial economies toward what Fourastié has called a "tertiary civilization."[27] In these theories the emphasis is placed on the various factors that limit the demand for industrial goods and the contribution the primary and secondary sectors can make to national income. As successive saturations of demand set in, rises in industrial productivity are not compensated by increases in demand, and the demand for labor falls in those industries.[28]

Whatever the mechanism that might link major investments in the energy and materials sectors to changes in the growth of output and employment, it seems undeniable that economic growth theory has tended to ignore issues of resource scarcity.

[C]ontemporary growth theorists, of either Cambridge, blandly ignore any mention of land or raw materials, assuming that somehow technological progress can assure that steady growth can go on forever. To her credit, Joan Robinson refers to such a state of affairs as a "golden age" to remind us of its mythical character, but the tough problems of how to deal with natural resources in models of growth do not seem to have been faced by anybody.[29]

A second line of argument focuses on the capital shortages that will purportedly result unless two demand trends are balanced by a corresponding increase in savings: on the one hand, the rising curve and sheer volume of the capital required to supply projected future energy needs, and on the other, the declining productivity of capital. A trend toward reduced capital productivity and a declining rate of profit has been observed for some time and seems to be accelerating. Rising energy prices and stable or rising consumption of energy will further exacerbate the problem. Commoner, for example, argues that the productivities of capital and energy are closely related and both vary inversely with the productivity of labor:

[M]ost of the newly introduced production technologies have reduced capital productivity (i.e., output/dollars of capital invested) and have increased labor productivity (i.e., output/man-hours of labor used). Energy links the two effects, for it is used to run the new, more capital-intensive machinery that produces goods with much less participation of labor than before.[30]

All of this threatens the capacity of the economic system to regenerate its essential resources. More and more capital is required to maintain the same level of output because the amount of energy produced per dollar of invested capital is falling. Since the energy producers and energy-intensive industries seem likely to continue to have preferred access to private capital markets and to public sector subsidies, a shortage of capital available to other sectors or a net decrease in private consumption seems a likely consequence. In either case, we would anticipate negative effects on the ability to produce and on long-run earnings potential.

Finally, the secular trend toward an expanding service sector is associated with an increase in government expenditures relative to GNP, as activities with low productivity are continuously transferred from the private part of the service sector to the state. This trend is only one element in the escalation of demands for public expenditures that has already given rise to "fiscal crisis," to "welfare backlash," and to actual cuts in expenditures on welfare services and income transfers in many advanced capitalist societies. Practically nobody imagines that the infrastructure investments, environmental costs, and direct investments in plant and equipment needed to increase energy supplies (especially nuclear, coal, shale oil) can be provided by the private sector. Heavy public sector expenditures will be required and will thus add to the fiscal crisis. Where will the extra funds come from? Some studies assume that adequate public surpluses will be generated as industrial economies return to *and sustain* rapid rates of economic growth and full employment.[31] But we may well question the extent to which this will actually take place. One obvious source of funds would be from cuts in private consumption and welfare and other public service expenditures, and these are already widely called for, especially by the business community. But this course is politically risky and can seriously undermine the legitimacy of the economic and political system. On the other hand, the attempt to meet all the competing demands on the public purse produces chronic deficits and forces the government into the capital market, thus "crowding out" other borrowers.

4. *We can expect that there will be limitations on the length of time the*

strongest industrialized nations will be able to "externalize" the adjustment problem to their own workers and consumers, to weaker industrial nations, or to the poorest countries in the developing world. Higher energy prices, inelastic demand for energy, and the capital demands of the energy sector are all powerful forces for economic instability and stagnation. We cannot predict the precise patterns that will exist from country to country or in the industrialized world as a whole, but lagging growth rates, high levels of unemployment, and frequent bouts of inflation will eventually bring about either a reorientation of the existing energy policy trajectory or the imposition of authoritarian or quasi-authoritarian measures to suppress the protests of the unemployed and those who will see their incomes steadily eroded. The sequences suggested in the foregoing pages clearly cannot go on indefinitely. But the longer the transition to an alternative energy policy strategy is delayed, the more skewed will be the income and wealth distribution, the more tenuous the legitimacy of national governments, and the more desperate and hostile the leaders of developing countries. In turn, these factors will make it even more difficult for governments to manage their economies and to rationally consider, implement, and have accepted the national and international measures necessary to deal with the energy macro problem.

Economic, Administrative, and Political Centralization

Political and economic theoreticians have always debated heatedly the complex problems involved in finding an optimal balance between centralization and decentralization. While this is not the place to review these arguments, we can, however, point to a number of centralizing trends inherent in energy policy choices. These can be summarized as they pertain to two broad propositions from the larger debate on centralization. Each suggests that present energy policies are leading us in distinctly undesirable directions.

1. *Increased economic concentration in market economies has adverse consequences for economic efficiency, price stability, and income distribution, which can only be countered by strong political regulation.* There is no doubt that the trend is toward larger and larger energy installations and larger and more complex and interdependent distribution networks. The increased importance of electricity is a case in point.[32] Heavy reliance on coal and nuclear energy seem likely to intensify the trend further. The scale of investments required, the long lead times, and the coordination and control that is indispensable all mandate an increased scale of energy production and distribution, the development of vertical and horizontal integration of activities, and an increasingly closed system of formal linkages among corporations and conglomerates in the form of consortia, joint participation agreements, and so forth.[33] This limits competition among producers, introduces price rigidities as the relative power of energy

buyers declines in favor of energy sellers, and militates against innovation in alternative fuels.

Effective political regulation seems to lag almost everywhere, either because of ideological or structural reasons or because of a failure to discover an appropriate strategy of intervention. Economic concentration itself can, of course, serve as a barrier to offsetting political regulation, as is most evident in the United States. Ways and means of "breaking up the oil companies" and of exerting meaningful control over the energy industry have once again entered the political debate in the United States, but with little sign that any substantial policy change is in the offing.[34] Considering the sheer volume of U.S. energy consumption and the global importance of U.S.-based energy multinationals, the outcome of this debate has important consequences for the rest of the world.

2. *Concentrated economic power and concentrated administrative power have the tendency to develop symbiotic relationships implying a degree of political centralization ("state capitalism" or "state socialism") that threatens democratic participation, unless it is countered by political mobilization through political parties, the legislature, or other specialized groups.* The most compelling case that there is a causal link between energy policies and political-economic centralization has been made by Amory Lovins. He argues that a high-energy, primary-supply-oriented, high technology, increasingly electrified, energy policy reliant on depletable resources

nurtures dirigiste autarchy, bypasses traditional market mechanisms, concentrates political and economic power, centralizes human settlements, persistently distorts political structures and social priorities, encourages bureaucratization and alienation, compromises professional ethics, is probably inimical to greater distributional equity within and among nations, inequitably divorces costs from benefits, enhances vulnerability and the paramilitarization of civilian life, introduces major economic and social risks, reinforces current trends toward centrifugal politics and the decline of federalism, and encourages—even requires—elitist technocracy whose exercise erodes the legitimacy of democratic government.[35]

The country studies that follow present substantial evidence in support of this position. The relationships are most clearly evident in the case of France. But a similar point is raised in the Swedish chapter where it is pointed out that the critical choice facing the country is whether to pursue a *flexibility* strategy preferred by the state power board, or a more decentralized *specialization* strategy preferred by energy consumers and distributors, especially the cities. The specialization strategy calls for adaptation to local situations, for matching the thermodynamic characteristics of supply alternatives to the specific uses envisaged, for a bringing together of consumers and suppliers, for cooperation between local initiative and central authorities. It closely resembles what Lovins has called a "soft energy path."[36] The principal conclusion is that certain otherwise desirable technological options may be foreclosed because they are incompatible with existing organizational arrangements or preferences, and that there will not be much chance to opt for conservation or for emphasis on renewable energy sources unless there is a prior decision to redirect the division of responsibility in the energy supply system *toward more localized control.*

In France, the commitment to a supply policy and the choice of the nuclear option have produced a state-industry control network. State administrative control over the energy sector was greatly extended as the push toward nuclear power intensified after 1973, and alternative technological options appear to have been effectively foreclosed by the scale of organizational and financial investment required by nuclear development. A set of interlocking holding companies with the French Atomic Energy Commission at its center organizes the whole of the nuclear fuel cycle and has become the real center of power and coordination in French energy policy. It concentrates the forces toward maximizing the size of the markets for reactors and nuclear fuels and toward rapid development and exploitation of nuclear technologies for export. Political parties, the parliament, and adversary groups have no active role to play in setting policy priorities—or even debating them—nor, it would seem, does the Electricité de France, which must buy electricity at prices over which it has no control. While similar trends toward hierarchically organized interpenetration of public and private sectors are evident in many countries, rather different offset roles have been played by legislative and party debate (especially in Sweden) and by the opposition of adversary groups (especially in the United States).

International Conflict

Energy policy choices, although severely constrained by international factors, are overwhelmingly determined by the push and shove of internal political life with very limited consideration of international consequences that may have new and more dangerous influences on subsequent policy. As we saw above, most governments seek where possible to lower the costs of national adaptation to the changing energy situation by directly or indirectly "externalizing" these costs to weaker groups or nations. Existing international political and economic structures (reflecting the distribution of wealth among countries) permit such outcomes and have allowed the governments of most advanced industrial nations to avoid or postpone complicated and politically difficult domestic policy choices, especially on the demand side.

But international consequences of such a potentially disastrous nature are implied by the current trajectory of energy policy that the international environment of future policy will become even more unstable, unpredictable, and conflict prone than in the past. It would seem to follow that the longer the advanced nations persist in their present policies, the fewer will be the options available to them and the greater will be the eventual costs. Even in terms of their own interests, then, these policies would seem to be extremely short-sighted. From the evaluative perspective of a more just global economic and political order, they are indefensible. Present policies are likely to intensify patterns of asymmetrical dependency and vulnerability, to militate against the evolution of consensual norms for the international management of interdependence, to strengthen the forces making for unequal development, and to increase the potential for war, aggressive countermeasures, and international terrorism. The case for this proposition will be summarized in the six arguments that follow. Each projects the international consequences of a major trend in national energy policies.

1. *By continuing to rely on petroleum imports, the advanced industrial countries will rapidly deplete the world's stock at the expense of the less developed countries, future generations, and alternative uses of petroleum as an industrial raw material.* The tacit international political "coalition" that would favor and benefit from this outcome in the short run would include most of the advanced oil-importing nations and the oil-rich developing countries. Dominant elements in each share a set of common interests encompassing preservation of the existing international economic and political order as well as integration into it of a *limited number* of states on the basis of reciprocal exchanges of capital, technology, and military support for guaranteed and preferred access to petroleum and other raw materials. This position also implies maintenance of the conservative domestic political status quo in major supplier countries, particularly Iran and Saudi Arabia. The imperatives of the domestic development and stability of oil-consuming and -producing states will limit the level of petro-dollar recycling to oil-poor developing nations. Incentives to create other commodity cartels will be increased because no real progress will be made toward a more general "new world economic order." The more effective of these will eventually be incorporated into the "club" of the rich and the newly rich.

2. *The effective monopoly of available oil resources by the advanced societies, combined with the rising price of all energy and the neglect of solar and alternative technologies, will make it increasingly difficult for the poorest of the developing countries to meet their development goals and will plunge them into chronic depression and ever greater dependency and vulnerability.* The long-run prospects for these countries are even gloomier than a mere extrapolation of the 1974-76 experience would imply.[37] To the direct impact on their economies of higher fuel and import prices and increased trade competition from better-endowed developing countries and even from Eastern Europe, as well as periodic recessions in the West that decrease their export earnings, we must add the progressive decline of their agricultural production due to the use of firewood and dung as fuel and an inability to pay the rising international price for fertilizers. As a consequence of the latter, these countries are being forced into a dangerous dependence on imported food supplies. Eckholm points out that North America occupies an even more dominant position in grains than

does the Middle East in oil and that the poor countries will have to compete with relatively affluent Europe, Japan, USSR, and oil-producing countries for access to these supplies:

[A] growing drain on exportable supplies [of grains] could well intensify inflationary pressures in all countries, as international demand pulls food prices up and forces costly investments that bring diminishing production returns in the agricultural sector of the advanced countries. The point could be reached where the sum of national grain import needs chronically exceeds the level North America is willing or able to supply, leaving heavy importers in a dangerous position. Furthermore, for the poor countries, the wholesale diversion of scarce foreign exchange from productive domestic investment to the purchase of food abroad would cripple economic development efforts.[38]

As this situation worsens, it is likely that some poor countries will be increasingly unable to bridge the food gap, and an even more dangerous degree of dependency and vulnerability will result. Food scarcity means rising levels of malnutrition and premature death and will present the more affluent countries with "choices and responsibilities so politically sensitive that they may not be able to deal with them rationally." For one-fourth of humankind the prospect is that

Marginal people on marginal lands will slowly sink into the slough of hopeless poverty. Some will continue to wrest from the earth what fruits they can, others will turn up in the dead-end urban slums of Africa, Asia, and Latin America. Whether the deterioration of their prospects will be a quiet one is quite another question.[39]

3. *Increased reliance on oil imports will likely contribute to a rising level of policy conflict among the United States, Western Europe, and Japan as they compete for access to oil supplies and for markets to offset the resultant balance-of-payments drain.* The failure of the United States to limit oil imports will be especially damaging for it could lead to deteriorating relations with Western Europe and Japan. These latter states simply do not *have* the alternative supply (and demand) options that the United States is *politically* unwilling or unable to take. The nascent conflict between the United States and its allies over multilateral versus bilateral strategies[40] for dealing with oil dependency will probably be resolved in favor of producer-consumer bilateralism and "the internal contradictions between the security and economic interests of the industrial countries will grow and their political coherence will dissipate."[41] Such a development would have wide repercussions. The developed countries could probably not achieve the degree of coordination in their economic policies they would need to control the rapid international transmission of business cycle fluctuations. What remains of European economic and political integration would be sorely strained, perhaps beyond the breaking point. International efforts to control and regulate the spread of nuclear technology and fissionable

materials would be doomed to failure. In sum, the process of economic and political realignment within the industrialized West might be accelerated to such a point that a collapse into a "new international anarchy" would be more likely than an ordered transition to a "new international order."[42] If such an ordered transition is to be at all possible, creative leadership would be required from precisely these countries.

4. *A "logical" response of governments to heightened uncertainties, issue conflicts, and strategic vulnerabilities is to increase military expenditures and adopt a more aggressive and interventionist foreign policy.* It will be critically important to sustain regimes with which bilateral supply agreements have been reached. Increased economic conflict breeds economic nationalism and competitive export drives. Commodity monopolies, as in food, would be used to maximum national advantage. The domestic political mobilization that would accompany such increased conflict would also be likely to strengthen the political coalitions in capitalist democracies favoring crash programs in nuclear energy and coal conversion as the keystone of national energy policy. Increasing the export market for nuclear reactors and fuels has already become a prime policy goal for balance-of-payments reasons and may eventually become part of a broader international power struggle.

5. *Governmental commitments to nuclear power as a long-term energy source entail the development of the breeder reactor, an ever-fiercer competition for export markets, the inevitable proliferation of nuclear fuel reprocessing technologies, and the emergence of an international plutonium economy.* In the situation of international conflict and asymmetric dependency described above, this commitment will raise the risk of accident, war, and the use of nuclear devices by terrorist groups.[43] Concentration on the very serious problems of direct safety risks, especially disposal of radioactive wastes and attendant environmental contamination, has until recently led to a relative neglect of a far more serious problem and one much less susceptible to "technological fix" solutions: the almost certain proliferation of nuclear power plants and nuclear fuels, fuel reprocessing, and the spread of conventional reactors. Twenty-one countries had commercial reactors in 1976, and this number seems likely to rise to forty or more by the year 2000.[44]

There is an already awesome dissemination of the capacity to make nuclear weapons, which, according to many experts in the field, markedly increases the likelihood of nuclear war.[45] But supplies of uranium ore appear to be insufficient to sustain conventional nuclear reactors for more than a few decades. Hence, the widespread introduction of the breeder reactor, which uses (and produces) plutonium as a fuel, seems inevitable if a decision is made to develop the nuclear option and will be the most fateful consequence of a decision to go nuclear. Plutonium is perhaps the most dangerous contaminant known to man. From as little as ten pounds of plutonium, a crude atomic weapon can be made without very great technological skill. It is estimated that a single breeder will produce 5,000 kilograms of plutonium per year and that a nuclear power program based on the breeder could involve up to one hundred and fifteen million kilograms of plutonium annually.[46]

It has been argued that proliferation can be kept manageable if the development of nuclear technology is stopped with conventional reactors, by treating this as a stop-gap measure until other sources become available. But by that time, the complex of pro-nuclear bureaucratic and private interests and the fixed commitments in technology and infrastructure will have accumulated to a point where they will be very difficult to overcome. If we are to go to the breeder reactor, enormous investments of capital and personnel will be required in the next decades. Even if the economics of the breeder and the enormity of the risks involved eventually bring about its abandonment, the world will have been exposed to a period of extreme vulnerability to war and health hazards and will have foregone (at least for a time) the advantages of alternative investments in more benign sources of energy.

6. *An international environment as dangerous and conflict-prone as that portrayed above will be likely to exacerbate further the difficulties of maintaining stable domestic economies and to intensify the centralizing tendencies noted earlier.* The breakdown of existing alignments, the resurgence of mercantilist protectionism, the related threat of trade wars or export controls, and the formation of new economic blocs seem to be sure consequences of present policies. These will disrupt established trade relationships, money flows, and security arrangements with adverse implications for the domestic stability of the advanced states. The uncertainties, anxieties, and tensions that will result may well be met by centralizing and authoritarian responses.[47] An intensified trend toward an embattled state capitalism or state socialism in the developed states does not bode well for their citizens or for the "human prospect" more generally. It will be most unlikely to allow for the policy reevaluations and international resource redistributions that will be more and more essential when the multiple trends postulated in these pages progressively increase the disarray of national and international political economies.

The Dynamics of Policy Response to the Changing Demands of Energy Policy

If the above scenario represents even in part a plausible extrapolation of present trends in national energy policies, it will behoove us to learn what we can about the historical origins of these policies, about the institutions and processes through which supply-oriented criteria have come to dominate, and about the political and organizational obstacles that stand in the way of the development of policies that are more sensitive to the broad political economy considerations that we have emphasized. Such a background will be indispensable to an effort to propose avenues of policy and institutional change.

The seven case studies that follow were designed to provide a crossnational perspective on these questions. Such a perspective is particularly useful in that it allows us to control for (and learn from) factors that presumably should be associated with policy variations or similarities. The authors of the case studies were asked to cover the following specific points:

1. A brief introductory account of energy policy decision-making arrangements, past policies, and internal political forces in the energy field, with special attention to be given to the roles of government bureaucracies, public and private enterprises, parliamentary committees, and interest groups.
2. A closer analysis of decisions, options, and strategies with regard to some especially salient or decisive dimension of energy policy. (In some cases, this point concerns the development of a particular alternative source of supply; in others, it involves questions of institutional design.)
3. A focus on how energy policy problems and energy planning have been perceived and understood by governmental and nongovernmental decision-makers and on how these perceptions have changed through time. (In particular, the authors were asked to what extent and in what directions did government policy change after 1973? How do their governments typically deal with uncertainty, urgency, and complexity in policy making? What is the influence of established administrative routines and ways of thinking? Has energy policy become salient and controversial in the larger political arena, and with what effects?)
4. An analysis of what broader policy objectives governments have sought to optimize in energy and how these have changed: economic growth and efficiency, national security and power, national autonomy and freedom of action, distribution of income and wealth, and so forth. (This point includes in particular an analysis of the interaction of policy sectors and the pattern of tradeoffs and unanticipated conflicts among objectives in present and past policies.)
5. An effort to account for and evaluate the current trajectory of national energy policy and the performance of national planning and policy-making institutions and to suggest measures or strategies for their reform.

The case study chapters differ in some interesting ways according to the special interests and backgrounds of their authors, and these differences add an important variety and richness to the analyses and comparisons. The authors come in roughly equal numbers from the ranks of the professional planner, the university researcher, and the governmental policy practitioner. Only a minority are energy specialists in a narrow sense. Most bring broader concerns for economic and spatial planning, science policy and technology assessment, and business and public administration to their responsibilities in the field of energy.

Two of the five authors of the chapter on Britain (Surrey and Chesshire) are members of the Science Policy Research Unit of the University of Sussex and specialize in energy policy research. The remaining three (Friend, de B. Pollard, and Stringer) are at the Tavistock Institute of Human Relations, a private, not-for-profit research organization that specializes in studies of processes of policy making and planning in regional and local governments. Their chapter is especially rich in its sensitive analysis of the possibilities and constraints of planning in complex and turbulent policy fields and in pluralist political settings.

David Fischer and Robert Keith, the authors of the Canadian chapter, are in the Department of Man-Environment Studies at the University of Waterloo. They summarize a much more extensive technology assessment study of petroleum development in the Canadian Arctic that they carried out for the Science Council of Canada. This work offers an especially useful account of the impact of political decentralization, bureaucratic inertia, and a multiplicity of actors on energy policy and planning.

The French chapter is written by Dominique Saumon and Louis Puiseux, both economists employed by the Electricité de France, the French nationalized central electricity generating authority. They offer the perspective and detailed knowledge of the policy "insider." Their analysis of how planning produces unplanned consequences and of the government-industry structures of control in atomic energy planning are outstanding contributions.

István Dobozi, an economist and planner at the Institute for World Economics of the Hungarian Academy of Sciences, describes the problems and the approach to policy and planning of an energy-deficit socialist planned economy. His analysis also offers a unique insight into the rapidly changing international contexts of energy and economic policy in the communist world.

T.L. Sankar is a high official of the Planning Commission in New Delhi. His account of Indian energy policy in Chapter 6 is written from the perspective of an economic planner in an oil-poor developing country that must emphasize a low-energy development strategy and the alternative sources and technologies appropriate to a relatively poor country.

Måns Lönnroth has a background in mathematics and in public administration and has served in the Delegation on Energy Policy attached to the Swedish Prime Minister's Office. He too writes from the perspective of an insider, one especially charged with developing conservation and demand restriction options in energy policy. His chapter is rich in insights into the relationships between technology and organizational structure and the dependence of policy innovation on organizational innovation.

Finally, Irwin Bupp is at the Harvard Business School and is a specialist on the nuclear power industry in the United States. His main preoccupations in Chapter 8 are with the ideological context of American energy policy (or nonpolicy) and with the politics and economics of nuclear power.

The selection of cases and the design of the questions each author was asked to answer approximates a quasi-experimental research design of the "interrupted time series" type. In the final chapters, we will be in a position to compare the policy and organizational behavior of a number of different nations over numerous time points before and after the introduction of a crucial stimulus: the 1973-74 boycott and price increases. Our purpose will be to look for both similarities and variations in response to this stimulus: we hope to be able to associate these with characteristics that are common to all our countries or that distinguish one from another. The value of this admittedly crude approximation of the experimental method depends critically on the choice of countries to be juxtaposed and compared. While we cannot claim to have selected the "sample" on a systematic scientific basis, our seven countries do display three central factors in common: All are net importers of energy, all have been adversely affected by price increases and prospective shortages or supply interruptions, and all have substantial organizational and technological capabilities for an active energy policy on both the demand and supply sides.

Five of our countries are highly industrialized and bureaucratized, have liberal-democratic political systems, and are capitalist economies. Yet, they contain an interesting range of variation: highly centralized to highly decentralized governmental arrangements; developed institutions and supportive ideologies for economic planning to a dominance of antiplanning in action and ideology; two-party to multiparty regimes and relatively nonmobilized to highly mobilized publics; very early and gradual industrial development to late and rapid industrialization; dominant elite ideologies and preferences as to policy goals and instruments ranging from egalitarian democratic socialism to free-market liberalism; substantial past reliance on nationalization as an instrument of public policy to a systematic rejection of such options. These five countries also vary substantially in GNP and GNP per capita; general economic performance, foreign policy involvement, and size of military budgets; as well as past and prospective energy resource endowments, energy consumption rate and distribution among sectors, and reliance on imported energy. Our sample also includes one moderately industrialized country with a centrally planned economy integrated into the Soviet-led bloc and one nonaligned Asian country at an earlier stage of industrialization with much lower levels of urbanization, a political regime dominated by a single party and at least rhetorical commitment to economic planning and a socialist economic program.

We hope that a careful juxtaposition of the energy policy experience of these seven countries in Chapter 9 will produce some useful empirical generalizations about the correlates of outcomes, bureaucratic rigidities, and political and institutional obstacles to change in energy policies. We will also rely on a comparison of these cases in Chapter 10 where we seek to extract conclusions as to the substantive policy implications of such empirical findings and as to organizational and political strategies and structures that might promote the adoption of different policies and the implementation of broader sets of policy criteria.

Notes

1. John Steinbrunner, *The Cybernetic Theory of Decision* (Princeton, N.J.: Princeton University Press, 1974), p. 45.

2. For excellent treatments of energy interdependence, see Nazli Choucri, *International Politics of Energy Interdependence: The Case of Petroleum* (Lexington, Mass.: Lexington Books, 1976).

3. Ibid., p. 192. Quote here from pp. 322-23 (in manuscript).

4. Bertrand de Jouvenel, *The Art of Conjecture* (New York: Basic Books, 1967), pp. 17-18.

5. Hugh Heclo, "Policy Dynamics," in Richard Rose (ed.), *The Dynamics of Public Policy: A Comparative Analysis* (Beverly Hills, Calif.: Sage Publications, 1976), p. 256.

6. Todd La Porte and C.J. Abrams, "Alternative Patterns of Postindustria: The California Experience," in Leon N. Lindberg (ed.), *Politics and the Future of Industrial Society* (New York: David McKay, 1976), pp. 21-22.

7. Heclo, "Policy Dynamics," p. 256.

8. See, for example, Wilson Clark, *Energy for Survival: The Alternative to Extinction* (Garden City, N.Y.: Anchor Books, 1974); Howard Odum, "Energy, Ecology, and Economics," *Ambio*, vol. 2, no. 6 (1973), pp. 1-8; and Carol Steinhart and John Steinhart, *Energy: Sources, Use and Role in Human Affairs* (North Scituate, Mass.: Duxbury Press, 1974).

9. La Porte and Abrams, "Alternative Patterns of Postindustria."

10. See Steinbrunner, *The Cybernetic Theory of Decision*, p. 16, and La Porte and Abrams, "Alternative Patterns of Postindustria," pp. 31-37.

11. Joel Darmstadter, "Energy Consumption: Trends and Patterns," in Sam H. Schurr (ed.), *Energy, Economic Growth, and the Environment* (Baltimore, Md.: Johns Hopkins University Press, 1972), p. 181.

12. See Lee Schipper and A.J. Lichtenberg, *Efficient Energy Use and Well-Being: The Swedish Example*, Energy and Environment Division, Lawrence Berkeley Laboratory, University of California, April 1976.

13. Denis Hayes, "Energy: The Case for Conservation," Worldwatch Paper 4, Worldwatch Institute, Washington, D.C., January 1976 and Energy Policy Project of the Ford Foundation, *A Time to Choose: America's Energy Future* (Cambridge, Mass.: Ballinger Publishing Company, 1974), especially Chapter 6. For a recent discussion, see Bruce Hannon, "Energy Conservation and the Consumer," *Science*, vol. 189, no. 4197 (July 11, 1975), pp. 95-102.

14. Philip Connelly and Robert Perlman, *The Politics of Scarcity: Resource Conflicts in International Relations* (London: Oxford University Press, 1975), p. 26.

15. For discussions on these points with regard to the whole range of raw materials see the Special Issue of *Science* on "Materials," vol. 191 (20 February 1976).

16. *Business Week*, March 22 and March 29, 1976.

17. James O'Connor, *The Fiscal Crisis of the State* (New York: St. Martin's Press, 1973). For a recent entry in the debate over public expenditure as a cause of economic instability see "Government Growth Crowds Out Investment," *Business Week*, October 18, 1976, pp. 138-145.

18. *Business Week*, March 29, 1976, p. 83. Connelly and Perlman, *The Politics of Scarcity*, p. 64 and Edward R. Fried and Charles Schultze, "Overview," in Edward Fried and Charles Schultze (eds.), *Higher Oil Prices and the World Economy* (Washington, D.C.: Brookings Institution, 1975), p. 63.

19. See Wilhelm Hankel, "West Germany Before and After the Oil Shock," paper presented at a conference on "Managing Domestic Economic-Political Crisis in the United States and Western Europe," Columbia University, April 23-24, 1976. See also Horst Mendershausen, *Coping with the Oil Crisis: French and German Experiences* (Baltimore, Md.: Johns Hopkins University Press, 1976).

20. Thomas H. Maugh II, "Natural Gas: United States Has It If the Price is Right," *Science*, vol. 191 (February 13, 1976). Also, Federal Energy Administration, *National Energy Outlook*, February 1976, p. 160.

21. *National Energy Outlook*, ibid., and Allen L. Hammond, "Coal Research (III): Liquefaction Has Far to Go," *Science*, vol. 193 (September 3, 1976), pp. 873-75.

22. *National Energy Outlook*, p. 297; "Can the U.S. Afford More Electricity?" *Electric Light and Power*, January 19, 1976, p. 12; and Irwin C. Bupp, "The Economics of Nuclear Power," *Technology Review*, February 1975, p. 15.

23. Earl Cook, "Limits to Exploitation of Nonrenewable Resources," *Science*, vol. 191, no. 4228 (February 20, 1976), p. 682. Copyright 1976 by the American Association for the Advancement of Science.

24. Barry Commoner, *The Poverty of Power: Energy and the Economic Crisis* (New York: Alfred A. Knopf, 1976), pp. 219-22. See also Steinhart and Steinhart, *Energy*, especially Chapter 6.

25. Burkhard Strumpel, "Induced Investment or Induced Employment—Alternative Visions of the American Economy," paper commissioned by Senator Hubert H. Humphrey, Chairman of the Joint Economic Committee of the U.S. Congress, for the study series, U.S. Economic Growth from 1975-1985: Prospects, Problems and Patterns (no date), pp. 1-2.

26. Ibid., p. 2.

27. J. Fourastié, *Le Grand Espoir du XXᵉ Siècle* (Paris, 1949).

28. For a brief review see "The Trade Union Movement and the Public Sector," speech delivered by Rudolf Meidner at the 20th convention of the Public Services International, New York, 10 October 1973.

29. Ronald Findlay, "Implications of Growth Theory for Trade and

Development," *Papers and Proceedings of the 87th Annual Meeting of American Economic Association, American Economic Review*, vol. LXV, no. 2 (May 1975), p. 327.

30. Commoner, *The Poverty of Power*, p. 226.

31. Barry Bosworth, James S. Dusenberry, and Andrew S. Carron, *Capital Needs in the Seventies* (Washington, D.C.: Brookings Institution, 1975).

32. For a full treatment of electrification and its relationship to centralization, see Amory B. Lovins, "Scale, Centralization, and Electrification in Energy Systems," Paper presented at Symposium on Future Strategies of Energy Development, Oak Ridge, Tennessee, October 20-21, 1976.

33. For an exposition of this point see James Ridgeway, *The Last Play* (New York: Mentor, 1974).

34. Alexander Cockburn and James Ridgeway, "Energy and the Politicians," *New York Review of Books*, April 15, 1976, pp. 19-25.

35. Amory B. Lovins, "Scale, Centralization, and Electrification in Energy Systems," p. 35.

36. See "Energy Strategy: The Road Not Taken," *Foreign Affairs*, vol. 55, no. 1, October 1976, pp. 65-96.

37. For the impact of the oil crisis on developing countries, see Fried and Schultze, *Higher Oil Prices*, pp. 33-37, and Wouter Tims, "The Developing Countries," ibid., pp. 169-196.

38. Erik P. Eckholm, *Losing Ground: Environmental Stress and World Food Prospects* (New York: W.W. Norton and Co., 1976), p. 180. See also James P. Gant, "Energy Shock and the Development Prospect" in James Howe (ed.), *The U.S. and the Developing World* (New York: Praeger Publishers, 1974).

39. Eckholm, ibid., p. 187.

40. Romando Prodi and Alberto Clô, "Europe" in "The Oil Crisis in Perspective," *Daedalus*, Fall 1975, pp. 109-10.

41. Thomas Enders, "OPEC and the Industrial Countries: The Next Ten Years," *Foreign Affairs*, July 1975, especially pp. 626-27. See also Klaus Knorr, "The Limits of Economic and Military Power," in "The Oil Crisis: In Perspective," ibid., pp. 229-44.

42. Geoffrey Barraclough, "The Haves and the Have Nots," *New York Review of Books*, May 15, 1976, pp. 31-41.

43. See Mason Willrich and Theodore Taylor, *Nuclear Theft and Safeguards: A Report to the Energy Policy Project of the Ford Foundation* (Cambridge, Mass.: Ballinger Publishing Co., 1974). See also Walter C. Patterson, "Exporting Armageddon," *The New Statesman*, August 27, 1976, pp. 264-66, and his *Nuclear Power* (Harmondswort: Penguin Books, 1976).

44. Denis Hayes, "Nuclear Power: The Fifth Horseman," Worldwatch Paper 6, Worldwatch Institute, Washington, D.C., May 1976, p. 8.

45. See for example the statements by George Rathjens, Herbert Scoville, Theodore Taylor, and George Kistiakowsky, "The Threat of Nuclear War," Granada TV Program; 29 March 1976 (transcript reprinted May 1976 by Granada TV, Manchester, England); A. Wohlstetter et al., "Moving Toward Life in a Nuclear Armed Crowd?" Report to Arms Control and Disarmament Agency, United States State Department, ACDA/PAB-263, 22 April 1976.

46. Mihaljo Mesarovic and Eduard Pestel, *Mankind at the Turning Point* (New York: E.P. Dutton, 1974). For other estimates see Hayes, "Nuclear Power," and Patterson, *Nuclear Power.*

47. For examples of such scenarios see Robert Heilbronner, *An Inquiry into the Human Prospect* (New York: Norton, 1974), and Bertram Gross, "Planning in an Era of Social Revolution," *Public Administration Review,* May/June 1971, pp. 259-96.

2

Energy Policy in Britain: A Case Study of Adaptation and Change in a Policy System

*J.H. Chesshire, J.K. Friend,
J. deB. Pollard, J. Stringer,*
and *A.J. Surrey*

Significance of the British Case

The recent prominence of energy policy in many countries arises from a variety of causes: the impact of higher oil prices, uncertainties about long-run fuel availabilities and prices, and the importance now attached to a variety of energy-related issues in international political relations. Reactions to the oil crisis vary among countries according to their fuel endowments, their dependence on oil imports, their technological capabilities, and the processes of policy formation they have developed for dealing with energy problems. The value of examining these policy arrangements in individual countries lies in the hope of identifying features that may be relevant to other countries facing broadly similar problems.

The British case is likely to be of wide interest for three reasons. First, since the Second World War, Britain has had an identifiable framework of energy policy that has permitted a variety of national interests to be taken into account in addition to purely commercial considerations. We do not mean to imply that Britain has succeeded in formulating a comprehensive and consistent energy policy that is ideally suited to its national needs and resources nor one that commands widespread public support. Nevertheless, there has been a degree of consistency in the approach to policy formulation and in the institutional structure over a period of three decades. Second, although Britain has retained a relatively large coal industry and has developed nuclear power and offshore natural gas supplies, like most other industrialized countries, it has become increasingly dependent on oil over the past two decades. Third, although suffering acute balance-of-payments difficulties—largely due to the increases in oil prices since October 1973—Britain stands a good chance of becoming self-sufficient in oil by 1980 (see Table 2-1) by virtue of the development of the fifteen oilfields in the North Sea that have been discovered since December 1969. There remains much uncertainty about the size of the physically and economically recoverable offshore petroleum reserves, but the North Sea oil discoveries now under commercial development should permit a high degree of independence for at least twenty years.

As awareness grows of the limited life of the reserves and of the uncertainties about the long-term world availability of different types of primary fuel, so attention is drawn increasingly towards the long-term problems of controlling the rates of oil and gas depletion, of improving the efficiency of energy

33

Table 2-1
North Sea Oil: Estimated Reserves and Production Buildup (000 b/d)

Field	Estimated Recoverable Reserves (m. barrels)	1975	1976	1977	1978	1979	1980	1981
Argyll	75	20	35	31	28	26	23	21
Auk	50		30	40	40	11	11	–
Forties	180	20	150	300	400	400	400	400
Beryl[c]	400		30	80	80	80	80	80
Brent	1750		20	50	170	250	350	470
Montrose	200		10	35	50	50	50	50
Piper	800		60	170	220	220	220	220
Claymore	400			20	65	110	110	110
Cormorant	160			10	25	45	75	45
Dunlin	400			10	40	60	80	90
Thistle	450			30	100	180	180	150
Heather	150				25	50	50	50
Ninian	1350				50	150	275	300
Alwyn[b]	500				25	75	100	100
Hutton[b]	300					25	70	100
Production from New Fields						130	320	670
Total (000 b/d)		40	335	776	1318	1862	2394	2856
Total (m. tons of oil)[a]		2.0	16.8	38.8	65.9	93.1	119.7	142.8

Source for North Sea Figures: Wood, McKenzie & Co., Ltd., *Petroleum Economist*, August 1975.

[a]Conversion factor of 20,000 b/d = 1 million tons of oil.
[b]Final development plans have yet to be announced for these fields.
[c]Two platforms may be placed on the Beryl field when peak production would rise to 130,000 b/d. These figures assume only one platform is installed.

conversion and use, and of determining priorities for energy research. Therefore, a new range of problems is arising that is very different from those of the past when attention focused mainly on the relatively immediate issues of fuel supply. These problems in turn can be expected to impose new stresses on the arrangements that Britain has developed over the years for forming and adapting its national policies in the energy sector.

In analyzing the British case, we will find it useful to refer to some general tools of policy analysis that can be briefly introduced at this stage and elaborated later by example. The first of these tools is the identification of *policy systems* both at the level of overall national energy policy and at the level of operational policy development in particular supply sectors such as electricity, oil, and coal. A policy system can be identified wherever a set of people exists with the acknowledged task of arriving at decisions relating to some class of problem situations and applying some set of recognized policy guidelines to which those concerned all subscribe, at least at a nominal level. As we shall discuss later, the nature and extent of these shared guidelines will vary from case to case. Figure 2-1 illustrates the importance of analyzing the way policy systems work and the way they adapt and change over time, by bringing together an understanding of the *issues* to which they relate, the *processes* through which these are tackled, and the *actors* who play roles within the system. Each of these, as the diagram indicates, is subject to a range of further influences, the nature of which may vary considerably over time.

Another analytical tool that will be found useful concerns the interpretation of the difficulties that people encounter in grappling with difficult and complex decisions in terms of three contrasting classes of *uncertainty*, as indicated in Figure 2-2. Difficulties in agreeing on the key policy choices may arise from (1) uncertainties about the policymakers' *operating environment*, which may be reduced by undertaking research or by seeking improved information through survey, prediction, or model-building techniques; (2) uncertainties about *policy values*, which typically involve formal or informal political consultations to cope with underlying conflicts of interest; and (3) uncertainties about choices in *related fields* of policy, which can be attacked through consultative processes

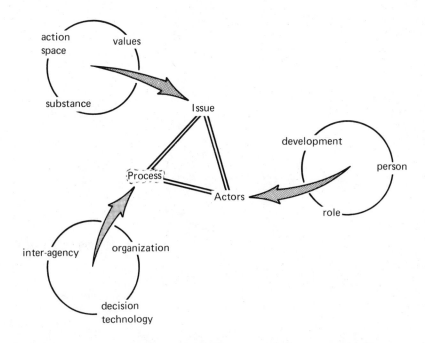

Figure 2-1. Influences on Policy.

36

between those in the focal "policy system" and those in other systems of policy making concerned with different but related issues.

At this point, we should give a brief introductory view of the "policy system" that has developed in Britain to deal with issues of general energy policy at a national level. This system focuses on the Department of Energy within the national government that is headed by a minister whose membership in the cabinet signifies the importance now attached to energy in national affairs. Although this department has only existed under its present name since 1974, it has essentially the same organization, responsibilities, staffing, and premises as its antecedents, the first of which was created in 1942 under the exigencies of the war economy. For thirty years, therefore, Britain has had a central government department responsible for coordinating the planning and operation of the major fuel industries.

At the operational level, other more specialized levels of policy system can be identified in the various main sectors of fuel supply. In the case of coal, gas, and electricity, publicly owned corporations have a virtual monopoly of supply; while in the case of oil, public control is exercized through powers of regulation over refinery building, licensing for exploration, fiscal measures, and—more recently—the setting up of the British National Oil Corporation. Public regulation and control first took root in the electricity and gas industries around the

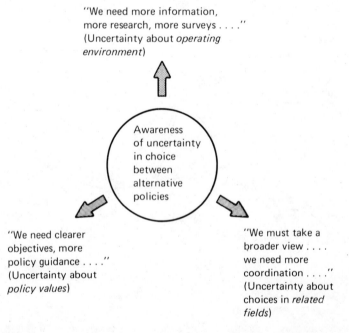

Figure 2-2. Three Types of Reaction to Difficulties in Policy Choice.

turn of the century, where efficiency required the creation of private or municipal undertakings with a regulated monopoly over the supply of gas or electricity within a given locality. To capture the economies of scale as more efficient methods of production and transmission became available, larger undertakings became necessary. In the case of electricity, statutory powers were obtained in 1926 to permit the development of a national electricity grid, first connecting local networks and then gradually permitting interregional power flows. This grid was largely complete in 1939.

After the war, the situation was ripe for full-scale public ownership. The first postwar Labour government had the necessary electoral mandate and was committed to a sweeping program of socialization in various fields. The fuel industries had been subject to central direction during the war and were still tightly controlled during the period of postwar austerity. Public ownership of the coal industry had been a prime aim of the miners since the troubled prewar years and was a precondition for their cooperation, which was crucial for postwar recovery. The electricity grid, already developed on a national scale, now permitted larger base-load power stations to be located near the lowest-cost coalfields. Like other basic industries, the fuel industries had been starved of investment during the war, and their manpower and capital requirements were vital elements in postwar governmental economic planning.

Apart from coal distribution, only the oil industry has remained largely under private enterprise. The main reason is that the oil industry is organized internationally: A large part of the British market was supplied by American-owned multinationals, and at the same time the two major British oil companies were themselves operating internationally. Provided that oil import prices in Britain were no higher than elsewhere, there seemed little to gain from nationalization. The American companies brought in much-needed technology and investment. The British government had long had a controlling interest in the Anglo-Iranian Oil Company (later BP, Ltd.) and could, at least in theory, use its powers of ownership and its control over refinery building to favor the British companies if circumstances warranted. Also lurking in the background was the fear that a move towards nationalization of the oil industry in Britain would provoke unwelcome reactions by foreign companies and governments. The Abadan crisis of the early fifties, which stemmed from the attempted takeover of British oil interests in Iran, pointed to the incipient dangers.

As in other West European countries, the main changes in Britain's energy pattern over the past thirty years have been an increasing dependence on oil, a retreat away from coal—especially in final energy uses—and a steady growth of electricity generation and other conversion processes that provide convenient and flexible forms of energy. Despite Britain's early entry into the field of nuclear power, it still supplies only 3 percent of the country's total primary fuel consumption. With the rapid exploitation of North Sea discoveries since 1967, natural gas in 1975 accounted for 17 percent of national primary energy

38

requirements. A general view of the shifting patterns of primary and final energy use in Britain is presented in Table 2-2.

Having sketched the central actors and the main trends in energy demand and supply, we can now examine how energy policy in Britain has evolved since 1945, in relation to the emergence of substantive issues and, equally important, the changing perceptions of key uncertainties over time.

Evolution of Energy Policy

The evolution of British energy policies since 1945 may conveniently be discussed under four headings, which, as illustrated in Figure 2-3, correspond

Table 2-2
Trends in British Energy Consumption and Supply

1. *Pattern of Primary Fuel Supply (mtce)*

	1950	1960	1970	1973	1974	1975
Oil	22.2	65.5	145.6	161.6	150.1	134.4
Coal	202.6	196.7	154.4	130.8	116.0	118.1
Natural Gas	–	0.1	17.6	43.6	52.1	54.5
Nuclear	–	0.9	9.4	9.9	11.9	10.8
Hydro	0.9	1.7	2.6	2.0	2.1	1.9
Total	225.7	264.9	329.6	347.9	332.2	319.7

2. *Pattern of Final Energy Use (mt, heat supplied basis)*

	1960	1965	1970	1973	1974	1975
Oil	12833	20163	27357	29696	27074	25753
Coal	31139	24634	17847	12829	11796	10139
Electricity	3372	5022	6567	7502	7292	7260
Gas	3187	3868	6182	11007	12127	12722
Total	50531	53687	57953	61034	58289	55874
Agriculture	601	663	750	883	747	732
Iron and Steel	7092	7497	7193	6575	5542	4890
Manufacturing Industry	14259	15798	17496	19215	18254	17061
Transport	8812	9437	11186	12876	12411	12261
Domestic	14425	14520	14643	14917	15086	14703
Public Services	2461	2781	3454	3542	3318	3228
Miscellaneous	2881	2991	3231	3026	2931	2999
Total	50531	53687	57953	61034	58289	55874

Source: Department of Energy *Digest of United Kingdom Energy Statistics* (London: HMSO, various years).

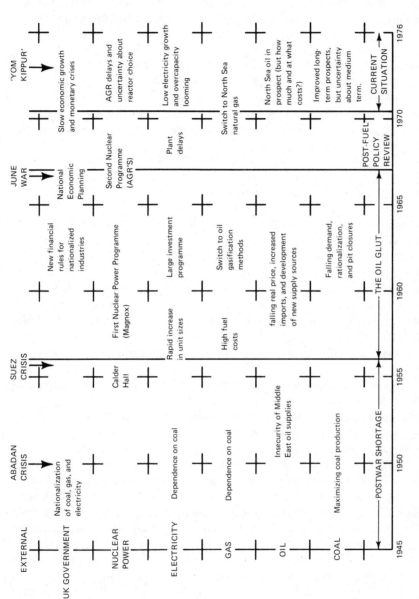

Figure 2-3. British Energy Policy 1965-1976: Major Problems and Uncertainties.

with four periods of different demand and supply conditions when perceptions of uncertainty were continually undergoing change. The first period, extending from 1946 to 1957, was one of postwar shortage and recovery when the central concerns of policy were the adequacy of coal supplies and the security of oil supplies. The second period, 1958 to 1966, was marked by falling real prices of oil on the world market, much reduced anxiety about the security of oil supplies, and a retreat from coal. The third period, 1967 to 1970, followed the Government's Review of Fuel Policy and represented a commitment to "cheap" energy and a controlled rundown of the coal industry. The fourth period, 1970 onwards, saw the virtual abandonment of the 1967 Fuel Policy due to increasing oil prices, major uncertainty about oil and nuclear power, and the discovery and development of North Sea oil.

Postwar Shortage: 1946-1957

In 1946, coal supplied 93 percent of British energy consumption and was a mainstay of the national economy. Shortages of indigenous coal meant an overall energy shortage and delays in reviving industrial production and exports. Starved of investment for many years (before as well as during the war), the mines were still largely unmechanized. Although marginal tonnage was therefore very expensive, the overriding aim was to maximize production. To maintain a sufficient supply of labor to the mines was therefore crucial, and this priority was reflected in the facts that miners' wages were high relative to average industrial wages and that working in the mines was a permissible alternative to military conscription. An especially severe winter in 1947, with resulting coal shortages and high unemployment, heightened the priority for expanding coal production.

The economic recovery under way in the early 1950s made apparent that indigenous coal supplies could not meet the increasing demands created by economic expansion. A great deal of refining capacity was still located in the Middle East, and the rise of Arab nationalism with designs on European-owned assets, such as the Abadan oil refinery and, a few years later, the Suez canal, created grave concern over the security of oil supplies. This situation was held to justify a strong military presence in the Mediterranean, the Near East, and the Indian Ocean. The background of high energy costs, prospective energy shortage, and insecurity of supply led the government to announce in 1955 a Plan for Coal with the aim of raising coal production to 240 million tons a year, together with a first Nuclear Power Programme, which led to the construction over the following decade of 4,000 MWe of nuclear plant based on the Magnox gas-cooled reactor design.

The dominant uncertainty in this early postwar period was whether British coal supplies would be sufficient to meet forecasts of a growing U.K. energy gap.

The policy settled upon was one of maximizing coal production despite the high costs of marginal tonnage and of making substantial investments in the mechanization of underground mining and transport. There was also an awareness during this period of the need to relate energy to other areas of policy, particularly in relation to foreign policy where the political crisis in Abadan and the closing of the Suez canal in 1956 demonstrated the inability of the United Kingdom (and French) governments to guarantee protection to oil companies' overseas assets. These events also signalled the arrival of the oil-producing states and their governments as important actors, even though the increase in supply sources and the fall in the real price of oil masked the probability that through time the interests of the oil-producing countries would diverge from those of the consuming nations and of the international oil companies.

The late fifties saw a diminution of uncertainties about fuel supplies. A paradoxical result of the Suez crisis was a surplus of oil in the United Kingdom—that is, as a result of a successful petrol rationing scheme that was rushed in as the canal closed and the installation of new refining capacity "upstream" in Europe. A contributory factor here was inertia in the oil and tanker trades: For many weeks after the canal closed, crude oil continued to flow to the West. The unexpected ease with which the crisis was met diminished the perception of political uncertainty that had dominated energy planning in the early fifties. Furthermore, the promise of nuclear power (in 1957, it was expected that within a decade 25 percent of electricity output would be nuclear) and the completion of the program of capital investment in the mining industry resolved much of the uncertainty which had dominated in the late forties.

To exemplify the changing perception of the various uncertainties, two shifts in related areas of policy may be mentioned. First, the substitution of diesel for steam traction on the railways, which contributed to the decline in the market for coal, was made possible by the massive injection of state funds for investment under the Railway Modernisation Programme announced in 1955. This was largely completed by 1963. Second, in the late 1950s the government had committed itself to a major program of motorway construction against a background of forecasts of exponential growth in the car population and effective lobbying by bodies representing private motorists, road haulage contractors, the motor car manufacturers, and the oil companies. The popular perception of the issues at stake, and indeed the dominant social value of economic growth, were such that it would have been difficult for any government to have pursued a radically different transport policy.

Gradually it came to be recognized, particularly after the Buchanan Report on "Traffic in Towns," that traffic planning is inextricably linked with urban planning and land use; but in many instances urban redevelopment continued on the assumption that priority had to be given to the rising tide of motor traffic. One of the outstanding challenges to this assumption came in the early 1970s, with the shelving of London's "Motorway Box" proposals that would have displaced several tens of thousands of Londoners by a network of urban motorways in and around the capital. As with the shelving of the proposals for the controversial Third London Airport, the public expenditure implications were probably at least as important as the level of public opposition aroused.

The uncertainty arising from the 1956 Suez crisis appeared to reinforce the wisdom behind the major investment programs for coal and nuclear power. The subsequent development of supertankers, for reasons of economies of scale, mitigated the effects of bringing crude oil from the Gulf around Southern Africa should the Suez Canal close once more—as indeed was to happen in 1967.

Uncertainty about policy values, on the other hand, played very little part at this time. As a generalization, the mood was one of expansion following two decades of depression and wartime austerity. The election of Conservative governments in 1951, 1955, and 1959 reflected a popular concern for rising material standards. In 1955, a senior minister was able to predict that the national standard of living would double over the next twenty-five years.

In this period, election speeches by leading politicians captured the public mood and reflected the underlying aspirations of the people. Aspirations were rising because of the success of postwar recovery, confidence in the continued successful application of science and technology, and confidence in the ability through Keynesian techniques of macroeconomic management to avoid the cycles of unemployment and widespread misery that had characterized the period 1890-1939. Expectations of increasing wealth and technological prowess contributed to the underlying view that the future could largely be left to take care of itself, for it was assumed that natural resources, capital, and technology would be sufficient to take care of any problems that might arise. Since economic growth was the generally accepted target, it followed that provision had to be made for additional energy supplies to sustain economic growth. The dominant social value was that energy demands had to be met, and little attention was as yet being paid to environmental and ecological issues. Certainly, when oil refineries and power stations were built, there was nothing like the outcry that one expects today. This attitude was not due to a callous or conscious disregard for nonmaterial values, however. The bulk of the British adult population had vivid memories of prewar unemployment and deprivation, and anything that seemed to assure future prosperity was generally accepted. Also, sensitivities about new sources of environmental degradation may well have been dulled for many people living in the great industrial connurbations in an environment of overcrowding, poor living conditions, and often an oppressive industrial landscape. All these were legacies of nineteenth century industrialization, and in the circumstances it was understandable that great hope was pinned on technological progress.

The Oil Glut: 1958-1966

After 1958, world oil prices fell dramatically due to the expansion of oil reserves in the Middle East. Substantial new reserves had been discovered in North Africa and Nigeria, and the United States introduced an oil import quota system that in effect left increasing supplies of cheap oil available to Western Europe and Japan. The foreign exchange costs of oil fell even further, because of a policy designed to ensure that refinery capacity in Britain matched requirements for the home market and bunkers and left a zero net balance of trade in refined products. In addition, the increase in the number of oil supply sources appeared to relieve the earlier anxiety over insecure oil supplies. Throughout the 1960s, both major political parties remained committed to economic growth and technological progress. The period of 1958-1966 therefore contained few of the sources of past anxiety and few indications of issues that were to become dominant later.

Despite considerable progress with mechanization and productivity, coal production fell steadily from a peak of 224 million tons in 1957 to 183 million tons in 1966. In addition to intensive competition from oil for heating purposes, the market for coal was steadily eroded by the spread of smokeless zones under the 1956 Clean Air Act, railway dieselization and electrification programs, the substitution of oil-based steam reforming plants in the gas industry for traditional coal-carbonization methods, substantial improvements in fuel efficiency in iron and steel production, and the switch away from open coal fires in the home—due to promises of cheaper electricity, increasing real disposable incomes, and competitive advertising by the fuel industries aimed mainly at the booming central heating market.

The government responded to the plight of the coal industry—falling production and inability to meet its financial targets—by imposing a substantial duty on oil to protect coal in competitive markets. A virtual ban on imports of foreign coal remained in force. The 1965 Coal Industry Act, by reducing the book value of the coal industry's obsolete capital assets, waived a substantial burden of interest charges. The electricity industry was also required to give coal a significant competitive advantage in its fuel purchasing decisions. Nevertheless, the early 1960s marked a decisive retreat from coal. Despite political pressure from the National Coal Board and the National Union of Mineworkers (a major force in the British Labour movement), the planning target for coal was revised downwards to 200 million tons and then (under the 1965 National Plan) to 180 million tons—25 percent below the target set a decade earlier.

Due to the falling costs of oil-fired electricity generation and the cost breakthrough claimed for early light water reactors in the United States, the position was only slightly more favorable for the nuclear power program. Technically, the new Magnox program was a success, since the plants were more or less built on time and achieved their design performance, but their high capital costs meant that their costs per unit of power generated were high compared with conventional steam plants during the period when oil prices were low.

Not unreasonably, the Central Electricity Generating Board (CEGB) took the view that if it was to install more nuclear plants, they would have to be capable of generating electricity at costs no higher than best-practice fossil fuel plants and American light water reactors. However, a sense of optimism due to nationalistic pressures to build another British reactor system and the desperate need of the British nuclear plant consortia for new orders, led the CEGB to choose the advanced gas cooled reactor (AGR). Long afterwards, it came to light that the bid price was excessively optimistic, that great technical problems would be encountered in modifying and scaling up the prototype AGR at Windscale to full commercial size, and that the cost advantages claimed for the early U.S. light water reactors were largely illusory. American firms had sustained huge financial losses on these "turnkey" contracts, and there has been rapid cost escalation on reactors ordered in the United States over the decade since 1965.

During the period of "oil glut," value-related uncertainties began to attract increasing attention. There was, first, an accidental escape of plutonium at the Windscale plant in 1957. Although its immediate consequences were small, it served later to reinforce the case of those who emphasized the inherent risks of nuclear power. Second, the success in 1956 of new clean air legislation, which led to the spread of smokeless zones, may well have heightened public awareness of the possibilities for reducing environmental pollution. Third, books such as Rachel Carson's *Silent Spring* drew attention to the dangers of pesticides and other forms of environmental pollution. Fourth, the major oil spillage when the *Torrey Canyon* supertanker ran aground provided dramatic confirmation of how a single accident could threaten the environment on a large scale. Even though in this case the effects on marine life and tourism were short-lived, the awareness of risk was heightened by further cases of major oil spillage and later by the explosion and complete destruction of a specialized petrochemical plant near a rural village at the cost of many lives. Even though those who voiced these anxieties were first seen as radicals or impractical idealists, the environmental issues to which they drew attention were to gain increasing prominence over the years.

When these energy issues came into the public limelight, little had as yet been done to develop a coordinated national energy policy. Although the responsibility of government to develop coordinated energy policies had been established in 1945, it was not until November 1967 that the first attempt at a comprehensive government policy statement appeared. Throughout most of the postwar period, uncertainties had not been consciously *managed*, but rather *displaced* onto the oil-supply sector. As yet, few foresaw the possibility that political interventions might "turn off the tap," either in the Near East or in other oil-producing countries. It was assumed that the annual growth of demand would continue and that the gap between indigenous fuel supplies and total demand could always be met by oil, whose availability at low cost remained unquestioned.

A Period of Reappraisal: 1967-1970

By 1966, two important choices arose for consideration in a wider policy context. The discovery of natural gas in the southern basin of the North Sea necessitated deciding to whom it was to be sold and at what "beach" price and final price. The former was relevant for purposes of the balance of payments and continued exploration, and the latter was relevant for the competitive position of other fuels. In the event, comparatively low "beach" and final prices were determined. The agreed objective was to supply most of the natural gas to "premium" uses where consumers were prepared to pay prices higher than actually charged for the advantages of convenience and flexibility. These were mainly domestic and commercial consumers, but there were also many industrial users who valued this clean and flexible fuel. This policy was thought to maximize the overall benefits to be obtained from natural gas, including the foreign exchange savings. But to obtain the lowest overall cost of supply it was necessary to agree to contracts stipulating a high level of offtake, thus permitting high utilization of the offshore and onshore pipelines. It was considered that the reserves would permit a peak supply rate of 4,000 million cubic feet per day (mcfd), and the target became one of building up supplies to this level as fast as possible. This goal necessitated a massive program of investment in transmission and of converting all existing gas appliances to take the higher calorific value of the natural gas. It also meant the retirement of oil-based gasification plants, many of which were no more than five years old and therefore only partly depreciated.

The second key choice concerned the future of nuclear power and its relationship to other primary fuels in the generation of electricity. Following the choice of the AGR in 1965, the government soon announced a second Nuclear Power Programme with the aim of installing 5,000 MWe of AGR capacity by 1975. But low economic growth and more especially low electricity growth (partly due to the increasing competition from gas) soon necessitated a cut in the electricity investment program that had been expanded to massive proportions during a burst for economic growth by the Conservative government in the runup to the 1964 General Election. Because of the optimism about oil and nuclear power costs, the cutback in the power station program fell first upon coal-fired plants and thereby further reduced the potential market for coal.

These two developments necessitated a comprehensive review of national fuel policy, the findings of which were summarized in the Fuel Policy White Paper of November 1967. This review had as its central themes the objective of cheap energy, measures to assist the controlled rundown of the coal industry during the transitional period (1968-1971), and the encouragement of competition between the fuel industries, thereby implying a high degree of autonomy for their managements and a comparatively commercial style of decision making. The uncertainties to be faced, especially those surrounding the basic judgments on oil and nuclear power, now appeared very limited, largely because the comparatively short time-horizon to 1975—no longer than the gestation period for many energy investment projects—had the effect of obscuring longer-term uncertainties.

An implicit assumption was that any deviations from the energy demand forecasted in the White Paper would be dealt with by variations in the level of oil imports. The oil companies, by virtue of their international operations, appeared ideally suited for this balancing role. Any net balancing effect was, of course, ultimately absorbed by the oil-producing states, and a latent source of uncertainty was in this way ignored. In the 1960s, however, the oil producers were still relatively poor, and their interest in boosting oil revenues through greater production coincided with the interests of the oil companies in maximizing sales and share of the market.

Since the strategies for nuclear power and natural gas were decided near the beginning of this review exercise, the focus increasingly fell on the position of coal. As a result of the use of statistical extrapolations of total energy demand, coupled with the judgments on nuclear power and natural gas, the target for coal production was reduced from 180 million tons to 150 million tons for 1970 and 120 million tons for 1975. The anxieties expressed by the NCB about an imminent collapse of morale and productivity in the industry were such that the government decided not to publish its estimate that the market for coal would fall to 80 million tons by 1980.

In this way, the 1967 Fuel Policy led to a significant cut in colliery investment and an acceleration of colliery closures during the following three years. Many of the collieries to be closed were in areas of high unemployment, and the social effects were to be alleviated by financial assistance to encourage transfers within the industry, retraining, and early retirement. The political repercussions were minimized by phasing the closures as far as possible to avoid aggravating local unemployment during the winter months when seasonal unemployment is highest.

Some people have claimed that this policy significantly reduced the coal industry's production capacity, but the closures were in fact concentrated on high cost mines and those approaching exhaustion. The NCB itself has said that the closures resulted in the loss of very little production capacity that would have been economic in the post-1973 situation of higher fuel prices and that the chief effect of this policy was to deny the NCB the incentive and finances needed for exploration, for the development of new low-cost production capacity, and for higher levels of research on coal mining and conversion technologies.

On the international front, 1967 saw the formation of OPEC, the association of Arab producers. In June 1967, the Arab-Israeli six-day war demonstrated that the major conflict in the Middle East was still far from resolution and had attendant risks for the worldwide security of oil supplies. Nevertheless, the Fuel Policy White Paper assumed that there was a virtually limitless world supply of oil at a price below the long-run marginal cost of home-produced coal and also that any future oil supply interruptions would be short-lived due to competition from newly developed sources, such as North and West Africa.

It followed that low oil prices would set a ceiling for the costs and quantities of British coal produced and that the most immediately practicable way to insure against temporary supply interruptions was to require the oil companies to maintain somewhat higher oil stocks in Britain than their commercial interests dictated.

A few weeks after the publication of the Fuel Policy White Paper, the government was finally forced to devalue sterling after a three-year struggle to avoid doing so. This action substantially increased the import costs of oil, but it failed to restore balance-of-payments equilibrium (apart from the short period of 1971-72). Despite the declared aim of the government to reduce its level of direct involvement in the operational policies of the energy industries, the period since 1967 has been characterized by increasing government interventions in the affairs of the nationalized fuel industries in the interests of the balance of payments and anti-inflation policies. The result has been growing conflict and antagonism between government and management of the industries that were at the same time under the injunction to act "commercially" and to meet the financial targets set by the government.

Adapting to Changing World Energy Politics: 1971 Onwards

The posted price of Saudi Arabian "marker" crude, which had remained at $1.80 per barrel for a decade, began its upward move in 1971 and rose in steps to $2.90 by mid-1973. During the same period, various forecasts were made that pointed to a global oil scarcity in the 1980s. By this time, many energy specialists expected oil prices to rise in the longer term. But no one was to predict the outbreak of the Yom Kippur War, the subsequent use of oil as a political weapon, and OPEC's readiness to raise the price of the marker crude to $11.65 per barrel on January 1, 1974. For Britain, the increase in oil import costs (which accounted for two-thirds of the massive visible trade deficit of £5,259 million in 1974) and OPEC's supply restrictions brought to the fore once more the anxieties about security of supply that had lain dormant so long.

By this time, however, numerous oil discoveries had been made in the more remote areas of the North Sea. They began with the announcement of the Ekofisk discovery in December 1969, and in the period 1971-73 starts were made on the commercial development of fifteen North Sea oilfields. The abrupt change in the world oil position towards the end of 1973 meant that even greater priority was placed upon the objective of displacing oil imports as soon as possible. The rise in oil prices greatly increased the expected profitability of North Sea oil and led the government, against great opposition from the oil companies, to impose a Petroleum Revenue Tax and to create the British National Oil Corporation to exercise a major degree of state control in the future development of Britain's offshore petroleum resources.

By the time oil prices soared in late 1973, very little remained of the 1967 Fuel Policy. The underlying uncertainties were fully exposed with regard to the basic judgments on oil and nuclear power. Although Britain faced a period of uncomfortably large trade deficits, pressure on sterling, and rising unemployment, the major investment in North Sea oil promised to reduce dependence on oil imports from 100 percent to zero by 1980-81 (see Table 2-3) and therefore to invigorate the national economy. Substantial new gas discoveries in the northern areas of the North Sea also promised to alleviate the problems of the rapid depletion of the gas fields in the southern basin that resulted from rapid exploitation since 1967. Energy, and oil in particular, now assumed macroeconomic significance through its effects on inflation, unemployment, the balance of payments, and the value of sterling, but the high priority attached to developing North Sea resources offered the hope that the acute balance-of-payments difficulties would be temporary.

Despite its earlier reluctance to order further nuclear plants until the AGR's were in operation, the Central Electricity Generating Board sought government approval in mid-1973 to build thirty-six light water reactors of American design. This move was reinforced when oil prices quadrupled a few months later. After the highly critical Parliamentary Select Committee Report and a mixed reaction by the press, the CEGB proposal was rejected by the government in favor of a much smaller program of steam generating heavy water reactors (SGHWR) based on experience with a prototype at Winfrith. This commitment—probably the minimum needed to keep the nuclear plant industry alive over the next five years—was influenced by technological nationalism, the intense worldwide debate about the safety of light water reactors, and the view that a larger nuclear program was unjustified since the expectation that coal and North Sea oil and gas would see Britain through until the 1990s, by which time it was hoped that the uncertainties surrounding nuclear technologies would be much reduced.

Shortly after the rise in oil prices, a national miners' strike challenged the government's anti-inflation policy and industrial relations legislation and thus precipitated a general election that brought the Labour party to power. The strike was settled by meeting the miners' wage demands. In addition, the government set up a tripartite group representing the government, the National Coal Board and the mining unions, to examine the future of the coal industry. This group recommended that long-term coal production should be stabilized at 130-150 million tons a year. To achieve this target, it recommended, on NCB advice, the development over the next decade of 42 million tons of new annual

Table 2-3
U.K. Natural Gas Supplies, 1967-1981 (mcfd)

North Sea–Southern Sector

	1967	1968	1969	1970	1971	1972	1973	1974	1975	1976	1977	1978	1979	1980	1981
West Sole	44	126	154	115	179	213	172	179	230	230	230	190	170	150	140
Leman Bank	–	73	290	781	1275	1317	1315	1571	1300	1300	1300	1200	1150	1100	950
Hewett	–	–	52	193	333	510	563	692	780	800	800	800	780	760	740
Indefatigable	–	–	–	–	16	445	451	553	600	700	700	700	700	700	700
Viking	–	–	–	–	–	134	345	471	550	550	550	550	490	450	400
Rough	–	–	–	–	–	–	–	–	50	150	150	150	150	150	140
Total (Southern Sector)	44	199	496	1089	1803	2619	2846	3466	3510	3730	3730	3590	3440	3310	3070

North Sea–Northern Sector

	1967	1968	1969	1970	1971	1972	1973	1974	1975	1976	1977	1978	1979	1980	1981
Brent											–		200	600	600
Frigg - U.K.											200	450	600	600	600
- Norway											200	450	600	600	600
Total (Northern Sector)											400	900	1400	1800	1800
Additional Possible Supplies													70	380	720
Total (mcfd)	44	199	496	1089	1803	2619	2846	3466	3510	3730	4130	4490	4910	5490	5590
Total (mtce)	0.8	3.0	7.4	16.3	27.0	39.3	42.7	52.0	52.7	56.0	62.0	67.4	73.7	82.3	83.9

Sources: For 1967-1973, Department of Energy, *Digest of United Kingdom Energy Statistics* (London: HMSO, 1974); for 1974, Department of Energy, *Development of the Oil and Gas Resources of the United Kingdom* (London: HMSO, 1975); and for 1975-1981, Wood, McKenzie & Co., Ltd., February 1975.

Note: Figures exclude natural gas production from the onshore Lockton field, which was closed in October 1974 and which produced small quantities of gas from 1971 onwards. They also exclude imports of liquified natural gas (approx. 78 mcfd in 1973).

production capacity (including a new coalfield near Selby) and an increase in investment over the decade from approximately £800 million to £1,400 million. The government accepted the proposals, although the NCB's investment program remains subject to annual review.

Whether the demand for coal will justify the new production target remains uncertain. The coal industry is heavily dependent on the power station market. If no new coal-fired power stations are built, power station coal requirements will be in decline by 1985, if not before. Forecasts of low growth in electricity demand and of considerable surplus generating capacity as the result of previous overordering give little scope for building new coal-fired power stations for some years. Moreover, given the pressures to restrict public expenditure, any further subsidization to maintain the market for coal would probably be resisted by the government.

Meanwhile, the rapid program of nationwide conversion to North Sea gas was carried through as decided in 1967, and an aggressive marketing program resulted in a correspondingly rapid build-up of natural gas sales. During this period, the inflexible supply contracts necessitated selling large quantities for crude heating purposes. By 1973, the natural gas transmission and distribution system had become highly centralized and local gas making was a thing of the past. In 1965, with the coming of Algerian liquified natural gas supplies—which were to be distributed to local area boards through a new trunk pipeline—the powers of the Gas Council had been strengthened. The conversion to North Sea gas saw a further strengthening of centralized responsibilities. The final demise of the area boards that had hitherto dominated supply came in 1973 when the British Gas Corporation was established with a monopoly over all public gas supplies.

The rapid build-up of natural gas supplies, although risky in that it meant that the southern basin gasfields would be exhausted by 1985-1990, actually turned out to be fortunate, for it meant that Britain was less dependent on oil when oil prices soared. The discovery of further large quantities of gas in the northern North Sea and the purchase of Frigg gas from Norway will postpone the problems arising from the depletion of the southern basin reserves. Nevertheless, a glimpse of future problems was seen in 1974 when the government empowered the gas industry to restrict the quantities offered to new industrial consumers. Since then, the gas industry has been reversing its policy of low prices to promote gas sales, and many industrial consumers have had to accept sharp price increases and longer periods of interruptibility when they were negotiating their gas contracts. Nevertheless, to the consternation of the CEGB especially, the price per therm of gas in early 1976 was only a fraction of the equivalent price of electricity in industrial and domestic markets.

For much of the period 1970-1974, the nationalized fuel industries were prevented from passing on their cost increases in full, and they sustained large deficits in the interests of the government's anti-inflation policies. In 1975, however, the government recognized the need to prevent further increases in public expenditure and taxation and agreed, in the interest of energy conservation, to permit energy prices to rise in line with costs.

The prospect of achieving self-sufficiency in energy by 1980-81—if only for a period of ten to twenty years—means that Britain's position is markedly different from that of countries such as Japan, France, West Germany, and Italy, all of which will remain at risk due to high dependence on oil imports and therefore have a major interest in seeking diversification through accelerated nuclear power programs and the development of new energy technologies. The situation of Britain, by contrast, requires no immediate crash programs. Rather, it suggests a balanced set of programs of energy research and development, with a view to opening up new long-run options when indigenous coal and offshore petroleum supplies can no longer meet the demand, and it calls for a greater emphasis on energy conservation and the control of depletion to extend the life of the reserves. The long-term uncertainties are being increasingly recognized as representing important challenges with which those who play a part in Britain's energy policy system must learn to cope.

The Challenges Ahead

Characteristics of Britain's Energy Policy System

When compared with other areas of public policy such as transport, housing and defense, energy has received only spasmodic attention from politicians, the media, and the wider public. Most of the time, it has been regarded as a technical problem best left to the experts. Energy is generally expected to be "on tap." Among the wider public, few have a well-developed understanding of energy problems or are accustomed to thinking on the time scales necessary for long-term planning. Usually, energy problems have come into the public limelight only at times of national shortage, international incidents that threaten the security of national energy supplies, or the announcement of major decisions that affect the interests of a significant section of workers or the wider public.

The 1956 Suez Crisis, and the accelerated program of colliery closures announced in 1967, were two salient events which attracted public attention, for a time, to certain aspects of energy policy. But the unparalleled prominence of energy in 1973-74 was caused by the coincidence of the world oil crisis, the probability of petrol rationing, the national miners' strike, and the CEGB's proposed massive commitment to light water reactor nuclear plants. By 1975, public attention had waned: oil and coal supplies seemed adequate, petrol rationing was now only a remote possibility, and the government's SGHWR decision had put the nuclear controversy into low key. It is true that in December 1974 the government introduced a package of energy conservation measures, but they were of a modest scale and probably signified to many people that the government itself felt that energy no longer represented a serious problem.

Whenever energy policy has come into public prominence, it has been evident that different people hold different ideas about the nature of "the energy problem." These variations are due to differences in their values, in their assessment of risks and uncertainties, as well as in their perceptions of the nature of the issues and constraints. The central actors engaged in policy formulation, however, are limited in number, and in some important respects, they form a relatively closed group. The policies adopted are heavily dependent upon their perceptions of the substantive issues, upon the organizational structures within which they operate, and upon the real and perceived constraints that limit their range of choice.

Traditionally, the central actors at the government level have comprised a few ministers (the Secretary of State for Energy and his junior departmental ministers) and a somewhat larger group of senior permanent officials. Ministers, however, come and go. They have little opportunity to familiarize themselves thoroughly with the problems, the technicalities, and the specialized concerns of the top managers of the fuel industries. Lord Robens has drawn attention to the fact that ten Ministers of Power came and went during his ten-year chairmanship of the National Coal Board.

Few of the senior career civil servants serving the minister have specialist knowledge gained directly in any of the fuel industries. During their careers, they are likely to occupy various posts, some remote from the energy field. While some of these senior officials may have much experience in government, they are often appointed to senior policy advisory posts in the energy field without relevant technical experience. In any case, their burden of day-to-day administration is heavy, and little time is available for systematic thinking on issues of longer-term policy.

The traditions of secrecy and of protecting the minister, which derive from the well-established British principle of ministerial responsibility, have meant that many of the more influential actors have had few opportunities to engage in public discussion and that their opportunities for learning about the technicalities of the fuel industries have tended to be limited to formal channels of communication. In these channels, the ministry's "sponsoring" role for the nationalized fuel industries means that the key civil servants must learn to play a subtle mediating role. In interdepartmental discussions, they tend to reflect the viewpoint of the fuel industries, whereas in discussion with the industries, they tend to reflect a wider government viewpoint. It is a difficult relationship, and the potential for conflict is considerable. The relationship is not always conducive to the free exchange of information needed if policies are to be coordinated effectively. On particularly difficult problems of coordination, where government officials request sufficient detailed information to enable them to form an independent view, the fuel industries may indeed tend to see this as an unwarranted intrusion into their own spheres of operational responsibility.

So far as the operational policies of the fuel industries are concerned, again the central actors are few. They tend to have spent most of their careers in the one industry and to have risen through internal hierarchies. Decision making tends to be comparatively centralized and technocratic due to the monolithic, centralized organizations involved, the often highly technical content of the problems, and the fact that many decisions are taken incrementally yet require an assessment of their effects in relation to the structure of a more complex, tightly interlocking supply system. This tendency is especially true of the electricity and gas industries that have large integrated networks, but it also applies to oil and coal. To cope with these complex decision problems, each fuel industry has invested in the development of complex mathematical models. The application of these models requires intimate knowledge not only about the technicalities of the industry, but also about the assumptions on which the computer models are structured. This required threshold level of knowledge further limits the ability of nonspecialists to participate effectively in discussion.

Despite recent concern for widening the scope of the energy policy debate, a number of factors tend to perpetuate the dominance of the central actors. First and foremost is the tradition of closed decision making in Whitehall, which retains its momentum despite evidence of the scope for cumulative errors on large-scale technology projects, such as the advanced gas cooled reactors and Concorde, and the setting up of Parliamentary Select Committees to probe government policy making. On the whole, these committees remain comparatively poorly informed, and despite their powers to call for witnesses and papers, it is not easy for them to penetrate adroit stonewalling by governmental and industrial witnesses. Second, the technical and incremental nature of many of the decisions tends to obscure the broader issues of policy. Third, potential new actors often have much difficulty in making their voices heard, partly because of the lack of adequate channels and partly because the media are rarely receptive to detailed arguments on technical subjects. So far, their role has been mainly confined to one of opposition at public hearings or to a propagandist one in technical or environmental journals.

Another characteristic is that the central actors tend to work through well-developed organizational structures and decision-making procedures where there are strong forces of inertia at work. The factors making for inertia include the long investment lead times, the existence at any given time of a large amount of obsolescent capital that is only partly depreciated, the existence of ingrained management philosophies that may reinforce resistance to change, and the statutory obligations that tie each of the nationalized fuel industries to a particular energy focus and impose other operational constraints. For instance, in the electricity industry there is an obligation to respond to all foreseeable demands, which implies that the industry has to carry much spare capacity to supply large, infrequent peaks of demands. Such forces of inertia have increased resistance to proposals for tidal barrage and district heating schemes, for an independent fuel advisory service, and for joint meter reading and joint showrooms for electricity and gas. Although in some cases the resistance has been justified, the general tendency to resist new ideas indicates that there is an underlying problem about the ability of the established decision-making processes and actors to deal with what they regard as "abnormal" problems.

In the formulation of national energy policy under conditions of multiple uncertainty, specifying clear and unambiguous operational objectives is not realistic. Of course, conceiving of a general objective expressed in terms of maximizing social welfare through time is possible, but this goal cannot be translated into objectives that are operationally feasible. In practice, a variety of national concerns have to be taken into account insofar as they impinge in different ways on different cross-sections of society: low resource costs, security of supply, the balance of payments, regional unemployment, and environmental considerations. Judgments have to be made pragmatically on the relative importance of these different objectives, and the priorities based on these judgments inevitably change through time. No energy policy can be ideally suited to both current and future circumstances, and at any given time there will be disagreement about the basic value judgments on which key decisions must rest.

Because of the impossibility of specifying clear objectives, and because the range of problems which are potentially relevant to energy policy is very wide, policy-makers find themselves forced to simplify both the objectives and the issues. Their actions are chosen from issues perceived selectively out of a wider range of problems. As the perceptions of issues, uncertainties, and objectives evolve over time, the boundaries of what is conceived as falling within the sphere of energy policy change accordingly. New interests and new issues become relevant, while inconsistencies and conflicts are likely to arise and to persist until the national policy system has adjusted to the changes which have taken place.

In recent years, new considerations have become important and many conflicts have arisen between the fuel industries and the government. Successive government interventions to assist employment in the selected development areas, the balance of payments, and the control of inflation have bred resentment in the nationalized fuel industries, whose leaders feel they have neither the autonomy necessary for efficient management nor clear guidance from the government. Recent examples include the requirement for the CEGB to burn six million tons of extra coal a year, the rejection of both the CEGB's proposed nuclear program and its proposals to convert coal-fired plants to oil, the bringing forward of the order for the Ince oil-fired power station in 1972, pressures to make the industries buy British steel pipe and platforms for North Sea operations, and the postponement of price increases that resulted in massive deficits for the fuel industries and prevented them from achieving the financial targets imposed by the government.

As a result, the financial and economic operating rules that emerged in the 1960s to encourage efficiency and autonomy—on the supposition that government interventions would be minimal and offset by appropriate financial compensation—have become increasingly inadequate as wider national considerations have come to dominate the processes of policy formation in the energy sphere.

Coping with Uncertainties

The British energy policy system therefore contains a number of features that cast doubt on its ability to cope satisfactorily with future problems. First, the dominant approach has for long been short term and supply oriented and therefore ill adapted to coping with the long-term problems of energy conservation, depletion, and research. This deficiency is underlined by the relatively tenuous links between energy policy and related policy systems for transport, housing and industrial development. Second, uncertainties have been obscured by reliance on comparatively short planning horizons, thereby leading to serious misjudgments about the future availability of oil and nuclear power. Third, the intrinsic difficulties of specifying an operational objective function and of devising adequate operating rules for the nationalized fuel industries have led to recurrent conflicts in formulating and implementing policies, which have tended to become submerged by the technical nature of many of the issues. Fourth, powerful forces of inertia, combined with the difficulty of keeping in balance the interests of consumers, local communities, workers, and the plant supply industries, make the energy policy system slow in responding to new circumstances and new challenges.

In the past few years, some major new challenges have arisen for the British energy policy system. They stem mainly from the uncertainties exposed by the world oil crisis and relate not only to the long-term availability and price of oil, but also to the problems associated with the growth of nuclear power (e.g., reactor reliability, construction delays and cost overruns, and public acceptance of the risks). These uncertainties mean that the time-horizons for energy policy must in the future be much longer than hitherto and that among the central concerns of British energy policy must be the rate of depletion of offshore oil and gas resources, the rate of growth of energy demand, and appropriate priorities for energy-related research. These represent major challenges to the energy policy system.

If Britain's offshore oil and gas supplies are to last well into the next century, the rate of production will have to be controlled, and the available supplies of oil may have to be used increasingly for nonsubstitutable, high-value uses such as petrol and petrochemical feedstock. If the rate of depletion is to be controlled, this policy in turn will require decisions to postpone the commercial exploitation of new discoveries; therefore, problems of equity and compensation are likely to arise. It is difficult to see how such a policy can be combined with one of encouraging vigorous exploration unless the recently created British National Oil Corporation acquires the necessary technical and financial resources to play an active longer-term role in exploration.

As yet, there is no sign that policymakers are developing adequate measures to control the future growth of energy demand. Given the public mood after oil prices soared, an opportunity existed to introduce effective conservation measures. In September 1975, a Parliamentary Select Committee report expressed the view that the opportunity had been passed by and recommended inter alia the creation of an Energy Conservation Task Force to coordinate and invigorate energy-saving efforts. The fall in energy consumption during 1974 and 1975, largely due to a recession in industry, has reduced the immediate urgency of government leadership in the introduction of conservation measures and has reinforced the apathy of the public towards the question of how energy may be used more efficiently.

As yet, there is little evidence that the national policy-making system has succeeded in adjusting to the intrinsically very difficult problem of curbing the long-term rate of growth of energy demand by identifying the critical choices in related policy fields, such as transport, housing, and industrial development, that will have a major bearing on future energy demands. On the basis of statistical projections, predictions have already been made of another national energy gap (this time arising after 1990) that some experts believe can only be fully closed by a rapid expansion of nuclear power. Given the expectation that a world uranium shortage will occur at about the same time, the perceived energy gap is being used by some interests to support the case for an early start on the development of a liquid metal fast reactor (breeder) of a commercial size.

Scottish nationalism and membership in the EEC represent further imponderables for British energy policy. Only time will tell if the moves towards greater political devolution for Scotland will discourage latent pressures towards separatism. Scottish nationalism hinges, to a large extent, upon North Sea oil, since many Scots regard the oil as a potential long-term source of income for the Scottish economy that would offer a better future than if Scotland were to remain as a less prosperous part of the United Kingdom. If the demand for separatism grows, the ownership and exploitation of North Sea oil would probably become major areas of dispute between England and Scotland.

Attempts to introduce a common EEC energy policy have so far failed because of the pressure of divergent national interests. If the EEC is to go forward to full economic and political integration, however, some form of harmonization of the energy policies of the various member countries will have to be achieved. Given the EEC's dependence on oil imports and the associated political and economic risks, North Sea oil is almost certain to become a major focus in any negotiations leading to political integration. It is clearly in Britain's national interest to retain full control over the use of the North Sea oil resources, since their depletion will be accelerated if the oil companies are allowed to export large quantities. If sufficient concessions could be obtained from other EEC members in other areas of policy, then it is conceivable that Britain might make some concession with regard to North Sea oil. This action might stop short of sanctioning large-scale exports, but it is not impossible to envisage deals concerning some of the marginal fields that might constitute a strategic reserve for the EEC in times of emergency. In addition to North Sea oil, a common EEC energy policy could impinge upon existing policies of the member countries for the protection of their coal, nuclear plant, and heavy electrical plant industries.

The scale and nature of the uncertainties and risks are such that it would be quite inappropriate to pin faith on a simple cost-minimization approach to energy policy. Optimization procedures only become realistic where the objectives are clear and the uncertainties small. For Britain, it is becoming clear that the challenge now is to develop policies that offer an inbuilt robustness and flexibility and that are therefore capable of adapting to a variety of possible future developments. Flexibility is, of course, by no means easy to achieve, given the long lead-times, heavy costs of investment, other sources of inertia, and the undesirability in present and foreseeable circumstances of using oil imports as the balancing form of energy supplies.

The nationalized electricity industry, a very large user of coal and oil, has occasionally been used to cope with short-run imbalances between supply and demand. This approach has produced much conflict and has never been seen as a continuing policy. If this role were to be thrust upon the electricity industry on a continuing basis, it would probably have to build more coal-fired power stations to obtain the requisite degree of flexibility. Financial compensation would also be needed, either through specific subsidies to the industry or through a relaxation of its financial target.

If the emphasis in energy policy is to shift to the longer-term problems of demand management, the control of depletion, and the priorities for energy research, there will have to be far less reliance on single-point forecasts that merely serve to obscure uncertainties and the scope for policy choices and more reliance on such innovative methods as the use of scenarios in order to identify courses of action that may be needed if blatantly undesirable outcomes are to be avoided. This approach, though fraught with difficulties in communication between different interest groups and professions and between different areas and levels of decision making, could offer the possibility of relating alternative policies for transport, housing, and industrial development to the context of long-term energy policy. Closer coordination would also be required between regional policies and an emergent national energy policy.

Despite the inherent difficulties, a resolve to move in these directions could do much to bring about a shift towards wider, more consciously connected policy making in which it is possible to see more clearly the links between key energy decisions and the development of policies in a whole range of interrelated fields.

Organizational Arrangements

If the energy policy system in Britain is to cope with the challenges ahead, changes will have to be considered in the organizational arrangements through which it functions. An overview of the present organizational structure is indicated in Figure 2-4, which shows the Department of Energy as one of several Departments of State whose concerns are formally brought together at the cabinet level. The Department of Energy itself is connected to a series of operational policy systems concerned with different supply industries, and as we have already discussed, the increasing range of concerns coming to bear on the future of national energy policy make it more and more difficult to draw a distinct boundary between the competences of these operational policy systems and the wider public policy system for energy supply within Britain. The issues of limiting future energy demands imply the creation of increasingly subtle links between the Department of Energy and other government departments, which themselves may exercise only indirect leverage over various industrial, commercial, and household energy demands.

It is easy to conceive a "rational" response to such problems of coordination by imposing new structures at a superordinate level—for instance, by merging existing departments into "superministries" or, as has been proposed, by setting up an independent energy commission. While such a commission could doubtless devote more time to thinking about fundamental long-term problems and could leave the administrative burdens arising from ministerial responsibility to civil servants, it might create new problems by coming into conflict with the government wherever the government wished to pursue nonenergy considerations through the fuel sector. On the whole, there are strong arguments that the government should be considered responsible for all such interventions. Also, an independent energy commission would be less well-placed than the Department of Energy for forging effective and informal links with other departments responsible for related fields of policy. Again, large "superministries" have been tried in the past as a means of achieving central coordination over mutually dependent policies. They have been found to carry the danger of inefficiency, of a further blurring of basic value issues, and of practices whereby policy conflicts tend to be resolved internally by civil servants rather than by ministers answerable to Parliament.

It may be argued that centralized systems can be more effective in dealing

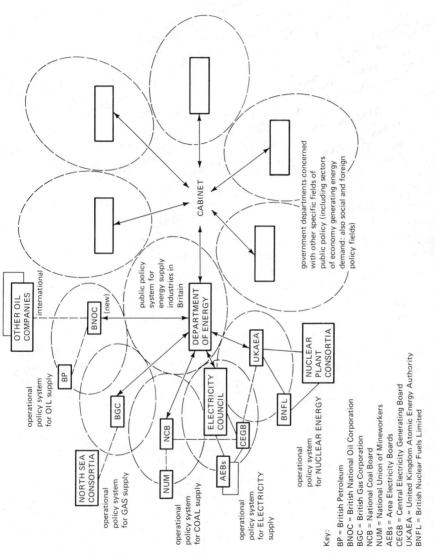

Key:

BP = British Petroleum
BNOC = British National Oil Corporation
BGC = British Gas Corporation
NCB = National Coal Board
NUM = National Union of Mineworkers
AEBs = Area Electricity Boards
CEGB = Central Electricity Generating Board
UKAEA = United Kingdom Atomic Energy Authority
BNFL = British Nuclear Fuels Limited

Figure 2-4. Organizational Structure of British Energy Policy Making.

with important perceived issues and in coordinating large-scale plans, but they are also likely to reduce flexibility, stultify local initiatives, and lead to the neglect of issues that may be important even though not perceived as such by central policymakers. The greater the degree of centralization, the greater the importance of counterbalancing its adverse effects by developing "pluralist" structures that permit alternative views to be heard.

Parliamentary Select Committees, although their effectiveness remains limited, are a welcome step towards greater pluralism. In recent years, new interests and agencies—environmental groups and trade unions among others—have begun to make their views heard, even if not always accepted, by policymakers. Informed public discussion through television, radio, and newspapers can have an important role to play in increasing the level of public understanding and thus making policy making more open. And for much the same reason—namely, to redress the tendency for policies to be dominated by the interests and values of the highly centralized, monopolistic organizations in the fuel sector—there is also a strong case for independent research on energy policy questions.

The desirability of conserving energy and preventing environmental degradation underlines the importance of seeking more sensitive forms of coordination between policies for energy, transport, housing, and industrial development and thereby of helping flexible, adaptive working links to develop between these mutually dependent policy systems. This process is bound to be largely experimental. The answer does not necessarily lie in reorganization and the creation of new institutions; sometimes existing mechanisms for achieving better coordination are inadequately exploited, whether because of differences of orientation between the actors concerned or because the languages through which they are able to communicate are not adequate to express the complex nature of the issues and interdependencies that they encounter. Possible solutions may lie in seeking to improve communication between existing institutions by encouraging more frequent movement of key people, thus changing their roles and broadening their understanding.

Britain is by no means alone in facing the apparent intractability of these fundamental problems: the difficulty in achieving adequate coordination between mutually dependent but internally complex policy systems, the problem of giving explicit consideration to value-related uncertainties, and the achievement of effective pluralism in the planning process. While the interrelationships between issues, processes, and actors, and the contributory variables indicated on Figure 2-1, are subtle enough even within comparatively specialized policy systems, such as those directed towards particular forms of bulk energy supply, the intricacy of such relationships increases manifold at the level of national energy policy with its ever-changing linkages to other national and international policy issues. Indeed, the fact that these problems are common to most industrialized countries makes it all the more necessary to compare and learn from the difficulties, experiences, and experiments that are to be found in a variety of different countries. In this light, it is hoped that the British case may contribute its own lessons for other countries that also face problems of adapting inherited policy systems to the challenges of an increasingly turbulent and interconnected world.

Postscript

The field of energy policy never remains static for long, and in the months since this chapter was drafted, two major developments have occurred in Britain. One was the decision by the Minister for Energy to take an initiative in stimulating public debate and in opening up exchange between the fuel industries on controversial issues by holding a national energy conference in public in June 1976. This action led in turn to demands both for further open discussions and for the setting up of an independent energy commission. The other significant development was the publication by the Department of Energy of a report on long-term research and development strategy. This report broke new ground by its use of scenarios and long-term time-horizons that extend to the years 2000 and 2025. It concluded that the main priorities for the future should lie with nuclear power, coal, and energy conservation measures. Yet it focused primarily on technological solutions and has been criticized for ignoring other policy instruments concerned with pricing, fiscal, and depletion strategies. Its projection of a widening energy gap after 1990, and its recommendation for a large nuclear program—especially a fast reactor program to avoid dependence on uranium—has served to prepare the way for an expected government announcement on whether to go ahead with a proposed fast reactor demonstration plant. Meanwhile, the long-term uncertainties continue to be as great as ever. The market for coal has not grown, and the estimated cost of the NCB's investment program has more than doubled. The size of offshore oil and gas reserves are still subject to a very wide margin of error, and despite the rapid escalation of costs and warnings against excessive optimism on the possibility of further North Sea oil discoveries, the announcement of two major new finds has brought about a very significant increase in estimated total British oil reserves. On the question of energy conservation, however, important uncertainties remain, for the government has yet to indicate in what directions its future intentions lie.

Bibliography

Ashworth, G. "Natural Resources and the Future Shape of Britain." *The Planner*, vol. 7, no. 60 (August 1974), p. 773.
Burn, D. *The Political Economy of Nuclear Energy.* London: Institute of Economic Affairs, 1967.

Department of Energy. *Coal Industry Examination*, Interim and Final Reports. London: HMSO, 1974.

———. *Development of the Oil and Gas Resources of the United Kingdom.* London: HMSO, 1975.

———. *Digest of United Kingdom Energy Statistics.* London: HMSO, annually.

———. *Energy R&D in the United Kingdom—A Discussion Document.* London: HMSO, June 1976.

———. *Fuel Policy*, Cmnd. 3438. London: HMSO, November 1967.

———. *Nuclear Reactor Systems for Electricity Generation.* London: HMSO, July 1974.

———. *United Kingdom Offshore Oil and Gas Policy*, Cmnd. 5696. London: HMSO, July 1974.

Friend, J.K., Power, J.M., and Yewlett, C.J.L. *Public Planning: The Inter-Corporate Dimension.* London: Tavistock, 1974.

Heller, R.A. "The Decision Process: An Analysis of Power-Sharing At Senior Organisational Levels." In Dubin, R. (ed.), *Handbook of Work, Organization and Society.* Chicago: Rand McNally College Publishing Co., 1975.

MacKay, D.I., and MacKay, G.A. *The Political Economy of North Sea Oil.* London: Martin Robertson, 1973.

National Economic Development Office. *Energy Conservation in the United Kingdom.* London: HMSO, 1974.

Pryke, R. *Public Enterprise in Practice.* London: MacGibbon & Kee, 1971.

Reid, G.L., and Allen, K. *The Nationalised Industries.* London: Penguin, 1973.

Posner, M. *Fuel Policy: A Study in Applied Economics.* London: Macmillan, 1973.

Select Committee on Science and Technology. First Report Session 1974-75, *Energy Conservation.* London: HMSO, 1975.

Surrey, A.J., and Walker, W.B. "Energy R&D—A UK Perspective." *Energy Policy*, June 1975.

H.M. Treasury. *The Nationalised Industries: A Review of Economic and Financial Objectives*, Cmnd. 3437. London: HMSO, November 1967.

Toffler, A. *Future Shock.* London: The Bodley Head, 1970.

Trist, E.L. "Action Research and Adaptive Planning." In Clark, A.W. (ed.), *Experimenting with Organizational Life. The Action Research Approach.* London: Plenum, 1976.

———. "Aspects of the Transition to Post-Industrialism." In Emery, F.E., and Trist, E.L., *Towards a Social Ecology.* London: Plenum Press, 1972.

3

Canadian Energy Development: A Case Study of Policy Processes in Northern Petroleum Development

David W. Fischer and
Robert F. Keith

Setting for Canadian Energy Policy

Because of Canada's geographic and climatic conditions and the quality of its peoples' lifestyles, Canada is second in the world in per capita energy consumption. Given the importance of energy to Canada, it is not surprising that much emphasis is placed on energy by its federal and provincial governments and that the energy industries are pervasive in the Canadian economy. The conflicts surrounding energy development and policy are increasing, and Canadian energy policy is in a period of flux. Within the energy milieu consisting of governments, public agencies, industries, consumers—some of whom bear the adverse impacts of new energy developments and some of whom defend Canadian identity and environmental sanctity—a broad range of actors or parties exists.

Canadian energy policy is therefore the ever-changing result of a complex and dynamic set of interactions among actors. Although specific energy policies have been developed for each energy source in relative isolation, this practice was found deficient during the energy crisis of 1973. This period of rapidly escalating prices found the federal government without a clear direction in regard to balancing energy producer and consumer needs, regional interests, price variations, and international pressures. Through a series of intergovernmental consultations, the federal and provincial governments have attempted to obtain some degree of consensus for future energy policy.

Canadian Energy Demand and Supply

In Canada as elsewhere, energy policy planning is characterized by numerous projections about future developments in supply and demand. Not surprisingly, projections even in recent years show marked differences. For example, in 1970 the National Energy Board approved new exports of natural gas to the United States based upon forecasts that showed Canada to have surpluses well beyond its domestic needs for twenty-five years. Only two years later these projections were being seriously questioned and no additional exports were allowed. In some cases existing levels of export were reduced as Canada now anticipates a petroleum shortfall in the late 1970s and early 1980s.

In its 1973 report on Canadian energy policy, the federal government (Department of Energy, Mines and Resources) forecast the consumption and possible development of primary energy use to the year 2050.[1] (See Figures 3-1 and 3-2.) Based upon a standard population growth, forecast energy consump-

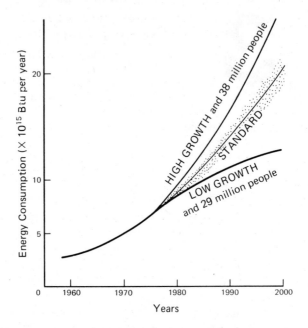

Source: Department of Energy, Mines and Resources, *An Energy Policy for Canada*—Phase 1, Vol, II, Appendices (Ottawa: Information Canada, 1973), p. 24.

Figure 3-1. Canada's Energy Consumption under High and Low Economic and Population Growth (1kWh = 3,412 BTU).

tion indicates an increasing dependence on electrical energy for a population two-and-one-half times as great as that of 1973. Natural gas will be replaced by electricity, and oil will be produced synthetically from oil sands and coal. In this case, assumptions about trends in price, demand, and technological break-throughs are couched in terms of past trends continuing into the future.

Of particular importance to Canada is the extent of its oil and gas resources. Table 3-1 provides estimates of proven remaining reserves, production, consumption, exports, and imports of both oil and gas. Reserve data show the beginning of a downward trend while production and consumption are both increasing. Exports, though shown to be rising, have since been reduced, while imports are steadily increasing. An apparent anomaly of technical self-sufficiency exists where production exceeds consumption; however, proved reserves are rapidly being depleted compared to increases in such reserves. Also, such sufficiency is indicated where exports exceed imports, but these export figures were based on a policy of dividing the country into two separate markets, one of which is dependent on foreign oil and the other, on exported oil. Table 3-2 is a comparison of oil and gas resources featuring proved, potential, and oil sands reserves in both the western provinces and the rest of Canada, particularly the

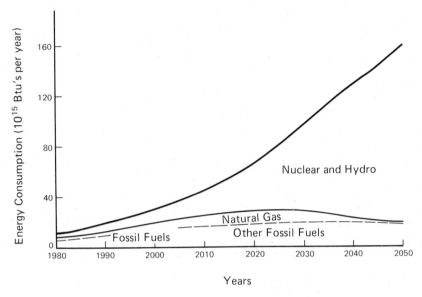

Source: Department of Energy, Mines and Resources, *An Energy Policy for Canada*—Phase I, Vol. I, Analysis (Ottawa: Information Canada, 1973), p. 101.

Figure 3-2. Example of a Possible Development of Canada's Primary Energy Use until the Year 2050.

frontier. Of interest is the present major role of the western provinces in providing Canada's oil and gas production and the potential dominant role of the frontier regions, the Arctic, and the eastern offshore.

The Alberta Oil Sands are also shown in Table 3-2. Given their known size they constitute a vast *proven* petroleum reserve of nearly one-half the size of Middle Eastern oil reserves. However, the technology for *in-situ* recovery is still nonexistent. Past Alberta government policies favoring its conventional oil industry did much to slow the rate of development of even the mineable reserves. Currently, the Alberta government favors rapid development of the oil sands, and one major plant, Syncrude Ltd., is under construction. Its output is scheduled to be 105,000 barrels of refined crude oil per day beginning in 1978.[2]

In a recent analysis from a private firm of the energy outlook for Canada, a projection based on all petroleum regions in Canada attempts to plot supply, demand, and project timing.[3] The projection in Figure 3-3 is based on the following assumptions:

1. The objective is maintenance of domestic self-sufficiency.
2. Demand for oil will continue its traditional 5 percent compound growth rate.
3. Oil will be readily found in the quantities forecast in geological, ultimate recoverable estimates.

Table 3-1
Canadian Oil and Gas, Basic Data

	1960	1962	1964	1966	1968	1970	1972ᵃ
Proven Remaining Reserves:							
Marketable Natural Gas [trillion cubic feet (10^{12})]	–	Not Comparable	–	43.2	47.4	53.1	52.9
Liquid Hydrocarbons [billion barrels (10^9)]	4.2	5.2	7.1	9.1	10.0	10.4	9.7
Natural Gas:							
Marketable Production [billion cubic feet (10^9)]	443.0	769.1	947.3	1,106.7	1,378.3	1,839.4	1,252
Canadian Consumption [billion cubic feet (10^9)]	332.0	432.0	555.7	702.0	850.6	1,043.7	1,256
Exports to United States [billion cubic feet (10^9)]	109.8	342.8	392.2	431.8	604.5	780.2	1,012
Imports from United States [billion cubic feet (10^9)]	5.5	5.5	9.6	44.6	81.6	10.9	16
Liquid Hydrocarbons:							
Production (thousand barrels daily)	543.4	731.2	847.7	1,012.6	1,196.3	1,476.1	1,819
Canadian Consumption (thousand barrels daily)	860.0	938.2	1,056.5	1,202.8	1,343.6	1,466.3	1,589
Exports, crude and products (thousand barrels daily)	122.9	252.4	303.4	385.7	517.4	763.0	1,144
Imports, crude and products (thousand barrels daily)	343.1	451.5	504.2	597.8	685.9	762.2	899

Source: Department of Energy, Mines and Resources, *An Energy Policy for Canada*–Phase 1, Vol. II, Appendices (Ottawa: Information Canada, 1973), p. 308.

ᵃFigures for 1972 are estimates.

Table 3-2
Canada's Oil and Gas Resources

	In Place	Recoverable	Cumulative Production	Remaining
1. Proved Oil Reserves (Conventional) Billion Bbls.				
NWT	0.5	0.1	<0.1	<0.1
W. Canada	43.8	15.9	6.2	9.7
E. Canada	0.2	0.1	<0.1	<0.1
Subtotal	44.5	16.0	6.3	9.7
2. Proved Natural Gas Reserves, Trillion Cu. Ft.				
NWT	2.0	1.3	–	1.3
W. Canada	116.5	69.1	17.8	51.4
E. Canada	1.1	1.0	0.7	0.3
Subtotal	119.6	71.5	18.5	52.9
3. Potential Oil (Conventional) Billion Bbls.				
Arctic Islands & NWT		70.1– 28.1	–	70.1– 28.1
W. Canada (Provinces)		6.5– 4.6	–	6.5– 4.6
East coast		41.7– 50.4	–	41.7– 50.4
Subtotal		118.3– 83.1		118.3– 83.1
4. Potential Natural Gas, Trillion Cu. Ft.				
Arctic Islands & NWT		481.1–341.7	–	481.1–341.7
W. Canada (Provinces)		100.5– 43.7	–	100.5– 43.7
East coast		253.1–326.1	–	253.1–326.1
Subtotal		834.7–711.5	–	834.7–711.5
5. Alberta Oil Sands, Billion Bbls.				
Open-Pit Mineable		65.0	0.1	64.9
"In-Situ" Recovery		235.9		235.9
Subtotal	710.8	300.9	0.1	300.8
6. Alberta Heavy Oil Billion Bbls.	75.0	30.0	–	30.0
7. Total Resource (BOE) Billion Bbls.	–	616.2–560.5	9.5	606.7–551.0

Source: Department of Energy, Mines and Resources, *An Energy Policy for Canada*—Phase 1, Vol. II, Appendices (Ottawa: Information Canada, 1973), p. 32.

Note: Totals may not add due to rounding.

4. Oil production from new areas and sources will come on stream at the earliest conceivable date and will not be subject to delay resulting from lack of finances, manpower, technology, pipelines, plants, or markets— that is, development is not impeded by social, economic or political restraints.

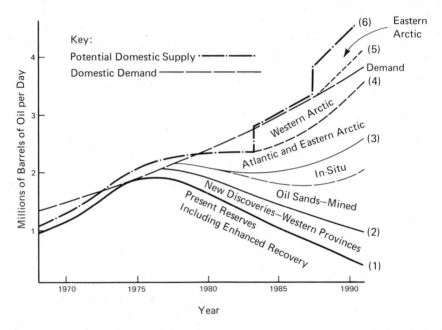

Source: Pallister Resource Management, Ltd., "Petroleum Policies in Canada: Issues, Forecasts and Outlook," Calgary, Alberta, May 1974, p. 23.

Figure 3-3. Potential Domestic Supply and Domestic Demand, 1970-1990 (millions of barrels of oil per day).

Although the authors admit that these assumptions are unrealistic, the scenario does provide a means for identifying the central policy issue of pace, scale, and timing of new petroleum regions. They further suggest that energy policy will be characterized by short-term self-sufficiency, slow growth, and alternate locations. They also indicate that social, environmental, and nationalistic pressures will be largely responsible for the shaping of Canadian energy policy.

The most recently published data on the Canadian supply and demand of oil and gas comes from the National Energy Board hearings in the fall of 1975.[4] Figure 3-4 shows the demand-and-supply situation for oil from 1975 through 1993. Two features are notable from this projection: (1) Canada is rapidly emerging from petroleum self-sufficiency, even with conservation practices being implemented; and (2) the Alberta Oil Sands along with oil imports will be the future major sources of petroleum, barring major finds in the Canadian frontier regions.

Thus, these three sets of demand-and-supply trends and projections demonstrate that Canada is in a period of flux from potential oil self-sufficiency to oil import dependence. Clearly, the most important opportunity to reverse or

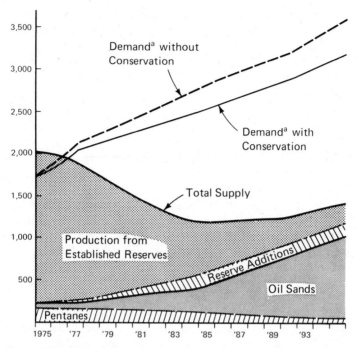

Source: National Energy Board, *Canadian Oil Supply and Requirements*, Ottawa, September 1975, p. 31 and Appendix E.

Note: Includes condensates and pentanes plus.

[a]Requirements for crude and equivalent, including losses and other adjustments.

Figure 3-4. Prospects for Demand and Supply of Oil, 1975-1993 (thousand barrels per day).

reduce this trend is to discover large petroleum supplies in its frontier regions. Therefore, much of the Canadian effort at the federal level is aimed toward furthering petroleum exploration. In recognition of Canada's lack of petroleum self-sufficiency, the federal government is striving to develop a greater supply of energy from a variety of sources and locations as well as to extend energy transportation corridors to the energy-deficient east. The federal government is involved in playing a multifaceted role as an energy consumer, a potential energy producer, a broker for less powerful provinces, an energy regulator, and a representative of other policy fields including economic development, immigration, employment, foreign control, and so forth.

Along with this greatly expanded energy role for the federal government the provinces are also stepping up their efforts to guarantee provincial energy self-sufficiency. Thus, conflicts exist over ownership of offshore lands and territorial lands in the Arctic, energy royalties and taxation, and the role of government energy investments. Table 3-3 presents an overview of each major energy source including the federal and provincial roles in their development. To demonstrate more fully the multiparty, multidimensional energy picture in Canada, this chapter will focus on how the development of a strategic new petroleum source has evolved. The area of study is the Canadian Arctic. The focus of study is the intensive search for petroleum in the Mackenzie Delta-Beaufort Sea and the Arctic Islands regions.

Much of the impetus for exploring the Canadian Arctic has come from the United States, which prefers to diversify its sources of energy and to rely on such sources that are considered politically stable. However, the Canadian government's response to its recent decline in discovery rates has been to conserve such petroleum supplies for Canadian users by limiting petroleum exports to the United States and to step up its frontier exploration efforts. Attention has been focused on the Arctic because of a longer drilling history there, discoveries of gas and oil there, and the recent formation of three transportation consortia to transport natural gas out of the Arctic.

Canadian Energy Jurisdictions

The complexity of energy jurisdiction and policy issues is perhaps greater in Canada than anywhere else. Canada, as a federal nation, is based on a confederacy with all primary governmental powers divided between the federal and provincial governments. The British North America Act of 1867 was the basis for the division of powers. It is, however, impossible to delineate a clear line between federal and provincial powers because of: (1) the extreme generality of the language used in the BNA Act, which creates overlapping jurisdictions; (2) either power can delegate to the other certain functions that would normally fall to that power; (3) neither power can limit the power of the other (interjurisdictional immunity), although some types of provincial law are applicable to the federal level; (4) jurisdiction varies depending on the kind of solution used; and (5) in the northern territories, the federal government acts as a province with all implied powers.[5]

Petroleum exploration, production, and transportation within provincial boundaries are totally under provincial jurisdiction. The provinces own 90 percent of the electricity generating industry; they presently control 100 percent of the oil and gas produced; they control nearly all of the coal fields; and when the oil sands potential is included, they control the bulk of Canada's future petroleum supplies. Any federal energy policy that ignores the provinces' interests cannot succeed. The transfer of energy resources across provincial boundaries is governed by federal regulation under the National Energy Board (established in 1959), which regulates the flow of natural gas and crude oil. The crossing of international boundaries also brings in the federal government for the

Table 3-3
Overview of Canadian Energy Sources

Energy Source	Reserve Situation	Demand Situation	Structure of Industry	Provincial Interest	Federal Involvement	Present Concerns
Coal	Massive but separated from demand centres	Stable but good potential	Private; crown corps	Leasing, royalties, safety, subsidies; some crown control	Subsidies for mining and marketing; finance R&D	Finding export markets; R&D on refining; modernize industry
Uranium	High proven and potential	Low but good potential	Private; one crown corp.	Leasing, royalties, safety	Subsidies for marketing; finance R&D	Finding export markets
Nuclear		High and growing	Provincial utilities; private mfg. of technology	Control, pricing, safety	R&D, safety; control exports; crown consortium	Finding export markets; R&D
Hydro	Potential sites but separated from demand centres	High and growing	Provincial utilities	Crown corp.; development	Subsidies; promote integrated river basin planning	Develop economic site; finding export markets
Gas	Production exceeds discovery rates; good potential but remote locations and high cost	Growing	Foreign private dominates; Canadian private; crown corp.	Leasing, royalties, conservation, transportation, R&D, safety, marketing, explore, pricing	Control exports and transportation; pricing when transferred; leasing, explore, planning; crown corp.	Determine reserves in frontier; curtail exports
Oil	Production exceeds discovery rates; good potential but remote locations and high cost	Growing	Foreign private dominates; Canadian private; crown corp.	Leasing, royalties, conservation, transp. R&D, safety, explore, pricing	Control exports and transportation; pricing; leasing, explore, planning; crown corp.	Determine reserves in frontier; ensure security of supply; curtail exports
Oil Sands	High proven but lack technology	Growing	Pilot plant (foreign private); consortium of private and crown	Leasing, royalties, production, safety, development	Subsidies; small equity	Ensure markets; develop technology; ensure orderly development

regulation of exports. The federal government relies on taxation and spending powers to influence petroleum decisions within the provinces.

Canada's federalism explains why many policies are a compromise among complex federal and provincial interests. The continuing task of the federal government is to attempt some kind of a national consensus through intergovernmental ministerial-level meetings. The objective of these disjointed but continuing meetings is the search for a petroleum policy that will serve the best interests of Canada as a whole.[6]

The Yukon and Northwest Territories, where the search for frontier petroleum is focused, come under federal rather than provincial jurisdiction. Should frontier oil and gas become available from the Canadian Arctic, the federal government will be thrust into the dual role of "provincial" and federal government.

The complexities surrounding the federal-provincial jurisdictions will continue to pervade the many decisions relating to energy policy. Satisfactory decisions on resource developments, leasing rights, and pricing policies will often be delayed unduly with subsequent higher costs. Although an overall Canadian interest should emerge, it will be an arduous process to reconcile the diverse interests of the producing and consuming provinces, such as Alberta and Ontario. Each of these provinces has vociferously defended its position, with Ontario legislating against a federally induced price increase passed to appease Alberta and with Alberta demanding a price increase to pay for its economic development so it can compete with Ontario.

Energy Capital Requirements

The capital requirements for the massive development of Canada's resources are themselves massive. One informed analyst recently commented on these capital requirements for sustained economic development:

... they aggregate well over $500 billion. I am referring here to the so-called "normal" needs of the energy, resource, and non-resource sectors. ... Add to that the special "super projects" about which there has been a great deal of discussion lately—the Alberta Tar Sands, James Bay Hydro and Arctic pipelines— and another $25 billion is tacked on to the capital investment bill ... requirements of this order of magnitude represent four to five times the total gross national product that Canada will likely achieve this year [1974]. ... To do so would require an average annual capital investment to at least 25 percent of Canada's annual output or GNP.[7]

The government has used an econometric model to project four scenarios of energy development in the Arctic.[8] This model, however, focused on incremental differences among the different rates of development rather than on the absolute amounts of capital required. One government analyst drawing on this approach, however, has suggested that the total development costs of oil and gas in the north through the year 2000 will range from \$49 to \$68 billion, depending on the rate of such development.[9]

Given the range of energy resource options open to Canada, the decision to develop Arctic petroleum, the oil sands, and coal gasification will be influenced by which source seems the most economic for Canada. The choice of which energy resource to develop depends critically on the amount of oil and gas found in the Canadian Arctic. Until the time when large commercial quantities are found in the north, however, Canada must rely on imports and oil sands plants as conventional oil reserves are depleted. Maxwell has compared the capital costs of new production capacity needed to produce one barrel of oil per day: Middle East, \$240; North Sea, \$5750; and Alberta Oil Sands, \$19,900.[10] Clearly, Canada is faced with varying risks in attempting to chart its course for meeting its burgeoning energy demands. Maxwell has noted that these risks include: imports, with their security risks; oil sands, with their cost risk; and frontier supplies, which are still subject to an exploration risk.[11] Given this situation, it can be readily understood why Canada is attempting to maximize the exploration effort in its frontier regions by giving more beneficial terms for the oil industry and, through its newly formed national petroleum company, Petro-Can, undertaking such exploration as its top priority.[12] Thus, this study will emphasize the policy concerns associated with northern petroleum development.

Northern Petroleum Development

Figure 3-5 shows the sedimentary basins that contain the potential oil and gas reserves of the Canadian north. To date, exploration has been concentrated in the Mackenzie Delta and the Arctic Islands with some lesser activity in Hudson Bay and the eastern offshore. Figure 3-5 also shows the proposed natural gas routes for transporting gas from the north to the south. Each of the four routes named are backed by different consortia. Three of the consortia are competing to deliver portions of the gas from the Prudhoe Bay-Mackenzie Delta regions.

Federal Government Oil and Gas Lands Regulations

A review of Canadian Arctic petroleum development clearly reveals a rapidly evolving program from a point of very little activity in the late 1950s to intensive action by many actors in 1975. In the spring of 1961, when the federal government issued statutes and regulations for petroleum exploration north of the 60th parallel, the stage was set for the Mackenzie and Arctic Islands developments. As Maxwell points out:

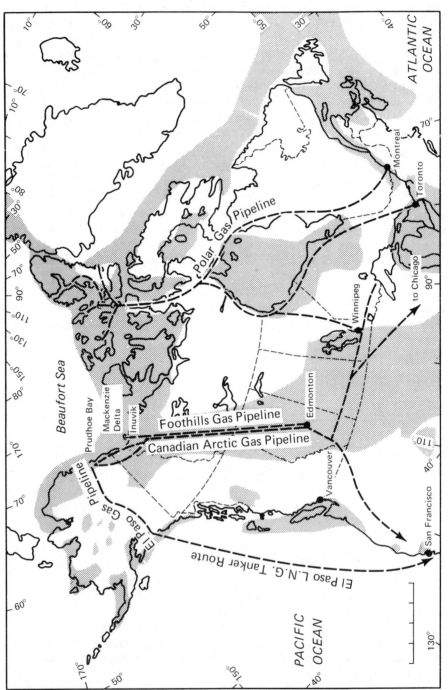

Figure 3-5. Proposed Transportation Systems for Arctic Natural Gas.

Within weeks the industry had snapped up permits for 60 million acres. The new regulations were different from those in most other producing countries, in that the government decided to forego revenues during the exploration stage and to give the companies long-term rights to the land. . . . In other words, the first priority was to get the exploration going.[13]

This action by the federal government in 1960 to allow petroleum exploration in the Arctic was clearly a fundamental decision. It induced immediate action on the part of the petroleum industry as permits were quickly taken out. The area involved covered virtually all sedimentary areas in the Northwest and Yukon Territories, both on land and under water. The decision required the government to allocate resources for the regulation and surveillance of exploration activity.

Imperial Oil's Decision to Remain

Although permits were taken up very quickly, exploration work was slow and arduous. In the early 1960s, some explorers relinquished their permits in favor of more promising areas of the world and less severe working conditions. However, not all explorers chose or were able to do so. Imperial Oil not only stayed, but also increased substantially their permit acreage in the Mackenzie Delta area. Thus, by 1964 Imperial had accumulated approximately 10 million permit acres, which thus made it the largest operator in the region.

The decision of Imperial to acquire such a vast permit area is seen as a fundamental decision. As prime explorers, they have set the pace in the Delta, have reported the first finds of oil and gas there, and have pioneered drilling in the shallow offshore area by the use of artificial islands. Moreover, other actors, encouraged by the Prudhoe discoveries and Imperial's lead, have followed Imperial to the Delta.

Decision to Form Panarctic Oils, Ltd.

While activity in the Mackenzie Delta progressed, so too did exploration in the Arctic Islands. This region was initially shunned by the "majors" with the result that the permits in the Arctic Islands were held for the most part by the smaller independents and a few foreign firms, two of which—Elf and British Petroleum— were controlled by the French and British governments, respectively. Growing government concern for Canadian sovereignty in the Arctic (among other factors) led the federal government in 1967 to participate in Panarctic Oils Limited, in which the government took a 45 percent equity position. This action allowed the independents to continue as cooperative explorers in the Arctic Islands, assured a Canadian presence there, and made government both a developer and regulator in the petroleum program.

Thus, for the Arctic Islands the decision in 1967 by the federal government to participate in and underwrite Panarctic Oils was a fundamental decision. It was fundamental in terms of both intent and consequences. Although discoveries and production were uncertain, the government intended to become a petroleum developer. It could have chosen to provide loans and favorable taxation conditions to the emerging consortium in 1966-67. Instead, it chose an equity position by which it could participate directly and thus exert even more influence over northern resource development.

Discovery at Prudhoe Bay, Alaska

Then in midsummer of 1968 the announcement came that vast quantities of oil and gas had been found at Prudhoe Bay on the Alaska North Slope. The effects of this find were immediate and great. The cabinet responded by creating the Task Force on Northern Oil Development to foster a permanent link between U.S. and Canadian oil and gas resources and markets. In response to this federal interest, seismic and drilling activities in the Canadian Arctic increased rapidly. Petroleum transportation planning began in earnest. Technical, social, and environmental research programs were launched. Federal government task forces and committees were formed and existing committees shifted their emphasis to northern petroleum programs. In Alaska itself, environmental interests began to pressure U.S. authorities to undertake comprehensive environmental impact studies. In addition, native groups in Alaska intensified their efforts to seek a settlement of their land claims and grievances. The emergence of environmental and native land claim issues in Alaska is one reason for their importance in the Canadian Arctic and for the ensuing level of activity and investment in research on these issues.

Decision Clusters

Since 1968 and the Prudhoe announcement there have been numerous decisions by a variety of actors affecting every aspect of petroleum development in the north. No single decision appears to have had quite the significance of those fundamental decisions already discussed. However, viewed as clusters of decisions very important trends emerge.

First Cluster. During the years immediately after Prudhoe, particularly 1970-71, a number of important decisions were taken by the federal government. In June 1970, both the Arctic Water Pollution Prevention Act and the Northern Inland Waters Act were passed by Parliament. The former was in response to the voyage of the Manhattan, an experimental U.S. ice-breaking oil tanker, which posed a threat to Canadian sovereignty in the Arctic.[14] The latter act was intended to protect inland waters, particularly the Mackenzie River.[15] Also in 1970, the Canada Oil and Gas Land Regulations were withdrawn as the government served notice it intended to revise them with a view to making them similar to those in effect in the provinces and Alaska, especially concerning "royalty rates and primary terms."[16] This same year the government introduced its Preliminary Pipeline Guidelines for Oil and Gas Pipelines in the Mackenzie Valley, which signalled their intent to support a pipeline. These guidelines served notice that the government intended to focus attention and priority on the Mackenzie Valley corridor concept, partly to maintain Canadian access to the U.S. market and partly to attract U.S. interest to a Canadian route for Prudhoe petroleum. In 1970 the National Energy Board also approved the last large gas export,[17] although the NEB still continues to approve substantial levels of export under existing agreements. In 1971 the government brought in the Territorial Land Use Regulations to complement the Arctic Waters Pollution Prevention Act and the Northern Inland Waters Acts, by providing comprehensive environmental protection through control of resource industries.[18]

These several decisions taken together mark the beginning of a change in the role of the federal government from that of an unobtrusive facilitator to an initiator of programs and policies. This cluster of government decisions in the early 1970s did much to raise the feeling of uncertainty among many groups. The combination of new and untried legislation with the withdrawal and pending revision of existing legislation left industry with a sense that the future was unpredictable. Environmentalists and native groups also saw the future as uncertain. Although legislation to protect the environment was passed by Parliament, the promulgation of regulations was seen as both slow and inordinately favoring the development process.[19]

Thus government decision making in the early 1970s had two important implications for northern development. The first was that the government moved to create a basis from which it could exert more influence over northern development. At the same time, however, it created serious uncertainty among many of those involved or affected by northern natural resource development.[20]

Second Cluster. A second cluster of decisions that emerges in this analysis concerns the evolution of northern native groups and the growing importance of the land claim issue. Three important decisions have affected the adversarial role of northern native peoples' groups. The first of these was the decision of Mr. Justice Morrow who ruled in favor of the request of the Indian Brotherhood of the Northwest Territories for a caveat on the use of lands involved in their yet-to-be-negotiated land claim. The second important decision was that of the three major native groups to identify "land, not money" as the basis of negotiation. While there are clearly important monetary aspects of the land claim, all three groups made the land issue their first priority. The third important decision was the establishment by the Department of Indian and Northern Affairs (DINA) of a Commission of Inquiry into the terms and conditions under which a natural gas pipeline may be built in the Mackenzie Valley. The importance of the inquiry to native groups stems from interpreting the terms of reference broadly.

The scope and timing of the pipeline inquiry and land claim negotiations may have a bearing on petroleum development. The strong consensus among northern natives for the land claim, supported by an active research program to substantiate the claim and prepare for negotiations, has made northern native groups active adversaries in the petroleum development process. This is not to say that native groups are against all development, only that they wish their land claim settled before development proceeds so they can exercise some control over the changing character of the north.

Third Cluster. As the roles of government and native groups underwent changes, industry activity increased despite high costs and uncertainty about regulations and land claims. Several important decisions by industry characterize the highly active period from 1972-74. In 1972, Imperial Oil built the first of its artificial islands in the shallow offshore areas of the Mackenzie Delta. Also in 1972 the formation of Canadian Arctic Gas Study, Ltd. (and its sister organization Alaskan Arctic Gas Study) occurred. The formation of CAGSL led to an intensive research program concerned with technical, environmental, social, and economic issues. In February 1973, Polar Gas, Ltd., was formed to study all possible means of transporting natural gas from the Arctic Islands to southern markets. This meant that now transportation studies were underway for both the Mackenzie-Beaufort Sea and Arctic Islands programs. Opinion was divided within industry on which of these two projects was likely to proceed first.

The year 1974 brought more important industry decisions. CAGSL filed an application to build a pipeline from Prudhoe Bay down the Mackenzie Valley to southern Canadian markets and the lower forty-eight states. Although incomplete at the time of filing, the application triggered a number of federal government responses. The previously discussed Commission of Inquiry was one.

Then in the summer of 1974, Alberta Gas Trunk Line, one of the founding participants of CAGSL, formally withdrew from the group. Shortly thereafter, AGTL announced the formation of Foothills Pipeline, Ltd., to build an "all-Canadian" natural gas pipeline from the Delta to Alberta.

In late 1974, El Paso Natural Gas Corporation filed an application with the U.S. Federal Power Commission and Department of Interior to bring Prudhoe gas to the lower forty-eight states via an Alaskan pipeline and LNG tankers. Like the Foothills Pipeline, Ltd., proposal, El Paso appealed to national interests and energy independence. Thus, with threshold volumes of gas in the Delta and Islands as yet unreached and with strong adversarial interests at work, four serious proposals for natural gas transport were brought forward.

Yet another significant development was the decision by Dome Petroleum in August 1974 to have two drill ships built for exploration in the Beaufort Sea. Until this time no company had been prepared to risk the cost of two drill ships—a duplication requirement established by the federal government.

In sum, decisions taken by various members of the industry block of actors represent significant developments in both the Mackenzie Delta-Beaufort Sea and Arctic Islands programs, particularly since they occurred in a climate of high uncertainty, high competition, and concerted adversarial action.

Fourth Cluster. The fourth major cluster of decisions focuses on the activities of governments from 1972 through the summer of 1974. During this period the provincial governments emerged as important actors in northern petroleum development. Alberta, British Columbia, Ontario, and Quebec have all moved toward involvement in one or another aspect of Arctic petroleum development. The governments of Alberta and British Columbia support the Foothills Pipeline, Ltd., proposal. Alberta's interest stems largely from a desire to expand its industrial base through the development of a petrochemical industry. British Columbia has similar ambitions, but it even now is experiencing a shortfall in natural gas due to production difficulties in its northern fields.

In the summer of 1974, the Government of Ontario announced the formation of the Ontario Energy Corporation. Indications were given that Ontario investment in some form—either in the Mackenzie-Beaufort Sea or Arctic Islands programs—was under consideration. Ontario as the industrial center of the country needs additional feedstocks to maintain and expand its industrial base. Thus, both Alberta and Ontario are vying for Arctic gas and petrochemical development projects.

Also in the summer of 1974, the Province of Quebec attempted to buy shares in Panarctic Oils, Ltd., and enter the Arctic petroleum game. Envisioning the need for future supplies of oil and gas, Quebec's move was seen as an attempt to secure energy for industrial development. The federal government blocked the purchase of these shares by Quebec. The federal Minister of Energy is quoted as saying, "This could cause conflict and perhaps even controversy between the various provinces holding an interest in Panarctic and those same provinces and the federal government."[21]

On the federal government side, several important decisions have been taken. In April 1972 Prime Minister Trudeau announced that construction of the Mackenzie Highway would begin shortly—a move many people thought was aimed at securing U.S. commitment to a Mackenzie Valley pipeline route.[22] Then came three decisions designed, it would appear, to strengthen the hand of the federal government and secure its position as an initiator and controller of the petroleum development process. Through the Department of Energy, Mines and Resources, the government served notice of its intention to form a national petroleum company, Petro-Canada. In addition, the 1974 spring budget statement, which contained more stringent taxation measures and disallowed high royalty payments to provinces as tax deductions for petroleum companies, evoked immediate displeasure from the petroleum industry. Then, in a move that further strained government-industry relations, the federal government announced in August 1974 that it would require detailed information on all "farmount" agreements in exploration programs and more complete seismic and drilling records from industry. While industry views these moves with extreme suspicion and displeasure, government sees these changes in the "rules of the game" as consistent with its announced intentions of 1970 to revise the Oil and Gas Land Regulations.

It is important also to note that the interplay between governments and governments and industry is now taking place in a climate of increased national concern for energy needs and supplies. A mood favoring energy independence in Canada has surfaced for each province. Whereas only a few years ago Canada sought to develop petroleum markets in the United States, the concern now has shifted to Canadian needs and strategies. The year 1973 was characterized both by the largest exports of oil to the United States in Canadian history (> 1 million barrels per day) and by the first imposition of export controls on oil.

Canadian Energy Actors in the North

Table 3-4 shows the sheer number of actors involved in petroleum development in the Canadian north. The typology used to classify these diverse actor groupings is described in an earlier effort.[23] This typology demonstrates possible competing interests by showing probable and actual roles between the various groupings. The complexity of issues that these groupings raise through their array of linkages is also quite large.

It is also important to note that the composition of actors is in flux. Not only are new actors emerging, but roles or priorities are shifting. Alliances and coalitions are constantly forming and reforming as groups strive to enhance their positions vis-à-vis other actors. Whether attempting to acquire information, to influence discussions, or to offset imbalances in power relationships, the evolutionary realignment processes are important to the overall northern energy development process. To a large extent high levels of regulatory, economic, and political uncertainty account for the system's being in flux. The classification of actors has permitted important relationships between actors in order to identify more clearly the nature of supportive and countervailing pressures at work. Although 1973 marks a turning point in energy emphasis within Canada, many of the actor groups to be discussed had either emerged or were emerging when the energy crisis of 1973 occurred.

In the northern frontier, core actors include leading members of the petroleum industry and the federal Department of Indian and Northern Affairs

(DINA). Allied actors generally include other ministries of the federal government, provincial governments, related industries, and high-level government-industry committees whose purpose it is to advise governments. Taken together, the categories of core and allied actors represent the greatest number of actors and the convergence of the greatest degree of financial, technical, and statutory power. Prior to the 1970s few other actor groups existed in Canada; and certainly, little formal opposition existed to energy development in the north.

Figure 3-6 identifies the key linkages surrounding northern petroleum development in the Canadian federal milieu. The major decision-making body is the cabinet, into which all information is fed via the ministers of the two concerned federal departments. The following sections discuss these actors in detail, but one factor stands out: the discretion of the government inner circle in information generation and policy formation.

Canadian Energy Regulatory Process

Because of the federal nature of Canada, a complete discussion of Canadian energy regulation would include both federal and provincial regulatory processes. Here we will only discuss the federal process that is limited by law to the frontier regions, including the north. The regulatory process in the Canadian frontier is characterized by uncertainty.[24] DINA designed and promulgated oil and gas land tenure regulations in 1961 and then withdrew them in 1970. To date, they have not been reissued.

Because most northern lands and offshore areas are already under permit or lease, the regulatory process begins with a Notice of Commencement of Exploratory Work from the Department of Indian and Northern Affairs (DINA) or the Department of Energy, Mines and Resources (DEMR), which control the way the permittee fulfills work requirements. Which of the two federal departments is involved depends on the location of the proposed exploration site (DEMR controls Hudson Bay and offshore from the provinces). Some exploratory work is required to maintain the permit or lease. In addition, exploration efforts require a land-use permit for disrupting the land surface. The exploratory work permit application is handled exclusively within the department having jurisdiction over the lands of interest. The land-use permit is also under the requisite department, but a Land Use Advisory Committee has been formed to advise the department. This committee has representation from the territorial governments and other federal departments having specialized environmental interests in the north. No native peoples are represented on this committee although they are to be given advance notice of proposed plans. Should a native community object to proposed exploration work, both the company and the department attempt to persuade the community; should the persuasion efforts fail, the minister of the department makes the final decision.

Table 3-4

Classification of Actors for Mackenzie and Arctic Islands Programs

Actor Type	Mackenzie	Arctic Islands
Core Actors	Petroleum Majors Indian and Northern Affairs (DINA) Arctic Gas (CAGPL) Alberta Gas Trunk (AGTL)	Panarctic Oils Ltd. Indian and Northern Affairs (DINA) Polar Gas
Allied Support Actors	Dept. of Environment (DOE) Dept. of Energy, Mines and Resources Treasury Board Departments of Transport and Public Works Advisory Committee on Northern Development Task Force on Northern Oil Development Federal Cabinet Dept. of Finance Pipeline Application Assessment Group Canadian Petroleum Association Independent Petroleum Assoc. of Canada Arctic Petroleum Operators' Assoc. Dome Petroleum National Advisory Committee on Petroleum National Advisory Committee on Pipeline Financing Government of Alberta Government of British Columbia Government of Ontario Steel Industry Transportation Industry (air, rail, boat/barge) Construction Industry Heavy Equipment Manufacturers Investment Companies and Financial Institutions Alberta Energy Resources Conservation Board	Dept. of Environment (DOE) Dept. of Energy, Mines and Resources Treasury Board Departments of Transport and Public Works Advisory Committee on Northern Development Task Force on Northern Oil Development Federal Cabinet Dept. of Finance Canadian Petroleum Association Independent Petroleum Assoc. of Canada Dome Petroleum Petroleum Majors National Advisory Committee on Petroleum National Advisory Committee on Pipeline Financing Government of Alberta Government of Ontario Government of Quebec Steel Industry Transportation Industry (air, rail, boat/barge) Construction Industry Heavy Equipment Manufacturers Investment Companies and Financial Institutions
Independent Central Actors	National Energy Board Commission of Inquiry	National Energy Board

Middle Range Actors	Government of the NWT Government of the Yukon Science Council of Canada	Government of the NWT Science Council of Canada Inuit Tapirisat of Canada
Rivals and Adversaries	Committee for Original Peoples' Entitlement (COPE) Indian Brotherhood of the NWT Council of Yukon Indians Federation of Natives North of 60° Canadian Arctic Resources Committee Railway Study Groups Committee for an Independent Canada	Federation of Natives North of 60° Canadian Arctic Resources Committee Committee for an Independent Canada Arctic Gas (CAGPL) Alberta Gas Trunk (AGTL)
Exogenous Rivals and Adversaries	El Paso Natural Gas Corp.	
Exogenous Independents	Federal Power Commission (U.S.) Department of Interior (U.S.)	
Supporting Exogenous Actors	Multinational Oil Corporations	Multinational Oil Corporations

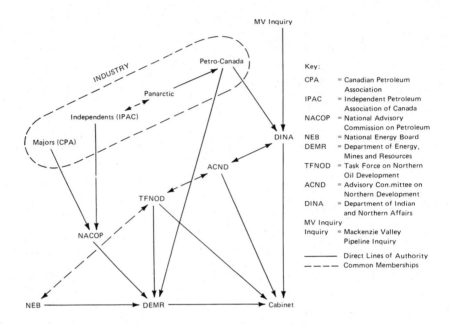

Figure 3-6. Key Actor Linkages in Northern Petroleum Development.

No offshore drilling has yet occurred in the Beaufort Sea other than in the shallows of the Mackenzie Delta from artificial islands approved under the land use permit process. The federal departments with jurisdiction have established an approval-in-principle for tentatively approving a designed but as yet unbuilt and unproved technology for drilling offshore. Industry is unhappy with the approval-in-principle since it feels the department has had adequate lead time for making offshore exploration technology regulations; the department, however, fears adverse public opinion over possible blowouts and is reluctant to authorize untried technology.[25] An internal departmental environmental review committee reviews the approval-in-principle for safety and environmental impacts. Other governmental reviews include transportation, pollution control, fisheries impact, and environmental information on weather, ice, and so forth.[26]

No development and production has yet occurred in the Canadian north. Transportation regulation, however, is under active consideration. The focal point within government is the Task Force on Northern Oil Development composed of federal departments and the National Energy Board (NEB).[27] This group is to coordinate the government's involvement in appraisal and policy studies including industrial supply, pipeline, economic impact, environmental-social, transport, and marketing. Each representative on the task force retains its own program and budget. A major output of the task force has been the corridor concept and guidelines for the pipeline consortia seeking to apply to the government for permits to build a gas pipeline.

Two permits are required for a pipeline: a right-of-way permit from DINA and a Certificate of Public Convenience and Necessity from NEB. (If the gas is to be exported then an export license is also required from the NEB.) The current pipeline applications are the first of their kind in the Canadian north. A minority government in the fall of 1972 forced DINA to create an ad hoc inquiry to investigate the economic, environmental, and social impacts of a pipeline right-of-way in the north.[28] One feature of this one-man inquiry has been its demand for public funds for supporting small public-interest environmental and native groups to do research in the field and to be present at the hearings. However, DINA has not provided all of the funds requested. Another unprecedented feature of the inquiry was the demand that all information be made public, including information from the applicants as well as from the government. When this inquiry has finished DINA will decide on a right-of-way permit, probably with the advice of the cabinet.

The final permit from NEB will emanate from another set of hearings that are proceeding simultaneously with those of the inquiry. While the right-of-way inquiry (also called the Berger Commission or the Mackenzie Valley Pipeline Inquiry) is an ad hoc response to the first northern pipeline application, the NEB, which began in 1959, has had a longer track record.[29] It has emphasized technical and financial feasibility, although it has the authority to investigate all matters affecting the public interest. The NEB must satisfy itself that the pipeline and any exports, if requested, are required. Formal application for intervenor status is required because the hearings are based on the adversary process. Cross-examination is done by the applicant, intervenors, and NEB staff. An unprecedented challenge of the chairman of the NEB was made by the public interest intervenors on the grounds of his past association with the pipeline applicant. The Supreme Court upheld this challenge (1976).

If the NEB decision goes against the pipeline, the applicant can only appeal through the courts on a point of law, not on a point of substance. If the NEB decision is for the pipeline, it can attach conditions to its decision that are unalterable. The NEB's affirmative decision is forwarded to the cabinet through the Minister of Energy, Mines and Resources for the final decision.

Whether or not the House of Commons becomes involved is at the discretion of the government. Certainly, the Canadian regulatory process as it is evolving is an ad hoc process that is reducing the role of such traditional institutions as the Parliament and the political parties.[30] The uncertainty surrounding this ad hoc process has heightened the concerns of all actors in this process, including those who are peripheral actors.

Northern Energy Actors

Major Petroleum Companies. The following "majors" are among the core actors in conducting exploration, development, and transportation activities in the Mackenzie Delta. Included are Imperial Oil, Ltd., Shell, Gulf, Mobil, and Texaco, which are dominated by American interests.

The Norman Wells oil field, one of the most northerly oil fields in the world, was discovered in 1920 by Imperial Oil, Ltd., 1,000 miles north of Edmonton along the Mackenzie River.[31] This field was concrete evidence of the presence of oil potential in the Canadian north.

By 1968 exploration in the Mackenzie Delta increased markedly because of the Prudhoe Bay strike. Much of this activity was undertaken by Imperial Oil, which had "10 million acres under permit in the Delta area."[32] In January 1970, Imperial announced a major oil show at Atkinson Point. Whereas the Prudhoe Bay discovery provided general encouragement for northern exploration, the Atkinson Point discovery was specifically encouraging for the Mackenzie Delta.

Gas finds began to occur more rapidly than oil finds, however, which resulted in attention being shifted to gas. The gas and oil finds at Prudhoe Bay and in the Mackenzie Delta gave new significance to the concept of transportation along a Mackenzie Valley "corridor" to southern markets.

This foreign-controlled industry has similar prevailing views, including: (1) Frontier petroleum must be brought to markets as soon as possible in order to avoid prolonged shortfalls; (2) the regulatory climate is uncertain; (3) the economic situation is variable due to taxation and royalty structures that fluctuate in a political atmosphere; and (4) other foreign investors are difficult to attract because of recent government moves to curtail exports and emphasize Canadianization of holdings. Nonetheless, exploration programs continue to be pursued vigorously under the assumption that the Canadian government will act "reasonably" toward them in setting its future energy policies.

Panarctic Oils, Ltd. The increasing presence of multinational and foreign government-controlled oil firms in the Arctic Islands was used to support the concept of a cooperative Canadian exploration venture.[33] By 1967 the exploration permits of a number of small Canadian companies were about to expire. Shortly thereafter, it was reported that only support by the government was needed in order to go ahead with a $20-million exploration program.[34]

Government support did come in the form of equity, and Panarctic Oils, Ltd., was formed on December 12, 1967, approximately six months before the Prudhoe Bay discovery. The government's choice for participation by equity rather than through loans was taken as a sign that the government viewed the program not in terms of Panarctic alone but of a whole new wave of development in the north.[35] Through Panarctic, the government could generate jobs. There was also an interest in establishing a Canadian "presence" in the Arctic Islands.[36] Another factor was the overall policy that resource development was good for the Canadian economy.

Panarctic took over 44 million acres of Canadian government oil and gas permits in the Arctic Islands. Major gas finds were made in 1970 and an oil discovery of commercial proportions was made in late 1975.

Department of Indian and Northern Affairs. Central to virtually all development north of the 60th parallel in Canada is the Department of Indian and Northern Affairs (DINA). The department's statutory powers and numerous programs make it preeminent and dominant not only in northern development but, by virtue of its control of northern natural resources, in national energy development and planning. The roles DINA plays in northern development are numerous. Statutory powers over land, water, forests, minerals, and petroleum make the department very much a *province-like* actor. As the majority equity position in Panarctic Oils, Ltd., is held by the federal government and two of four government company directors are from DINA, the department acts as a corporate *developer.* DINA is also represented on the board of Canada's new national oil company, Petro-Canada. In its role of *regulator*, DINA issues licenses and permits for petroleum exploration and development as well as considers issues of environmental impacts. As an *administrator* of northern programs, DINA is concerned with the evolution of political and administrative functions in the Northern Territories. The operating premise appears to be that centralization is the only way to encourage an evolutionary process that will ultimately lead to provincial status. Of considerable importance to the process of northern development is the role of DINA as a *coordinator* of federal government interests in the north. Its statutory and regulatory powers have been augmented by departmental roles in various interdepartmental committees and task forces.

In the 1972 publication, *Canada's North 1970-1980*, the Government of Canada sets out its national objectives for the north and indicates that "the heaviest emphasis in current thinking is on the needs and aspirations of the native peoples."[37] From DINA's perspective one of the important priorities is to maintain "a reasonable pace of northern development." Maximum benefits to northerners will only be realized if an optimum pace of economic and social development is achieved.

Critics maintain that DINA is in a continuous conflict of interest position because of its wide array of conflicting roles in the north. Certainly, the decisions emerging from DINA indicate that contrary to its stated policy goals in *Canada's North 1970-1980*, northern development has priority over both Indian affairs and environmental concerns. Several findings that support the critics of DINA have recently been disclosed:[38]

1. DINA chaired the Advisory Committee on Northern Development (ACND) which advised the Cabinet on energy matters related to the north and encouraged the oil industry in its development planning.
2. The Minister of DINA worked in the Cabinet to secure approval-in-principle of a gas pipeline down the Mackenzie Valley which would tie the Canadian north directly into the North American energy economy.
3. DINA did not accept (prior to 1972) that the northern natives had any role in the planning for northern development which included pipeline routing, exploration locations and highway routing.
4. Panarctic Oils Ltd., on which DINA representatives sit, employed only six

natives in 1970 even though the new pipeline guidelines stressed native employment.

5. DINA actively worked to delay a settlement with Canadian natives through 1972 by rejecting the notion of aboriginal rights and by stressing that construction of a pipeline would proceed prior to any native settlement.

6. DINA gave approval-in-principle in 1973 to offshore drilling in the Beaufort Sea without consulting native groups and in advance of environmental studies.

7. DINA recommended an all-weather highway to Cabinet in advance of native consultations and any environmental studies in order to signal to the U.S. that Canada was serious in its bid for a rapid pace of northern development.

8. DINA has blocked the federal Department of Environment from conducting environmental impact studies for development projects in the north.

9. DINA has attempted to restrict the scope of the Mackenzie Valley Inquiry (Berger Commission) by restricting it to one gas pipeline, not allowing it to recommend for or against the pipeline and attempting to cut its budget for supporting native and environmental groups.

National Energy Board. The broad purpose of the National Energy Board (NEB) is to ensure the people of Canada the best and most effective use of energy resources in this country.[39] The NEB has both regulatory and advisory responsibilities that constitute a conflict of interest. One must question the independence of the board inasmuch as its chairman sits as a member on the National Advisory Committee on Petroleum. This group of senior executives from industry and government advise the cabinet on matters pertaining to petroleum development. Thus, the board was in the position of advising the government to speed up the pace of northern development via an approval-in-principle of a gas pipeline that it would later have to assess impartially as to its propriety.[40] Potential conflict with the government can exist because the board is to exercise independent judgment and is not to accept viewpoints from other agencies or interests, including ministerial statements favoring a particular project. Given its dual function of advisor and regulator of energy, the NEB is placed in a difficult position in the government milieu. For example, its former chairman played a crucial role with respect to oil exports to the United States, was part of a committee attempting to persuade the U.S. oil and gas industry to build pipelines in Canada, and advised the cabinet on energy policy. In addition, the chairman oversees the impartial hearings of the NEB on exactly the same concerns about which he advised the government.[41]

In recent years concern has arisen both within and outside the NEB for the sufficiency and accuracy of its information, particularly that related to reserve estimates. The NEB is not set up to collect detailed information but draws heavily on other branches of the federal and provincial governments, from the knowledge and experience of its staff, and from the information submitted by the public and energy industry during public hearings. A recent report showed that the NEB as well as the cabinet had relied on the Canadian Petroleum Association for their information concerning Canadian oil and gas reserves.[42]

Based on these figures, in 1970 the Board approved the largest export license for natural gas in Canadian history. Barely one year later the NEB began to reject new export requests because of pending shortages. It was impossible to substantiate Canada's petroleum reserves because neither the NEB nor the government had any independent information on Canada's reserves. Nevertheless, as late as 1972 the NEB was still of the opinion that Canada had extensive reserves of natural gas available to carry it into the twenty-first century and beyond. Hearings on reserves were finally held in 1975 and showed that Canada is in a precarious position with less than twenty years' supply at current rates of use.[43] Even the cabinet has been remiss in relying too extensively on information supplied by industry and on criteria that do not adequately reflect the changing nature of supplies and deliverability.[44]

Another point of contention regarding reserves is that in the past the NEB has considered them only in physical terms. No consideration of their value in an economic sense has been given. Presumably their value would increase as the reserves are depleted.[45] One NEB official said that in a "few years" the board will consider reserves in an economic sense.

Beyond advising the government and assessing energy information the NEB is also charged with regulating the transportation of petroleum and electricity across provincial and international boundaries. This regulatory process involves hearings on such applications with the hearing process determined by the Board itself. The NEB must approve pipelines, transmission lines, and exports. The form of the hearing process (whether or not to allow witnesses to contest the views of the applicant) and who would be allowed to intervene in this process is at the discretion of the board. Critics outside of the oil and gas industry have charged that the NEB is the captive of the industry it is to regulate.[46]

Advisory Committee on Northern Development. This Committee was established to advise the cabinet on northern resource development policy. It was composed of senior civil servants and chaired by the Deputy Minister of Indian and Northern Affairs (DINA). It contained many of the same conflicts of interest that plagued DINA, but it did have a direct role in advising the cabinet during the decade of the 1960s. During this time, it also worked closely with the oil and gas industry. The Prudhoe Bay oil discovery showed that the committee was ill prepared to handle the perceived implications of this discovery for the Canadian north so the Task Force on Northern Oil Development was formed in 1968.[47]

Task Force on Northern Oil Development. This task force was also composed of senior civil servants (deputy ministers) as well as the chairman of the National Energy Board. The Deputy Minister of Energy, Mines and Resources chaired the task force, which was to plot the Canadian response to the Alaskan oil find. The task force became the most important advisory body on energy to the cabinet over the period 1969 to 1974.[48] Its initial mandate was to "protect" the Canadian oil industry by maintaining its access to the U.S. market. The task force was also the main point of contact between the cabinet and the industry. Its basic thrust was to push for both oil and gas pipelines down the Mackenzie Valley from Alaska to the United States to link the Canadian north to the U.S. market. The oil pipeline "sales" effort failed; however, the gas pipeline question is still open.

National Advisory Committee on Petroleum. This committee serves as an interface between industry and the federal government and is made up of representatives from industry. It is an advisory body designed to give the government the views of the industry and to obtain early warning of pending changes in government policy. Both its membership and its proceedings are secret.

Northern Energy Actors since 1973

Industrial Actors. 1. In June 1972, *Canadian Arctic Gas Study, Limited* (CAGSL)—and its U.S. counterpart, *Alaskan Arctic Gas Study Corporation*— were formed to study the possibility of transporting Alaskan and Canadian natural gas to southern markets.

Extensive research into technical, social, and environmental issues has been conducted by CAGSL following the pipeline guidelines developed by the federal government's Task Force on Northern Oil Development. The CAGSL view of the Mackenzie Valley route proposal is that such a development is rational on economic, technical, and environmental grounds.

To many industry actors, the fundamental uncertainty at this time is the lack of proven reserves of natural gas (and oil) in the Mackenzie Delta. Until such time as threshold volumes are proven, CAGSL's proposal hinges on the availability of Prudhoe gas, which in itself is an uncertainty. Whether a joint U.S.-Canadian route will be acceptable to U.S. regulatory and political decision-makers is uncertain.

2. *Alberta Gas Trunk Line Co., Ltd.* (AGTL) was one of the initial members of a Prudhoe Bay-Mackenzie Valley natural gas pipeline group. In September 1974 AGTL formally withdrew from the CAGSL consortium. In doing so, it formed Foothills Pipeline, Ltd., and filed an application to build a natural gas pipeline from the Mackenzie Delta south to Canadian markets.

Increases in the price of natural gas, particularly for export, and the emergence of the El Paso proposal combined to emphasize the uncertainty of future exports. Also, limited success in finding gas in the Mackenzie Delta region raised doubts about an exportable surplus. These factors led AGTL to develop the "Maple Leaf" proposal, an all-Canadian gas pipeline from the Delta. AGTL in announcing its application recognizes that the timing of its pipeline construction will be somewhat later than that proposed by CAGSL. In AGTL's view, this additional time will permit the proving up of further reserves, the gathering of better economic and financial information, and the coordination of an approach to materials supply. Moreover, the financial requirements will have a lesser impact on the Canadian economy.

3. *El Paso Natural Gas Corporation* is a U.S. firm that proposes an alternative to CAGSL for constructing a natural gas pipeline from Prudhoe Bay to Point Gravina, Alaska, where a liquefaction facility will be constructed, and liquified gas will be shipped by LNG tankers to California. In the view of El Paso, their proposal has several advantages over that of Arctic Gas. The first is that of exclusive U.S. control, which is argued on the basis of efforts of certain foreign countries to exploit the U.S.'s energy shortage and "recent actions by the Canadian government in doubling the price of natural gas flowing across the border to United States customers and in requiring, contrary to existing contracts, that the burden of gas supply shortage be borne exclusively by U.S. customers rather than equitably shared with Canadian customers."[49]

A second advantage seen by El Paso is that their project will incur no effect on the nation's balance of payments, whereas the Arctic Gas project as viewed by El Paso would leave $10 billion in Canada through taxation and profit. Tax revenues to the U.S. from El Paso will be double those from Arctic Gas. Environmental impacts will be negligible since the pipeline will be in the utility corridor with the oil pipeline. Arctic Gas would cross a wildlife range plus many miles of permafrost. El Paso envisions completion of its project in a shorter period than Arctic Gas. The lack of proven Canadian reserves and the doubt about how much Canadian gas, if any, will be exportable are also seen by El Paso as a further advantage of their project.

Thus, in both Canada and the United States a proposal oriented to energy independence now rivals the Arctic Gas Pipeline, Ltd., project. There is little doubt in anyone's mind that the decision on Prudhoe gas will be made in Washington, D.C. Whatever happens, the impact of one country's decision will clearly affect options in the other.

4. *Polar Gas, Ltd.*, was formed in February 1973 when Panarctic Oils, Tenneco, Canadian Pacific Investments, and TransCanada Pipeline joined forces to study various methods of transporting Arctic Islands natural gas to southern markets. Since then, the group has expanded. Financing has come from the participants in the project. U.S. interests have been guaranteed first right of refusal on exportable supplies of natural gas and have also been required to state that they would not "block" a pipeline in which there would be few if any benefits for them.

Environmental and social impact issues will hinge to a large degree on the route selected for a pipeline and/or liquefaction and tanker transport system. Polar Gas is actively considering a liquefaction and LNG tanker program to bring

Islands gas to market more quickly. Some provincial government money was attracted when Ontario provided additional funding.

Government Actors. 1. An organization that will soon exercise a major role in northern petroleum programs is *Petro-Canada*, the new national oil crown corporation begun in January 1976. It is anticipated that federal government equity positions in Panarctic Oils and Syncrude Oil, the second Alberta oil sands plant, will be turned over to Petro-Can.

The initiative for a national oil corporation came out of a minority government in 1974. Its actual beginning was delayed for nearly two years while the government sorted out its role and decided on a head officer.

Considerable uncertainty exists over this new crown corporation on the part of the major oil companies. They prefer it to be one among equals with no favor given to it by the government. On the other hand, the government sees Petro-Can as an instrument of public policy that will be subject to the needs of the country and not the needs of the industry. Certainly, one key role is the development of a vigorous exploration program to demonstrate quickly Canada's proved petroleum reserve situation. In this task the corporation will be a leader in exploring areas of high risk and cost. Further roles can only be hinted at the present time, but they would include retail operations and investment in other parts of the world similar to other multinational oil companies.[50]

2. In March 1974 the Minister of Indian and Northern Affairs appointed a *Mackenzie Valley Pipeline Inquiry* to make recommendations to him "regarding terms and conditions" that should be attached to any right-of-way that might be granted for a natural gas pipeline.[51]

The significance of the Berger Commission clearly lies in the view which Mr. Justice Berger takes of his terms of reference:

Both the Order-in-Council and the Pipeline Guidelines are cast in broadly worded language. They say I am to conduct a social, economic and environmental impact study. It is a study without precedent in the history of our country. I take no narrow view of my terms of reference.[52]

This interpretation requires a consideration by the inquiry of the land claims of native peoples since settlement of such claims is considered by the native groups to be one of the terms or conditions that should be imposed by the government before any right-of-way is granted. All native groups will have the right to urge this position at the inquiry. Although the commission has an advisory rather than decision-making role, Berger clearly hopes the inquiry will set a precedent and serve as a model for future evaluations of the possible consequences of government and industry decisions.

Native Peoples' Groups. The following groups of native peoples have been actors in northern energy since 1973:

1. Federation of Natives North of Sixty;
2. Committee of Original Peoples' Entitlement (COPE);
3. Indian Brotherhood of the Northwest Territories;
4. Council of Yukon Indians;
5. Inuit Tapirisat (Eskimo organization).

Usher's account of some of the native peoples' views on the historical background of current events in the north reveals much that is at issue.[53] According to Usher, the growth of the native movement in Alaska, especially its success in holding up oil development while trying to get a fair land claims settlement and the discovery of oil at Atkinson Point in January 1970, spurred the growing belief of some native people that the moment has arrived to speak up.[54] This the native peoples have done.

The native peoples' view of government activities is extremely negative and emphasizes government's long-time failure to consult native people about social, political, or economic changes. Exploration for oil and gas, according to Usher's report, is the most recent catalyst of too-rapid change and, as conducted, an "assault on the land."

Central to the position of native peoples' groups is the land claim issue. The approach to land settlement currently proposed has as its basic premise: "Land not money is the focus of the land settlement."[55]

Government, and industry as well, are portrayed as agents that push ahead as they wish, whether with experiments in education and social programs that affect native life or with pipeline construction. Government efforts to involve native people in resource development through job programs alone are seen as inadequate and perhaps harmful in the long run. Similarly, government research priorities are viewed as placing environmental ahead of social impact concerns.

The Inuit Tapirisat of Canada was formed to represent and serve all Inuit groups in Canada and to prepare and negotiate the Inuit land claims. The conflict between oil exploration activities and Inuit concern about the environment is considered the most difficult problem the ITC has had to face.[56] The ITC position on a land claims settlement is being worked out separately from those of the other native groups in the NWT and the Yukon. The ITC is primarily interested in negotiating for control over certain land areas, with an eye to long-term benefits for the Inuit as a group rather than any monetary lump-sum settlement on the Alaskan model.

Independent Groups. 1. The *Canadian Arctic Resources Committee* (CARC) was formed in March 1971 "to maintain a watching brief over industry and government plans for northern resource development."[57] The committee included both scientists and nonscientists who were alarmed at the lack of citizen input into government policymaking for the north, as well as foreign control of resource development. By 1973 CARC had begun to assume a greater role as a "watch-dog" in the north.

A comprehensive statement of CARC's objectives stresses the committee's aim to act as a catalyst of public discussion and a monitor of research and participation programs relating to the north. CARC supports a settlement of native land claims as a prerequisite to any major northern development undertaking. It also urges the institution of land and resource planning procedures in the north (as distinct from the Land Use Regulations, which provide a control but not a planning apparatus).[58]

2. The *Committee for an Independent Canada* (CIC) was formed in 1970 to lobby for stricter government control over foreign investment in Canada and is currently planning to intervene as a major adversary in the NEB hearings on the CAGPL gas pipeline proposal.[59]

The CIC sees as its most important task for the next few years the stopping of the Mackenzie Valley pipeline project. The committee's objections are:

1. That construction of the pipeline is designed to meet U.S., not Canadian, energy demands, at least initially, and would "seal Canada's fate as a supplier of raw resources to a voracious industrial giant."

2. That the large financial stake of U.S. companies in the pipeline will jeopardize Canada's ability to control future development of her own energy resources.

3. That the large amounts of money that will have to be borrowed will disrupt the Canadian economy, either because of upward pressure on the Canadian dollar (resulting in higher export prices and danger to jobs in the manufacturing industries) if the money comes from the United States or, if the money must come from Canadian capital markets, because there would be virtually no funds left to finance other important, or even essential, projects.

3. The *Committee for Justice and Liberty* (CJL) was reformed in 1973. The CJL is an "independent Canadian people's movement which seeks to develop political, economic, and social policies and action programs from a Christian life-perspective." It attempts to present an alternative vision from the viewpoint of Christian justice, stewardship, love, and compassion.

This group has made energy research its major interest and has intervened in the NEB hearings. It successfully helped to challenge the NEB chairman's credibility in these hearings by carrying the case to the Supreme Court of Canada.

Issues Arising from Northern Petroleum Development

Given the scale and pace of proposed and pending energy projects, the federal government has had to break new ground in learning to cope with the scope of these decisions and the impacts emanating from them. One political decision to launch a particular project by giving it precedence over other projects initiates a host of subsequent decisions and potential impacts of major political significance. For example, the cabinet at the federal level wished to signal to the United States its favorable attitude toward an oil pipeline from Alaska through Canada to the U.S. mainland.[60] Its statements in advance of technical, economic, and environmental studies cast doubt on the validity of information garnered from such studies for decision-making purposes. In fact, such statements were seen by many to render the entire regulatory process superfluous and "cosmetic." The impact of these advance statements was to set in motion consortia to begin the actual process of applying for a pipeline approval as well as to cause many others to become suspicious of the government's role in this process as well as the possibility of premature development of the Mackenzie Delta region.

From discussions with many of the actors, each with their varying and sometimes conflicting objectives, information needs, and decision processes, the following five broad content-based issue categories have been identified: (1) technological, (2) environmental, (3) economic, (4) social, and (5) political. In spite of great differences among actors, these categories are quite readily identified by them. They seem to form a common basis for the organization of perceptions and concerns, though always with the recognition that a given concern may cut across more than one of the above categories. What complicates an analysis of issues, however, is the ever-changing dynamic character of the petroleum development process itself. As the development program proceeds through its various phases, it gives rise to different mixes of actors and it generates new or different information and decision processes. This dynamic means that the issues themselves change.

Over and above this aspect, however, and as revealed through the analyses of the Arctic petroleum development programs, is the nature of the assessment systems and processes themselves. The balance (or lack) of participating interests, the quality and accessibility of information, the nature of decision-making processes, the relationships among actors are also vital issues in northern development and, in fact, may be more important than those identified as substantive issues. The nature of the assessment system itself may influence to a considerable degree the perceptions and understandings of actors and hence their definitions of issues and objectives.

Substantive Issues in Petroleum Development

The substantive issues are listed by categories in Table 3-5, as they are perceived and reported by actors in the technology assessment system. There did not appear to be a significant difference among general issues between the Mackenzie

Table 3-5
Substantive Issues in Northern Petroleum Development

Technological

Drilling in the deep sea	Pipelines and sea bottom scour
Transportation alternatives	Liquefaction in Arctic
Oil spills under ice	Laying pipeline through ice
Alternative energy sources	Icebreaking ship technology

Environmental

Impacts on aquatic and terrestrial regimes	Waste disposal
Impacts on fish and wildlife	Impacts of infrastructures
Oil spills	Pipelines in permafrost
Lack of baseline information	Artificial islands and marine ecosystems

Economic

Pacing of development	Incentive and controls
Impacts on prices, interest rates, exchange rates	Impacts on industry, labour, markets
Impacts on financial capabilities	Industrial strategy
Consumption pattern	Investment pattern (capital flows)

Social

Lifestyles	Transient populations
International equity	Education priorities
Aboriginal rights	Health and welfare
Native employment	Community disruption

Political

National independence versus global community	Petroleum exports
Foreign ownership and participation	Territorial sovereignty
International realignment	Regulatory uncertainty
Industry-government complex	Responsible government in Territories

Delta-Beaufort Sea and Arctic Islands situations, although their relative importance would presumably differ. The issues as listed in Table 3-5 do not imply a rank order of importance. Rather they are a listing of important recurring unresolved questions raised by different actors.

Technology Assessment System Issues

Ideally, the purpose of a technology assessment system is to conduct assessments of technology that generate a balanced overview of information and issues about the internal and external consequences of applying technology in the short and longer run. To the extent that any given technology assessment is wanting, it may well be due to inadequacies and limitations in the assessment system itself. Thus, by identifying and analyzing the weaknesses in the assessors and assessment processes, one can account for observed deficiencies in the particular technology assessment that was carried out. An analysis of the assessment system should focus on actors and relationships among actors, information, and decisions. From a discussion of these aspects of the assessment system a number of general observations can be made to help focus on the important issues stemming from the assessment system itself.

Issues Involving Actor Groups. In the context of the Mackenzie-Beaufort Sea and Arctic Islands programs, there do not appear to be significant actors who have not become involved in some manner. The establishment of the Mackenzie Valley Pipeline Inquiry, perhaps more than anything else, has assured numerous groups of an input to deliberations about terms and conditions of a right-of-way for a natural gas pipeline. Moreover, the provision of some research funds to native and environmental organizations from the federal government to prepare for land claim negotiations and assess negative environmental impacts has provided a greater opportunity for participation by the native groups and environmentalists.

In both the Mackenzie-Beaufort Sea and Arctic Islands programs, the system is disproportionately weighted in favor of federal government and industry participation. Historically, this pattern has always been the case. While it might be argued that government and industry have made substantial efforts to involve and consult northern groups in the formation of their plans and programs, the nature of these efforts is questionable. While they appear to seek the involvement of all parties, the practice seems to consist of consultation after the fact, with the only change seen as a desire for longer warning periods. Rather than encouraging involvement, the strategies of industry and government appear to have generated more hesitancy, uncertainty, and even mistrust.

Recognition of conflicts in objectives is another important issue that emerges. Perhaps foremost among those actors with conflicting objectives is DINA. Several writers have elaborated on this point.

Where conflict occurs between the needs of the people, environmental maintenance and resource development, the government's tendency is to either deny the existence or possibility of such conflict, or to dismiss those who oppose resource development as uninformed, emotional or reactionary.[61]

It does not appear, however, that DINA completely dismisses the existence of conflicts among its objectives. The department suggests that such conflicts must ultimately be resolved and that the normal machinery within the department is both capable of doing so and is the appropriate forum. The difficulty here, however, lies in the scope of interests that can effectively be brought to bear on decisions. The predominant role of the "Northern Development Program" of DINA is such that the economic development thrusts appear to have a decided advantage in shaping the outcome of such decisions. If "development-people" tradeoffs were to be made outside the department where a wider array of interests and values could be brought into perspective then very different decisions might result with very different consequences.

DINA is seen by other federal government departments, the territorial governments and northern residents as an agency exercising extensive and preemptive powers in the north. The basis of this power is both statutory and managerial—that is, managerial in the sense that DINA occupies central coordinating (in some views co-opting) roles in the federal government.

DINA's underlying assumptions about northern development reflect a limited view of development possibilities and the means by which they can be realized. DINA sees the fate of the north as inextricably linked to the petroleum exploration and transportation programs now in progress. DINA views its "Hire North" program as a demonstration of its concern for ensuring that development programs respond to northern native needs. However, other actor groups in the territories see that once again the natives are being presented with only temporary and low-skill job opportunities.

Apprehensions exist about large development projects conducted over short periods of time, which stem in part from past experiences with the DEW-Line project and mineral projects.[62] In spite of these experiences the federal government remains firmly committed to large-scale natural resource developments, especially with regard to petroleum. This commitment combined with highly centralized control over development in the north places DINA in the center of the decision-making process.

Considerable uncertainty has resulted from the absence of revised Canada Oil and Gas Lands Regulations. The inability to arrive at a decision on these regulations is linked to the East Coast petroleum program and the dispute between the federal government and the Maritime Provinces over offshore rights. This example highlights one of Canada's more important dilemmas at the present time: the role of the federal government and the provinces in resource development and benefit sharing. Although some form of compromise is likely in the East Coast offshore dispute and the dispute between Ottawa and Alberta over taxation and royalties, strong indications of moves by several provincial governments into the Arctic energy scene do not conjure up images of federal-provincial cordiality.

Issues Involving Information. Nearly every actor interviewed expressed some sense of concern either implicitly or explicitly over the following issues:

1. Secrecy of information,
2. Independence of sources of information,
3. View taken of information,
4. Information networks,
5. Uncertainty of information,
6. Uses of information.

Each of these issues surrounds the substantive issues listed in Table 3-5. *Secrecy* overrides in importance all other information issues. Even given that a certain degree of secrecy is important to maintain a position vis-à-vis other actors, the question remains: How much secrecy is justifiable and from whose point of view? The overall reliance on secrecy is expensive from many points of view including the requirement for more extensive information and duplication of information systems. Secrecy also fosters mistrust among actors in their attempt to offset such secrecy.

Examples of secrecy are legion throughout the petroleum technology assessment system. In his analysis of decision-making in the Mackenzie Valley pipeline development, Dosman indicates that on a number of occasions the federal government took decisions in consultation with industry but without any advance discussions with other interested parties.[63] Within the federal government also, some departments proceed with plans that significantly affect other departments without prior discussions. The proposed petroleum taxation and royalty measures of May 1974, developed by the Department of Finance, were reported not to have been made known beforehand to some of the other departments with extensive interests and responsibilities for petroleum development. The announcement by the Prime Minister in April 1972 that construction of the Mackenzie Highway would commence immediately to link existing sections to the Delta was not preceded by discussion with many of those in the north who saw themselves being affected. The government's task forces and advisory committees are conducted secretly. The petroleum companies do not share seismic data; each company requires reruns over the same area. DINA has shown frustration over industry secrecy and has stated that they consider such secrecy to be "unreasonable with respect to Canada's North" because of the large concessions made in land disposal policies.[64] On the other hand, DINA itself is accused of secrecy by both the environmentalists and native peoples. Indeed, DINA kept the offshore drilling proceedings held in December 1972 secret while complaining of industry secrecy at the same meeting.[65] Natives have complained of DINA secrecy where they feel information is not only not passed on to them but deliberately denied them. The overriding concern for the native peoples as well as for the environmentalists is the need for information. Even industry and DINA see the lack of information as their basic problem; yet all actors seem to be caught up in a system of secrecy with no basic questioning of the need for it.

Independence of sources of information is another major information issue. Every actor group interviewed saw a necessity for maintaining separate information sources or information-gathering systems even at a high cost. Their concern is to be seen by other actors in the assessment system as independent of all others.

Native groups hire their own social and economic experts to gather and present information to support their land claims. Environmentalists hire their own ecological staff to do separate studies of environmental impacts. The government undertakes a multimillion-dollar program of environmental-social studies in order to be in a position to assess the industry studies independently.

The CAGSL consortium sponsors an Environmental Protection Board to independently assess its own studies. Each company within the industry does its separate studies and analyses of exploration.

In addition, independence of information is linked to actor goals and the knowledge that information is designed to be gathered to support such goals. Thus, independence is used as an information strategy to offset secrecy and bias. How should such actor goals be analyzed and integrated to reduce the need for excessive independence? As yet there is no way of resolving this problem.

The view taken of information is also important. Here, actor goals determine the width or narrowness of the view taken toward the kinds and amounts of information necessary for decision making. Often the information base of one actor group does not coincide with another actor's information base because their respective perceptions of the issues do not match. For example, industry tends to use a quite narrow information base consisting mainly of geologic data, technical feasibility studies, and financial rates of return. The government, on the other hand, is being pressed through the political processes to develop information including social and environmental impacts before any decisions are taken. Thus, past government actions are no longer the norm for their future decision making. This mismatch over the view of the requisite information base is a constant source of conflict between these actors and thus leads to communications barriers.

One strategy over the Mackenzie pipeline is to retain a narrow view of the project while giving the appearance of a broader view of it. Thus, two aspects are stressed by industry and government: the resource development of the north and the availability of that resource in the south. The desire of the natives for participation in resource development is being interpreted as "pick-and-shovel" participation rather than participation in decision making. Socioeconomic impact is seen solely in terms of the number of jobs created and the number of natives employed in those jobs.

The network or channels used to obtain information would also appear to be a major information issue. The search for and use of an informal network is used to circumvent the publicly visible, often cumbersome, network. The government created the Task Force on Northern Oil Development partly to aid the oil industry in maintaining contact with government people. The emphasis is on gaining access to and influencing the direction of policy as well as on obtaining an early warning of pending changes in policy and the nature of such changes. These informal liaisons are also often used to gain a competitive edge on other actor groups.

The main problem with a reliance on informal channels is the exclusiveness inherent in their use. Many actor groups who should have access to the same information at the same time are excluded. Industry and DINA have "regularized" informal contacts whereby information is transferred without affording similar opportunities to environmentalists, natives, or other actors.

One major area of concern is the downgrading of Parliament's traditional role in debating government policies. The government has deliberately allowed the role of Parliament to deteriorate to that of an after-the-fact disclosure of government initiatives.[66]

Reliance on both secrecy and informal channels of communication contribute to *uncertainty* of information. Uncertainty can take several forms: uncertainty over the existence of information, uncertainty over the sufficiency of information, uncertainty over the quality of information, or even overall uncertainty from rapid changes in the information base. Uncertainty, of course, is always present to some degree, but when does excessive uncertainty occur?

Both industry and government have become more uncertain over Arctic petroleum development. Contributing to industry uncertainty has been the withdrawal of land regulations, change in oil and gas regulations, change in provincial royalty rates, change in federal tax rates, creation of an export tax, controlled prices, fluid nature of ownership of northern lands, and creation of a national petroleum company. Government uncertainty has come about through such events as the possibility of native title to northern lands, gas and oil discoveries (or the lack thereof), energy shortages, lack of precedent, lack of information, heightened interest in environment, heightened expressions of nationalism, and in general the shifting of the Arctic from a liability to an asset. Given this overall context of uncertainty, it is not surprising to see industry shift exploratory activity elsewhere or government lengthen the application process, both of which are reactions to the untoward uncertainty surrounding petroleum development in the Arctic.

Actual use of information in the decision-making process is the last major information issue. Here information is to be matched to the knowledge requirements for making a decision; however, it is often the case that information gathered bears little relationship to the decisions to be made. For example, one perception of the social and environmental studies undertaken by industry and government is that they constituted "add-on" information to decisions already made.

Even for the environmental study requirements, far more studies were suggested and carried out than were necessary to decide on the environmental feasibility of the pipeline or its routing and design. Scientists involved in such studies collected information as defined by their disciplines, often with little or no clear idea about its role in planning, designing, or deciding about a pipeline.

Without question, a monumental information search effort went into operation, albeit belatedly, to support petroleum development in the Canadian Arctic. Nearly every actor group has been involved in this search in one way or another. Actor perceptions of this information vary considerably. As one critic has noted:

The Mackenzie Valley gas pipeline has provoked a sheaf of engineering and environmental studies, economic analyses and public policy reviews on a scale that is claimed to surpass anything in our history ... for the most part their purpose is not public education. Rather they are sponsored by investors, environmentalists and tax collectors attempting to overcome our ignorance of the complex technical, ecological, sociological and economic consequences peculiar to Northern resource development. As a result, they are fragmentary both in their coverage and in their point of view.[67]

Canadian Responses to Energy Development

Canada is a nation that has both an industrial base and the long-term potential to be self-sufficient in energy production, although at a very high cost. This apparent "blessing," however, is tempered by an important factor: The present sources of energy are generally remote from their place of consumption so that it has been more economic for Canada to import energy rather than transport energy over vast distances. Although Canada has been a net exporter of oil, only half of the country's oil supply is met through domestic production; the remainder is met through imports. To become totally self-sufficient in energy, however, is a policy choice completely open to Canada, especially if exploration in the frontier regions reveals large commercial deposits of petroleum. To do so will mean that Canadians will be paying higher prices for fuel, electricity, and steel and its related products to obtain control over fuel supplies.

The crucial problem in energy sufficiency is the total dependence of the eastern provinces on imported crude oil. By 1980 eastern Canada will consume over one million barrels of crude oil per day. Oil consumption in the eastern provinces is growing at a greater rate than in the rest of the country. This situation shows that oil supply and its security is a growing issue in Canada. In the short term, there is very little that Canada can do except to stockpile a greater supply. In the medium term, an extension of the pipeline from Sarnia to Montreal was seen as necessary. This effort began in 1975. In addition, a greater exploration effort is being mounted in the eastern Arctic and in the eastern offshore regions for commercial deposits of petroleum. By diverting western Canadian crude oil to eastern Canada, exports to the United States will drop. An oil exchange agreement with the United States has also been under discussion whereby Canadian oil destined for eastern Canada would be diverted to the U.S. Midwest in exchange for oil destined for the U.S. East Coast being diverted to the Canadian Maritimes.

Institutional Responses to the Energy Crisis

The post-1973 period is marked by a major shift in policy implemented in response to the energy crisis. The federal government is attempting to emerge from the Canadian milieu as the dominant energy actor—decisionmaker, coordinator, and initiator of energy policy—in Canada. The federal government has recognized many of the problems outlined in this study and has begun to develop its response to them. These responses can be outlined as follows:

1. The creation of the Mackenzie Valley Pipeline Inquiry to add credibility to the government's position, to aid in setting the terms for subsequent approval, and to provide a forum for northern native peoples to air their positions: Whether or not this commission-style technology assessment will be formally institutionalized has yet to be seen, but whatever its form this kind of assessment can no longer be ignored.

2. The review by the National Energy Board of the oil and gas reserves of the country and of its own rules for determining such reserves and their economic life: This review is in response to the realization of the seriousness of Canada's reserve situation and the need to develop a source of information independent from the U.S.-dominated oil industry that it regulates.

3. The creation of a section concerned with energy demand and conservation within the federal government: This group is charged with examining and creating measures to reduce energy demand and has been given a $2.5-million program for promoting energy conservation through the media. Their research has shown that the annual increase in Canadian demand for energy could be reduced by 2 percent if Canada allowed world petroleum prices to prevail within the country.

4. The attempt by the federal government to dominate national energy policy through its budgetary and taxation regulations: The federal government precipitated a confrontation with Alberta by disallowing royalties for income tax deductions and placing an export tax on oil in order to achieve a dominant role in setting prices for oil.

5. The attempt by the federal government to gain greater awareness and control of the oil industry's activities in the north and offshore: The government demanded information from the industry on all of its farmout agreements and drilling operations.

6. The federal government agreement to become a partner in Syncrude Canada, Ltd., the oil sands plant currently being constructed: When one oil company pulled out of the consortium, the Alberta, federal, and Ontario governments provided the 30 percent equity financing needed to ensure the successful completion of the project. This oil sands plant, the first commercial-scale production unit, also received pricing and taxation concessions from the federal government that will allow it to compete with conventional oil.

7. The creation of Petro-Canada, the national oil company, as a signal that Canada intends to become more directly involved in the development of its petroleum resources: Although born out of a minority government, this promising approach appears to be widely acclaimed. Petro-Can will offset the foreign-dominated oil industry by leading the way in high-risk exploration regions in the frontier, by competing with them in other countries and in the evolution of retail operations, and by providing the government with first-hand experience in petroleum development for obtaining more accurate operational data.

8. The continued large-scale commitment to nuclear energy by attempting

to have provincial and foreign governments adopt the CANDU reactor system: Federal consumption projections show that nuclear energy will perhaps be the most important energy source (barring major frontier discoveries and major technological breakthroughs in oil sands processing) in the twenty-first century.

9. At the provincial level, the establishment of energy portfolios in the cabinet by nearly every province: Depending on whether the province is an energy exporter or energy importer, this energy ministry has taken on a variety of functions. In Alberta, an energy exporter, an energy research and development group has been created to study the oil sands and coal gasification. Alberta has also created an energy company that has taken an equity position in energy-related industries. Alberta has also taken equity in its oil sands via the Syncrude consortium. These functions have been added to its continuing roles in regulating and supporting the oil industry in the province. Ontario, on the other hand, as an energy importer has sought to increase its nuclear capability and to take an equity position in future energy efforts such as the oil sands and the Arctic Islands. It is also considering ways to reduce demand although no concerted effort has occurred in this area as yet. These provincial energy ministries provide important and continuing planning and contact points for interprovincial and federal-provincial energy planning. These ministries will also enhance the province's position in negotiating with the federal government over energy priorities.

Demand and Supply Responses

The dominant Canadian effort in energy is directed toward enhancing its supply base through exploration for oil and gas in frontier regions and elsewhere in the western provinces, further development of its CANDU nuclear program, research into coal gasification, development of its massive coal reserves, development of the Alberta Oil Sands, and research into unconventional sources such as wind, solar and tidal energy. This emphasis in energy supply involves many factors, some of the more important of which are summarized below.

1. Governments have historically been organized and oriented toward supply considerations.
2. Industry has organized around energy sources and is oriented to its further development.
3. Both government and industry have worked together to enhance energy resource development.
4. The energy policy field is dominated by two federal departments neither of which have to share their policy prerogatives with other departments.
5. The BNA Act does not recognize the influence of "demand" as a basic power; therefore, residual powers belong to the provinces which makes for

an uncoordinated approach. Also the BNA Act gives control over natural resources to the provinces who emphasize energy supply.

6. Federal energy research is oriented to supply through increasing reserves, exploring the frontier regions, and diversifying energy sources.
7. Since demand depends on individual responses to incentives of various kinds, controls and predictions are very difficult for government.
8. Government persists in its confidence that the frontier regions hold vast amounts of oil and gas only awaiting discovery.
9. The government hopes to improve its balance of payments via the export of energy and its associated equipment while it minimizes imports of same.
10. To date only a beginning has been made by the government for using its regulatory powers to change the rules for house and building construction, automobile manufacture and operation, industrial use of energy, and so forth.

In particular the federal government has emphasized exploration for oil and gas in the Arctic on a large scale through very lenient oil and gas land regulations and provision of key elements of the infrastructure. Some of the more prominent reasons for its massive interest in the Arctic include:

1. The large find at Prudhoe Bay in Alaska gave promise for a large find in Canada.
2. The initial attempt to link Canadian petroleum to U.S. markets by having the oil pipeline and the subsequent gas pipeline to bring oil/gas through Canada to the United States.
3. The large earnings possible from selling its gas to aid in the Canadian balance of payments.
4. The interest-free loans from U.S. utilities given to Canadian-based gas exploration efforts in the Arctic.
5. The need to find sufficient Canadian gas reserves to make a Canadian pipeline route viable and timed with available gas from Prudhoe Bay.
6. The need for massive gas reserves to support the large pipeline efforts necessary to transport the gas.
7. The need for an infrastructure to service industry exploration efforts.
8. The need to supplement Alberta's declining discovery-depletion ratio with new discoveries elsewhere.
9. The desire of the federal government to make the Canadian Arctic into a vital part of Canada by showing sovereignty in the Arctic, "bettering" the lifestyles of the natives, and making the Arctic into an overall asset rather than a liability.
10. The desire to control resource development directly without going through the provinces.

Interaction among Policy Sectors

The interaction among policy sectors has played an important role in the evolution of federal energy policy. Certainly, the federal government foresaw the aggressive responses of the provinces in protecting their spheres of influence in the energy policy field. It has made aggressive policy thrusts of its own to widen the scope of federal prerogative in this area.

In the Canadian milieu, the appropriate vehicle for dealing with the impacts between policy sectors is the cabinet. At both federal and provincial levels, the cabinet is prominent in attempting to resolve such issues. Between these levels of government, cabinet-level meetings are used to negotiate settlements acceptable to these governments.

Foreign Policy and Energy Policy

The United States responded to Canada's oil-marketing problem by allowing it to export oil to the U.S. Midwest in the early 1960s up to an agreed quota. As the energy needs of the United States increased later, the quota was lifted. However, Canada is now in the process of decreasing exports of oil to the U.S. Midwest. In addition, gas exports have been reduced in some cases and the price of gas raised. The United States has interpreted these moves broadly by now calling into question all areas of commercial policy for review and change. Foodstuffs and automobiles have been affected in this "review."

Energy security has played a role in the formation of both energy and foreign policy. Canada exports oil and gas to the United States; Canada imports coal from the United States; Canada is tied into the U.S. electrical grid system; Canadian pipelines cross U.S. territory; and the Canadian government favors a combined U.S.-Canadian pipeline crossing Canadian territory. Thus, the two countries are intimately linked together in the energy policy field. Yet both countries have elected to pursue separate energy self-sufficiency policies regardless of the costs of doing so. How this search for energy independence will evolve is uncertain. Canada has given notice to the United States that oil and gas exports will be phased out after the current contracts expire and after the U.S. Midwest gains an alternative supply source.

The U.S. domination of the Canadian oil industry, with U.S. firms controlling over 91 percent of the industry's assets and over 95 percent of the industry's sales, has caused growing concern among Canadians. Canadian coal is also dominated by U.S. interests, although to a lesser degree. This massive degree of U.S. involvement in Canadian energy development (as well as in other industries) has led to the passage of the Foreign Investment Review Act of 1974. This act created a board to review foreign investment in Canadian industries and either to allow or disallow these investments. The impact of this act has yet to be totally felt, but it has led to certain foreign investments being blocked and to a general downturn in foreign investment in Canada.

In the exploration and transportation planning efforts in the Arctic, U.S. and Canadian energy and foreign policy fields have been involved. The early emphasis on exploration and pipeline planning in the Arctic was on maintaining and even increasing exports of gas to the U.S. The projects were to be export oriented and of such a scale as to permit such exports on the lowest possible per unit cost basis. A consortium of U.S. and Canadian firms dominated by U.S. industry put together the Alaskan Arctic Gas Pipeline-Canadian Arctic Gas Pipeline Study Group to explore the feasibility of transporting Prudhoe Bay and Mackenzie Delta gas together through Canada into the United States. This project is now going through regulatory procedures simultaneously in each country. In addition, two nationalistic rival pipeline groups have evolved to transport separately the gas from Alaska and from Canada, which would keep each country's gas within their respective country. So far a decision has not been taken; however, the key decision will be made in the United States with Canada following suit.

Both Canada and the United States have suffered from problems of coordination between energy and foreign policy fields. Timing of announcements from energy and foreign policy officials has not been adequate, and certain key groups of actors have felt cut off. For example, the U.S. Senate has complained that the U.S. State Department withheld information on Canadian energy intentions when deciding on the oil pipeline.

The North American energy crisis (so-called) has been mainly felt in the United States. Canada has not really experienced any such crisis of its own, but Canada has been affected by the U.S. energy crisis. Because Canada both exports and imports energy to and from the United States, the two countries are tied closely together. The United States is not short of energy but rather short of clean, low-cost energy. For the short term, the United States is dependent on large amounts of energy imports, which account for nearly half of its total energy demand. Of this amount, however, Canada exported only about 6 percent of total U.S. demand for oil and about 5 percent of total U.S. demand for natural gas. Therefore, Canada will never be able to play a significant role in U.S. petroleum-related consumption. There is no need for Canadians to think they are in an excellent bargaining position regarding energy nor is there a need for the U.S. to assume a retaliatory role toward Canada. Both positions have little bearing on the actual amount of Canadian oil and gas consumed by the United States.

Canadian responses to the energy crisis can only be readily understood by noting the ever-present massive capability of the United States to penetrate into Canadian policy space at any time. For example, Canada has assured the United States that it will not immediately cut off oil and gas exports to the United States should extreme shortages develop. Instead, Canada would share such shortages equally with its U.S. customers. On the other hand, the government of British Columbia has abruptly changed prices of natural gas for the United States upward and reduced the quantity available to the United States. Such provincial prerogative causes Canada to be seen from the United States in a confused way, which is then compounded by a crisis situation where decisions with lasting consequences may be made quite quickly.

In response to public pressures for a greater Canadian identity and to technologies with great potential adverse impacts, Canada had begun to exercise greater unilateral decision making. In fact, Canada has demonstrated a willingness to make unilateral decisions that are against U.S. interests if it perceives its self-interests are being blatantly denied. For example, when its sovereignty was threatened in the Arctic by the presence of the U.S. Coast Guard, Canada, after considerable hesitation, unilaterally extended its jurisdiction one hundred miles out into the Arctic Ocean through its Arctic Waters Pollution Act of 1970.

In the energy policy field, Canada and the United States appear to have opted for energy self-sufficiency rather than the continental energy approach into which each country was drifting. Even though strong energy ties exist between the two countries, each seems determined to follow separate routes to self-sufficiency. These decisions by each country constitute a watershed in Canadian-U.S. energy relations, since they come on the heels of a long history of joint or shared planning in energy. The United States developed Canada's oil industry at terms beneficial to itself, and Canada continues to export oil to the United States. Although Canada is to have the same relationship to the United States through its Project Independence as the OPEC countries, U.S. decisions can only work to the benefit of Canada. Self-sufficiency in energy policy will allow Canada to maintain a more independent stance in foreign policy.

Given the size of Canadian petroleum reserves in relation to world supplies at a price high enough to induce development of the oil shales and sands around the world, Canada's role as an exporter is insignificant. Canada will never really be in a position to export major amounts of petroleum to other countries. Even if security of supply for eastern Canada were not an issue, the U.S. would absorb all available Canadian oil and gas at world prices.

With regard to multinational corporations, Canada has been deeply concerned about intrusion from these firms in its energy policy space. In response to these trends, Canada has passed legislation for a foreign investment review board, a national oil company, a holding company for buying back control of Canadian resource industries, and a directive to obtain more information on petroleum reserve figures and farmout agreements. In addition, Canada has maintained its position in the high Arctic by participating in Panarctic Oils, Ltd., a consortium of independent Canadian oil firms exploring for oil and gas.

Thus, Canada has become more active in the international policy sphere and is attempting to define its place as an independent country. Given its historic dependence first on the United Kingdom and later on the United States, Canada has been slow to evolve a national identity with the active policy fields to support it. An independent posture has now been struck, and the momentum is increasing for fulfilling this posture. Certainly, there are limits to a Candian expansion of policy space, but these limits will be determined via high-level bilateral negotiations rather than in a unilateral fashion from the United States. The attempted independence in the energy field may only be a forerunner to later independent thrusts in other policy fields.

Economic Policy and Energy Policy

The interdependency between economic and energy policies is integral to the development of a stable energy program. Economic policies that affect the energy policy field include the following kinds of concerns:

1. How would changes in the development, timing, and exportability of energy affect other areas of trade and access to existing markets for other goods and services?
2. How would changes in energy development and export affect the international balance of payments position?
3. How would changes in energy development affect Canadian capital requirements and access to foreign capital markets?
4. How would increases of capital into the energy sector affect other capital projects or even competing energy projects?
5. How would increases of foreign capital for energy resources development affect Canadian interest rates, the Canadian dollar and Canadian manufactured exports?
6. How would changes in the amount of foreign capital affect foreign control and ownership?
7. How would energy development affect employment opportunities in other industries and in total?
8. How would capital, equipment, and labor requirement for energy development affect the rate of inflation?

These questions at the interface of economics and energy illustrate some of the basic problem areas in an economy with large-scale energy development. Great concern over energy development impacts on the Canadian economy have been discussed by independent economists, but the core actors in the energy industry and in the energy ministries have remained singularly silent on this issue.

One significant area of interaction occurred when the Minister of Finance in his budget of May 1974 recommended new taxation policies for the oil and gas industries. He intended to disallow provincial royalty payments as tax deductible items on the federal income tax. This budget item provoked an instant reaction from the industry and the provinces. Industry threatened, and indeed some followed through, to pull out of Canada and certainly out of the high risk frontier areas.

Energy development impacts on the economy and economic impacts on energy development are of a major magnitude. Many studies have been carried out by banks, financial institutions, private research institutes, and university economists, in addition to those by government and industry. Given this myriad of economic assessments, it should not be surprising that little agreement has occurred among them. One thing they would all agree on, however, is that the linkage between energy development and the economy is direct and is crucial to Canada's economic position in the world, especially since planned spending on energy development could go as high as 25 percent of GNP.

Regional Development Policy and Energy Policy

While some development of frontier regions in Canada will occur through large-scale energy projects, this development has not been the impetus behind the location of these projects. Rather the obvious factor influencing location is the expected presence of petroleum in an economically viable quantity for exploitation. Attention has instead been focused on the negative impacts from energy development in the regions involved. Even though the core actors in both government and industry have stressed the regional employment benefits from such development, they have spent much of their time answering their critics.

These negative regional impacts include housing and material shortages, labor shortages, higher prices and wages, displaced labor and local business, and especially impacts on the native culture. With the government emphasis on large-scale projects, such negative impacts are beginning to receive far more attention.

Because Canada is a federation of provinces each province tends to promote its own regional development over that of other provinces.[68] The federal government has opted to direct some economic activity toward the poorer provinces via its Department of Regional Economic Expansion (DREE). With the prospects of massive energy projects that will be delivering large amounts of energy, competition has evolved between the provinces for capturing the economic spinoffs such as secondary industry for upgrading crude oil and natural gas. Both Alberta and Ontario are building world-scale production facilities for upgrading natural gas feedstocks into methane for export. In addition, the material and labor shortages created by all of these energy-related projects may have offset the DREE objectives of providing greater economic impetus to the have-not provinces, the prairies, and maritimes. Labor is being attracted from all points in Canada and indeed from outside of Canada into the energy projects of Quebec, Alberta, and the frontier regions.

The frontier regions' development has been of a cyclical nature—that of the "boom-bust" phenomenon. Given the phasing of these large-scale energy projects, this traditional "boom-bust" cycle can be accentuated or attenuated. Development of such phasing plans has not been evident, especially with both the federal and various provincial governments competing for energy projects.

Industrial Policy and Energy Policy

Conflicts between the manufacturing and the energy industries have evolved from the government's emphasis on energy development. The major sources of conflict include the following:

1. Differential tax rates between the two kinds of industry, with the energy industry getting lower effective taxes;
2. Possible displacement of manufacturing through emphasis on large-scale energy projects;
3. Effects on manufacturing exports from energy development impacts on the Canadian dollar;
4. Displacement of capital, labor, and material from the manufacturing sector to energy development;
5. Contribution of energy projects to the rate of inflation;
6. Problems of cyclical energy project component requirements on manufacturing capacity (e.g., the problem of building to scale to meet large-scale energy industry needs and then being left with excess capacity);
7. Lack of emphasis by the energy industry on the Canadian content of manufactured components;
8. Large changes in price for fuel for manufacturing during short periods of time.

These conflicts have not all occurred as yet but are seen as potential problems by those involved. When more energy projects begin, these conflicts in policy will have to be resolved.

Immigration Policy and Energy Policy

One area of policy conflict that was not wholly anticipated is the shortage of Canadian labor for energy development projects. Labor shortages have occurred at all levels, including unskilled. Even though the contractors use government manpower offices, severe labor shortages still occur. Thus, recruiting is done in the United States and Europe for both unskilled and skilled labor. Labor constraints have held up energy projects, and these delays are exacerbated by government requirements that Canadians be hired if possible.

Severe labor competition occurs among the federal and provincial govern-ments identified with the energy projects within their jurisdiction. Wages rates in energy projects exceed those in other construction areas or in manufacturing so that labor conflicts occur between these industries. Thus, immigrant labor is required for all industries even though overall Canadian unemployment remains high at around 7 percent. Canadian labor unions and other interested organiza-tions oppose additional immigrants even though indigenous labor is insufficient for the labor demand generated by the energy projects.

Conflict exists in immigration policy over where immigrants settle, where they work, and the fact that they occupy some jobs that Canadians could fill. Energy projects underway or planned have such large and lumpy labor require-ments that these problems are intensified.

Environmental Policy and Energy Policy

The potential conflicts of energy development impacting on environmental quality in the Arctic have been pronounced. The public expectations raised through previous publicity on environmental travesties have caused the federal government to respond cautiously to energy development in the fragile Arctic environment. This cautiousness, combined with uncertainty over how to proceed to implement environmental constraints, caused the federal government to proceed slowly in the approval process. In addition, due to the lack of baseline studies on environmental conditions in the Arctic, the government required pipeline project applicants to undertake massive environmental studies to support their applications. At the same time, the government had to undertake similar studies to use as a gauge to test the applicant's information. While these massive information requirements have delayed these projects beyond industry's original timetable, the resulting information has also made these projects more visible and hence more political.

Further delay has occurred because of the need for the government to adopt a visible, nonpartisan, and unbiased approach to the right-of-way decision for a pipeline. The governments' previous public responses to energy development clearly demonstrated the cabinet's desire for early development of oil and gas pipelines across the Arctic. With this past public record favoring rapid develop-ment of Arctic energy sources, the government did not enjoy public credibility for environmental protection. In addition, the federal unit (DINA) responsible for both northern development and environmental protection has a past record favoring development at the expense of environment. The mechanism chosen to provide this visible response to environmental and native protection was an independent commission headed by a former provincial Supreme Court justice with experience in northern native affairs. The terms of reference of the commission do not allow it to recommend for or against pipelines. Rather it is to identify the terms and conditions under which a pipeline should be built. The final decision is to remain with the cabinet.

Because environmental policy is still in its infancy in Canada, no set process or even framework has totally evolved. However, the outlines of such policy in relation to energy development are becoming known. Anticipatory environmental studies are being required, but approval-in-principle for pilot development is being given in advance of study findings. In addition, social aspects of environment are now being stressed. Some government funding of native and environmental research groups for counterbalancing industry and government studies has also been provided. Whether or not an independent commission will again be used depends upon the government's political view of its role in its current hearings (1976).

Concluding Note

Intensive oil and gas exploration activity in the Canadian Arctic has given rise to numerous and varied issues. The long-term commitments of Canadian petroleum to the United States, the massive capital investments by American utilities in Canadian petroleum exploration, the largest pipeline project ever proposed, the unknown Arctic environment, the growing power of native northern peoples, the foreign relations between Canada and the United States, the magnitude of the energy economy in Canada, the dominance of U.S. multinational firms, the emergence of crown energy corporations, the anticipated energy shortages in Canada as soon as 1976, and the uncertainty of supply continuity and price from the Middle-East and South America have all combined to focus the search for oil and gas in the extensive sedimentary basins of the Canadian Arctic. These developments abound with issues and problems, several of which have national and international consequences.

From this analysis of Canadian energy policy processes, one notes an impressive amount of talent, effort, and expenditure in energy development. While at the level of particular activities there is a sense of purpose, organization, and controlled performance, in the larger overall context there is a much greater sense of drifting—of being constantly caught up in an unfolding dynamic that demands that actors react and respond to emergent situations but without any sense of overall purpose and direction.

This problem points to what may well be the most fundamental issue: How to address the question of the Canadian, and undoubtedly global, capability to create normative planning processes and within these, comprehensive and timely assessments in multiparty, multidimensional settings.

Notes

1. Department of Energy, Mines and Resources, *An Energy Policy for Canada—Phase I,* Vol. 1, Analysis (Ottawa: Information Canada, 1973). This section describing the current overall energy projection has been summarized from this report.

2. J. Maxwell, "Developing New Energy Sources: The Syncrude Case," (Montreal: C.D. Howe Research Institute, November 1975).

3. Pallister Resource Management, Ltd., "Petroleum Policies in Canada: Issues, Forecasts and Outlook," mimeo, Calgary, Alberta, May 1974. See also, E.R. Mitchell, "The Future of Fossil Fuels in Canada," Fuels Research Centre, Report FRC 74/70 (Ottawa: Canadian Combustion Research Laboratory, October 1974).

4. National Energy Board, *Canadian Oil Supply and Requirements,* (Ottawa, September 1975).

5. Dale Gibson, "Constitutional Jurisdiction over Environmental Management in Canada," background paper prepared for the Government of Canada, National Library, Government Publications Collection, Ottawa, June 1, 1970. This section has been summarized from this document.

6. See Department of Energy, Mines, and Resources, *An Energy Policy*, pp. 57-60, for a discussion of federal-provincial relationships in the energy policy field.

7. R.C. Frazee, "The Financial Problems of Canada's Energy Needs," speech prepared for the Association of Professional Engineers of Ontario, Toronto, October 5, 1974, p. 9.

8. See Department of Energy, Mines and Resources, *An Energy Policy*, Vol. II, Appendices, pp. 181-216.

9. R.W. Crowley, "Large Scale Energy Investments and the Public Finances: The Canadian Pipeline Case," paper prepared for the International Institute of Public Finance, Bucharest, September 1974, p. 8.

10. Maxwell, "Developing New Energy Sources," p. 22.

11. Ibid.

12. "Top Priority Given Frontier," *Kitchener-Waterloo Record*, March 29, 1976, p. 26.

13. J. Maxwell, *Arctic Energy: Facts and Issues* (Montreal: C.D. Howe Research Institute, 1973), p. 19.

14. E. Dosman, *The National Interest: The Politics of Northern Development 1968-75* (Toronto: McClelland and Stewart, 1975), pp. 54-57.

15. Peter J. Usher and Grahame Beakhust, *Land Regulation in the Canadian North*, Canadian Arctic Resources Committee (Ottawa: November 1973), p. 12.

16. J. Maxwell, *Arctic Energy*, p. 10.

17. Ibid., p. 6.

18. Usher and Beakhust, *Land Regulation*, pp. 12-13.

19. Ibid., pp. 5-7.

20. For a description of the federal decision-making process see Dosman, *The National Interest*. Also see R.F. Keith, D.W. Fischer et al., *Northern Development and Technology Assessment: A Study of Petroleum Development Programs in the Mackenzie Delta-Beaufort Sea Region and the Arctic Islands*, Background Paper No. 34 (Ottawa: Science Council of Canada, January 1976).

21. *Globe and Mail*, Toronto, October 22, 1974, p. B10.

22. Dosman, *The National Interest*.

23. Keith, Fischer et al., *Northern Development*, Appendix A.

24. Ibid., pp. 44-56. See also A. Thompson and M. Crommelin, "Legal Constraints on Petroleum Policy Options in Northern Canada," in P. Pearse (ed.), *The Mackenzie Pipeline: Arctic Gas and Canadian Energy Policy* (Toronto: McClelland and Stewart, 1974), pp. 80-97.

25. A. Yates, "Wrap-Up Remarks—Government," Northern Canada Offshore Drilling Meeting, DINA, Ottawa, December 5-6, 1972, pp. 328-34.

26. Canadian Arctic Resources Committee, "Offshore Drilling in the Beaufort Sea," *Northern Perspectives*, vol. 2, no. 2 (1974).

27. Dosman, *The National Interest* pp. 20-26, 63-84.

28. Canadian Arctic Resources Committee, "Mackenzie Valley Pipeline Inquiry," *Northern Perspectives*, vol. 2, no. 5 (1974).

29. Canadian Arctic Resources Committee, "Preamble to the Hearings," *Northern Perpsectives*, vol. 1, no. 6 (1973).

30. A.P. Pross, "Canadian Pressure Groups in the 1970's: Their Role and Their Relations with the Public Service," *Canadian Public Administration*, vol. 18, no. 1 (1975), p. 131.

31. E. Gray, *The Great Canadian Oil Patch* (Toronto: Maclean-Hunter, 1970), p. 79.

32. R. Rohmer, *The Arctic Imperative* (Toronto: McClelland-Stewart, 1973), p. 73.

33. *Oil Week*, July 5, 1965, p. 8.

34. *Oil and Gas Journal*, November 17, 1967, p 44.

35. Ibid., December 18, 1967, p. 47.

36. Dosman, *The National Interest*, pp. 42-46.

37. "Canada's North: A Statement of the Government of Canada on Northern Development in the 70's," presented to Standing Committee on Indian Affairs and Northern Development, March 28, 1972, p. 11; and A.D. Hunt, "Welcoming Address and Opening Remarks," Northern Canada Offshore Drilling Meeting, Ottawa, December 1972.

38. Dosman, *The National Interest*. See also a summary of Dosman in Canadian Arctic Resources Committee, "Canada's Energy Crisis: A Bizarre Case of Bungling," *Northern Perspectives*, vol. 4, no. 1 (1976).

39. National Energy Board, *Functions and Responsibilities*, Ottawa, January 28, 1974.

40. Dosman, *The National Interest*, pp. 67-68; Canadian Arctic Resources Committee, "Canada's Energy Crisis," pp. 9-11.

41. Canadian Arctic Resources Committee, ibid., p. 11.

42. Ibid., pp. 10-11.

43. National Energy Board, *Natural Gas Supply and Requirements*, Ottawa, August 1975.

44. Eric Kiernans, "The Day the Cabinet was Misled," *Canadian Forum*, Toronto, March 1974, pp. 4-8.

45. P.G. Bradley, "Energy, Profits and the National Interests: Three Perspectives on Arctic Natural Gas," in P.H. Pearse (ed.), *The Mackenzie Pipeline* (Toronto: McClelland and Stewart, 1974).

46. I. McDougall, "The NEB: Let's Give Credit Where Credit Is Due," *Canadian Forum* (June-July 1973), p. 31.

47. Dosman, *The National Interest*, pp. 7-8, 20.

48. Ibid., pp. 20-26, 63-84.

49. El Paso Corp., Press Release, Washington, D.C., September 24, 1974.

50. "Multi-national Role Seen for Petro-Canada," *Kitchener-Waterloo Record*, January 6, 1976.

51. "Information Sheet on the Mackenzie Valley Pipeline," mimeo, Research Bureau, National Liberal Caucus, no date.

52. The Hon. Mr. Justice T.R. Berger, *Preliminary Rulings, Mackenzie Valley Pipeline Inquiry*, Yellowknife, July 12, 1974.

53. Peter J. Usher, "The Committee for Original Peoples' Entitlement," mimeo, Ottawa, April 25, 1973. Also see Dosman, *The National Interest*, pp. 148, 191-95.

54. Philip Sykes, "Billion Dollar US Settlement Raises Canadian Native Hopes," *Toronto Star*, September 30, 1972.

55. James J. Wah-shee, "A Land Settlement, What Does it Mean?" presented to the conference, *Delta Gas: Now or Later?* sponsored by the Canadian Arctic Resources Committee, Ottawa, May 24, 1974.

56. "Inuit Magazine Boosts Eskimo Pride," *Ottawa Journal*, September 3, 1974, p. 7.

57. Kitson Vincent, "Cornelius Vanderbilt is Alive and Well: DIAND and the Public Interest," address to the Canadian Political Science Association Convention (draft), June 5, 1974, p. 2.

117

58. Canadian Arctic Resources Committee, *1973: Summing Up*, Ottawa, January 1974.

59. *Toronto Star*, June 1, 1974, p. B1.

60. Dosman, *The National Interest.*

61. Usher and Beakhust, *Land Regulation.*

62. K. Scott Wood, "Social Indicators and Social Reporting in the Canadian North," panel presentation, Proceedings of a Seminar, *Social Indicators*, The Canadian Council on Social Development, Ottawa, January 1972, p. 51.

63. Dosman, *The National Interest,* p. xvii.

64. H.W. Woodward, "Other Departments' Interests and Channels for Government/Industry Coordination," Northern Canada Offshore Drilling Meeting, Ottawa, December 5-6, 1972, p. 128.

65. CARC, *Northern Perspectives*, vol. 2, no. 2 (Summer 1974).

66. Pross, "Canadian Pressure Groups."

67. Peter H. Pearse (ed.), *The Mackenzie Pipeline: Arctic Gas and Canadian Energy Policy* (Toronto: McClelland and Stewart, Ltd., 1974), p. xi.

68. See P. Mathias, *Forced Growth* (Toronto: James Lewis & Samuel, 1971), for a study of five development projects sponsored by governments for regional development purposes that failed.

4

Actors and Decisions in French Energy Policy

Dominique Saumon
and *Louis Puiseux*

A Period of Great Changes

By 1950, postwar industrial reconstruction in France was already well under way. In almost all sectors of the economy, the production levels of 1938, the record production year of the prewar period, had been matched or surpassed. Simultaneously, the signs of a demographic surge, which contrasted with the stagnation of the period between the two world wars, and a very strong consensus regarding the objectives of industrialization and modernization in an economy where agriculture still held a very strong position, signalled the beginning of a period of much more rapid change.

In effect, a period of sustained economic growth that was accompanied and strengthened by increasing abandonment of protective measures for French industry had begun. In the autumn of 1973, however, the sudden increase in the price of petroleum revealed one of the weak points in the situation that had evolved: France was importing more than three-quarters of her energy, and the bill had become very high (more than fifty billion francs a year in current prices). In 1950, French energy production had provided 70 percent of national requirements. In 1960, this figure was already down to 60 percent, and it fell below 25 percent from 1972 on.

This development is summarized in Table 4-1, which shows clearly the increase in energy imports between 1960 and 1970. The growing dependence on imports resulted from a rapid growth in consumption, on the one hand, and an invasion into the energy field by petroleum products, on the other. Figure 4-1 illustrates this development, and Figures 4-2 and 4-3 show that it had not been at all foreseen by French policymakers. At the end of the 1960s another element was added: The "national" technology for the production of nuclear electricity (the natural uranium-graphite-gas cycle) was abandoned in favor of systems using enriched uranium developed by American industry. This decision postponed by several years the industrial development of nuclear energy, which the French central administration had actively promoted.

Preparatory to a more detailed analysis of these decisions, and of the economic factors underlying this evolution, we feel it is important to describe in detail some of the more important developments.

The Consumption Explosion

From 1960 to 1973, French energy consumption more than doubled (corresponding to an average annual growth rate of approximately 6 percent). Growth

119

Table 4-1
French Energy Consumption, by Origin (National or Foreign; in mtce)

	1954	1960	1964	1970	1973	1974
Coal						
production	56.3	58.3	55.8	40.6	29.1	26.8
imports	10.9	12.0	18.5	16.6	16.6	20.1
Petroleum						
production	0.6	2.8	4.0	3.2	1.8	1.5
imports	24.8	37.5	63.0	127.8	172.7	165.9
Natural Gas						
production	0.4	4.5	7.6	10.0	10.6	10.6
imports	0	0	0	3.9	11.8	13.5
Primary Electricity						
production	8.0	13.4	12.5	20.4	19.4	23.3
Production	65.3	79.0	79.9	74.2	60.9	62.2
Net Imports	35.7	49.4	81.5	148.3	201.2	199.5
% Covered by National Resources	64.6	62.0	49.1	33.4	23.6	23.8

Source: EDF compilation of data from *French Committee for World Energy Conference* and *Commission de l'energie du plan.* La Documentation Française (Paris, 1975).

during this period was much more rapid than it had been previously (3.66 percent per year from 1949 to 1960). It was also more rapid than the rate for Western Europe as a whole during the same time (4.8 percent per year between 1960 and 1970). The increase in consumption was accompanied by a redistribution of the roles of the sources of supply (see Table 4-2).

This spurt in growth came as a surprise to a large number of experts in the energy sector. In works produced in 1964 and 1965 after the movement had clearly begun, the Energy Commission of the Fifth Plan forecast a growth of energy needs in France of between 60 and 70 million tce's (tons of coal equivalents)[a] for the period 1960-1970, whereas growth actually was 95 million tce's. It is tempting to attribute this phenomenon to the acceleration of general economic growth and the entry of French society into the "era of mass consumption," but this answer does not suffice as a general description or explanation. Some complementary findings permit us better to pinpoint how this acceleration of needs came into being.

Worldwide economic growth does not provide a sufficient explanation. The growth rate of the gross national product between 1960 and 1970 was only slightly higher than between 1949 and 1960. On the other hand, the coefficient of elasticity of total energy consumption in relation to the GNP, which had been around 0.8 between 1949 and 1960, approached unity during the 1960s. This data show very clearly that between 1960 and 1970 there was a 20 percent increase over the previous decade in energy consumption per unit increase in GNP.

[a]That is, an annual growth of between 3.85 percent and 4.3 percent.

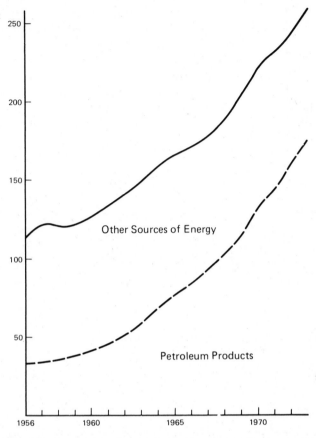

Source: *French Committee for World Energy Conference* and *Commission de l'energie du plan.* (Paris, 1975).

Figure 4-1. Consumption of Primary Energy in France (mtce).

This increase in consumption was distributed in a very uneven fashion across the various sectors of the economy, and it is this unevenness that most surprised the forecasters, as is seen in the final distribution of consumption (in millions of tce's). As Table 4-3 shows, in twelve years, the share of the domestic, tertiary, agriculture, and transport sectors grew from 47 percent to 55 percent of total consumption.

The importance of the transportation sector derives directly from the massive increase in the use of the automobile. This increase was forecast by the planners, but here again events surpassed the predictions, both from the point of view of the number of vehicles and of the use made of them. In 1972 private vehicles accounted for 80 percent of the automotive trade, whereas in 1960 the Fourth Plan had forecast that their proportion would be on the order of two-thirds.

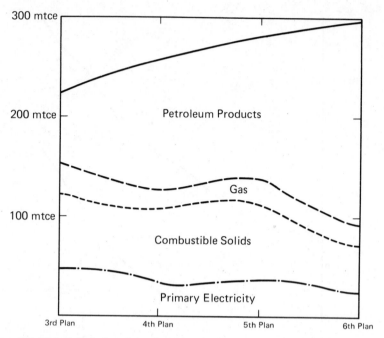

Source: Established with data from *Rapports de La Commission de l'energie du plan.* La Documentation Française (Paris, 1956-1976).

Figure 4-2. Successive Forecasts of the French Energy Balance.

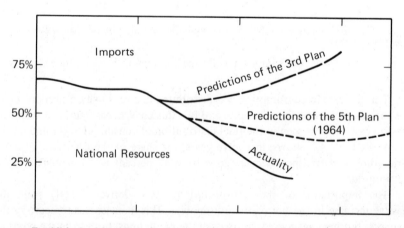

Source: Established with data from *Rapports de La Commission de l'energie du plan.* La Documentation Française (Paris, 1956-1976).

Figure 4-3. National Resources as a Percentage of Needs.

Table 4-2
Development of Primary Energy Consumption in France (m tce and %)

	1954	1960	%	1964	%	1970	%	1973	%	1974	%
Lignite coal	67.2	70.3	54.7	74.3	46.0	57.2	25.7	45.7	17.3	46.9	17.9
Petroleum	25.4	40.3	31.4	67.0	41.5	131.0	58.9	174.5	66.6	167.4	64.0
Natural Gas	0.4	4.5	3.5	7.6	4.7	13.9	6.3	22.4	8.6	24.1	9.2
Primary Electricity	8.0	13.4	10.4	12.5	7.8	20.4	9.7	19.4	7.4	23.3	8.9
Total Consumption corrected for temperature	101.0	128.4	100.0	161.4	100.0	222.5	100.0	262.1	100.0	261.7	100.0
Total Consumption without correction	101.0	127.4		163.1		225.5		265.1		257.3	

Source: EDF compilation of data from *French Committee for World Energy Conference* and *Commission de l'energie du plan. La Documentation Française* (Paris, 1975).

Table 4-3
Consumption Increases in France, 1960-1970 (mtce)

	1960 Consumption	1972 Consumption	Estimates of the 5th Plan for 1972 (reconstituted)
Domestic and Tertiary Sectors plus Agriculture	32.5	84	57-60
(Annual Growth)		(8%)	(5%)
Transport	20	43.5	35-38
(Annual Growth)		(6.5%)	(4.5%)
Industry	58.5	105	95-104
(Annual Growth)		(4.5%)	(4.5%)

Source: *Rapports de La Commission de l'energie du plan.* La Documentation Française (Paris, 1956-1976).

The domestic-tertiary-agriculture ensemble merits a more detailed examination, and some indication of the changes in consumption patterns is furnished by examination of consumption by type of energy product (see Table 4-4). The threefold increase in electricity consumption is almost entirely explained by improvements in lighting and, above all, by the movement of French households toward standards of household comfort imported from the United States[b] (in spite of relatively rapid development, electric heating and air conditioning still weigh light on this scale at approximately 1 tce). The increased need for fuel has been much more surprising to the experts. Even though its use is practically limited to heating (heating of buildings and provision of hot water) and the kitchen, total French consumption has increased in twelve years from 28 million tce's to 66 million tce's. This multiplication by nearly 2.4 results partly from the particularly rapid increase in the number of residences during this period, but it cannot be completely explained without taking note of the profound changes in consumption within these residences, principally as concerns heating. Two elements seem to predominate:

> The promotion of a certain image of comfort; to wit, living very lightly dressed in an apartment maintained permanently at a Mediterranean temperature;

> An evolution towards more and more "light" construction techniques such that technical norms imposed on construction do not lead to careful thermal isolation, which would otherwise be technically possible.

In a country with a relatively temperate climate, demand for fuel per household has practically doubled, which on the national energy scale amounts to nearly

[b]But they are still far from them, since electricity consumption per household is 4,000 to 5,000 kWh less than that of U.S. households.

Table 4-4
Energy Consumption in France, 1960-1970 (mtce)

	1960 Consumption	1972 Consumption	Estimates of the 5th Plan for 1972
Electricity[a]	5	18	15 to 16
Gas	2	8	6
Petroleum Products	8	49	24 to 25
Coal	18	9	13

[a]Using the French convention 1,000 kWh = 0.33 tce, which values electric energy as a function of the thermal energy necessary for its production.

Source: *Rapports de La Commission de l'energie du plan.* La Documentation Française (Paris, 1956-1976).

four times as much as the introduction of other elements of domestic comfort. Nevertheless the energy profile remains lower than that of the other countries of Europe and the northwest (see Table 4-5).

The Invasion of the Energy Field by Petroleum Products

Representing less than 15 percent of total consumption in 1949 and 31 percent in 1960, the share of petroleum reached 65 percent in 1972 and was still growing—up to 67 percent in 1973 in spite of the October energy crisis. In 1969, the Energy Commission of the Sixth Plan forecast that the importance of petroleum in the French system would not begin to decline until after 1980. The automobile was responsible for beginning the increase, and the rapid rise in fuel needs since the Second World War has required massive imports of crude oil and the development of a refining capacity (which was developing at a rate of 15 percent per year in 1960). Refining simultaneously produces domestic fuel oil and heavy fuel that from 1960 onward reached prices competitive with "national fuel." Domestic fuel oil provided an impetus for further petroleum development in the same way gasoline had. It took on increasing importance for industrial purposes and also for domestic use where it played a major role in the open market due to increased consumption and the decline of coal. This process made significant quantities of heavy fuel oil available to industry, and consumption in turn showed impressive increases, especially after 1965 when it became the most important energy source for installations providing steam and space heating. This phenomenon is amplified by the collapse of international petroleum prices between 1966 and 1969.

Although underestimated in all the forecasting studies, this expansion of petroleum led to a reaction from the central administration. An exploration

Table 4-5
Energy Profile of Western Europe, 1973

	GNP per Inhabitant ($)	Energy Consumption per Inhabitant (tce/inhab.)	Energy Consumption per km²	Electricity Consumption per Inhabitant (kWh/yr)	Share of Electricity in Energy (%)	Degree of Energy Dependence (%)
Norway	4,780	8,930	107	17,020	63.5	69.9
Sweden	6,140	7,460	134	9,380	41.6	66.0
Belgium	4,650	6,813	2,173	3,870	18.9	86.3
Netherlands	4,410	6,502	2,379	3,660	18.7	5.7
Germany	5,610	6,111	1,522	4,650	25.4	54.9
United Kingdom	3,100	5,660	1,302	4,660	27.4	48.2
France	4,900	4,938	469	3,300	22.2	76.0

Sources: OECD and CEE.

effort, stemming from the double concern for assuring "politically reliable" reserves and for limiting the impact of petroleum imports on the balance of payments, led the state to spend 10 billion francs in fifteen years (from 1945 to 1960) to discover more than 700 million tons of reserves in what was then called the French Union. The state had created the Autonomous Petroleum Administration (Régie autonome des pétroles) in 1939 and then in 1945 the Bureau of Petroleum Research (BRP) as tools for this policy. Aside from some success in France (Parentis, from which Esso drew more than 2 million tons annually), in Gabon, and in the Central Congo, the most important discoveries were made in the Sahara. The rise to independence of countries in the ex-Union considerably modified the status of these reserves and the interests that they represented. Until 1970 imports of Algerian crude oil were regulated by the state-to-state agreements of 1965, but already the francs used to pay for Saharan petroleum were freely convertible.[c] At the end of 1970 the price paid for Algerian petroleum was in practice aligned to the world market. A *tous azimuths* (all directions) policy evolved, in which the two French companies, CFP and then ERAP (created in 1966), tried to diversify their sources of supply. Africa, Indonesia, Canada, the North Sea, and recently South America have been the object of French prospecting. Simultaneously, the search for oil on domestic territory—above all around the French coasts that had been somewhat neglected after the effort of the 1950s—was revived and intensified after 1969 when the euphoria about petroleum dissipated and the first symptoms of the crisis appeared.[1]

The development policy of French companies reached at least for a time

[c]In fact, until 1968, about one-third of Algerian francs in reserve were converted into foreign currency. See Jean-Marie Chevalier, *Le nouvel enjeu petrolier* (Paris: Colman Levy, 1973).

(the policy of producer control of production has now changed the parameters of the problem) its first objective, which was to assure them control of a total production at least equal to total French consumption. But one must not forget that a large part of this "French" production is in fact redistributed on the international market; companies belonging to the international cartel continue to dominate the French market. A second objective, the diversification of sources of supply, is still very far from attainment. As can be seen in Table 4-6, the increase in imports was possible because of supplies from the Persian Gulf, which now account for two-thirds of French imports. Algeria, which has held control of its own resources since the Franco-Algerian crisis brought an end to the accords signed in 1965, has chosen diversification of its markets and now occupies only a secondary place in the French supply system.

In 1973, in spite of the perturbations resulting from the oil crisis which began in October and slowed down consumption in the last two months of the year, the demand for petroleum products still rose by 11 percent.

The Decline of Coal

The reconstruction of productive potential and then its rapid development were objectives given to the nationalized coal companies at the time of the French liberation. In March 1946, the Planning Council (Conseil du Plan) adopted a resolution that began with the following sentence: "The recovery of the French economy is strictly dependent on coal." The same resolution gave 50 million tons (the same as the 1939 figure) as a production goal for 1946, and 65 million tons from 1950 on. In fact, although the first objective was reached, the second

Table 4-6
French Petroleum Supply According to Origin (millions of tons)

	1962	1965	1970	1972
Algeria	13	18.5	26.9	10.2
Gabon, Congo, Nigeria	1	1.5	7.0	14.5
Mediterranean	7	12.5	23.8	20.4
Persian Gulf[a]	14.4	20.7	38.4	64.7
Other	2.7	3.5	4.2	3.7
Domestic	2.4	2.8	2.2	1.5
Total	40.5	59.5	102.5	114.0

[a]This includes all petroleum shipped from the Persian Gulf, and the figures include imports of Iranian origin as well as part of those coming from Iraq.

Source: D. Beauchard, op. cit.

was not. In spite of numerous difficulties with recruitment of miners and modernization of equipment, production grew regularly to a maximum level of 60 million tons per year in 1959.

This weak rate of growth took place in very difficult financial circumstances: Any profit to the coal producers was effectively eliminated by the fixing of the sale price to the mean cost. (By taking into account unforeseen technical and salary costs, we can even say that this price fixing led to a chronic deficit.) The method of price fixing lowered the price of energy and perhaps somewhat increased the volume of the coal market, compared with the probable results of marginal taxation. In any case, it led to deficits in numerous mines because nearly half of the production had prime costs superior to the average price.

During the whole period from 1950 to 1958, energy consumption grew more rapidly than domestic coal production, with the deficit being made up by importing coal and petroleum products. In fact, the share taken up by imports grew very rapidly, and the conquest of more and more markets by fuel oil was almost inevitable because the equipment chosen by the consumer depended on this type of fuel. The presence of petroleum in the competitive domain (domestic and tertiary uses and steam production in industry) became established, and with petroleum at an equivalent price during 1958-59, the prospects for sale of coal seemed less secure.

Almost simultaneously, transatlantic freight costs declined and leveled off at three-to-five dollars per ton. It was the beginning of wide sweeping structural changes in the world ore shipping fleet. This movement to specialized ships that were faster and increasingly large strengthened the position of American coal in the French market.

Although the effects of the general crisis of coal in Western Europe from 1958 to 1960 were dampened by policies of stockpiling and reduced imports, a coal adaptation plan was published in July 1960. Based on a 10 percent reduction in annual production by 1965, the first phase of the plan was carried out nationwide. But the objective of redressing the financial situation remained out of reach. Whereas the costs of production grew in spite of regular increases in productivity (where personnel costs representing almost two-thirds of the total increased along with other wages), the sale price did not increase because it was adjusted to the price of fuel adopted by the government as "guideline prices for French energy." The production objective was revised downward several times (the plan for 1968 envisaged a production of 25 million tons for 1975) and manpower difficulties had a tendency to accelerate the decline.

The Breakthrough of Gas

Until 1955 natural gas consumption in France was essentially limited to the area around the small oil field of St. Marcet in the Southwest. The 400,000 tce's produced and consumed annually counted for little in comparison with the gas production of the coking plants, blast furnaces, and gas factories whose production corresponded to 12 million tce's in 1965. The discovery of the Lacq oil field, in the same region at the foot of the Pyrenees, revolutionized the gas market in France. The size of this resource permitted the almost immediate establishment of a local industry based on the use of gas (chemicals and electric power stations) and a network of gas distribution in France, from south of the Loire at first, then towards the Paris region. The use of this new fuel was facilitated by the existence of the Gaz de France, which provided a framework for distribution and commercialization. Natural gas replaced manufactured gas; the Gaz de France liquidated its production machinery and created instead a nationwide network for gas transport. The fixing of the price at a low level in relation to other fuels (taking into account the ease of using gas) contributed to its success in industrial use.

Natural gas consumption increased rapidly. Even though Lacq has not had a significant successor, the recourse to imports, which became important from 1966 on, permitted the continuance of growth, as can be seen in Table 4-7.

The sources of these imports also evolved very rapidly. Essentially assured by the deposits of Gronigen (Netherlands), they were completed by Algerian gas as soon as the necessary techniques for liquefaction and shipment of methane were developed. Norwegian gas (Ekofisk), followed by imports from the USSR, should take up the slack when the current sources of supply level off. Concurrently, the type of control that the Gaz de France exercises over supply will become modified. After making various contracts directly with the producers, it will become a member of the buying consortiums formed by various European distributors for contract negotiations with Algeria and Ekofisk.

Electricity, Prisoner of Petroleum

In 1959 fuel oil accounted for barely 5 percent of electricity production, whereas in 1973 its share reached 40 percent. This proportion will continue to grow for another six or seven years and will then exceed half of the total production (regardless of efforts undertaken in the realm of nuclear power

Table 4-7
Development of Natural Gas Consumption (mtce)

	1950	1960	1966	1972
Total French Consumption	0.4	4.5	8.4	19.3
Share of Imports	0	0.5	0.8	8.7

Source: *Rapports de La Commission de l'energie du plan.* La Documentation Française (Paris, 1956-1976).

plants, since current investment decisions will not bear fruit until about 1981). Three elements have played an important role in this evolution: the ceiling on hydroelectric installations, the reduction in the use of coal, and the absence of nuclear programs from 1966 to 1970.

The economically feasible hydroelectric potential has always been estimated at between 60 and 80 billion kilowatts. Current policy calls for stopping development of the French potential at a little over 60 billion kilowatts, a figure that will be reached by about 1980. Almost three-quarters of this development was already completed in 1965. Thus it can be seen that the rate of development of hydroelectric power has been slow for ten years and much slower than the rate of growth in electricity consumption, which continues to nearly double every ten years.

For this reason, a greater and greater proportion is taken up by electricity of thermal origin, largely due to the growth of the Electricité de France (EDF). Production from the thermal installations of the EDF, which until 1960 accounted for less than half of French thermal production (thus less than a quarter of the total electricity production), increased tenfold in a little more than twenty years. Prior to the installations begun in 1963, coal was used in the great majority of cases, but from this date forward, there was an almost complete turnabout towards heavy fuel oil, with the exceptions being a few coal units in mining regions that were begun between 1963 and 1967. A laboriously negotiated agreement in 1965 between the coal producers and the EDF guaranteed an annual production that could have grown to 15 million tons by 1975,[d] but it was revised and the EDF only consumed 7 million tons of domestic coal in 1970. Some of the installations originally intended to burn coal were converted to fuel oil at this time.

The growth of petroleum was accented further by a marked slowdown in the program for nuclear plants. Whereas the Fifth Plan (1966-1970) had foreseen 500 MW per year, this program guaranteed by a complementary program 1,000 to 1,500 MW at the end of the period covered by the plan, just one plant (St.-Laurent II) was begun by 1970. The second plant provided for in this program (Fessenheim sur le Rhin) was decided on in 1967, postponed from year to year, and then finally launched in 1970 after the decision to adapt the American chain of light water reactors. Only with the elaboration of the Sixth Plan was the decision taken to commit in principle a minimum of 8,000 MW to nuclear plants. This decision was confirmed in 1973, and beginning in 1974, when the price of petroleum tripled in a few months, this program was vigorously accelerated: 12,000 MW were installed in two years and a comparable rate of investment continued over the following years.

These delays and hesitations in the nuclear program had the effect of reducing energy production from uranium to half of the initial objectives of the Fifth Plan between 1972 and 1975. In addition, the decision in favor of the

[d]On the other hand, EDF would have been free to import foreign coal.

Fessenheim plant marked the end of the French chain (natural uranium-graphite-gas).

The Nuclear False Start and the Abandonment of the French Chain

In 1945 the Atomic Energy Commissariat (CEA) was created and charged specifically with the organization and control of prospecting, of exploitation of reserves of primary resources necessary to the development and utilization of atomic energy,[2] and with carrying out research on the various types of reactors using this energy. The search for ore was a success from the beginning both on domestic territory (France is not lacking in granite formations) as well as in the colonies (Madagascar, the Congo, the Ivory Coast, and later, Nigeria, and Gabon). From 1950 on, uranium production was sufficient to permit consideration of the construction of large reactors. The CEA acquired some competence with regard to heavy water reactors, but beginning in 1952, it concentrated its efforts on a modified system using coal and carbonic gas (for cooling) that was somewhat similar to the one that had been developed in Great Britain. To symbolize the marked interest in nuclear electricity production, the Electricité de France decided to install a turbine to recover the heat produced by the first reactor at Marcoule in spite of the very small amount of retrievable power. A collaboration between the EDF and the CEA for the development of a program of prototypes was begun, and between 1959 and 1966, five prototypes were rapidly put into service on the sites of Marcoule (on the Rhone north of Avignon) and Avoine-Chinon (on the Loire).

Even though the objectives defined by Parliament in July 1957 had not been completely accomplished (the 800 MW foreseen for 1965 were only achieved in 1966 with the completion of EDF 3, the third plant at Chinon), one utility was in place at the end of 1966 and three of the industrial series (Burgey I and St.-Laurent I and II) had already been ordered. The relationship between the EDF and the CEA was not completely harmonious, however, because the boundary defining the respective responsibilities of the two organizations was difficult to decipher.

The choice in favor of the natural uranium-graphite-gas chain did not suppress all work on the other processes. The Euratom Treaty resulted in 1960 in a decision to build the plant at Chooz (enriched uranium, light water, Westinghouse type), and a step was taken in the direction of heavy water in 1962 with the Brennilis plant that was far from being a success. Important efforts were undertaken with regard to fast breeder reactors. In 1967 an experimental reactor was laid out (not producing electricity), and in 1973 Phénix was put into service as a prototype at the industrial level.

The rapid takeoff of the natural uranium-graphite-gas chain (the French chain) was followed by a series of hesitations. The decision to construct the plants planned by the Fifth Plan at Fessenheim was blocked. The EDF began to test American techniques during this time (1968-69) in large power plants at Tihange in collaboration with Belgian producers and at Kaiseraugst in collaboration with the Swiss and Germans. In November 1969 the government published its decision for renewed effort in the development of nuclear production. It gave the EDF the mission of launching a program of so-called diversification, which would begin in 1970 and involve several large power plants using the enriched uranium process.

In actual fact, this decision marked the end of the French chain. The Energy Commission proposed as their minimum objective a program of 8,000 MW in plants using enriched uranium and ordinary water, and the orientation of the Sixth Plan derived from that decision. As we have already seen, this program would be broadly doubled by the decisions taken in January 1974 following the oil crisis in the autumn of 1973. The EDF concentrated all its efforts on a single technique for which the only experience was the Franco-Belgian plant at Chooz since the plant at Tihange did not come into service until the end of 1974.

Apart from some contract commitments, until the end of the 1970s autonomy was encumbered mainly by the failure to regulate the supply of nuclear fuel according to domestic need. Enriched uranium came from the United States and in lesser degree from the USSR until the European plant at Tricastin in southeastern France was put into service. The fuel elements were manufactured in Belgium by a company run by Franco-American capital.

The Decisions, the Actors

The developments described in the preceding section radically changed the physiognomy of the French energy sector in less than a quarter of a century. Not only did consumption habits and sources of supply change greatly, but there were also profound changes in the roles of the various actors and the patterns of relationships among them, which until then had regulated the sector as a whole. This situation was the outcome of a series of decisions, whether explicit or not (laissez-faire played an important role). Table 4-8 pinpoints those decisions that seem to us to have most strongly influenced the evolution of the market in energy products and the structure of the energy sector.

Doubtless it would be possible to investigate which interests were involved for each of the decisions thus defined and what the resulting arbitration was. But the interdependencies implicit in the fact that they all belong to the same sector would lead to numerous repetitions; one finds the same actors following nearly identical goals through the various developments in the sector as a whole. It seems simpler to choose some of the decisions that had the greatest effect on the energy market and the structure of the energy sector. We will concentrate

Table 4-8
Principal Energy Decisions Since 1945

	Consumption	Investments and Production	Research Developments	Prices	Legal and Structural Framework of the Energy Sector
Coal		Decline starting in 1959, accelerated after 1965		Sale at mean prices	
Petroleum	Promotion of fuel-oil consumption in domestic and industrial sectors		Effort up to 1980 and recent resurge in petroleum research	Few specific taxes on fuel (maintenance of TWA until 1968)	Creation of Elf-Erap
Gas	Extension of the use of gas in industry and in the production of electricity	Development of the mass transportation network		Price for gas from Lacq set deliberately low	Nationalization of gas
Electricity and Nuclear Power	Commercial turning point in 1969	End of the importance of hydro power in thermal production; gap in nuclear development 1965-70. Take-off of American nuclear technique after 1970	Nuclear research resumed after liberation; choice of gas-graphite cycle. Its abandonment in 1969.	Electricity priced at marginal cost	Nationalization of electricity. Foundation of CEA; modification of legal and functional status of CEA
Other Sources of Energy			No expenditures for geothermal, nor for solar		Research cut off from industry until end of the 1960s
Decisions Affecting All Sources of Energy				Norms of feasibility aligned to imported petroleum from 1960 on	Evolution of the role of the plan in public enterprises; "Nora" policy; criteria for development based on rules of the market; adoption of the strategies of big business and the multinationals

particularly on those that seem most likely to reveal the conflicts that set the various actors in opposition to each other in the various time periods.

After describing briefly the various organizations concerned with energy problems and the broad lines of organization in this sector, we will examine successively: the exploitation of the gas at Lacq, the reduction in the use of coal, the regulation of the petroleum market, and the takeoff of nuclear production.

The Organizations and the Structures

As in numerous other sectors of the French economy, there is a confrontation between: (1) *private interests*, upon which depend a large part of the production and distribution of petroleum products, the marketing of some coal production, and basic equipment for consumer industries as well as producing industries; (2) *public enterprises* devoted to industrial and commercial functions, which have in practice a monopoly over the production and distribution of electricity and gas, coal extraction, research, and some nuclear activities; and (3) an *administration* whose role is to respect the general objectives of government policy, but also to arbitrate among the various interests present.

The consumption requirements come from domestic and tertiary consumption and individual transport on the one hand, and from industrial consumption on the other hand. The most important consumers are concentrated heavy industries, with practically all of them being in the private sector. The government administration therefore has no direct control over them.

The sectors of engineering and construction of mining or refining equipment are relatively less concentrated, and each is composed of partners who are relatively marginal in relation to the global problems of energy. In contrast, the construction of electromechanical equipment has been marked by a very pronounced concentration dominated by two very important groups: the Compagnie Générale d'Electricité and the Groupe Creusot-Loire. They control a large part of the market for the construction of generating plants, and in turn their development is strongly influenced by technological choices in electricity production. The importance of the public sector, which controls a large share of production, is noteworthy, as is the power of the administration, which in theory provides for tight control over the petroleum sector.[e] Coordination is facilitated by the large administrative agencies involved (mines,[f] gas and electricity, motor fuel), and these agencies are all under the aegis of the Ministry of Industry and Research (including, since 1970, the Commissariat of Atomic Energy).

Table 4-9 summarizes the relative positions of the various organizations. It is

[e]By a group of laws making the petroleum sector a public monopoly delegated to private enterprise.

[f]Abolished in 1971, because of the decline of coal.

Table 4-9

Organigram of Energy in France

	Industrial and Commercial Activity		Scientific and Technological Research	Administration		
Coal	Extraction in France: Charbonnages de France and its affiliates Houillières de Bassins Imports: Association Technique de l'Importation Charbonnière	Commercialization: Charbonnages de France and wholesalers	Centre d'Etudes et de Recherches des Charbon- nages de France	Direction du Gaz, de l'Electricité, et du Charbon (DGEC)		
Petroleum	Prospecting and production in France and over- seas: Elf Aquitaine and Compagnie Française des Pétroles Petroleum imports: groups Elf and Total—Shell—Esso— BP—Mobil—Fina— Agip Petroleum products: 75 importing dis- tributors	Distribution: Companies author- ized to import and some merchants	Institut Français du Pétrole and Companies	Direction des Carburants (DICA)		
Gas	Imports: Transport: GDF GDF and Aquitaine	Distribution: GDF and local dis- tributors	GDF	DGEC	General Secretariat for Energy[a]	Ministry for Industrial and Scientific Development
Electricity	Electricity pro- duction: Electricité de France Independ- ent producers Transport: EDF (monopoly)	Distribution: EDF and some local distributors	EDF	DGEC		
Nuclear Energy	Provision of nuclear materiel, research and development of processes	General responsibility of the Commisariat for Atomic Energy	CEA and other companies			
	Independent activity, or in cooperation with other companies (outside of commercial production of electricity)					

Source: Internal Document of the CEA.

[a]Changed to General Delegation for Energy in France in 1974.

useful to elaborate on this table insofar as it ignores the organizations less directly involved in production and distribution.

We will note first that the role of the Ministry of Finance, which often exercises direct control over public investment, is most important when it involves long-term strategies because they require investments. The Commissariat Général du Plan is charged with the preparation every five years of social and economic development plans. On this occasion, it redefines the development perspectives of all industrial sectors and of the energy sector in particular. But the ability of these actors to play a role, to define, and to execute strategies on the energy scene depends, of course, on their political and economic importance and also on the research funds at their disposal.

The government agencies with strong regulatory power have hardly any permanent funds for study. For example, the specialized agencies of the Ministry of Industry are small teams of high-level civil servants. This weakness in infrastructure makes studies of a truly global character impossible. It behooves us, nevertheless, to note some individual cases.

The Commission de l'Energie du Plan (Energy Commission of the Plan) has a permanent staff and is concerned with long-term problems and with the evolution of the national energy balance in particular. But its funds are limited and its most important studies are carried out at the time the plans are elaborated, within specialized groups essentially involving the representatives of producers.

The Direction de la Prévision (Forecasting Agency) in the Ministry of Finance has substantial funds and plays an important role in the definition of short- and medium-term policies. The role of this agency expanded around 1965 as the relative importance of the Commission de l'Energie du Plan declined.

The Délégation Générale à l'énergie (General Delegation for Energy) was set up at the end of 1973 to strengthen the role of the secretariat of energy that it replaced and has at its disposal the Agence Nationale pour les Economies d'Energie, which selects and promotes measures to economize energy.

Public enterprises represent a significant share of the national value added and a significant number of salaried workers (120,000 for the EDF-GDF; an equivalent figure for the CDF in spite of a rapid decline in growth; and 30,000 for the CEA before its reorganization). They all have services for technical and economic studies and participate in the elaboration of the plans.

The oil companies present similar characteristics. They also have important study funds available, but seem to be oriented primarily toward short-term forecasting and management. One sees here an effect of the habitual expectation that large profits will permit the rapid amortization of investments.

The Exploitation of the Gas of Lacq and Its Price

Until the mid-1950s the operation of the French energy market was characterized[3] by the predominance of a "national system" that followed two criteria:

(1) a strictly national basis of the market and of supply to enterprises concerned, and (2) close and privileged relationships between these enterprises and the state to assure the cohesion of the system. Because it was based on natural resources in French territory, this national system assured the distribution of rather expensive energy in relatively limited quantities. The first important changes in the workings of this system would coincide with the beginning of production from the natural gas deposits at Lacq.

These changes created an interesting conflict. Should this resource be reserved for the region, exploited parsimoniously, and sold at a price high enough to release resources necessary for self-financing of petroleum prospecting in France? Or, on the contrary, should it be exploited as fast as possible on a large scale and at a price near the marginal cost so as to maximize the collective gain rather than the profit of the seller, notably by improving the competitive position of industries that were large consumers of energy?

The actors present were:

1. The DICA (Direction des Carburants—Fuel Board), the department of the Ministry of Industry responsible for policy with regard to hydrocarbons, gave priority to financing petroleum research and therefore defended a policy of prudent exploitation. It permitted maintenance of a high price so as to obtain maximum profit.
2. The DIGELEC (Direction du Gas et de l'Electricité—Gas and Electric Board), another department in the Ministry of Industry, defended the contrary thesis and marginal pricing in the name of "public service."
3. The SNPA (Société Nationale des Pétroles d'Aquitaine—National Society of Aquitaine Petroleum), an association where the state controls a majority through the intermediary of the BRP and the Gaz de France, had the concession for the gas, but was startled by the size of the discovery and did not favor rapid exploitation.
4. The BRP (Bureau de Recherche Pétrolière—Bureau of Petroleum Research), a public body presided over at the time by M. Guillaumat, naturally defended the restrictive position.
5. The Gaz de France, a public utility, hoped to benefit its customers by providing this new resource with the least delay, at the best price, and in the greatest quantities possible. The costs of production were obviously much lower than for manufactured gas, which still accounted for nearly all of the production, transportation, and consumer use of gas in France.
6. The Electricité de France, a public enterprise, held a position and goals identical to those of the Gaz de France.
7. The consumers were represented only by local collectives in the region that sought to keep the gas for their own exclusive profit.

These various points of view were brought into confrontation with each other at the Commission de l'Energie du Plan, whose favorable opinion at the time was indispensable for any granting of credit. Let us remember that the context for national economic policy at the time was marked by an energy shortage with respect to the development of industry and by a clear tendency toward deficit in the balance of payments. After long and difficult discussions, the Commission de l'Energie du Plan decided in favor of the second solution (extensive exploitation and public pricing at marginal cost). It was influenced principally by the Minister of Economy and Finances (Félix Gaillard) who subordinated financial profitability to the advantage to the consumers of low prices from the perspective of long-term competition between Europe and the United States: "Natural gas will be Europe's oxygen balloon while awaiting nuclear energy," and lightly accepted in return destroying the markets from which the petroleum companies drew large profits. This decision was facilitated further by the offer of the EDF to consume as much natural gas as necessary to make the investments in production and transport immediately profitable while waiting for industrial or domestic consumers to take up the slack.

In 1956, the SNPA at last presented a program of investment and exploitation that was resolutely expansionist.

The Apogee and the Decline of National Coal

The Period of Reconstruction. The ambitious objectives spelled out to the coal companies in 1946 reflected a consensus that was too general (comprising as it did political and labor forces, administration, and managers of newly nationalized industries) for the concerns over profitability manifested by some cautious souls[4] to be taken seriously. It was necessary to reestablish a national energy base in order to assure the recovery of French economic activity, and this role could only be filled by coal. The initial objectives were somewhat lowered with the elaboration of the Second Plan, but as Michael Toromanoff points out, even if the most clairvoyant of the coal company directors believed that it was time (between 1949 and 1952) "to rethink the programs of the coal producers in a realistic way, taking into account the special handicaps of the French mines . . . ,"[5] the only perspective acceptable to the public authorities remained the expansion of production.[6] However, there was still a debate over the technical conditions for development of this production potential. According to Pierre Massé, whether from a refusal to pose the problem in economic terms or from a choice of the easiest policy, the expansion of coal production was decided without seriously considering the problem posed by the development of a modern sector (essentially corresponding to the Lorraine basin) replacing the older and more costly mines.

The difficult financial conditions that the nationalized coal industry was to experience came in large part, as we have seen, from the sale price that had been fixed for coal. The sale at a median price, which maintained only a precarious equilibrium, did not free the resources that would have permitted self-financing of investments for development or modernization by the coal industry. The resulting indebtedness, when combined with the social changes that took on more weight as receipts declined along with production, was one of the causes of the deficit that continued to grow in spite of the plan for adaptation. According to Pierre Massé, even the directors of the coal industry would have favored a policy of low prices leading to a wider market. However, this opinion is not held by M. Toromanoff who believes it was imposed by the public administration for reasons that varied in relative importance over the years: (1) to prevent a nationalized industry from making "profits," (2) to put a brake on inflation, and (3) to lower the price of energy.[7]

In fact, the refusal on the part of the consumers to pay more for a domestic resource was reinforced as the international climate passed from energy scarcity to energy abundance. This refusal was as strong on the part of the national enterprises (the EDF only agreed to a "premium for security of supply" of 10 percent above the price on the international market) as on the part of the private sector. The limit of 10 percent of the "premium" that one could accord national fuels would reappear in studies carried out to determine the market for coal, after the decision to reduce production.

The Coal Crisis and the First Adaptation Plan. The decline of coal appeared "unavoidable" to all the experts as soon as they were certain that large petroleum reserves were available at very low cost. They thought that consumers would not tolerate prices that were significantly different from those obtainable on the international market. But in 1959, the French economy opened up to the world market, and the principal concern of the economic and political powers was to strengthen the competitive capability of domestic industries. They became sensitive then to the arguments of management against the handicap of high energy prices. Thus, distribution of abundant energy at the lowest possible price appeared to be a necessary condition for assuring the competitive position of French products.

A question arises at this level: Was there an offensive strategy on the part of the petroleum companies? A high official has pointed out that after the first debates over the reduction of coal production, the petroleum companies favored the maintenance of the coal mines (perhaps to maintain prices at the highest level) while at the same time they were known to be practicing a policy of lively competition, notably by means of a rebate of the sale price (up to 20 percent). For M. Hincker,[8] the signs of a European petroleum offensive were unmistakable. France would be the most vulnerable zone in Western Europe for the following reasons:

1. The French price for energy was the highest because of the difficulty of exploiting French coal deposits.
2. For the Common Market countries taken as a whole, the petroleum

companies maintained refining capacities clearly in excess of anticipated demand.

3. In 1958, the fall in petroleum prices in Germany and in the Netherlands reached 40 percent to 45 percent in relation to the preceding year (in the view of this author, this voluntary lowering of price could very well have been avoided by the large companies).

Finally, in addition to its support for a policy of low prices, the world of industry and finance affected the outcome by its contribution to the importing of American coal. A financial group comprised of the Banque de Paris et des Pays-Bas, the Banque Lazard and the Banque de l'Union Européenne created the *Union Navale* in 1957 for the purpose of constructing a coal fleet destined for traffic between the United States and France.[9] We must connect the creation of the Union Navale with the development of the metalurgical complex at Dunkirk (Usinor and the Banque de Paris et des Pays-Bas), the location of which was designed to assure the "proximity" of American coal just as much as that of Mauritanian iron ore.

Faced with these interests and this new consensus, there was very little resistance. In July 1958, the public authorities asked the coal companies for a study of the financial consequences of a reduction in production, and when Minister M. Janneney announced the elements of a plan of adaptation in June-July 1960, the most violent reaction came from the employees of the coal companies. This worker resistance was mainly symbolic[10] (except for localized conflicts such as the one at Décazeville) until the explosion in the spring of 1963, when the reactions of the labor unions became differentiated. CFTC (then the CFDT) accepted the "economic conditions of the problem," which was not the case with the CGT, and the Décazeville affair pointed up these differences in attitude.

The Speeding Up of the Retrenchment. According to P. Massé, and to R. Bonety as well, psychological factors played an important role. The general strike of miners in March-April 1963 lasted more than six weeks and did not result in any fuel shortages. As a result, there was a change in the collective French consciousness that understood that the era of coal was finished. When the miners understood that they were no longer indispensable to the functioning of the French economy, they lost their moral and social status. No reason remained for accepting such a hard vocation and there was a loss of the will for survival in the mining world. Young people no longer went into mining and a growing proportion of the personnel was made up of immigrant workers. These personnel difficulties partially explain the accelerated decline in production, and according to a director of the EDF, the failure to fulfill the 1965 contract between the EDF and the coal companies.

But the new rules of the game (i.e., considering the price of petroleum as a

reference price for energy, to which only the Communist party and CGT showed
any noticeable opposition) contributed to the accelerated decline of the
"competitive core" of coal production. Until the end of 1960, this norm had
almost unanimous approval from energy enterprises and large consumers, and
until this date petroleum prices were in rapid decline! In spite of the gains in
productivity and the reliance on the most competitive mines, the coal production aimed at for 1975 was reduced in 1968 to 25 million tons. Only following
the general rise in prices for energy products in the fall of 1973 was this
objective reexamined and were studies begun foreseeing a slower drop in
production from the Lorraine and Central Midi basins.

The Regulation of the Petroleum Market. The petroleum sector in France is
characterized by the strong positions held by the international petroleum
companies. Nevertheless legislation passed in 1928 instituted a system of import
and refining quotas that would permit promotion of the domestic refining
industry by limiting imports of refined products and by using these refining
preferences to favor French companies and encourage the consumption of
petroleum products. The public authorities used these regulations to encourage
the creation of a French refining industry and to give a growing share in the
distribution of domestic petroleum products to French interests. But these
methods were never used to limit or to direct the use of petroleum products.

To summarize the French policy on this matter, one can say that the state,
for the main part, left the law of the international market free rein in the
petroleum sector. This laissez-faire attitude led the French to adapt very quickly
to consumption levels well above national resources and to a dependence, as
dramatically revealed in 1973, on the principal petroleum-producing countries.

Aside from the international companies everyone knows, the DICAC
(Direction des Carburants, the department of the Ministry of Industry responsible for petroleum policy) and the BRP (Bureau de Recherche Pétrolière—Bureau
of Petroleum Research), it is useful to note among the decisionmakers involved
in this sector the following:

1. The French petroleum companies, such as CFP (Compagnie française des
   Pétroles), ERAP, and so forth, that although controlled[g] by the public
   authorities have followed essentially the same policies as the international
   companies for twenty-five years;
2. The very reduced role of the Commission de l'Energie du Plan, where the
   persons involved have almost never participated except as observers;
3. The considerable role in the rise of petroleum consumption of the industries
   (the great majority of which are privately owned) whose activity is directly
   tied to the consumption of motor fuel (the first and foremost of which are
   the manufacturers of automobiles and trucks).

[g]In fact, ERAP is owned by the French government, which is the only main stockholder of
CFP.

The incursion by petroleum products into the French energy system (to the detriment of coal at first and then to the detriment of nuclear energy development) began with the growth of the automobile, a development that was more rapid in France than in any other European country. The need for automobile fuel led to the importation of crude oil and then to a large surplus of fuel coming from the refineries, which replaced coal and favored the development of excessive or wasteful uses of energy (both industrial and domestic). French policy regarding transportation has obviously favored this evolution. The priority given to individual vehicles to the detriment of public mass transit in France for the past twenty years is evidence of a tacit consensus that reflected (1) the seduction of the general public by American civilization, the big winner in the Second World War; (2) the interests of private industries who found a considerable source of profit in the development of this market; and (3) the pressure of the labor unions as well, who saw the automobile as one of the elements of comfort they claimed for the workers. When the harmful effects appeared, the fear of unemployment led them to continue to support the automobile industry.

Faced with this balance of forces, the public authorities allowed an allocation of credits for public investment that always favored individual solutions over collective solutions, and the state consistently defended an aberrant tax system. For example, the user of the railway was made to pay all the costs his transportation involved for the collectivity, but on the contrary, the use of the automobile in large cities was subsidized as was the congestion that created, as everyone knows, employment, value added in the national accounts, and some heart attacks.

In the course of the 1960s, the petroleum companies concentrated their commercial efforts on the promotion of domestic fuel oil (FOD), a low-priced product that permitted large profit margins. If we add to this commercial effort the convenience of using the product when compared to coal and a sale price that made it a very cheap source of energy for domestic use especially after 1965, it becomes evident that conditions were ripe for a spectacular breakthrough of this product. Its use increased tenfold between 1959 and 1972, and more than half of the 34 million tons consumed in 1972 went to household use.

From 1965 on, the large consumption of "white products" put important quantities of heavy fuel (FOL) at the disposal of industry at prices that corresponded to the decline in the world price for crude oil. When consumption of heavy fuel experienced in turn a sudden expansion as a substitute for coal in industry, the public authorities refused once again to tax petroleum products more heavily. Rather than limit their use at levels less threatening to the security of supply, the state favored maintaining the lowest possible cost in an attempt to favor the competitive position of French industry while the Common Market was going into effect. The Energy Commission of the Sixth Plan affirmed its principles very clearly:

... the evolution of prices and of the fiscal system should take into account the option in favor of industrial development. Concern for the competitiveness of French industry should guide all action in this domain, notably in the framework of European harmonization.[11]

In Great Britain and in West Germany, fuel-supported use taxes were much higher than in France[h] where the value-added tax became deductible in 1968. After the "regularization of monetary parities" in 1969, the "ex-refinery" price of French heavy fuel, aside from deductible taxes, became the lowest in the European Community. This evolution naturally met with the favor of industry, which supported anything that would lessen their costs.

Beginning in 1966, when prices began to decline more quickly—with the petroleum industry accentuating this situation by their practice of systematic rebates—one can speak of a veritable gluttony for fuel oil that infected the end users as well as the industry. To some observers of this period, dumping was evident. The Fifth Plan announced a relatively rapid breakthrough for nuclear power, but a place still had to be found for the important petroleum discoveries of the 1960s. To most, it seemed rather to be an amplification of factors inherent in the French situation in a market characterized by worldwide euphoria with regard to petroleum that stemmed from the accumulation of important discoveries, notably those of independent American companies in Libya and the lowering of freight costs. As we have just indicated above, the public authorities favored the reduction of costs borne by French industries that were just beginning to feel the effects of international competition resulting from the Treaty of Rome. Simultaneously, they wanted to broaden the French petroleum market (ERAP in particular, which had just been created and was trying to break into the markets of its competitors). By allowing the total volume of the market to expand, this end could be accomplished without too much deterioration in the relationships with the multinationals.

But in trying to achieve their goals, the national companies would show themselves similar to the private American companies against whom they were trying to compete. This patterning of the national companies on the behavior of private companies and their power politics led the French oil companies to maximize sales and thus to stimulate demand through their pricing policies, their publicity, the building of freeways, and so forth. They wound up with a paradoxical result: The competitive position of French companies was achieved to the detriment of the very goals for which it had been promoted, because the effort toward diversification of supply undertaken at the same time had only mediocre results. Dependence on oil producers grew rapidly, especially in the

---

[h]In West Germany this tax was forty francs per ton and designed to aid the coal miners. This type of transfer was always defeated in France where subsidizing the coal mines was regarded as a general responsibility rather than the specific responsibility of energy consumers.

Middle East, for at the same time the crisis between France and Algeria considerably reduced the supply of Algerian oil in the French market.

From the government point of view, the rapid growth of energy consumption was normal, if not desirable, because French consumption was still lower than that of other developed countries, and the only way to continue this growth was to import petroleum. Finally, at least until 1969, the belief in a continuation of low prices for petroleum products was generally accepted among those responsible for the energy sector, those involved in the Plan, as well as those in the ministries and public enterprises. This belief justified the lax response to the reduction in the part played by domestic resources.

The problem was posed explicitly only from 1970 on. At the beginning of 1971, the following series of measures was proposed at a closed meeting of the Council of Ministers:

Creation of a fund to finance a supplementary effort at prospecting by ERAP (offshore and in black Africa);

Diversification of supply among the various countries of the Middle East;

Supplementary stocking of ten million tons (above and beyond the three months' worth of consumption already imposed by law);

Encouragement of long-term contracts with producing countries (Iran for the CFP, Iraq for the ERAP);

Increasing the French share in petroleum transport.

But the opposition of the Ministry of Finance, which found the costs too great, prevented putting these measures into effect.

In part, then, dependence on foreign energy sources stemmed from the fact that nature had not rewarded the technical and financial efforts to find petroleum deposits in France and thus diversify the supply of domestic companies. The misadventures of decolonization, which led to rapid loss of control over Algerian deposits, played a role of prime importance. In addition, government policies had the effect of accelerating energy growth whereas the concern for diversification was shown to be illusory from the moment the consumer countries were no longer able to play off the producers against each other. For France at least, the only real diversification would have been to begin the development of nuclear energy earlier.

The Launching of the French Nuclear Industry

The Beginnings of the French Nuclear Effort and the Choice of a Process. Between 1951 and 1952, the argument in favor of the natural uranium-graphite-gas process was spelled out. All the decisions were taken by the governments of the time based on various sorts of considerations, including the following:

1. One could not, at that time, contemplate a procedure in France for enriching uranium, so a technique using natural uranium was necessary.
2. The production of heavy water necessary to the installation of powerful reactors using this moderator appeared to be too costly.
3. It was hoped that procedures would be prepared to produce energy that would also produce fissionable materials. In fact, the conditions were already being created for the perfection of a French atomic bomb, and the production of plutonium that could be used for military purposes was easier in this type of reactor.
4. These procedures permitted a rapprochement with the English who were using similar techniques that were also chosen for their military implications.

This orientation coincided with the retirement of Juliot-Curie, whose political opinions were not considered compatible with the role of the CEA in military uses of atomic energy. The first five-year plan (spelled out by Félix Gaillard, Secretary of State for Atomic Energy, and covering the period 1952-1957) was based mainly on the production of plutonium and led to the completion of the three units at Marcoule. The Consultative Commission for Production of Electricity of Nuclear Origin (called the Commission PEON) was created at this time as a meeting point between the CEA-Electricité de France and the industries involved in manufacturing nuclear materiel.

The Industrial Development of the French Chain. The public sector still held first place with the construction of the three units at Chinon resulting from the collaboration CEA-EDF. The installation of the first reactor actually destined for electricity production, EDF 1, was somewhat delicate because it was a first try. Installation of EDF 2 was much easier. With EDF 3, which was the biggest unit in the world at the time of its installation (480 MW), the aim was to try out a prototype of the industrial series that was to follow. Major disappointments followed the installation of this third unit (autumn 1966), and an inquest into the technical causes revealed faults in construction—attributable to the builders—in two groups of components.[i] A press campaign at the end of 1966 threw the responsibility on the EDF. This establishment itself undertook extremely detailed studies, and the builders complained of not having seen the complete plans that would have allowed them to carry out the various construction tasks correctly. This cabal against the EDF was linked to the preference on the part of

---

[i]It concerned, on the one hand, elements of heat *exchangers* between the carbonic gas cycle and the steam cycle, and on the other hand, metallic conductors in the devices for the detection of ruptures in the sheathing of the fuel assemblies.

the electromechanical sector of the construction industry for global markets for turnkey contract delivery, which was the practice in most foreign countries. This method of drawing up markets gave the builders a large share of the engineering responsibility, which until then had been assumed by the Direction de l'Equipement of the EDF. It met with lively opposition from the labor unions, for it might have diminished control over the price of materials.

When a first try was made on the global market at the end of 1967 (for the nuclear part of the Fessenheim project), the proposal presented by a group made up of Babcock, Schneider, and the CGE seemed very expensive in comparison to the prices obtained for the units at St.-Laurent des Eaux. Following the usual methods of project studies and the signing of agreements, the EDF refused to start the project.

The Abandonment of the French Chain. By the end of 1966, three units had already been ordered by EDF: St.-Laurent I in 1963, then in 1965, and in 1966; St.-Laurent II; and Bugey. This latter choice, according to a director of EDF, was made with some hesitation.

The refusal of the EDF to undertake the installation at Fessenheim resulted in a complete end to orders. More than three years passed without a new commitment or any firm option for the technique that would be used. It was then a matter of setting the conditions for building a nuclear capability at the current stage of industrial development, and in addition to the three initial partners (government, CEA, and EDF), French heavy industry (manufacturers of boilers and electromechanical equipment) played an important role. It is useful to point out the positions of those involved.

According to the CEA, it was necessary to continue to develop the French process now that it had been decided upon. Besides, the commission was prepared to build the nuclear installations that EDF did not want to build and questioned the seriousness of the problems the electricians foresaw in nuclear development, while it reprimanded them for behaving as niggling headmasters with regard to the construction work. EDF had a hard time criticizing the contradictions in the position of the commission, which proclaimed the necessity for a "strong and adult" industry, while it tried to maintain as much control as possible over nuclear development, which it regarded as its domain.

All this happened at a time when the commission was under strong attack. The government was increasingly critical of the behavior of this budget-devouring organization (four billion francs per year in 1969, of which two billion were for military purposes) whose activities were barely under control.

The management of the EDF had greatly modified its point of view since the enthusiasm at the beginning, which had lasted, so it seemed, until the first installation of St.-Laurent des Eaux. The first doubts arose in 1964, when the English abandoned this type of reactor as too expensive. The technique, which used natural uranium, lent itself with difficulty to extrapolation—that is, to the construction of plants with the large capacity that would be necessary to lower investment costs. Its complexity, especially the continual recharging of the fuel elements, gave rise to fears about its reliability.

The American methods with light water continued their early successes, and export of the French technique looked unlikely. The EDF management then laid its hopes on technical progress that it hoped would be faster than for the American techniques. During the winter of 1967-68, it opposed undertaking the second generator foreseen by the Fifth Plan (Fessenheim) when the bids for construction came in with costs that were much too high. In 1968, it asked for authorization to try the American methods as soon as possible.

The manufacturers of electromechanical equipment expressed considerable hesitation about the graphite-gas process; they made almost no effort to bid for contracts for the generator at Fessenheim. But nobody got the contract and the various technical jobs were scattered about among the CEA, the EDF, and the construction industry itself. The industrial policy of the Fifth Republic (the public sector prescribes the techniques that should then be developed by the private sector) went badly. The industrial groups concerned were reluctant to enter into alliances promoted by the government in order to develop an industrial structure that would be capable of taking charge of nuclear development. They had their own strategies. This absence of an industrial partnership interested in promotion of a graphite-gas "product" doubtless accounted for much of the difficulty in finding a market for it. The public authorities sold the installation at Vandellos in Spain, and to do so, it had to create a new company from bits and pieces so that it could be built.

But French industry, at least in the beginning, did not reject the graphite-gas technique, because there was the possibility that its development in France might represent an important protected market. Nevertheless, the builders did not believe in its export possibilities and did not want to take financial risks to develop it. This accounts for the high level of the bids for Fessenheim, but it became the pretext for the EDF to stop the project. Builders preferred, however, to work under a license (the CGE had gotten the license GECO for boiling water reactors for its affiliate SOGERCA, whereas Schneider had an affiliate, FRAMATOME, licensed by Westinghouse for pressurized water from the installation of the Euratom reactor at Chooz). The desire to enter the international market became predominant, particularly when three years passed with no French order and the principal world builders[j] chose the American chains. The CGE soon adopted a frankly hostile attitude toward the French chain; it counted on benefits from a turnabout toward light water reactors because the government hoped thus to strengthen its industrial position.

Starting in 1968, a general offensive of Westinghouse in Western Europe[k]

[j]Siemens-AEG in Germany, Brown Boveri in Switzerland, Asea in Sweden, and Mitsubishi in Japan.

[k]Apart from its participation in FRAMATOME, Westinghouse had affiliates in Belgium and in Italy. In 1969, it would also try to buy back Jeumont-Schneider from the baron Empain but the French government opposed this.

increased the pressures in favor of moving toward the American chain. The American company also moved into a strong position in the area of nuclear fuels. In association with Péchiney-Ugine-Kuhlman, it installed a manufacturing plant in Belgium and refused to cooperate in any way with the CEA.

The government no longer showed the same determination with regard to the gas-graphite chain. On the one hand, the military motivations were much less strong for with the shift from the A-bomb to the H-bomb the need for plutonium decreased. On the other hand, it was looking for external markets for French companies since it considered the domestic market too small to support them in a competitive position. To this end, it wanted to encourage regroupings and associations with other European companies, which was difficult and incompatible with the development of a technique that was by then purely French.

In fact, continuance of the option in favor of the gas-graphite chain was tied to the possibility of finding a market for it. But governmental action in this area fluctuated curiously. After a major commercial and financial effort had led to the construction of the generator at Vandellos in Spain, it was practically *une fin de non recevoir* that opposed a request from Argentina for the construction of a French chain reactor. Contacts with other countries were equally erratic and clearly reflected the absence of a financial and industrial group truly interested in the sale of reactors.

In spite of the recommendations of the Fifth Plan to undertake one or two reactors per year, the cessation of nuclear investment lasted more than three years without any official decision having been taken. There were two main reasons for this: (1) As noted earlier, the belief that the prices for petroleum products would continue to decrease (a belief shared until 1969 by the directors of the EDF and the government) led to the feeling that the matter was not urgent; and (2) besides, this pause in nuclear investment lightened the financial load in the energy sector, and the Ministry of Finance, which was trying to reduce public investments, was hardly favorable to a relaunching of the nuclear effort.

In 1968 the PEON Commission took note of the economic advantages of the enriched uranium-light water chain put forward by the EDF. It recommended building an installation of this sort, whereas the EDF negotiated with Belgian and Swiss producers for the installation of two "international" generators using American techniques at Tihange (Belgian Ardennes) and Kaiseraugst (on the Rhine above Basel). The CEA, for its part, tried to work out programs permitting a transition from graphite-gas to light water.

Only at the end of 1969, after the defeat of General DeGaulle, did the government make a decision. The negotiations with Algeria marked a turnabout in the trend of opinion in the petroleum sector and EDF pushed for a rapid decision. This decision was taken in the direction hoped for by the EDF, and also by the CGE and FRAMATOME.[1] Under a so-called program of diversifica-

---

[1]I.e., by the tandem Westinghouse-Empain of which FRAMATOME is an affiliate in common.

tion, the installation of several American reactors was approved and no further construction of the graphite-gas generator was envisaged.

Movement to the American Technique. The movement toward concentration in the electromechanical and boiler industries began to gather speed. The CGE, which had taken control of Alsthom, was a classic electrotechnical corporation. Although it could not itself build the tank—the centerpiece of the nuclear reactor—and planned to subcontract it out to the Italian BREDA, it had in fact an advantage over the other industrial combinations involved because it was more "French."

The Creusot-Loire group, the result of the fusion of the Ateliers du Creusot (Schneider, affiliate of the Belgian corporation Empain) and of the Ateliers et Forges de la Loire, intervened for its affiliate, FRAMATOME, which it held in common with Westinghouse. Better integrated vertically and thus likely to produce a greater portion of the nuclear reactor within the same corporation, it would be able to offer the best prices and bring the first generators into the market.

The EDF, preferring to play on the competition between two builders, continued long negotiations with the CGE, which obtained some orders and a series of options in 1974, only to see them annulled during the summer of 1975. The public service resigned itself then to a single supplier of nuclear boilers, since the other potential suppliers (Babcock and Compagnie Electro-Mécanique) had abandoned the competition.

The government tried to promote the development of French groups at each link in the chain of nuclear activity, as follows:

For the boilers and generators, those "licensed" for light water, about which we just spoke;

For uranium mines, the affiliates of Péchiney Ugine Kuhlmann and the group Rothschild le Nickel;

For nuclear fuels, the affiliates of the CEA and PUK;

For enrichment, the European factory, EURODIF, where France occupied the main position.

In order to build the project EURODIF the CEA engaged in a great amount of activity between 1973 and 1974. Perhaps the petroleum crisis accelerated the beginning of the project, but the clumsiness of the United States in writing very hard-nosed clauses for their clients buying enriched uranium facilitated the decision of the European partners in the affair.

The industrial schema was nearly settled when, in March 1975, the decision to progress to an investment rate of 6 or 7 million nuclear kilowatts per year was taken.

The Politics of Response to the Energy Crisis

We must note to begin with that the quadrupling of the price of petroleum posed a more formidable problem for France than for any other country in Europe except Italy. The portion of petroleum imports in the overall energy balance was higher in France (over 70 percent) than the average for the Europe of the Nine (60 perçent), and France's natural resources in fossil fuels (coal, gas, and petroleum) were not adequate to permit counting on their development alone.

Governmental Policy

At the beginning of 1974, the French state saw the acceleration of the nuclear program as the best step toward a strategic solution to the crisis. The resistance created by this policy led it in the spring of 1975 to a more reserved, more wait-and-see position.

Aside from measures explicitly directed against waste—such as raising standards of thermal insulation in new buildings, prohibition of heating above 20°C, restrictions on public and commercial lighting at night, speed limits on freeways, anti-waste publicity, and so forth—the government plan of 1974 included some slowing down in the development of general energy consumption in the course of the coming ten years. These plans included halting the decline in production of domestic coal, some increase in imports of coal and natural gas, and finally and most significantly, a strong speeding up of the nuclear program. The program would move from 2 x 1,000 MW pledged in 1973 to 6 x 1,000 MW pledged in 1974 (PWR) and 7 x 1,000 MW pledged in 1975 (6 PWR and 1 BWR)[m] and would continue at the same rate of six or seven units of 1,000 MW per year until 1980 in order to increase as quickly as possible the part played by nuclear energy in electricity production and the share of electricity in the total production of energy. From 1981 on, each new nuclear unit that comes into service will save 1.3 million tons of petroleum imports.

In the spring of 1975, the government declared that no commitment had been made for following an accelerated nuclear program in 1976 and beyond. Official sources let it be understood that the rate of growth could be reduced from six or seven units of 1,000 MW per year to only four or five. (Note that the slumping levels of industrial activity in all Western countries and the slowness of the expected economic recovery made creation of new methods of energy production somewhat less urgent.) On the other hand, the public authorities took the following measures: underlined the prospects for recovering heat from nuclear installations (until then conceived exclusively as producers of electricity); looked for new possibilities for imports of natural gas and coal; began

[m]This plan became modified following abandonment of the BWR process in August 1975.

serious prospecting for petroleum off the Brittany coast (mer d'Iroise) where nothing had been done; and announced their intention to develop new forms of energy (solar and geothermic) by naming a person who would be responsible for this development but who was given only modest funding.

The Forces Involved

The Dispute over Nuclear Energy. Nuclear energy had long been the *bête noire* of the French ecological movement, which is supported by two main news-papers, *Le Sauvage* and *La Gueule Ouverte.* But the ecological dispute in France represents only a small minority, since it is without finances and is incapable of mobilizing any large groups.

The new fact of the year 1975 with regard to the discussion of the energy problem in the Parliament was the taking up of the nuclear dispute by important sectors of student and scientific opinion and by a part of the general press. The arguments developed on this occasion centered mainly on the ecological aspects of the problem (radioactivity, risks of accident, nuclear waste) and emphasized the following points:

1. The serious uncertainty over the future price of nuclear energy and the performance of the installations;
2. The technological dependency involved in the French nuclear program with regard to the granting of licenses for the construction of plants (Westing-house) and also with regard to the supply of enriched uranium (EURODIF will not begin operation until 1981);
3. The extremely centralized nature of nuclear power and the police state (to prevent risks or blackmail) implied in its eventual development;
4. The "totalitarian" nature of nuclear energy that drains away all research and development funds to its own advantage to the detriment of other energy technologies, especially "new" sources of energy;
5. The choice of civilization implied by an energy program, and the illusion that we will enjoy a truly superior lifestyle from an indefinite increase in levels of energy consumption.[1,2]

Labor Unions and Opposing Political Parties. Traditionally, labor unions and the parties of the Left (the Communist and Socialist parties) have relied on nationalized industry to promote the best technological choices, and they have based their criticisms of energy policy on a denunciation of the ascendency and the profits of private industry (national and international) over the public sector. In the discussion of the nuclear program, this traditional position was for the first time more critical and more reserved with regard to nuclear expansion, despite the guarantees of the two public enterprises, the CEA and the EDF. This reserve, this prudence, which never reached the point of frank and complete opposition to the nuclear program (because maintenance of medium-term employment remained the priority) was most noticeable in the non-Communist organizations (Socialist party and CFDT labor union). In the Communist party and the CGT, the positions clearly reflected the Promethean aspects of Marxism, where the development of nuclear energy was regarded as "progress," and only the conditions of this development were open to dispute.

The Public Authorities. Within the administration, only the Ministry of Industry—guardian of the EDF, the CEA, and so forth—defended the accelerated electronuclear program proposed by the EDF, which it adopted as its own. The ministry regarded this program as the centerpiece of its industrial policy, and as the basis for the credibility of the French electronuclear industry in the international market. The Ministry of Finance, although put off by the cost of the operation, certainly did not oppose the nuclear option, but looked for ways to make it less financially burdensome. In 1975, the local governments, which were closer to the people, began to reflect the opposition of some of their citizens to nuclear development and often rejected projects for building generators that were submitted to them.

The Petroleum Industry. The petroleum companies—the French ones as well as the affiliates of international companies—were on the defensive. A parliamentary report (the Schwartz report, September 1974) accused them of having profited outrageously from the crisis, of having entered into illegal contracts with each other, and of falsifying their tax returns. In the short term, the antiwaste policy of the public authorities caught them on the wrong foot: Refining capacity in 1973 was already somewhat ahead of demand. The companies thus searched actively for ways to renew demand[n] without further tarnishing their image. In the long term, the strategy for replacement of petroleum (e.g., hydrogen production) became the object of careful studies.

The Gas Companies. The gas companies, conforming to the instructions of the Plan, looked forward to increasingly substituting gas for petroleum in order to diversify the energy supply, while at the same time maintaining the share of hydrocarbons in the domestic balance sheet. New networks of transport and distribution are envisaged to support hydrogen in the place of (or in combination with) natural gas, but this substitution is not foreseen before the 1990s.

The Small and Medium-Sized Enterprises Directly Involved. The heating companies saw the rapid development of "all-electric" new construction (nearly 50

---

[n]Manufacturers and users of the automobile, who constituted a powerful pressure group in France, pushed in the same direction; cf. their opposition to speed limits on the freeways, finally settled at 130 km/hour instead of 120.

percent in 1975, compared with less than 5 percent in 1970) as a threat. Electric heating, which requires almost no maintenance, reduced or even eliminated the role they had played as intermediaries in traditional solutions (gas, fuel oil, or district heating).

The subcontractors in the electronuclear construction industry felt themselves even more vulnerable in the current situation than when they dealt directly with the EDF or the CEA. The acceleration of the nuclear program made them bear considerable risks.

The Commissariat of Atomic Energy (CEA). Deprived of its main hope by the abandoment of the French chain (natural uranium-gas-graphite), the CEA found in the present situation the occasion to play a central role in the electronuclear system. On the one hand, it became involved in the system of financial and technical relationships that connected the large industrial holdings in nuclear energy by buying shares (majority control in some cases) in the enterprises working on different links of the nuclear energy chain. On the other hand, by the orientation of its research techniques, it attempted to diversify the market for nuclear energy not involved in the production of electricity (which had been taken on by the EDF)—that is, miniaturization of the generators, district heating, steam production, production of hydrogen, and so forth. This point will be further developed when we talk about structures in the nuclear industry.

The Electricity of France (EDF). The EDF for some ten years had based the main part of its development strategy on the replacement of petroleum by nuclear energy. Slowed down by the indecision over reactor types, this strategy had been accompanied since 1968-69 by vigorous commercial activity designed to help consumers anticipate the relationship of future prices (the price of a nuclear kWh being based on the decline in prices for other forms of energy) in order to make them change over quickly to electricity in their choice of equipment, then to increase the portion of electricity in the total energy balance, and thus eventually to decrease the dependence of France on energy from petroleum-producing countries.

The energy crisis was, for the EDF, a "too" good affair. In the long term, the public authorities renewed their support for the strategy of replacing petroleum with nuclear energy, but in the short term they reproached the EDF for having outrageously encouraged the development of consumption through its advertising and various commercial advantages. Public opinion, hitherto confident of the "public service mission" of nationalized enterprise, was surprised by the scale of the advertising campaign with its slogans for "all-electric, all-nuclear," and the EDF was accused by agitant minorities of "totalitarian imperialism," thereby likening the EDF to any giant capitalist enterprise trying to maximize profits.

Faced with these opposing forces, the EDF tended to withdraw into a position of executing governmental policy as approved by the Parliament and suspended all public advertising. Nonetheless it continued its commercial practices and research and development devoted mainly toward the development of electrical energy (the solar house was given token attention). The EDF was reluctant to become involved in related activities such as the sale of steam power, the recovery of lost heat from nuclear plants, or the production of hydrogen.

The Structure of the Nuclear Industry

The nuclear program occupies a central place in governmental policy. Its size and its conditions of production will determine to a large degree the independence of the French energy supply. It is thus useful to examine the existing structures that provide for development of construction and fuel supplies for nuclear installations. Since both French and international industrial groups have been jockeying for place in this structure for some ten years, we find an evolving situation that has had some setbacks. Taking account of its size, French "economic space" represents a market of exceptional importance that is dedicated to rapid growth. The construction of electronuclear generators will represent a business figure of three billion francs per year in the course of the next decade, but part of this business will replace the traditional outlets of the electromechanical industry and the manufacturers of boilers. Most impressive is the expansion of the production of nuclear fuels: Less than one billion francs annually at present, it should reach three billion per year about 1980, and surpass the figure of ten billion per year before the end of the 1980-1990 decade.

Aside from the CEA, the principal industrial groups battling for position will be groups working in the areas of electromechanics, boilers, chemicals, and mines. To this end, they will deploy strategies at several levels: technological, industrial, and financial. While they must begin by placing their stakes on the techniques that will effect the breakthroughs, the necessity of joining in a game of alliances becomes immediately apparent. This phenomenon is singularly reinforced by the relatively small size of the French companies and the exigencies of a market that remains essentially national. The enormous cost of research and development in the nuclear field has forced the various groups to look for a maximum of already-existing "know-how" (hence the links with American licenses for light water reactors and high temperature reactors[o] that will create a system of alliances at the international level), while at the same time it has forced them to arrange for a sufficiently solid financial base for even with the licenses the investments required remain high. Then, apart from the initial

[o]And the utilization of the "acquis" and the scientific potential of the Atomic Energy Commissariat.

treatment of uranium, the choice of equipment and the processes required at different levels of the fuel cycle are more or less tightly linked to the type of reactor employed. The market of one group is actually dependent on that of others who have chosen the same technological option. Finally, from the point of view of the client (essentially EDF at the present time) and governmental decision making, the choice of a technique is based more upon its support by a credible financial and industrial ensemble than upon its intrinsic advantages.

The following description corresponds to the situation in September 1975.

The Industrial Poles. Diverse industrial activities are carried on by companies, very often of medium size, that specialize in one particular aspect of the nuclear industry and are only the executive arms of large industrial groups or coalitions. For example, FRAMATOME, builder of the nuclear boiler, is a common affiliate of Creusot-Loire and Westinghouse, and Uranex, a sales group for concentrated uranium, is a common affiliate of the Commissariat à l'Energie Atomique, Péchiney Ugine Kuhlmann, and the mining companies of the Groupe du Nickel. The industrial holdings are the true center of coordination in the nuclear industry, and it is around their respective zones of influence that guidelines will be set.

The predominating five of these poles have medium-term production capacity; three others are less well placed and seem mainly rich in hopes. Domestic petroleum companies, finally, in contrast to their big international brothers, have only recently entered the nuclear arena where they represent only a balancing force in the sector of prospecting for and using uranium.

The CEA, after the governmental decisions of the summer of 1975, definitively moved in a direction that should make it the main large industrial holding in the nuclear sector. It had taken on, over nearly twenty years, the pioneering of nuclear power (as much for military as for civilian uses) with a public statute in which the first job concerned technological research and development. Progress to the reactor construction stage in the course of the 1960s and activities in the prospecting and exploitation of uranium had led it to develop industrial and engineering activities in the civil sector (Mining Department, Direction of Production, and Direction of Piles). At the end of the 1960s, a policy for the creation of common affiliates with various private groups emerged, principally with Péchiney Ugine Kuhlmann for the treatment of uranium and with the Groupe Nickel Rothschild for prospecting, extraction, and concentration of uranium. The next logical phase would be to make affiliates out of certain current departments of the Commissariat. But this action is likely to raise political and labor problems, particularly since this change would permit private interests to participate in activities until now reserved for public monopoly.

When it became a shareholder in FRAMATOME, currently the only French builder of nuclear boilers, the CEA was once again involved in all aspects of the nuclear industry. It was in a monopoly position in the areas of uranium enrichment (where it regroups French participation at the European enrichment plant, EURODIF) and in the treatment of irradiated fuels. It occupied a predominant position for the extraction of uranium on French territory and for the development of the chain using fast neutrons (the company for engineering sodium reactors—CIRNA—was created, controlled by the engineering affiliate of the CEA, TECHNICATOME). It was present once again in the construction of electronuclear equipment through its participation in FRAMATOME and was well ensconsed in the treatment of uranium and its commercialization by its participation in the companies responsible for concentration: Société Industrielle des Minerais de l'Ouest (in France), Mines de l'Aïr (in Nigeria), Mines de Franceville (in Gabon), the conversion to hexaflouride (COMURHEX), and commercialization (URANEX). The CEA, however, was only rich in hopes in the area of manufacturing fuel elements because the Société Industrielle de Combustibles pour Réacteurs Electrogènes (SICREL), the creation of which the CEA had supported at the end of 1972, found itself for the moment at least on the outside. The French electronuclear generators had to use fuels produced by the company belonging to Westinghouse, the Compagnie Européenne de fabrication de combustibles à base d'uranium pour réacteurs à eau légère (EUROFUEL), at least at first.

The Commissariat remained at the same time the center for nuclear research and development in France. It promotes new techniques (in the case of energy applications one will note the importance of its role in the perfection of *fast neutron breeder reactors*). Even when techniques are imported, its supporting role remains important. For high temperature reactors, it holds the Gulf-General Atomics license while a private group studies the possibilities for promotion of the process in France. Finally, it conserves para-administrative functions, mainly in the matter of nuclear security, which further increases its control over the nuclear industry.

The Creusot-Loire group (which was involved in a banking battle at the beginning of 1975 that confirmed the preponderance of private interests traditionally oriented toward metallurgy) remains mainly under the control of the Belgian group, Empain, and owes its success in the nuclear field to its alliance with the American Westinghouse. The alliance dates from the beginning of the 1960s[P] and Euratom's efforts with light water techniques at Chooz. Through its affiliate FRAMATOME, it controls the French market in light water reactors, and it can hope for a significant complement of orders for export. It is very well integrated and in a position to provide a large number of the components for nuclear reactors directly through its various affiliates. But orders for turbo-alternators have so far escaped its allies, Jeumont-Schneider and CEM.

[P]It was in fact part of the group Schneider, one of the elements at the origin of the concentration between the plants of Creusot and the group of the Ateliers et Forges de la Loire.

On the other hand, it has managed to establish itself in the sector of nuclear fuels where it already participated in the Compagnie pour l'Etude et la Réalisation des Combustibles Atomiques (CERCA), which provided gas-graphite reactors before becoming a partner of Westinghouse and Péchiney Ugine Kuhlmann in EUROFUEL. For fuels in the future, Creusot-Loire has taken an interest in CORHAT (fuel for high temperature reactors).

Péchiney Ugine Kuhlmann, another recently formed group (1971), is the result of the fusion of Péchiney and Ugine Kuhlmann, which were already present in the various stages of dealing with nuclear fuels. The new group has considerably enlarged its position in the sector as a whole through: participation in the CFMU (Compagnie Française des Mines d'Uranium) in French mines and presence in companies mining the deposits in Nigeria, Gabon, the Central African Republic, and Canada; participation in SIMO (concentration), URANEX (marketing of concentrates), and in COMURHEX (conversion to hexaflouride), which assures the group of control over activities concerning concentration and conversion of uranium; and majority control in EUROFUEL with Westinghouse and Creausot-Loire (an affiliate located in Belgium will be the industrial agent for EUROFUEL). Finally, in looking out for the future Péchiney Ugine Kuhlmann participates in the economic interest group for the study of high temperature reactors.

The Rothschild group intervenes by way of the mining companies (Nickel, Mokta, and Pennarroya). It dominates the cluster of private corporations that are involved in the search for and mining of uranium ore, often in association with the CEA in France and in the former colonies, and with local groups in Australia, Canada, and the Union of South Africa. These activities are extended further through participation in the sales group URANEX and in SICREL.

The Compagnie Générale d'Electricité (CGE) had participated in the construction of the gas-graphite chain through its various affiliates. It became associated with General Electric[q] in order to utilize the license for the boiling water reactor (BWR) and has exerted a great deal of effort since 1968 to become the second-place French supplier in reactors using light water. An agreement at the beginning of 1974 provided for eight reactors of 1,000 MW each and confirmed the success of its efforts. However, a decision at a closed meeting of the Interministerial Counsel on August 6, 1975, voided this agreement and eliminated the procedure the group had relied upon from the French market.

This change appeared to be a severe setback and noticeably reduced the activity of the CGE in the nuclear field. But the group still occupies an important position and holds strong cards for the future. In the short-run market for turbo-alternators, its affiliate Alsthom has obtained all the orders to equip the Westinghouse reactors using pressurized water. For the near future, the position of Alsthom remains predominant in a tripartite cooperation (Creusot-

[q]And became the champion of an alliance of European firms working on boiling water reactors.

Loire, Compagnie Electro-Mécanique, and Alsthom), which should lead to a common structure for the export of complete "turnkey" reactors. For the second generation of nuclear reactors, CGE continues its role as industrial master. Its common affiliate with Babcock—the Groupement Atomique, Alsacienne, Atlantique[r]—has played an important role in engineering the French prototype of the fast neutron reactor (Phénix) and since January 1975 has been the partner of the CEA in the Compagnie d'Ingénierie pour les Réacteurs au Sodium (CIRNA) that is supposed to provide the engineering and promotion for Phénix. The creation of this affiliate prolongs and reinforces an alliance already established by the same partners in the framework of the Groupement des Neutrons Rapides (GNR).

We categorize as *the second line* groups those that are currently unable to occupy a really predominant position in any link of the chain.

Babcock-Fives-Cail suffered a costly setback in proposing its nuclear reactor (license Babcock USA) and in 1972 effectively retired from competition in the market for light water reactors. Its possible successes in the nuclear field appear to be linked to those of the CGE and to the success of breeder reactors since its principal involvement there now is its participation in GAAA.

The Compagnie Electro-Mécanique, affiliate of the German-Swiss group Brown Boveri, is a potential supplier of turbo-alternators. This group suffered repercussions from the elimination of the CGE, for it was going to provide the electromechanical materiel to equip boiling water reactors (BWR) ordered *or in option.* In the future it should share with Alsthom the turbo-alternator groups of pressurized water reactors (PWR) for which the real nuclear components are supplied by Creusot-Loire.

The petroleum companies stand in contrast to the international corporations, since neither the French groups (CFP and ELF-ERAP) nor the French affiliates of the "majors" have invested in the development of nuclear technology. The domestic petroleum companies came late to the nuclear scene, taking up shares in the groups for prospecting and exploitation of uranium (Australia and Canada).

Saint-Gobain—Pont-à-Mousson, also of recent origin (1971), is a group with activities simultaneously in the areas of metallurgy and chemistry. It has developed its nuclear sector much less than its competitor PUK. Its principal interventions are in the fuel cycle where it plays an important role in the study and building of plants for the treatment of spent fuels—for the account of the CEA—and it builds treatment stations for the effluent from electronuclear generators. Because of its experience in this domain, it has built a treatment plant in Japan. It is a copartner of SICREL with the CEA and the Nickel group.

The Control of the Different Phases of the Nuclear Cycle. Nuclear activities can be broken down into zones corresponding to the different phases of the

[r]Which has become the Groupement pour les Activités Atomiques et Avancées.

production cycle. Each zone focuses on a particular technology (heavy boiler for the nuclear reactor, for example). We can distinguish eight zones (or phases) in the process of building and using electronuclear ensembles: (1) prospecting and mining uranium ore, (2) concentration of uranium ore and conversion to hexaflouride of uranium, (3) enrichment of uranium, (4) manufacture of the fuel elements, (5) nuclear engineering, (6) building of nuclear reactors, (7) building of turbo-alternators, and (8) treatment of spent fuels. The development of new types of reactors constitutes a ninth zone of activity.

Examination of the nuclear activities of the various industrial groups described in the previous section shows that each of them concentrates its activities on one part of the process. Table 4-10 lists the principal affiliates "mainly occupied with nuclear activity" of each of the industrial groups that we have examined and reveals that for each of the groups corresponding to the columns in the table the recorded affiliates are grouped along a limited number of lines.

But to get a more precise idea of the division of activities among our different poles and, above all, of the consequences of this division in terms of control of nuclear energy production, it is interesting to run a zone-by-zone analysis that takes into account the actual state of affairs, the means of production, and the orders credited to each group. This examination reveals the measure to which control of each zone is apportioned among the various poles we have described.

1. *Prospecting and Mining.* The CEA still largely dominates these activities on domestic territory. In spite of the development of the Compagnie Française des Minerais d'Uranium (controlled by the Nickel group), the mining divisions of the Commissariat (La Crouzille, Vendée, Forez) provide 80 percent of French production.

The Commissariat still occupies the most important position for prospecting and exploitation overseas, primarily because the mines being developed in Nigeria are expected by 1980 to account for more than three-quarters of the overseas production controlled by French interests. This production will be divided between the Société des Mines de l'Aïr (SOMAÏR) and the Compagnie Minière d'Akouta (COMINAK), in both of which the CEA is the principal investor (respectively, 33.5 percent and 44 percent of the capital). Secondly, its important position is also due to its ownership of 99.4 percent of the Société d'Etude et de Recherche d'Uranium (SERU), a holding company whose affiliates are responsible for prospecting in Australia (AFMECO), in South Africa (FRAMCO), and in Canada (SERU Nuclear).

Péchiney Ugine Kuhlmann (which controls the Société Centrale de l'Uranium et des Minerais and Métaux Radio-actifs in France and participates in the Mines de Franceville in Gabon, in the Mines de l'Aïr in Nigeria, and in the mines of Saskatoon in Canada) and above all the Nickel group (which controls the Compagnie Française des Minerais d'Uranium and holds important interests in

Table 4-10
Nuclear Activities of French Industrial Group Affiliates

Financial Poles	*DE WENDEL*	*EMPAIN*	*PARIBAS*		*CGE*	*SUEZ*	*ROTHS-CHILD*	*OTHERS*
Holdings	CEA	Creusot Loire	Fives-cail Babcock	PUK	CGE	St. Gobain Pont à Mousson	le Nickel	
Mining Activities	*Mining departments Limousin Vendée Forez SOMAIR-COMUF-SERU*			SOGEREM *Minière Péchiney-Mokta*			*CFMU Péchiney Mokta*	TOTAL Compagnie minière
Concentration and Conversion to UF$_6$	*COMURHEX SIMO URANEX*			*COMURHEX SIMO URANEX*		*COMURHEX*	URANEX	
Enrichment	EURODIF			*USSI*		*USSI*		
Nuclear Engineering	Technicatome *FRAMATOME* CIRNA	*FRAMATOME* SHTR	G.A.A.A. CIRNA	SHTR	SOGERCA G.A.A.A. CIRNA			SHTR (CEM)
Manufacture of Fuels	*SFEC CICAF SICREL CORHAT*	*CICAF CERCA EUROFUEL CORHAT*		*CERCA SION EUROFUEL CICAF*		*SICN CERCA SICREL*	SICREL	*SICN (ALSPI)*
Recycling	*Usine de la Hague et de Marcoule*					St. Gobain Techniques nouvelles		
Building Nuclear Boilers	*FRAMATOME*	*FRAMATOME* Creusot-Loire	Babcock-Atlantique		Neypic			
Turbo-Alternators		Jeumont-Schneider			*Alsthom Rateau*			Cie électro méchanique (CEM)

Source: Compiled by authors from internal documents of the CEA and from French financial reviews.

the same mining companies (either directly or through the intermediary of the CFMU) play a definitive role. The interests of these groups are no greater than those of the CEA except for the Mines de Franceville (Gabon) and of Saskatoon (Canada). However, the private groups are making a large effort to increase their share of the market now that the large price increases of the last couple of years have made it more profitable.

2. *Concentration of Uranium Ore, Conversion into Uranium Hexaflouride, and Marketing.* We should begin by noting the leading role of the Péchiney Ugine Kuhlmann group in this zone of activity. First, PUK has a monopoly on the technology for concentration of uranium ore in France. It planned and built the installations near the mining fields that transform ore into concentrated uranium as rich as possible in metal, and it is the principal stockholder of the Société Industrielle des Minerais de l'Ouest, which directs the three French factories for concentration of uranium ore (SIMO holds two, that of Forez belonging to the CEA). Second, through the intermediary of the Usines Chimiques de Pierrelatte (UCP, affiliate of PUK which owns 99.9 percent), Péchiney Ugine Kuhlmann controls the company COMURHEX that has a monopoly on the conversion of uranium-bearing concentrates to flouride for enriched uranium and to metal for direct uses in the form of natural uranium. Finally, the mining company Péchiney-Mokta holds a third of the stock in URANEX, an economic interest group that assures the marketing of domestic uranium as well as that of the African companies.

The CEA holds only a blocking minority (34 percent in URANEX and a minority share (29 percent) in COMUREX. The Nickel group only intervenes through its participation in the CFMU and the mining company Péchiney Mokta of URANEX.

3. *The Enrichment of Uranium.* Currently France depends heavily on American and, to a lesser degree, Russian supplies of uranium to meet its needs. Beginning in 1979, the supply will be assured by EURODIF, a company in which France, Italy, Spain, Belgium, and now Iran participate. The French share in this company is nearly half (47 percent, after having been a majority before the entry of Iran into the club). The plant will be situated in France, and the CEA owns the French shares. The Commissariat provided the technology and will doubtless play the main role in competition for contracts. One can thus assume that in the short run it will have a monopoly on the enrichment of uranium in France. But it must be noted that the construction of a new EURODIF will be necessary to satisfy the increasing needs for enriched uranium in Europe from 1985 on.

The members of EURODIF are reassembled in the Société de construction d'usine de séparation isotopique (USSI), which was formed to take advantage of the experience of the CEA and promote its export.

4. *The Manufacturing of Fuel Elements.* The manufacturing of natural uranium fuels for the reactors of the gas-graphite chain is divided between two

companies in which Péchiney Ugine Kuhlmann holds minority shares: (1) the Société Industrielle des Combustibles Nucléaires (SIGN), which is allied with the group of the CGE,[S] and (2) the Compagnie pour l'Etude et la Réalisation de Combustibles Atomiques (CERCA), which is allied with the Creusot-Loire group. These two companies have been given General Electric and Westinghouse licenses respectively for the manufacture of fuels for pressurized and boiling water reactors, but in fact the competition for fuels for light water reactors, which should experience their fastest growth during the coming decade, will involve two other companies: SICREL and EUROFUEL.

The Société Industrielle de combustibles pour réacteurs électrogènes (SICREL), which was first founded at the initiative of the DEA (which holds 34 percent of the stock) and in which Saint-Gobain, Nickel and l'Alsacienne participate, is for the moment outside the market. Because of strong links between the technology of the reactor and the fuels used and, above all, the conditions laid down to benefit the builder of the reactor, the first fuels used in pressurized water reactors (PWR) will have to be manufactured by a company under Westinghouse.

EUROFUEL was put together by Péchiney Ugine Kuhlmann (51 percent), Westinghouse, and Creusot-Loire. It will have, for the coming years, a monopoly on the supply of fuels for light water reactors. Its Franco-Belgian affiliate, Fabrication de Combustible (FBCF), will provide the greatest part of the production in its factory of DESSEL in Belgium.

The PUK thus controls, for several years at least, the entire market in fuels for light water reactors.

5. *Engineering and Construction of Nuclear Boilers.* A very large majority of nuclear installations put into service during the decade 1980-1990 will have PWR reactors of the Westinghouse type. FRAMATOME (Creusot-Loire, 51 percent, and Westinghouse, 45 percent) will adapt the American-type installations to French conditions and assure the construction of industrial nuclear reactors, for which a large portion of the elements will be manufactured by the companies of the Creusot-Loire group. The decision, taken by the government during the summer of 1975, to bring the CEA into FRAMATOME (to the detriment, it seems, of the part played by Westinghouse) should not call into question the dominance of Creusot-Loire in the building of nuclear installations. Rather it envisions using the CEA more directly to carry out the electronuclear program and to accelerate the acquisition (the Frenchification) of the technology of high-powered PWR reactors.

These positions could doubtless be changed by the development of a second generation of reactors, but, at the present, the importance each industrial group might take in the building of reactors seems to be linked to the option taken on the technical level, for each one in practice concentrates all its efforts for

[S]For controlled by participation by Lille, Bonnières, Colombes, and l'Alsacienne, companies of the Suez group, who are the dominant stockholders of CGE.

research and development on one process (be it fast neutron reactor cooled by sodium or be it high temperature reactor cooled by gas).

Creusot-Loire is associated with the Compagnie Electro-Méchanique and with Péchiney Ugine Kuhlmann in the Société pour les Reacteurs à Haute Température (SHTA, in 1974), thus continuing a group that has allied the same partners for several years. In this way, they remain partners of the CEA since the Commissariat holds the license for Gulf General Atomic.

The option taken by the CGE and Babcock is more consistent with the line of development hoped for by the public administration since they are the partners of the CEA (through the intermediary of GAAA) in the Compagnie d'Ingénierie pour les Réacteurs au Sodium (CIRNA), which should develop the French chain of breeder reactors at the end of the current phase of building prototypes. GAAA had already played an important role in building the prototype generator Phénix (250 MW) and is continuing studies and preparing proposals for the future European reactor with 1,200 MW of power (Superphenix), which should be built by NERSA in the framework of French-German-Italian collaboration.

6. *The Electromechanical Aspects of Nuclear Installations.* A compensation has in effect given the CGE the greatest share in the construction of the electromechanical parts of the PWR reactors for which the nuclear elements were handled by the Creusot-Loire group. The largest piece consists of the turbo-alternator groups that will be built by Alsthom and Rateau. This division of tasks has held for a little more than fifteen units within the French nuclear program. It is probable that in the medium term the supplying of turbo-alternators will be divided between the CGE group and the Compagnie Electro-Méchanique (of the Boveri-Brown group), since they will complete the turbo-alternators designed for boiling water reactors (BWR) abandoned in August 1975. In the longer run, much will depend also on the success of the different chains. Some companies have already put their stakes on the success of one technique as partners in the Groupement pour les Hautes Températures (and in the SHTR) that is studying a turbine using fluid gas adapted to the HTR and THTR reactors.

7. *Reprocessing Spent Fuels.* Reprocessing is currently under the complete control of the centers under the Commissariat a l'Energie Atomique (Marcoule and the Hague) but the important contribution of St.-Gobain Techniques Nouvelles in the perfection of the processes and in the construction of reprocessing plants must be noted. Besides, these activities are the subject of a broad effort toward European cooperation in the United Reprocessors company that unites the CEA in France by using the installations of the Hague and Marcoule; British Nuclear Fuel, Ltd., in Great Britain by using the plant at Windscale; and KEWA, which combines German industries and plans the construction of a third plant in Germany. Destined from the beginning to produce an excess capacity for reprocessing (a result of the British and French

military programs), United Reprocessors will have the task of harmonizing the increase in European capacity made necessary by the acceleration of the nuclear programs.

By providing the atomic installations on domestic territory, while also being for the moment the only industry for recycling, the CEA occupies a monopoly position. Nevertheless its freedom is limited by a European agreement directed toward rationalization of investments and adaptation of the recycling capacity to international needs.

Autonomy of the System, Internationalization, and Margin of Action for the Central Administration. Two aspects of the structure seem particularly characteristic of the nuclear industry: (1) The ensemble of nuclear activities is controlled by a small number of industrial groups of a "multimonopolist" character; and (2) the development of new technologies, mining activity, and the enrichment of uranium are areas in which the international aspect is particularly important. We would like to describe, in a few lines, these two ideas and attempt an evaluation of the consequences of these two characteristics of the French nuclear system.

1. *A Multimonopoly.* We would like to say here that *there is practically no competition in the short and medium term* in the various zones of activity we have described. Currently, each of these zones is in fact controlled by one of the five principal industrial poles presented in the previous section (see Figure 4-4).

To grasp all the consequences, we must understand the difficulty (acquisition of "know-how" and lead time of necessary investments) that the launching of a new activity or the resumption of one that has been abandoned presents in the nuclear field. This organization of nuclear activity is the result of the decisions taken in the course of the five past years and a framework that will install and nurture the techniques that will be dominant for at least the next fifteen years. And it can be changed only slowly and at high cost (except in the direction of greater concentration, of course).

We see that this monopoly over allied products creates a strong solidarity of interests among the various poles holding this monopoly. They are all interested in a market that is as broad as possible, but they are in a position of power and have at their disposal margins of maneuver in price fixing since the only boundary they have to respect is the competitiveness of traditional electricity generators.

The client (EDF in this case) and the public authorities have almost no means to control prices and to direct short-term activity: Almost nowhere is there the possibility for competition between groups.[t] There is solidarity among

---

[t]For the turbo-alternators, there remains a small possibility of competition between Alsthom and CEM, but there seems to be an orientation towards division of the market; in the longer term, the possibility for competition between EUROFUEL and SICREL could appear in the domain of fuels.

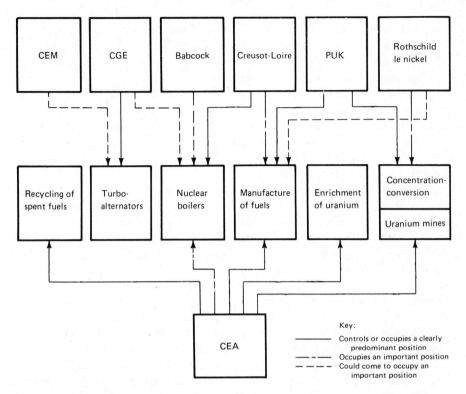

Source: Compiled by authors from internal documents of the CEA, FORATOME 79, and financial periodicals.

Figure 4-4. Control in the Nuclear Electricity Sector (September 1975).

the suppliers of nuclear energy, and it is at the service of profits that this market will devote itself to rapid development. To increase their size, they must rely on two variables: (1) prices and (2) volume of activity. For the first, there is almost no action possible, and the level of the second is guaranteed in effect by the policy of energy independence.

If there is any competition between the various partners, it is rather for the future, for the control of technologies for future generations of nuclear installations. At this level, the state retains some means for control insofar as its role remains important. The CEA is far and away the most important center of research and the transfer of knowledge from the public sector to private industrial groups allows for favoring one or another among them.

Let us note finally that the public sector tends to be involved in the zones that require the highest investments or in which the profits are neither immediate nor assured (development, mines and enrichment, retreatment).

2. *Internationalization Very Unequally Divided Among Sectors.* In the

medium term, one can look forward to a certain amount of autonomy for French nuclear activities. But until the end of the 1970s a relative dependence will continue, principally because of uranium enrichment. The conditions for disengagement from American tutelage seem to converge on several levels: EURODIF and the entry of the CEA in FRAMATOME creates the conditions for the rapid Frenchification of the PWR chain. In the longer run everything rests on a bet (the fast breeder reactors) and on a real diversification in the supply of uranium. Unless there is a shift to a second generation of reactors that are more sparing in the use of fuels, a dependence will evolve with regard to countries producing mineral ore.

In the areas of research and development and of mineral prospecting and exploitation, we see a very strong internationalization of activity: the breeder reactor prototypes that will follow Phenix will be constructed in collaboration with Germany and Italy; the alternative (the high temperature reactor) will require, for its perfection, recourse to foreign assistance, American or German; and the various mining companies described previously are "shared" with the countries owning the deposits and also with the "joint ventures" of the Germans, Italians, Spanish, Japanese, and so forth.

Perhaps it is not just by chance that the areas where internationalization reaches the greatest degree of importance are those where development and competition were underwritten by the public sector in the beginning stages of the nuclear age. As we have just pointed out, investment in these areas is heavy, or else it has to be made without immediate return, and this would explain the public involvement in these sectors. Thus the desire to limit public investment in France could well explain the evolution toward internationalization.

Degrees of Freedom

Having completed this descriptive panorama of the forces at play and the directions they take, let us go back and see what results various alternative strategies might have, without taking sides with any of them.

The growth of demand for energy is evidently not linked in a rigid way to general economic growth. At a given level of French GNP, in the year 2000, for example, one could certainly change the corresponding energy needs by as much as one-third according to the rigor of the antiwaste campaign; the level of the reference or target price for energy in the long term; determining the optimum balance between energy and investment (currently, the implicit price would assume a brilliantly successful nuclear program, the breeder reactors having begun in 1990 to relieve the burden on slow neutron reactors); also investment in thermal isolation in residential buildings as well as in the choice of techniques in industry. Energy need would also depend on the composition of the GNP, especially with regard to industrial products using a lot of energy—for which importing, guaranteed by long-term cooperative agreements with countries rich in energy, could cover part of the needs—and the style of urbanization and the development of the corresponding system of transportation. Naturally, putting these possibilities into effect would require significant delays (e.g., diversification of the activity of automobile producers), especially in sectors touching on lodging and urbanization.

In *the choice of energy techniques*, the crucial variable is obviously the part nuclear energy will play. The quick reestablishment of equilibrium in the French balance of payments in 1975 seems to demonstrate that the maintenance of a large volume of imported fossil fuel is not as intolerable as the proponents of nuclear energy would have us believe, provided, on the one hand, that part of its physical composition (gas, coal, or oil) and its place of origin are sufficiently diversified, and on the other hand, that the principal contracts for supply are signed with an arrangement for long-term cooperation with the supplier countries, including reciprocal guarantees.

The development of new forms of energy (solar, geothermal) could bear fruit from the year 2000 on, if research efforts, preferably at the European level, were agreed upon, with a provision for lost funds such as are indispensable to the development of any new technology and without which nuclear energy itself would never have been developed.

The same holds for the recovery of heat lost in the nuclear production of electricity where the use of chemical vectors such as ammonia offers an immense field for research that is almost untouched today. Since energy currently lost represents two or three times the volume of the corresponding electric energy, procedures permitting its use could provide for an important portion of the needs of the domestic sector and some of the need for low temperature heat in industry.

In each of these areas, the margin for freedom in the long term is thus considerable. The government plan of 1974 seems to represent a limiting of the possibilities to the maximum development of nuclear energy.[u] Even if a complete renunciation of nuclear development during an intermediary phase is difficult to conceive in the French case, it remains true that the global volume in the year 2000 could easily vary from the single to the quadruple according to the play of the actors and the system of values underlying their behavior, in particular according to the value attached to the stability of the ecosystem in the very long term and to the social advantages of decentralization.

Conclusion: Energy Policy Subordinated to the Dominant Pattern of Industrial Competition

France had on hand all the institutional means necessary to provide for the development of national energy policy under the best possible conditions of

---

[u]But where its absolute importance could reach higher levels in a situation of return to a rapid rate of growth in energy consumption.

self-determination. However, these were not used or were used poorly, and a policy was followed that had little coherence and that by the end of the period studied had led the French economy into a situation of dangerous dependence on petroleum-producing countries. This apparent incoherence becomes clarified if one places energy policy in the framework of the larger policy pattern of this quarter century, which was aimed at enabling France to rise to the level of a great industrial power, competitive in the world market.

Such is the thesis we propose in conclusion. Let us take up each of these three points in greater detail.

The French state had on hand powerful and diverse means to control the energy sector. Coal, gas, and electricity were a monopoly controlled by public enterprise; the law of 1928 gave the public administration considerable powers for intervention in the petroleum market; and the state controlled the ELF-ERAP company and owned a majority interest in the CFP. These latter two groups, which are of international dimensions, succeeded in developing a complete roster of petroleum activities, from prospecting to petrochemical operations. The CEA, a public organ, is the chief coordinator, pioneer, and sole agent for the acquisition of technology in most segments of the nuclear industry. It perfects procedures and transfers them to private enterprise when they become profitable and thus guarantees to private enterprise a large market as well as remunerative prices. The CEA thus plays the role of "launching pad" for private nuclear industry. In the Commissariat of the Plan, energy planning was given special attention from the beginning, and even served as the methodology laboratory for all French planning (e.g., the "actualization rate"). Finally, the Ministry of Finances has the power of discretionary intervention—with regard to the public enterprises of the sector—for taxation and financing. The largest share of investments in energy was financed by the capital endowments of the state and by low-interest loans from the Fund for Economic and Social Development (FEDS).

In spite of these impressive potential means of control, toward the end of the 1960-1970 decade the French state seemed to lose the leadership in energy development—to abandon it to the competitive fluctuations of the world energy market. The plan for coal production was lowered several times; the nuclear program spelled out in 1965 was abandoned; the growth of demand for petroleum defied all predictions; and while French energy dependence of petroleum-producing countries grew, the French state refused to tax imports of crude oil as the English and Germans had already done.

With the exception of the first plan to decrease coal production (1958) and the abandonment of the French nuclear chain (1969), which gave rise to a lively public reaction, policy making took place almost entirely among technocrats (high officials of the government and the administration and managers of public enterprises). The Parliament was hardly consulted except to approve the plans, and the Council of Ministers resolved conflicts between administrations. An implicit point of view emerged from these decisions: Of the two traditional criteria, the minimization of energy cost was given priority over energy independence. General deGaulle could very well blow the trumpets for national independence at the front of the stage; the executors of his policy—those of whom he said, not without disdain, "the administration will follow"—did not in fact act completely in accord with his scale of values, especially after 1967-68.

This verdict, however, would be unfair if one forgets the historical context within which what we might call the French energy misadventure took place. In the aftermath of the Second World War, the French were fascinated by the model of the United States and fearful of being surpassed by Germany (after 1950, one spoke of the "German miracle") in this school of industrial competition where Uncle Sam was the professor. To catch up with America and Germany in the race for industrial development, to succeed in exporting French technology around the world, to substitute success in business for the dwindling colonial empire—such were the elements of the grand design in this quarter century.

In the energy sector this involved strengthening the competitive capacity of French industry by providing it with energy at the best possible price. Antagonism between the "minimization of cost" and the "security of supply" was resolved with what seems in the light of history to have been a naive intrepidity—that is, overestimation of the regulatory and balancing role of international market competition and underestimation of the strategic positions first of Anglo-Saxon companies and then of states holding reserves in the battle for petroleum revenues.

It also meant that public enterprises in the energy sector should use their markets, their capital, and their know-how to promote the creation and rise of industrial groups of international scale. (Thus the EDF insured the profitability of the investments of Creusot-Loire and Alsthom; the CEA passed on to private groups, through the intermediary of common affiliates, nuclear techniques as soon as they were perfected; and so on.) The nuclear programs in particular—if their realization had been dependent on the existence of industrial structures strong enough to assure the development of a quite costly, new, and delicate technology—would have been at the same time a tool for accelerated growth and concentration in the electromechanical industry. The launching of a new chain of generators currently being discussed is posed explicitly in these terms: The government requires as a condition for its involvement that an "industrial combination" be put together, this time an international one capable of guaranteeing the building and promotion of "commercial" generators—that is, generators that are competitive on the export market.

The energy crisis of 1973-74 has doubtless strongly revalidated the criteria of autonomy and security of supply, while upsetting the scale of costs. But the subordination of energy programs to the totality of French industrial policy, methodically led by the public administration, still seems to predominate. In spite of the acute problems involved in the conversion of the petroleum industry, which some people would like to avoid, the attitude of the administration still seems by nature to favor the priority development of the nuclear industry.

Notes

1. Denis Bauchard, *Le jeu mondial des petroliers* (Paris: Le Seuil, 1969).

2. François Perrin, quoting the decree founding CEA (private discussion).

3. Jean-Marie Martin, "L'évolution des relations étât-entreprises dans le domaine des activités energetiques en France, mimeo (Grenoble: University of Grenoble, October 1973).

4. Michael Toromanoff, *Le drame des houillières* (Paris: Le Seuil, 1969).

5. Ibid., p. 34.

6. See, for example, the general report of the Commission de l'énergie du IIe Plan, published in March 1957.

7. Toromanoff, *Le drame des houillières.*

8. "L'energie en Europe et en France," *Economie et Politique*, November 1959.

9. Henri Claude, "La leçon de Décazeville," *Economie et Politique*, February 1962.

10. According to R. Bonety.

11. "Rapports des Commissions du 6e Plan," (Paris: La Documentation Française, 1971).

12. These ideas are elucidated in the brochure, "Alternatives to Nuclear Energy," signed by researchers of the Institut Economique et Juridique de l'Energie at Grenoble. It was published in February 1975 and rapidly sold out.

Bibliography

Information and analyses on the subject of this chapter are very sparse in the literature. The works and publications listed here contain much of the information used and also points of view that are sometimes in contradiction with those expressed in the text.

Commissariat Général du Plan. *Rapports des Commissions de l'Energie des III, IV, V et VI Plans.* La Documentation Française, Paris. These reports present, illustrate, and defend the five-year programs (investments, different energy markets, and corresponding energy balances) in the framework of a long-term forecast of the development of the energy sector. Interesting information is also found in the reports of other Commissions of the Plan (gasoline and transport notably).

Revue Française de l'Energie. This monthly provides a forum where those responsible for energy policy present financial data, projects, and prospects. The voice of the nationalized sector predominates.

Economie et Politique "Revue Marxiste d'Economie." This monthly is frequently devoted to studies of heavy industry and the energy sector.

Scott and McArthur. *L'industrie française face aux Plans.* Paris: Dunod, 1969. This work, now somewhat dated, tries to analyze the evolution of French business and the role of the plan in this evolution.

Alain Cotta. *Inflation et croissance en France depuis 1962 (PUF).* This work furnishes some interesting facts about the distribution of the fruits of French industrial growth.

Philippe Brachet and Jacques Gallus. *Les Nationalisations (Objectif—Le Cerf),* 1973. This work is an attempt to analyze whose interests were served by the nationalizations after the Second World War.

François Morin. *La structure financière du capitalisme français.* Paris: Colman Lévy, 1975. This work provides an analysis of the movement toward financial concentration in French industry and its effects on group strategies.

André Oizon. *L'évolution récente de la production et de la consommation d'énergie en France.* Paris: Larousse, 1971. This work contains a detailed examination of the energy sector.

Michel Toromanoff, *Le drame des houillières.* Paris: Le Seuil, 1969. The rise and fall of French coal as seen from the inside is presented in this work.

Denis Beauchard. *Le jeu mondial des pétroliers.* Paris: Le Seuil, 1970. In addition to a description of the world energy problem, this work contains a description of French strategy in the 1960s.

Jean-Marie Chevallier. *Le nouvel enjeu petrolier.* Paris: Colman Lévy, 1973. This work contains in particular the history of Franco-Algerian relations as they affected petroleum.

G. Pilé and A. Cubertafond. *Pétrole, le vrai dossier.* Paris: La Cité, 1975. The French oil companies, as they are perceived and as they would like to be perceived, are presented in this work.

FORATOM 74: The Nuclear Power Industry in Europe (Deutsches Atom forum 1974). Complete repertory of the European nuclear industry.

Beaud, Danjou, David. *Une multinationale française, P.U.K.* Paris: Le Seuil, 1975. This work describes the past and present situation of a big industrial corporation (a result of recent mergers) that is very involved in nuclear activities.

Rapports annuels d'activités of the Electricité de France, Charbonnages de France, Gaz de France, Compagnies pétrolières, Compagnie général d'électricité, Groupe Creusot Loire, and so forth. In addition to facts about the various activities of these companies and corporations, statements of the directors regarding plans and strategies are generally included.

Studies of specialized organizations, such as files and announcements of DAFSA and SEF (who publish specialized studies of branch organizations or groups, financial connections), and *Annuaire Desfossés* (makeup of the administration consuls and the important companies in the stock exchange).

Economic and Financial Press. *Les Echos, La Vie Francaise—L'Opinion, Entreprise, Les Informations,* and *ENERPRESSE.*

Rapport de la Commission de l'énergie. Paris: La Documentation Française, 1971.

5

Energy Planning and the Energy Situation in a Socialist Planned Economy Lacking Energy: A Case Study of Hungary

István Dobozi

Some Methodological Questions of Energy Planning

Some General Problems

The significance of energy in the economy is recognized equally in socialist and capitalist countries despite the different economic systems. It is generally believed that one of the most important factors that determines economic growth is meeting of the energy demand of national economies safely and economically. Wide-ranging studies have been started over the past fifteen or twenty years in almost every country to predict long-range energy demand and to optimize energy supply, and there has been a steady increase in the number of central organizations and institutions engaged in such centralized activities.

This direction in the development of the energy economy is related to the following internationally valid peculiarities of the energy industry.

1. Energy consumption affects almost all of the production, servicing, and subsistence functions of societies.

2. The gestation time of large energy investments is extremely long. In some cases the time span between preparatory studies, research, and the actual preparation is eight to ten years while the economical life span of investments is twenty-five to thirty years. Decisions on energy, then, should be made in the present, but so that efficiency and the general operation of the project would come up to requirements even twenty to thirty years thereafter. Since existing capacities will always have a compelling effect on future energy development, these fixed assets will create an environment difficult to change.

3. Energy production, transformation, and transport belong to one of the most capital-intensive branches of the economy. Energy supply thus has significant economic implications. Throughout the world, one-third of industrial investments is devoted to the development of energy; at the same time, demands on investments are on the increase.

4. In the energy economy a comparatively small number of investment decisions is made at the macroeconomic level. These, however, have an immense impact on the development of other branches of the economy and on the general advance of technology.

5. The necessity for stability and continuity of production and imports creates a fundamental problem in a balanced energy supply—that is, energy must be received continuously through complicated transport systems practically day

by day, at a rate and in a quality and quantity determined for the long term. Any energy shortfall may cause a fall in production value of 50 to 100 times its own value.

6. The ever-increasing costs of ensuring energy supply will influence the lines of economic development in advanced consumer countries because of the great reliance on imported energy. Thus, the following questions should be reckoned with: How great is the energy demand in each of the various development patterns? Is there any significant difference between alternatives from the aspect of energy demand? What should be the goods content of the export equivalent of energy imports, and so forth?

These peculiarities require that decisions in the sphere of energy economy should everywhere be painstakingly prepared. Naturally, the dimensions of the problem vary according to whether the given country is a socialist planned economy or an advanced capitalist market economy. In the socialist countries—thus in Hungary, too—the necessity for energy planning goes without saying.

In the socialist countries, a variety of up-to-date economic-mathematical-statistical analyzing methods has been elaborated and used to examine questions related to the energy sector. From the methodological aspect, the problem of *long-range planning* in the energy sector lies in the following: in long-range planning there is a close connection between planning in a strict sense—that is, planning the balance (proportions)—and selection of the most effective solutions (economic efficiency) from the viewpoint of the national economy. Planning demand for energy in a socialist planned economy is not confined to adopting the various extrapolation methods recommended to survey demand for energy, or to project—in one way or another—past development, because the objective is the selection of the most effective method from the viewpoint of the whole economy. The most suitable methods for planning may naturally vary according to the length of the planning period (short term, medium term, or long range).

Long-range energy planning may conveniently be divided into the following (not strictly separable) main parts (phases):

1. *Preparation of a long-range energy plan* based on the study of major technological and economic tendencies in the past both at home and abroad and on the general survey and evaluation of the situation of the energy sector;
2. *Projecting the anticipated trends in the energy processes under investigation*, primarily in energy consumption, by using methods and techniques based, first of all, on the analysis of past development or on various methods of extrapolation, correlation calculations, and international comparisons;
3. *Planning the equilibrium (proportions)* by using mainly energy balances or rather the separately detailed uses of various forms of energy;[a]

[a]In Hungary regular information has been supplied over some fifteen years on the basis of yearly energy balances (i.e., a data supply that must be provided by any industrial or

4. *Long-range optimum investigation of energy supply*, through which optimum policy outcomes are sought, taking into account the interactions of decision possibilities.

Since in a socialist planned economy the most reasonable and optimum exploitation of resources can only be understood at the level of the national economy, taking into consideration all of its complex interrelations, long-range investigation is highly complicated and forms the most important part of the whole energy planning process. A brief outline follows of the situation of optimum investigations at the level of the national economy in Hungary.[1]

Optimum Investigations of Long-Range Energy
Supply in Hungary

Over the past fifteen years or so optimum investigations of long-range energy supply have been continuously carried out in Hungary. Their objective is to ensure meeting the ever-increasing long-range demands on energy in a manner that is efficient and economical from the viewpoint of the national economy in spite of the regular uncertainties of planning. On the basis of practice evolved so far, methodologically these investigations are being carried out in two directions:

1. Determination of an *optimum distribution* (by energy type and consumption) for a source composition defined arbitrarily and in advance;
2. Determination of the *optimum source composition of energy* (finding the optimum distribution for each source).

Obviously, information on the economic efficiency of the distribution and structural composition can be expected from the optimum investigation, which presupposes the consistency of the plans for the national economy, and its results will only serve further to improve them. It can neither replace demand calculations nor ensure the consistency of the plan for the national economy, since the latter is the task of various input-output models.

The optimum investigations of energy supply may only be related to a certain long-term period (five-, ten-, or fifteen-year long-range plans)—that is, the individual investigations are static in character. The dynamic approach is replaced by calculations examining the supply of subsequent years and the relationships between them in their development. The dynamic approach is, then, replaced by a series of static examinations.

transport organization with an energy consumption of over 10^9 kcal/year). These balances provide the possibility for detailed analyses of the complete energy-consuming process of the above users broken down by energy transformation, immediate consumption, specific uses of energy, and so forth.

Model of Investigation

The model serving for optimum investigation is shown in the form of a matrix in Figure 5-1. In the lines marked with i consumers are indicated in groups that are homogeneous according to the character of the energy consumption (homogeneous energy consumers), particularly as regards the replaceability of various forms of energy. The j-marked columns indicate the kinds of homogeneous energy forms that, from the viewpoint of consumers, may be regarded as practically equivalent. For the meeting point of any i and j line, a series of parameters can be determined (quantitative factors mean yearly quantity). Such are:

E_{ij} : the energy demand of the ith consumer in terms of kcal, if it is fully met by the jth energy;

x_{ij} : the quantity in terms of kcal distributed from the jth energy to the ith consumer;

η_{ij} : degree of efficiency ensured by the use of the jth energy in the case of the ith consumer;

c_{ij} : specific cost factor in the case of meeting the full demand of the ith consumer by the jth energy in terms of forint/year/kcal;

E_j : distributable quantity of energy available from the jth energy (Σx_{ij});

E_i : the full energy demand of the ith consumer when it is met by several kinds of energies.

The optimization investigation of the long-range energy supply is described by the following equations:

$$x_{ij} \geqslant 0. \tag{5.1}$$

$$\Sigma_j \frac{x_{ij}}{E_{ij}} = 1 \ (i = 1, 2, 3, \ldots . m). \tag{5.2}$$

$$\Sigma_i x_{ij} = E_j \ (j = 1, 2, 3, \ldots . n). \tag{5.3}$$

$$\Sigma_i \Sigma_j c_{ij} \cdot x_{ij} \rightarrow \min. \tag{5.4}$$

The first equation expresses the natural fact that the consumer may receive but not give energy. The second equation means that the energy demand E_i of consumers should be met. The economic content of the third equation is that the sum of the total energy sources available equals the total demand of consumers (not counting an insignificant change in demand resulting from η_{ij}).

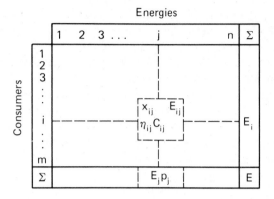

Figure 5-1. Model for Investigation of Energy Supply.

The target function of the investigation makes possible the realization of an energy distribution in which the total cost per year for energy supply at the level of the national economy is at a minimum.

The total energy costs of the individual energy sectors may be calculated by the relation $\Sigma_j E_j \cdot p_j$, where p_j is the specific production cost of the individual forms of energy in terms of forint/10^6 kcal. The total cost of the national economy's energy supply for a certain energy sector is composed of the above energy cost plus the minimum costs resulting from the optimum distribution defined by the target function (5.4). In the case of the minimum of these two kinds of costs—that is, of $\min/\Sigma_j E_j p_j + \min \Sigma_i \Sigma_j c_{ij} x_{ij}/$ we can obtain the *optimum energy source structure* representing the smallest cost for the national economy.

Results of Optimum Investigations

Investigations carried out so far—which were models reduced to "simple transportation task" solved by linear programming—have already produced significant practical results in shaping energy policy, although the models examined were highly aggregated of about 20 x 30 matrix size. The role of these investigations is considerable in the quantitative evaluation of the effect of hydrocarbons, in the prevalence of the national economy level approach, and in the exploration of the close interrelations of energy supply (thus, for instance, also in the determination of relations between the energy consumption of the individual sectors).

The details of the optimum investigations carried out on the basis of the model outlined above gave the following information.

They have confirmed our general practical and experimental knowledge relative to the improvement of the energy structure; at the same time, they have quantified it both technologically and economically (in calorie and forint), which was impossible while using the traditional methods.

They have pointed out some *close interrelationships* within the energy supply. By taking into account costs and economic aspects, they have made it possible to evaluate how intervention at the level of the energy consumer makes its effect felt on other forms of energy and other consumers. In other words, there exists no long-range oil or gas program by itself, or, for instance, a separate and economically efficient energy supply for industry and population. All that can exist is an efficient complex energy supply at the national economy level.

Supported by figures, these investigations have confirmed the general experimental knowledge that the limited amount of high-quality energy (hydrocarbons) should be allocated first to the "small consumers." *Individual and communal consumers* should be supplied with hydrocarbons, mainly with gas and fuel oil, although consumption is generally under 200 hours/year. The continuous adaptation of this type of consumer to hydrocarbons seems to be efficient even with the additional costs of the summertime buffer consumption of gas.

In meeting the demands of *industry and technology*, energy for furnaces— mainly in the machine industry—can also be provided by hydrocarbons. The most economical fuel for the new smaller-capacity industrial furnaces is also hydrocarbon. Moreover, in many cases the adaptation of the existing coal-fed equipment to hydrocarbons may also be economical.[b] Within this category of consumers, gas for steam production that operates throughout the year with a large number of exploitation hours can also be justified.

The greater part of coal remains for feeding the big boilers of power plants. The relatively better quality and smaller shares are left partly for the still coal-fed but economically efficient boilers and partly for certain industrial furnaces, while the best quality coal is for meeting the heating requirements of individuals and communities. The latter mainly serves where other energy sources cannot be introduced in an economical way or where the adaptation of the existing equipment is not economically efficient.

Knowledge of interrelationships among the individual decisions is of particularly great moment. One of the most important is that the increase in the proportion of fuel gas consumed by individuals and communities requires a large buffer consumer capacity; otherwise it requires the creation of significant alternative possibilities for heating (power plants, big boilers, furnaces) that would operate with coal or fuel oil as necessary during the winter months.

The investigations also provided important information regarding shadow prices. When expressed as cost at the national economy level, these quantitative-

---

[b]It should be pointed out here that these calculations were made before the large-scale rise in oil prices. The increase in the world market price of oil affected Hungary, too, although not so seriously as the advanced capitalist countries. This will be dealt with later.

ly underlined the value differences between domestic mining of inferior quality, uneconomical coal and the import of hydrocarbons, thus providing a cost guideline for future changes in the energy structure.

Regarding the future of optimum investigations, the main objective is to reconcile the method of investigation with its demand on data information. Detailed information processing offers the possibility for the study of models of considerably increased matrix size.

The methodological problems of energy planning in Hungary are naturally more complex than could be fully reported in such a brief chapter. The present objective was simply to offer an example of some methodological problems in long-range energy planning.

Energy Situation in Hungary

Hungary is fairly poor in energy that is economically exploitable. Like several other economically developed countries, Hungary is increasingly compelled to import energy. According to figures in Table 5-1, in 1960 26 percent of energy consumed in the country came from imports while the corresponding figure for 1970 was 37 percent and 48 percent for 1975. According to long-range plans, dependence on import sources will increase further in the future.

Trends in Energy Production

Coal Mining. After 1945, the Hungarian coal mining industry had an extremely big task. Energy necessary to the country's reconstruction and industrialization had to be produced almost completely from domestic coal. In 1964 coal mining reached its maximum output of 31.5 million tons. With the structure of energy demand transformed since 1965, coal production has continuously decreased—to 27.8 million tons in 1970 and to 25.8 million in 1974. The coal produced is for

Table 5-1
Percentage Distribution of Domestic and Import Sources

	1960	1965	1970	1975	1980	1990
Domestic Production	74	69	63	52	44	32
Import	26	31	37	48	56	68
Total	100	100	100	100	100	100

Sources: Gy. Szekér, "Energiagazdálkodásunk helyzete és távlatai" (The Situation and Prospects of Our Energy Economy), *Társadalmi Szemle*, no. 6 (1974), p. 34; M. Szőcs, "Energiaigények kielégitésének lehetőségeiről" (On the Possibilities of Meeting Energy Demands), *Gazdaság*, no. 1 (1974), p. 63.

the most part lignite, which is of low heating quality. The economic efficiency indices of Hungarian coal mining are very unfavorable. The output of a domestic shaft of average capacity, for instance, accounts for only 20 percent to 50 percent of the corresponding index number of countries with up-to-date mining.

On the basis of geological research, Hungary's coal reserves are estimated at some 7 billion tons, of which about 6 billion are exploitable and a good part can be drawn by open-cast mining as well. In the future, Hungarian coal mining can be set at a higher level of production than the present. The sudden increase in the price of petroleum and the difficulties with energy imports have improved the relative economic efficiency of coal mining, and coal production has been given greater attention than before. The plans predict that the decline in coal production will come to an end. It is expected that the yearly output will still be 25 to 26 million tons for some years to come; then, after the completion of new investments, it will rise again. The long-range target figure for 1990 is a yearly 30 million tons. Geological research at present is directed at guaranteeing the coal base of big up-to-date power plants of 1,500 to 2,000 MW capacity.

Increased coal production is based on accelerated technological development and rationalization and large-scale concentration of production. The more moderate production tasks have made the concentration and modernization of coal mining possible. Between 1965 and 1973 the number of shafts decreased by 50 percent, while the output per shaft increased by 40 percent. Currently, almost one-third of coal production comes from open-cast mines, which are more productive than deep working mines. This structural change shows that the prospects for coal mining lie primarily in the large-scale mining works and in the related large consumers.

As a result of concentration and technological development, the productivity of coal mining increased by almost 60 percent in 1965-1973; thus the output—which was only 15 percent lower than the maximum output—was achieved by an almost 40 percent smaller number of workers. As a result of modernization, coal mining has become more effective and competitive in the energy economy.

Hydrocarbon Production. Of Hungary's present area of 93,011 square kilometers, some 77,000 square kilometers are suitable for hydrocarbon exploration at the present technological level. Geological research in hydrocarbons is being carried out at a high professional level according to defined plans. About half of the country's estimated reserves has already been explored. Hungary, with her modest hydrocarbon production, is the third-largest producer—after the Soviet Union and Romania—among the socialist countries.

The production of petroleum has been stabilized at the level of 2 million tons per year. In all probability, this level can be maintained until 1980, but because of the exhaustion of reserves, after that a gradual decline in production is expected.

The stabilization of domestic oil production and the rapid increase in oil imports made it necessary to develop a large-scale processing industry. The capacity of the oil processing industry increased from almost 5 million tons per year in 1965 to over 10 million tons in 1975. Large new projects have been put into operation while obsolete, low-capacity refineries have been closed.

Natural gas production in Hungary was insignificant until the mid-sixties. Natural gas reserves discovered recently resulted in a rapid increase in production and servicing. Natural gas production rose from 1.2 billion m^3/year in 1965 to 5.2 billion m^3 in 1974. Prospects for the development of natural gas are promising; production will increase by some 40 percent by 1985. Even so, this amount will be insufficient to meet domestic demand.

To transport and distribute natural gas, a pipeline system covering the whole country has been built and is in the process of being put into operation.

Production of Electric Energy. The Hungarian electricity industry is developing at a very rapid rate. The built-in output of the country's power plants rose from 2,087 MW in 1965 to 4,400 MW in 1975. Electricity production increased from 7.6 billion kWh in 1960 to 18.9 billion kWh in 1974.

More than half of the present machine stock of power plants consists of high-performance machine units, and the plants themselves are characterized by the increasing size of their machines. The power plants under construction now contain turbines and generators of 215 MW unit performance. These are the products of Hungarian industry and of the socialist camp, and their operation and technological parameters have led to favorable results. The basic technological indices of the power plant system have improved. The amount of fuel used to produce 1 kWh has decreased by 20 percent over the past decade, but the specific input is still high in international comparisons. Power plants increasingly meet a considerable part of the steam and hot water demands of industry and individuals. The supply of heating has increased fivefold over the past ten years.

Atomic Energy. Since Hungary is poor in energy, the idea of building nuclear power plants was taken up rather early. It appeared from the economic calculations that the specific costs would considerably decrease with increased built-in performance. Thus, only the building of reactor blocks of several hundreds of MW capacity could be considered. In the Soviet Union in 1965, the design of a nuclear power plant of 800 MW capacity, equipped with pressurized water reactors, was elaborated and sent to the socialist countries. This "Druzhba Project" anticipated that between 1975 and 1980 the nuclear power plant would be economically competitive. In 1966 Hungary had already concluded an intergovernmental agreement with the Soviet Union for the construction of the plant. For various reasons the construction was put off and the agreement was modified. The construction of the first Hungarian nuclear power plant was started in Paks in 1974, and its first 440 MW block is scheduled to be put into operation in early 1980, while the second block will be completed by 1981. The power plant is so designed that later it will be possible to enlarge the capacity to 2,000 and then 4,000 MW.

This long postponement in the building of the nuclear power plant is regarded as unfavorable by many experts, since it will exert an obvious negative influence on the Hungarian energy economy in the next few years and thus necessitate a considerable increase in oil imports. (The intake of the oil power plant, substituting for the nuclear power plant, is some 1.5 million tons of fuel oil.) In putting off the date of the establishment of the nuclear power plant an important role was played by economic calculations that have changed in the meanwhile.

The long-range plans—within the framework of a close cooperation with the Soviet Union—envisage a rapid development of electric energy production in nuclear power plants, so that 15 percent of the country's energy consumption will be provided by nuclear power plants in 1990.

Trends in Energy Consumption

Hungary's energy consumption in the 1950s increased at a rapid rate. There were years when the country's energy demand increased by 13 percent to 15 percent in one year. Characteristically, the rapidly increasing energy consumption was linked to the extensive-type economic policy of that time and with the related quantitative way of thinking. As a result, fulfillment of the quantitative objectives of industrial production was preferred to the reduction of energy consumption. Adding significantly to the high level of energy consumption was the high specific consumption, too. In that period, the coefficient of elasticity of energy (calculated for the national income) showed an unfavorable tendency, about 1.2 to 1.3. In the early 1960s the growth rate for energy consumption became more moderate and amounted to 5 percent (see Table 5-2). In the later 1960s the intensive-type development of the power economy has begun to decrease the growth rate of energy consumption. The value of the coefficient of elasticity of energy has decreased to 0.6 to 0.7.

This favorable change is largely the result of the *energy policy conception*

Table 5-2
Trends in Energy Consumption (mtce)

1960	1970	1980	1990
20.6	30.5	45.8-46.0	69-70

Source: J. Drecin, "Iparpolitika Magyarországon" (Industrial Policy in Hungary), *Gazdaság*, no. 2 (1975), p. 32.

adopted by the Hungarian government in 1964, which was aimed at the economically motivated reduction of the country's total energy demand, as well as at the modernization of the energy balance.

Since 1950 a shift in the energy structure toward hydrocarbons has been observable in Hungary. In the beginning this change was moderate in its pace, and followed the international trend with a ten-year time lag. Since 1965, however, in pursuance of the energy policy conception, the transformation of the energy balance has sped up (see Table 5-3).

The structural rearrangement of energy was not only a technological necessity, but also the only real possibility for meeting the increasing energy demands of the national economy. This change has yielded significant technological and economic results in several branches of the national economy.

Between 1970 and 1975 it was possible to replace $2.8 \cdot 10^{12}$ kcal of coal by switching over to hydrocarbon consumption through an energy rationalization program consisting of 200 large projects with a total investment of 1.43 billion forints. This is equivalent to 711,000 tons of coal of which 609,000 is produced domestically. Due to the difference in efficiency of coal heating and hydrocarbon utilization, 244,000 tons of coal are saved yearly in this program that, when calculated at current coal prices, is equivalent to 181 million forints/year savings. The average period of return of investments in energy rationalization is 2.8 years. Such a large-scale transformation of the energy structure resulted in the investment demand of the national economy decreasing by a yearly amount of 5 to 7 billion forints. By using hydrocarbons as fuels of greater efficiency, the savings of consumers may be estimated at several billions of forints. In alumina factories and in the cement, glass, and ceramics industries, the specific energy consumption decreased by 25 percent to 40 percent due to the use of hydrocarbons. There are only a few European countries that—like Hungary—can run their entire fertilizer industry on natural gas. Iron metallurgy and the steel industry are also pushing the advantages of natural gas, thereby improving quality and lowering production costs.

Table 5-3

The Structure of Energy Consumption (% of total consumption) (as % of total consumption)

	1960	1970	1975	1980	1990
Coal	73	50	34	24	16
Petroleum and Gas	21	43	59	68	62
Atomic Energy	–	–	–	1	15
Others	6	7	7	7	7
Total	100	100	100	100	100

Source: J. Drecin, "Iparpolitika," p. 32; Gy. Szekér, "Energiazazdálkodásunk," p. 34.

The transformation of the structure of energy is no longer regarded as so unambiguously favorable a process as before. As early as 1973, a government report established that in fuel consumption the switchover to hydrocarbons had been going on—mainly in industrial plants—at a higher rate than desirable. Coal heating was given up even in places where technology had not made it imperative. In the course of transforming the energy structure there was a bottleneck in the supply of some consumer categories where consumption sped up in some cases well above the plans. The increased rate of transformation appeared to be harmful in the service industry, too, which had been unable to make preparations in time, and the resulting difficulties could be eliminated only by significant additional investments (storing and transport capacities, building new pipelines, and so forth).

The skyrocketing prices of crude oil on the world market considerably lessened the economic advantages of oil over solid fuels. In consequence, the large share of liquid fuels in the energy balance no longer signifies the unambiguous advantages it used to.

Participation of Hungary in International Energy Cooperation among the Socialist Countries

Trends in the Energy Imports of Hungary

Because the possibilities for energy production in Hungary are limited by the geological situation, the share of imports in total energy consumption is growing at a rapid rate. As has been seen in Table 5-1, in 1960, 26 percent of the country's energy consumption came from imports, but the corresponding figure for 1975 will be almost 50 percent and 68 percent for 1990. Hungarian energy imports have very drastically increased in recent years (see Table 5-4).

Table 5-4
Increase in Energy Import (1970 = 100)

	From Socialist Countries	From Capitalist Countries	Total
1968	79.4	*	76.7
1969	88.2	*	85.5
1970	100.0	100.0	100.0
1971	111.8	179.9	114.6
1972	116.5	214.9	120.7
1973	124.2	195.8	128.9
1974	126.9	187.7	138.0

Source: *Külkereskedelmi Statisztikai Évkönyv 1974* (Statistical Yearbook for Foreign Trade, 1974), (Budapest: Központi Statisztikai Hivatal, 1975).

*Turnover did not reach 0.5 percent of total turnover in the commodity group.

In addition, economic considerations, at least in the case of oil, encouraged the rapid increase of imports. By comparing the cost of various forms of energy in the period before the oil price "explosion," we can see that—similar to international tendencies—the cost of hydrocarbons, both domestic and imported, is lower than the average cost of domestic coal. These proportions expressed numerically are shown by the following data:

Domestic coal (average), 100

Domestic natural gas, 35

Domestic oil, 52

Imported oil, 66

Imported natural gas, 70-80

The greater part of Hungary's imported energy comes from the socialist countries, mainly from the Soviet Union, although imports from the capitalist countries—especially from developing countries—have increased considerably in recent years (see Table 5-5). In 1974, the share of energy imports from developing countries in the total suddenly rose to 15.9 percent. This increase may be due to the fact that while oil from the developing countries was purchased at the greatly increased world market price, imports from the Soviet Union were coming at unchanged prices (much lower than the world market price). In 1974, Hungary imported some 6.3 million tons of oil from the Soviet Union and 1.4 million tons from the Middle East.

Some Problems in Energy Cooperation among
the CMEA Countries

For some decades, the CMEA countries have deliberately worked on establishing a common raw material and energy base. A common raw material and energy

Table 5-5
Energy Imports by Sources (percent)

	Socialist Countries	*Capitalist Countries*
1965	89.9	1.04
1968	99.5	0.41
1970	96.1	3.9
1971	93.0	7.0
1972	92.4	7.6
1973	90.7	9.3
1974	81.4	18.6

Source: *Külkereskedelmi Statisztikai Évkönyv 1974.*

base of their own would free, to a large extent, the CMEA countries from speculative and unpredictable price changes in the capitalist market. The advantages have been particularly observable over the past two years when the price of energy (and raw materials) has been skyrocketing, and there have been substantial difficulties in the supply, too. The CMEA countries taken together have potential energy reserves that can guarantee the safe energy supply of the region even in the long range.

The main supplier for the energy import demands of the CMEA countries is the Soviet Union. In the years between 1961 and 1974, the Soviet Union multiplied her energy exports to the socialist countries by six while Soviet energy production doubled. In 1973, 57.3 percent (or 67.8 million tons) of Soviet oil exports, totalling 118.3 million tons, went to the socialist countries (40.1 percent went to the advanced capitalist and 2.5 percent to the developing countries).

The extent of energy cooperation among CMEA countries is shown by the fact that international socialist economic integration has come into full play precisely in the energy industry of the CMEA countries. This fact is also attested to by a number of important integration projects. It was more than a decade ago that the European CMEA countries set up a common electric energy system. The unified "Peace" energy system made possible the exchange of 17 billion kWh of electricity in 1973 alone. New vistas of development are opened up by the decision that the CMEA countries will begin construction of an international transmission line of 750 kW, which is an outstanding performance even from the purely technological aspect. One important junction point of this system will be in Hungary. The 860-kilometer transmission line will be put into operation in 1978 and will join the unified energy system of the socialist countries with the Southern Unified Energy System of the Soviet Union, thus making possible the better fulfillment of the increasing electricity demands of the socialist countries. This highly important transmission line connecting the CMEA countries will offer several advantages. It will facilitate the lessening of the peak load, save on investments in power plants, and make the energy supply more even and safe in the participating countries.

A similarly outstanding role is being played in the energy supply of the socialist countries by the "Friendship" oil pipeline, which from 1962 up to 1975 has transported over 300 million tons of petroleum to Hungary, the GDR, Poland, and Czechoslovakia from the Soviet Union. The construction of a transcontinental gas pipeline has also started. It comes from Orenburg in the Ural region of the Soviet Union to the western border of the country and is a joint effort of the socialist countries. When completed, it will be the biggest gas pipeline in the world and will transport 15.5 billion m^3 of natural gas yearly to the socialist countries. The gas pipeline called "Brotherhood" was put into operation in 1975, and in 1976 it supplied some 10 billion m^3 of natural gas to member countries, including Hungary.

It is widely known that the production of energy is highly capital intensive and needs extremely large investments with long lead times. This characteristic imposes disproportionately serious burdens on the energy-exporting countries (within the CMEA primarily on the Soviet Union), since energy production and its development tie up a good part of the financial resources originally devoted to accumulation. This situation may cause a certain lag in investments immediately serving the improvement of living standard. In addition, the main focus of Soviet energy production is rapidly shifting to regions beyond the Urals, which will further increase the burdens of investment due to the greater distances of transport and unfavorable conditions for production.

The energy-importing CMEA countries, therefore, recognized that they should use their own resources for the development of the Soviet energy industry to ease the burdens on the Soviet Union and, consequently, to ensure security of their own long-range energy supply. In their Comprehensive Program, adopted in 1971 to deepen and promote integration, the CMEA countries drew up several forms of cooperation by which the importing countries may participate directly by using their resources to develop the capacity of the exporter countries in the interests of meeting their own demands. Czechoslovakia and the GDR, for instance, with credit cooperation, participate in developing the Soviet oil industry, while the Soviet Union, in exchange, substantially increases her oil exports to these countries.

The CMEA countries, in various forms of economic cooperation, attach a great deal of importance to energy saving achieved through such cooperation. To cite only one example, according to the Hungarian-Soviet Aluminum Agreement, Hungary, which abounds in bauxite, will develop aluminum production by transporting alumina to the Soviet Union where it will be turned into aluminum by energy intensive processes and then returned to Hungary. This cooperation enables energy-poor Hungary to save 2.7 billion kWh/year of electric energy. (This quantity is equivalent to 12 percent to 14 percent of Hungary's electric energy consumption.) According to calculations, aluminum thus produced is 16 percent to 18 percent cheaper than that produced in Hungary.

The international energy cooperation among the socialist countries ensures the stability necessary for the energy-importing countries to engage in medium- and long-range planning. According to intergovernmental commercial agreements, the member countries fix—for five years—the volume of energy imports and exports within the socialist community. Foreign trade prices, used in the energy trade, are determined by the CMEA countries in much the same way as for other products, on the basis of the capitalist market prices so that price fluctuations of a speculative nature will be eliminated. Before 1975, the foreign trade prices of each new five-year plan were based on the average capitalist market prices of the previous five years. Foreign trade prices within the CMEA were thus fixed for a period of five years. Prices used in 1971-1974 were the average capitalist world market prices of the period 1966-1970. The drawback of the stability offered by such a price system was that prices within the CMEA occasionally fell away from the world market prices to a great extent and in such periods could not ensure mutual advantages. This condition occurred during the sudden rise of oil prices in 1973 and 1974. In these years the CMEA countries received oil at unchanged (and very low) prices from the Soviet Union. Naturally, their oil imports from the developing countries were paid at the actual world market prices. The oil-importing CMEA countries, too, are interested in having energy trade go on at real prices. Only in this way can the member countries ensure mutually favorable conditions in their trade among themselves, as well as a sound orientation and incentive for both the producers and consumers, and the dynamic further increase in their mutual energy trade. Therefore, the CMEA countries, at the session of the Executive Committee of the organization in January 1975, agreed that the prices used in their mutual trade would be adjusted yearly to the average prices in the world market over the previous five years. Thus the 1975 prices are based on the average world market prices of the period 1970-74, while prices for 1976 will be based on the average prices of the years 1971-1975, for 1977 on the average prices of 1972-1976, and so forth.

The new method of foreign trade pricing within the CMEA ensures the relative stability and elasticity of prices and lessens the danger of a wide discrepancy between the prices in the socialist trade area and those of the world market. This method of pricing will—in a few years—also modify the price distortions of the past few years and will draw nearer to the *lasting* tendencies and proportions of the world market from which the CMEA countries do not wish to fall away.

On the basis of the new price system, the price of the Soviet oil within the CMEA trade has increased more than twofold since January 1, 1975. Thus in 1974, Hungary purchased oil from the Soviet Union at the price of 16 rubles a ton, transported to the Hungarian border, while from January 1, 1975, it costs 37 rubles, which is equivalent to $7/barrel, compared with the capitalist world market price of more than $11. The energy cooperation of the socialist countries, then, protected the oil-importing countries from the damaging consequences of a sudden big price increase (not to mention that it shields them from supply restrictions resulting from political or other reasons), and the change in prices, regarded as lasting, will be permitted to make its effect felt only gradually in the socialist trade. At the same time the Soviet Union showed its readiness to help by its willingness to give long-term and very favorable credits in 1975 and in the coming years as well to Hungary and the other socialist countries to solve the temporary problems of payments resulting from the price increases.

With regard to the future, it is expected that the high-level regional energy self-sufficiency of the CMEA community will remain, and integration in the CMEA energy economy will deepen further. Over the past few years, the meeting of energy and raw material demands by joint efforts has been a major concern in the cooperative planning of the CMEA countries. In the coming years, the time horizon of cooperation will widen, particularly in energy planning, since the member countries recognize that the solution to such common problems as energy supply requires long-range projection of fifteen to twenty rather than five years. (The member countries are making prognoses concerning anticipated energy demand until 1990 and 2000 and the possibilities for cooperation.)

The cooperation of member countries in the exploration and development of energy will increase further in the fields of atomic energy and other nontraditional sources of energy. To achieve this end the CMEA countries have already established several international organizations.

The Soviet Union will remain the main energy supplier of the member countries. The energy cooperation of the CMEA countries will in the future protect the member countries from the price fluctuations in the capitalist world market and from supply difficulties. The rise of energy costs will increasingly pressure the CMEA countries to move toward an energy-saving economic development as well.

The Role of Developing Countries in the Energy Supply of Hungary and the Other CMEA Countries

Although the European socialist countries tend to meet their energy demand through internal cooperation, their cooperation with the developing world is also gradually taking shape. In 1975 the CMEA countries purchased some 30 million tons of oil from the Middle East and North Africa. This quantity accounts for only 2 percent of the total energy consumption of the CMEA countries. By 1980, the oil imports of the CMEA countries from developing countries will probably double, and the share of nonsocialist oil imports in total energy consumption in some smaller countries like Hungary will be over 10 percent. As has been mentioned above, primarily due to the difference between the socialist and capitalist oil prices, the share of energy from developing countries in Hungary's total energy import in 1974 was 15.9 percent. After 1975, with the increase in socialist foreign trade prices, this share will decrease considerably.

With regard to the increasing Middle Eastern and North African imports, Yugoslavia, Hungary, and Czechoslovakia decided jointly to build the Adria oil pipeline to transport oil economically. The pipeline is expected to be complete in 1978. Of the 34 million tons of oil passing yearly through the pipeline, 24 million tons will go to Yugoslavia, 5 million to Czechoslovakia, and 5 million to Hungary.

The costs of energy imports from developing countries have increased considerably in recent years as shown by Table 5-6. In the summer of 1975,

Table 5-6
Trends in the Price Index in the Energy Import of Hungary (1970 = 100)

	Capitalist Countries	Socialist Countries	Total
1968	*	99.2	99.2
1969	*	98.8	98.8
1970	100	100	100
1971	120.8	102.7	103.6
1972	118.1	105.4	105.9
1973	175.5	107.4	109.7
1974	457.6	118.2	128.3

Source: *Külkereskedelmi Statisztikai Évkönyv 1974.*
*Turnover did not reach 0.5 percent of the total turnover of the commodity group.

Hungary purchased crude oil from developing countries at the average price of $90 per ton.

The socialist countries may begin to establish their relations with developing countries under favorable conditions, since power relations in the international capitalist oil industry have shifted to the advantage of developing countries and to the disadvantage of international monopolies. The CMEA countries tend to establish relations mainly with the state sector of the developing countries. Cooperation may range from the simple exchange of goods to joint enterprises. To achieve all this, the CMEA countries, especially the Soviet Union, are giving powerful support to and are participating in building up the national petroleum industry of several developing countries.

Prospects for East-West Energy Cooperation

Although energy trade between the European socialist and capitalist countries existed until the late 1960s it accounted for only 3.6 percent of the total energy consumption of Europe (except the Soviet Union).[2] In the past two decades two different and only slightly related energy systems have been formed on our continent: a West European system based mostly on oil imported from other continents, and a socialist system, traditionally based on coal, but gradually becoming organically intertwined with the oil and natural gas system of the Soviet Union.

Attempts to lessen the energy crisis afflicting the developed capitalist countries and the dependence on energy from other continents, as well as the demand for additional energy supplies, have understandably enhanced Western European interest in energy cooperation with the East European countries and have pushed to the fore inquiries regarding possibilities for a wider European cooperation.

In the East-West energy trade, Poland has been exporting significant amounts of coal for years. The Soviet Union is exporting oil to West European countries, and this trade can be expected to increase in the coming decades. Soviet oil export capacity will be limited by the fact that the largest Soviet oil fields are far from industrial centers, particularly from Europe and, in addition, are in places where building up the infrastructure requires considerable additional expenditure. Because of this, the increase in the quantity of oil flowing from the Soviet Union to Western Europe will be determined partly by the rate at which big pipelines can be built to transport it.

The cooperation in natural gas and electric energy supply deserves special attention from the aspect of East-West cooperation. It is well known that extremely good prospects are opened up for East-West energy cooperation by the Soviet plans foreseeing a large-scale transport of gas to Western Europe from Soviet reserves (mostly in Central Asia). Due to the increasing volume of European international gas transports and because the main gas pipelines pass through several countries, international cooperation will not consist simply of agreements between exporters and importers; it will be much more comprehensive. It is not unrealistic to suppose that in the long run this cooperation will lead to the construction of a *united European gas pipeline system*. It is therefore feasible to put the construction of an all-European uniform gas pipeline system on the agenda, and to work—with the collaboration of the European countries concerned—on outlining this system and then on the steps to be taken towards its implementation.

No organic relations between the electric energy systems of the socialist and capitalist countries have been established to date, and no high-capacity permanent connections have been made. Exchanges of electric energy of minor importance, however, have already taken place between certain members of the two systems (Hungary and Austria, Czechoslovakia and Austria, and Yugoslavia and her neighbors). It is likely that in the foreseeable future there will be a transmission line between Czechoslovakia and the Federal Republic of Germany and between East and West Germany.

The three largest electricity systems of Europe (the unified European part of the energy system of the Soviet Union, the UCPTE, and the unified system of the CMEA countries) are currently working separately. Calculations show that the larger the regions whose energy system becomes unified are, the larger are the savings. In addition, the safety of the electric energy systems increases, and more possibilities are available for mutual assistance. All this raises the question of the organic connection of East and West European electric energy systems. International reconciliation and establishment of the European Security System create favorable conditions for such a large, comprehensive European cooperation.

Economic considerations from the outset favor such immense all-European projects. According to estimates by the UN Economic Commission for Europe, the harmonization of electricity demand at the peak load periods at an all-European level would save about 10 percent in electric energy investments over the next decade.

Due to the endowments of both socialist and capitalist European countries, the possibility for energy exchange related to the seasons is of greater importance. Water-power plants in Western Europe can produce more energy in spring and autumn than is necessary to meet the demands of Western Europe. However, because of limited energy storage capacity, part of the water flows away unutilized. Therefore, with wider cooperation, water-power plants might work at full capacity, and the surplus energy could be taken up by the CMEA unified electric energy system. Thus in the seasons with abundant water, less fuel would be consumed in the CMEA countries where the greater part of electric energy is produced by heat power stations and where the fuel might be stored more easily. The West European energy system, on the other hand, would get back the electric energy in seasons poor in water, mainly at night, when the water basins could be refilled by operating the water-power plants at low capacity. Such an energy export would have a further advantage for the CMEA countries, too, since heat power plants would operate at higher capacity and electric energy production would be more efficient.

Cooperation between the electric energy systems could provide mutual assistance in the case of breakdowns. The volume of this assistance would not be large, but it would give a sense of security to industry and would make it possible to avoid restrictions or damage resulting from a lack of electricity or the breakdown of technological processes difficult to repair.

The agencies of the CMEA that take part in the work of the Electric Energy Committee of the Economic Commission for Europe are preparing studies on the feasibility of the unification of Eastern and Western energy systems, and will, in the future, do their best to realize this large-scale plan of cooperation.

In the opinion of the socialist countries, energy cooperation among European countries would be largely cooperation in research and development. Now these activities are being performed by the East and West European countries separately.

To summarize, the three most important fields for all-European energy cooperation are: (1) harmonization of plans for gas supply and building a uniform European gas pipeline system; (2) connection of regionally unified electric energy systems and, in the long range, the construction of a uniform European transmission line; and (3) analysis of long-range energy demands and cooperation both in widening the technological basis of energy production and in the exploration and utilization of new sources of energy, as well as in austerity measures for energy.

The favorable political atmosphere created by the European Conference on Security and Cooperation will certainly have a stimulating effect on the implementation of these large-scale cooperation projects. The final document of the Helsinki conference established

The participating countries,

... believing that their economic potentials and natural resources permit cooperation in the long range by the joint realization of large-scale projects they are mutually interested in, either in regional or subregional dimensions, and that these projects may further the acceleration of economic growth in the cooperating countries,

... think that the exploitation and processing of energy sources, particularly crude oil, natural gas, and coal, as well as mineral raw materials, particularly iron ore and bauxite, all prove to be a suitable field for strengthening long-term economic cooperation and, as a possible consequence of it, for developing trade;

... think that projects of common interest aimed at long-term economic cooperation are possible in the following fields.

Exchange of electric energy within Europe to exploit—in the most reasonable possible manner—the capacity of electric power plants;

... cooperation in exploring new sources of energy, particularly in the field of atomic energy. . . . [3]

Energy Policy and the Institutional Pattern of Energy Management

General Problems

In the latter half of the 1950s it became increasingly obvious to Hungary that energy was to play a key role in economic and social development. The need to organize the energy economy under a central management was just as clear. Government resolution No. 1044/1958 (December 9), issued in 1958, served this purpose. To this very day this government resolution and the decrees issued by the ministries under the authorization of the resolution are the key to the organization of the energy economy. [4]

Energy management is a subject involving all areas of the national economy using energy. Central management is the job of the Minister for Heavy Industry. He works through the National Authority for Energy Economy, a body operating under his jurisdiction and within the framework of the Ministry for Heavy Industry. The National Authority for Energy Economy, for the most part, handles management within the sector. However, since the Minister for Heavy Industry is responsible for the energy economy within the whole of the national economy, the work of the National Authority for Energy Economy really covers all areas where energy is used, no matter in what sector this may take place, and therefore its sphere of operations is also *functional*.

Within the present system of economic control and management, the major tasks of central sector management regarding energy are the elaboration of a national economy-wide plan for the energy economy to lay the foundations for implementation and coordinate the conditions required for execution of the general national economic development plans.

The National Authority for Energy Economy works *in cooperation* with the National Planning Office, the National Committee for Technical Development, and the National Materials and Price Office. National economic planning related to energy is within the authority of the National Planning Office, while development in the energy field together with product development research related to energy and energetics is coordinated by the National Committee for Technical Development; issues related to product turnover are under the jurisdiction of the National Materials and Price Office.

Working out energy policy objectives is broad technical and economic work; in other words, it is principally scientific analysis. Execution of the long-term energy policy principles approved by the Council of Ministers and aimed at by a system of economic regulators requires both direct intervention of an administrative nature and scientific analysis.

In addition to energy management tasks on the level of state theoretical guidance, there are also those concerned with the central economy and management, and some of these are the job of the administration. These are handled by the State Energetics and Energy Safety Technological Authority operating under the National Authority for Energy Economy.

All ministries (nationwide bodies of authority), trusts, and economic organs involved in energy management have energetics chiefs or energetics offices to handle energy management operations, while the executive committees of the Budapest Municipal Council, the county councils, and the rural municipal council delegate energy management to specialized council bodies maintained for this purpose. The sum of all this is the energetics organization.

In the socialist economies, including the Hungarian one, the long-term management of energy policy forms a part of general economic policy and is clearly a direct state task. Therefore, state management is directly responsible for the overall dimensions of prospective energy policy within the framework of the national economic plan, as well as for determining the quantities included in interstate import agreements and the signing of such agreements. As a part of this, determining the general structure of energy resources is also the job of the national economic plan. In general it may be said that state influence is particularly strong in those countries where a significant part of energy requirements are imported and/or the rapid transformation of the energy pattern is a definite objective.

State management is also responsible for determining the optimum composition of energy consumption and for determining and elaborating the measures through which the optimum can be achieved. This includes prescribing the energy resources to be used by large-scale consumers (stipulation is individual and irrespective of enterprise interest) and the formation of an economic environment that ensures that enterprise interests are also aimed at achieving a national economic optimum during the course of execution.

After forming an economic environment of the type required by the state, including the long- and medium-term development tasks and an optimum energy pattern, there are comparatively greater possibilities within the short-term energy supply system for the operation of "market" relations although these, too, are strongly and definitely limited. In the case of the few large users, which account for the decisive ratio of energy use, the market cannot function in any real way. (The prices of energy sources are determined administratively, while the types of demand are determined externally and for the most part rest on administrative decision, and so forth. It is not in the interests of the national economy to allow the market to operate more freely in this area. Decisions on large uses of energy are closely related to realizing energy policy objectives so decisions cannot be left to individual enterprises. But even in the areas other than the large-scale consumers, *the functioning of the market is limited and controlled.*

Since the decisive ratio of energy use in Hungary involves but a few consumers (e.g., roughly two-thirds of domestic coal is used by only three large-scale consumers), it is possible to regulate the overwhelming majority of the energy sector with comparatively few direct prescriptions. At the same time it is essential that the concepts and material interests of the ten to fifteen large-scale enterprises most influenced by the regulators be, to a certain extent, centrally coordinated with national economic interests.

Long- and medium-term energy policy concepts are elaborated regularly in Hungary's socialist national economy, as has already been mentioned. In Hungarian practice, the Ministry for Heavy Industry calls on the three large-scale sectors of energy production (coal, hydrocarbons, and electric energy—each of which operates within the framework of a single large trust) to present their proposals for an energy policy concept. Since the enterprises (trusts) are influenced decisively by long-term energy policy decisions, they try to keep approved energy policy concepts available so that they have sufficient information on which to base their own long-term decisions. However, the optimums of the various subsectors do not necessarily result in a national economic optimum. For this reason the initiatives taken by the enterprises (trusts) are controlled through the National Committee for Technical Development, the various research institutes, and the functional bodies (National Planning Office, Ministry of Finance). There are also consultations on an international scale to determine the quantity and composition of energy which can be imported in the given period. Since the country is highly dependent on imports, the energy policy concept cannot be completed without data on energy sources available for import. The draft concept of energy policy is subject to the criticism of the Energy Policy Council, which serves as a means of social control, and the State Planning Committee. Once the energy policy concept is fully elaborated and prepared in final form, the actual decision on acceptance is made by the government.

The Energy Management System Prior to 1968:
The Old System of General Economic Management

The role of management in the energy economy is to ensure the continuous and full satisfaction of domestic demands within an optimum pattern based on the economy, technical requirements, way of life, and environmental protection. In a socialist economy a management activity this comprehensive in nature is clearly the job of the state.

Energy management, by its very nature, was an organic part of national economic planning. On the basis of national economic balances, the plan determined production, imports, and available resources and divided the energy among the user enterprises, the portfolios, and exports. The balances were, therefore, also administrative means of distribution. In addition, the plan determined the funds that the energy user enterprises could devote to the energy sources needed for their activities, which were also stipulated in the plan. In this case, a turnover system based on the supply plan, broken down into details and using quotas, was used.

The role of the National Planning Office was to handle national economic planning of the energy sector. The nationwide energy balances were prepared by the National Planning Office that thereby determined the main lines for producing basic energy resources, as well as their distribution, turnover, use, and inventories, while it also marked out the energy management tasks for the different national economic sectors. Organizing the execution of the annual and quarterly plans prepared by the National Planning Office and approved by the government and managing the country's energy economy was the job of the Ministry for Heavy Industry (more precisely, the National Authority for Energy Economy operating within the ministry). As the central manager of the country's energy economy, the National Authority for Energy Economy coordinated the control and supervision of planned management with the types of energy and also handled some of the direct execution.

The system of operative management in the pre-1968 energy economy had the following *advantages:*

1. Professional management of enterprise energy economy ensured taking national economic interests into consideration.
2. Energy management was centralized on a national economy scale and therefore the resources could also be centralized.
3. Detailed and full-scale information was rapidly available for preparing decisions. Management built up an information network with the organizational units on all levels of the economy and management.
4. Central decisions could be made to dissolve tension as it appeared, which made possible the ranking of demands to correspond to national economic interests.

5. Comparatively little time elapsed between decision making and practical execution. The decisions were of a directive nature, to be executed immediately.

The above advantages were accompanied by the following *disadvantages:*

1. There was no direct relationship between the producers, the distributors, and the users. Therefore, they were not sufficiently acquainted with one another's possibilities and requirements.
2. Centralization was exaggerated and central decisions were also required on comparatively unimportant issues. The exaggerated centralization also meant that there could be no satisfactory operation of material interests, individual responsibility, or risk-taking for either producer, distributor, or consumer.
3. Management was too rigid. It concentrated on detail. As a result, activities to influence the production and use pattern or to regulate the process became neglected.
4. The economy and efficiency aspects were almost forgotten, or at least, they did not operate in a satisfactory manner.

In other words, the pre-1968 system of the energy economy was fundamentally centralized, corresponding to the general system of economic control and management of that time. In addition, the chronic shortage of energy the Hungarian national economy suffered until the mid-1960s led to increased application of the methods of central management in the energy supply.[5]

The System of Energy Economy under the New Management System

By the middle of the third Five-Year Plan period (1966-1970) it became possible to end the "shortage economy" in energy. From 1966 on, energy resource possibilities were constantly in excess of demand, thereby making it possible to include energy when introducing *the indirect ways and means of economic regulation* in the new system of economic control and management in 1968. The new features in energy supply made it possible for socialist market relations to play a greater role together with direct contacts and agreements between producers and consumers.

Of course, the central planning organs of the national economy continue to elaborate the prospective development objectives and the main lines of development for the different sectors according to the national economic plans prepared under the conditions of the new economic mechanism. However, tasks are not broken down into compulsory plan indices for the different economic units.

Instead, elaboration and application of those means of economic regulation that fully ensure the realization of the targets under the conditions of the new economic mechanism have become the criteria of guidance.

In energy turnover, administrative restrictions and forced channels of distribution were ended. This change not only means that the system of quotas for energy sources was ended but also that detailed observation and evaluation of the processes were reduced. With the exception of concepts related to prospective development, the significant part of decisions on energetics have for all practical purposes been shifted to the enterprise spheres of authority. Due to the fundamentally unrestricted nature of distribution, the reform assumed that in certain areas it would be necessary to maintain administrative prescriptions. These included satisfaction of demands by the population, and to prevent disequilibrium, measures basically affecting the balance of payments. Although socialist organizations (such as enterprises) may sell energy sources to any other socialist organization, for national economic considerations the Council of Ministers has the authority to regulate product turnover within a definite sphere.[6] The means of regulation are the following:

1. *Central management*, which controls the full-scale distribution of a product among the users by taking into consideration both resources and demands (the supplier takes on an obligation by contract, and a specific supplier can only make sales to a specific buyer and only up to the amount determined by contract);
2. *Quota prescriptions*, which determine the quantity of a product that may be procured or the quantity that can be sold to a specific sphere of buyers;
3. *Stipulation of the realization body*, when the products may only be distributed on the domestic market by stipulated bodies and can only be procured by the users from that specific body;
4. *Contract obligation prescriptions*, when the supplier may only refuse to undertake a contract if it can prove that it would be incapable of meeting it, or if signing such a contract were opposed to the interests of the national economy;
5. *Prescriptions on inventory level*, in which the stipulated users can be obliged to maintain certain inventory levels of certain definite products to ensure disturbance-free product turnover.

Energy Policy Decisions under the New Energy Situation in Hungary

Although the rise in energy prices in the last years did not affect Hungary's economy as seriously as the economies of the advanced capitalist countries, it still does not mean that changes in the world's energy economy would not influence Hungarian economic policy. First of all, the degree of centralization of energy decision making has been increased rather substantially. There is a general policy goal to lower the rate of growth of energy demand. To achieve this, important changes have been introduced into the energy price structure (to favor the use of coal and natural gas), and the role of the administrative quota system in the energy supply has been greatly increased.

As an effect of the rise of energy prices (and generally of the rise of raw material prices), a partial *producer's price adjustment* was made on January 1, 1975, by which domestic producers' prices were adjusted to foreign trade prices. It was simply impossible to evade the price problem. A price that is wrong will give rise to erroneous decisions at both the micro and macro levels. A structural policy that keeps international competitiveness and rational energy thrift in view and an export policy that deals realistically with foreign terms of trade can only be conducted in an economically well-determined price system.

In the new situation, energy conservation has come to the fore, and thus the Hungarian government has obliged the companies to work out a plan of energy (and raw material) austerity measures. To this end, the government issued general directives that make clear to the companies that there is no need for falsifying results, and savings that are harmful to the national economy are to be avoided. The government's decisions on energy austerity included several other measures, too (e.g., revision of the energy economy of the 500 most significant gas and fuel oil consumers, removal of automobiles in poor condition from the road, organization of central dispatching offices to lessen empty runs of trucks, and so forth).

The energy troubles of the Hungarian economic policy, however, are related to future development and the orientation of development; therefore they are the troubles of the late 1970s. This situation justified the elaboration of a medium-range raw material and energy policy conception as an organic part of the Fifth Five-Year Plan (1976-1980). The Fifth Five-Year Plan is the first to assign energy saving a high priority as a research and development task to the sector-specific research institutes.

The future will answer three particularly important questions: (1) From what structural and import sources can increasing energy demands be met? (2) What price effects can be expected, and how can we deal with these effects? (3) What changes will be necessary in the structure of production?

As regards the first question it can be established that the increase in energy consumption in the next ten to fifteen years cannot be lower than 4 percent, and the increase in electric energy consumption cannot be lower than 6.5 percent to 7.0 percent per year. On the other hand, it can be taken for granted that the share of energy imports will rise from the present nearly 50 percent to a minimum of 66 percent in six years, and in fifteen to sixteen years it will be in the vicinity of 70 percent. Considering Hungary's present level and rate of development, the most dynamic development can be expected in fuel oil consumption that will increase at a rate 2.5 times more rapid than the total energy consumption. In the field of energy imports from the CMEA countries, the strongly trade-oriented nature of the present cooperation will change and will be shifted to the sphere of integrated production (investment) cooperation. In addition, Hungary will also make efforts to develop cooperation with the energy-exporting developing countries under mutually favorable conditions.

As to the second question, the traditional energy structure will certainly have to be modified to the advantage of the solid fuels—beginning with the production of electricity. The increased prices of hydrocarbons throw a new light on the economic efficiency of Hungarian coal mining, too. In spite of this, due to the limits of the country's economically exploitable coal reserves and to manpower shortages, increased coal consumption cannot be seriously expected. Lignite mining and deep working (of which only lignite production is growing) can jointly ensure the long-range achievement of a power plant performance of 4,000 to 5,000 MW. Hungarian long-range energy policy relies primarily on atomic and coal energy in developing electric energy plants. Atomic energy, which will certainly play a leading role in the long-range plans of the energy structure, will not yet offer a complete solution in the coming decade mainly because of the technological problems of its implementation. Therefore, in the next decade, coal energy should be utilized to a larger extent than was anticipated a few years ago.

The new world market prices of hydrocarbons modify not only the value system of the domestic energy structure, but also the industrial production costs—the degree of which varies from one sector to another. Since in present industrial production we have certain technological reserves as regards energy consumption, part of the effect of rising prices will be counterbalanced by a speed-up of technological development. Accordingly, technological development serving energy conservation will be given priority in our technological development policy.

The third question is related to the change in the structure of production. The structure of production in the Hungarian economy is highly energy intensive and is not in harmony with the country's natural endowments. The energy intensiveness of production is partly responsible for the large specific energy consumption. One goal of the structural transformation of industrial production, therefore, will be a growth rate of the energy-intensive sectors (except, naturally, the chemical industry) that will be slower than the average. This goal will be emphasized in the Fifth Five-Year Plan, and later, too, a production structure ensuring a decrease in the specific energy (and raw material) consumption and technological development will be one basic ordering principle of the Hungarian economic development policy. It has become essential to abandon uneconomical activities and to limit production or its growth rate in some places, thus saving expensive energy and raw materials and freeing manpower.

The transformation of the production structure is made imperative by the fact that under present world market price conditions, the export of finished and semifinished products based on the utilization of imported energy and raw material has become less economically viable. This situation arises because prices of raw materials and energy on the world market are rising at a more rapid rate than those of semifinished and finished goods. Hungary, therefore, is continuing central development programs and reconstructions at an accelerated rate and devoting more energy to building up as soon as possible a vertically integrated production in aluminum, petrochemicals, and other branches that will enable the country to turn available raw materials and energy into products representing more value and work. For a country lacking energy (and raw materials)—thus for Hungary—it may be advantageous to develop the production and export of sophisticated high-quality products, based on imported raw material and energy, provided they can be produced effectively and competitively.

Summary

In the planned socialist economy of Hungary, energy planning forms an important organic element of general economic planning. For some fifteen years, investigations of optimum long-range energy supply have been continuously carried on in Hungary. In this chapter, a model serving optimum investigation is demonstrated in a simple form, and some findings of investigations carried out so far are outlined.

Hungary is very poor in economically exploitable energy. With the structure of energy demand transformed, coal production has gradually decreased since 1965. The greater part of the coal produced is lignite, which is of low heating value. In the new energy situation, the downward trend of coal production will stop and the trend will begin to rise again in a few years. Oil production in Hungary can provide slightly more than one-fifth of the country's requirements and has become stabilized at the level of two million tons per year. Since the late 1960s, natural gas production has developed vigorously, but it will not be able to meet the domestic demand in the future. As a result of the rapid increase in the demand for electric energy, the electric energy industry is developing rapidly. In 1974 the construction of the country's first nuclear power plant began, and a significant increase in the future quantity of electricity produced by nuclear power plants is anticipated.

The increase in energy consumption has slowed down since the second half of the 1960s. Between 1970 and 1975, a 1 percent increase in the national income was achieved by a 0.75 percent increase in energy consumption. According to international experiences, under Hungarian economic conditions this ratio can be regarded as favorable. The transformation of the energy balance has accelerated since 1965, but the switchover to hydrocarbons was taking place at a rate higher than desirable.

Almost half of the present energy consumption of Hungary is being provided by imports, and dependence on imports will significantly increase in the future. The majority of energy imports comes from the Soviet Union. In 1974, the share of developing countries in imports suddenly increased as a result of the difference between the socialist and capitalist energy prices.

Hungary is vigorously participating in the international energy cooperation of the CMEA countries. International socialist economic integration has come into full play in the energy supply of the member countries. This fact is shown by a number of important integrative projects. The integrative production (investment) cooperation of the member countries has recently become more intense in the interests of developing the export-oriented energy capacities of the energy-exporting member countries (of the Soviet Union primarily). The socialist foreign trade prices of energy ensure the relative stability and elasticity of prices. Changes in world market prices, which are expected to be lasting, are only gradually introduced by the socialist countries in their mutual trade in modified form. This arrangement protects the energy-importing countries from the damaging effects of a sudden large-scale price rise. In the coming years, the time horizon for the cooperation of the member countries will widen since the joint planning for energy supply requires a fifteen- to twenty-year rather than a five-year planning time.

The role of the developing countries in the energy supply of the CMEA countries, in sharp contrast with the advanced capitalist countries, is only marginal, although in the future their significance in our supply will increase to some extent. The CMEA countries establish relations mainly with the state sector of the developing countries.

East-West cooperation in the field of energy is still of marginal importance. In the past two decades two different and only slightly related energy systems have been set up in our continent. Within an all-European energy cooperation, real development can be expected in the following three fields: construction of a uniform European gas pipeline system, connection of the regionally unified electric energy systems, and in the long range, the development of a uniform European transmission line system and cooperation in research and development in energy.

Regarding the institutional setup of the energy management system, in the socialist Hungarian economy the comprehensive, long-term management of energy policy, as a part of general economic policy, is clearly a direct state task. The state influence has been particularly strong in Hungary, since a significant part of energy requirements is imported and the rapid transformation of the energy pattern has been a definite objective. In the field of energy, the functioning of the market is limited and controlled. The energy management system prior to 1968 was highly centralized and corresponded to the general system of economic control and management of that time. The new system of economic control and management, introduced in 1968, has made it possible for *socialist market relations to play a greater role* together with direct contacts and agreements between producers and consumers. In the new energy situation of the last few years, the degree of centralization of energy decision making has been increased rather substantially, and there is a general policy line to lower the rate of growth of energy demand. Demand management has gotten more attention than before.

Radical changes taking place recently in the world energy economy have had an effect on Hungary's energy economy, too, although not as severe as in the advanced capitalist countries. Due to the new international energy situation, some modifications had to be made in Hungary's energy policy conception determining the operative long-term tasks that would lessen the costs of energy supply. Comprehensive measures were taken to save energy. Measures were taken to effect the utilization of coal-fed plants to the largest technologically possible extent. The previous energy structure had to be modified to some extent to favor primarily solid fuels in electric energy production. Hungary's long-range energy policy relies primarily on coal and on atomic energy for the development of electric power plants. Part of the effect of rising costs for hydrocarbons will be counterbalanced by the acceleration of technological development. Modifications are to be made in the structure of production so that the growth rate of energy-intensive sectors will be slower than the average. Hungary will devote more energy to building up vertically integrated production in several branches of industry, which will thus enable the country to turn available raw materials and energy into sophisticated, competitive products representing more value and work. Energy saving in all branches of the national economy is regarded as a highly important long-term task. To achieve this end, the government is giving significant central support.

Notes

1. In elaborating this part, the author has relied on a study by P. Erdös, T. Füredi, and P. Ligeti, "Uj eljárások az energiaellátás távlati tervezésében és optimalizálásában" (New Procedures in the Long-Range Planning and Optimization of Energy Supply), *Energiagazdálkodás*, no. 6 (1970).

2. J. Szita, head of the Secretariat of the Hungarian International Economic Relations, gives an excellent survey of the East-West energy cooperation in his monograph, *Az összeurópai gazdasági együttmüködés távlatai* (Prospects of the All-European Economic Cooperation), (Budapest: Kossuth Publication House, 1975), which was heavily used in preparing this part of this chapter.

3. *Final Act*, Conference on Security and Cooperation in Europe, Helsinki, August 1, 1975.

4. L. Bódi, "Az energiagazdálkodás és jogi rendje. 1" (Energy Economy and Its Legal Order, Part 1), *Energiagazdálkodás*, no. 1 (1976).

5. *Energiagazdálkodásunk időszerü kérdései* (Topical Issues in the Energy Economy), written and compiled by a team of authors within the Ministry for Heavy Industry (Budapest: Kossuth Publication House, 1969), p. 50.

6. See L. Bódi, "Az energiagazdálkodás," p. 31.

Alternative Development Strategies with a Low Energy Profile for a Low GNP/Capita Energy-Poor Country: The Case of India

T.L. Sankar

The objective of this chapter is to explore the factors that determine the supply and demand schedules of the energy equation in a country with a low per capita GNP and relatively poor energy resources. The case of India will be examined in detail with a view toward drawing certain conclusions that might be of relevance to all poor countries with similar energy resources. In so doing, we recognize that the trends in energy consumption are determined not merely by the levels of production of goods and services and the relative price of different fuels, population dynamics, and technological changes, but also by the complex interplay of government policies, institutions, and agencies concerned with the planning and production of different fuels and related matters. The study will include an analysis of the consumption trends not only of coal, oil, and electricity, but also of cow dung and firewood and energy consumed in the form of animate energy (the last is a form of energy normally neglected in such studies).

The chapter is in four sections. In the first section, the trends in energy consumption in India during the past two decades are broadly surveyed, the energy-GNP relationships are analyzed, and the important changes in the trends are identified. The second section contains an analysis of the manner in which the different agencies concerned with the planning, production, and distribution of different energy forms interact and influence the formalization of energy plans. The third section attempts to explore the extent to which the analysis of the agencies and their interactions can help us to understand the major shifts in energy consumption trends identified in the first section. The fourth section seeks to forecast, in the light of the analysis in the first three sections, alternative patterns of energy growth with an examination of the critical factors that could shift the development towards a low-energy growth profile.

Trends in Energy Consumption in India

In India, even in 1975, almost half of the total energy consumed in the economy was in the form of forest fuels, animal waste (dung cake), and vegetable waste. The rest of the fuel-derived energy is obtained in the form of coal, oil products, or electricity. The former category of fuels is called noncommercial fuel and the latter, commercial fuel. Besides these, a significant share of energy consumed in the rural sector is derived from animate power for which very little quantitative information is available. We shall first analyze the data on commercial and noncommercial energy and then examine the available information on animate power to add to our understanding of the Indian energy situation.

Table 6-1 shows energy consumption by type of fuel in India from 1953-54 to 1970-71. As the different fuels vary in their energy content, the coal equivalent[a] measure has been used to present the consumption data in a comparable form and to aggregate the total energy consumption. The specific fuel consumption in original units and the conversion factors used in deriving the table are described in Appendix Tables 6A-1 and 6A-2.

The significance of noncommercial fuels in India's total energy consumption has been steadily declining over the years as can be seen from Table 6-2.

There has been no serious attempt to quantify the animate energy still used in large quantities in India. Even the Fuel Policy Committee (1974), which made a very detailed analysis of the energy situation in India, merely stated:

In addition, mechanical energy derived from animal power and man-power used for drawing water and ploughing is also used in significant quantity. No records of the quantum of such utilisation are available.[1]

Since the studies have been concerned with the use of fossil fuels and electricity, the researchers could afford, to some extent, to neglect the implications of the widespread use of animate energy. On the other hand, this chapter, which seeks to explore the possibilities of changes in lifestyle and a low-energy growth profile has to take the use of animal power into consideration. Based on the Planning Commission assessment that the quantity of animate power used in 1960-61 was on the order of 76 million tons of coal equivalent and on detailed information on the working bovine population in the Livestock Census, we have

---

[a]Almost all energy studies relating to India have adopted the coal replacement ton as the common measurement for energy. This scale was first adopted in the *Report of the Energy Survey Committee* of 1965 (for details, see pp. 322-29 of this report). The coal replacement ton is the amount of coal that would have been needed in the economy if no other source of energy were available. In other words, the coal replacement measure indicates the quantity of coal that would be needed to substitute for other fuels taking account of the efficiencies in typical cases of substitution. But in all energy studies relating to other countries the coal equivalent measure is used. UN energy statistics are given in that measure. The coal replacement measure makes it difficult to compare the findings of this chapter with papers regarding other countries that may be discussing energy trends in coal equivalent measures. At the same time, the adoption of coal equivalent measures for noncommercial fuels would give a distorted picture of energy use in India vis-à-vis energy use in countries without significant quantities of noncommercial fuels. If noncommercial fuels were not available in India, the amount of commercial fuel that would be used in their place would be given by the coal replacement measure. I have therefore adopted the coal replacement measurements for noncommercial fuels and the coal equivalent measurements for commercial fuels. Adoption of this unorthodox scale for energy measurement, in my view, presents the energy situation of the developing countries in a form that can be compared with that of developed countries. For those who like to examine the data purely in terms of coal equivalent or coal replacement measures, the conversion factors and the basis for deriving these factors are explained in Appendix B.

Table 6-1
Consumption of Energy in India, 1953-54 to 1970-71 (mtce)

| | Commercial Energy | | | | Noncommercial Energy | | | | Grand |
Year	Coal	Oil	Electricity	Total	Dung	Firewood	Vegetable Waste	Total	Grand Total
1953-54	28.70	7.33	7.60	43.63	18.60	82.20	25.10	125.90	169.53
1954-55	28.50	7.92	8.40	44.82	19.10	83.30	25.60	128.00	172.82
1955-56	28.80	9.33	9.40	47.53	19.60	84.40	26.30	130.30	177.83
1956-57	30.70	9.34	10.20	50.24	20.10	85.60	27.00	132.70	182.94
1957-58	34.60	10.44	11.80	56.84	20.60	86.90	27.70	135.20	192.04
1958-59	36.10	11.11	13.20	00.41	21.10	88.50	23.40	137.80	100.21
1959-60	35.70	12.33	15.40	63.43	21.30	91.70	28.70	141.70	205.13
1960-61	40.40	13.48	16.90	70.78	22.15	95.99	29.53	147.67	218.45
1961-62	44.10	14.93	19.37	78.40	22.44	97.27	29.93	149.64	228.04
1962-63	49.10	16.78	22.57	88.45	22.70	98.40	30.28	151.38	239.83
1963-64	48.60	17.30	25.21	91.11	23.43	101.54	31.25	156.22	247.33
1964-65	48.20	18.58	27.76	94.64	23.72	102.78	31.62	158.12	252.76
1965-66	51.80	19.88	30.56	102.24	24.51	106.23	32.69	163.43	265.67
1966-67	52.30	21.25	33.21	106.76	25.04	108.50	33.38	166.92	273.68
1967-68	54.50	22.57	36.76	113.83	25.63	111.07	34.17	170.87	284.70
1968-69	53.00	25.32	41.46	119.78	25.99	112.61	34.64	173.24	293.02
1969-70	56.66	27.71	45.02	129.39	26.37	114.24	35.15	175.76	305.15
1970-71	51.35	29.90	48.65	129.90	26.91	116.62	35.88	179.41	309.31

Source: Computed from Table 6A-2.

made a rough computation of the likely magnitudes of animate energy used in India in selected years from 1953-54 to 1970-71.[2] These results, along with the levels of commercial and noncommercial energy use are set out in Table 6-3.

As can be seen in Table 6-4, animate energy contributed nearly 27 percent of all energy consumption in 1953-54, and although it is slowly declining in importance it still contributed 20 percent in 1970-71. It is noteworthy that since 1960-61, the amount of energy contribution by animal power has remained constant. The reason is because the working bovine population tended to level off at around 80 million throughout the 1960s, which probably represents the maximum cattle population that can be supported with the available land and fodder resources. The amount of noncommercial energy consumed has slowly increased during the last two decades, though its share in total energy consumption has steadily declined.

Relative Importance of Coal, Oil, and Electricity

The share of commercial energy in total energy consumption has steadily increased during the last two decades. It is interesting to examine the change in

208

Table 6-2

Relative Share of Commercial and Noncommercial Energy in India, 1953-54 to 1970-71 (percent)

	1953-54	1960-61	1965-66	1970-71
Commercial Energy	25.7	32.4	38.5	42.0
Noncommercial Energy	74.3	67.6	61.5	58.0
Total	100	100	100	100

Source: Computed from Table 6-1.

Note: Data is based on coal equivalent measures. The noncommercial energy is used almost exclusively in the domestic sector. Some available waste is still being used in the mining and manufacturing sector, such as the use of begasse in sugar factories, but the quantity is negligible when compared to the total energy used in industry. It has therefore not been taken into account.

the relative importance of commercial fuels. The relative share of the different fuels consumed is given in Table 6-5.

The relative share of coal declined steadily during the period 1953-54 to 1970-71 while the share of oil and electricity increased very rapidly. This is in keeping with the general trend in most countries in the world, both developed and developing, the exceptions being a few centrally planned economies. During this period, the average compound rate of growth of consumption for different fuels, as well as growth during different sub-periods, may be seen in Table 6-6.

The rate of growth of coal consumption declined sharply since 1965-66. The rate of oil consumption steadily increased during each subperiod, while electricity consumption increased during the subperiods up to 1965-66 and then declined somewhat. It is interesting that in the period 1965-1970, when the growth rate of total commercial energy declined to 4.9 percent (as compared to over 7 percent in earlier periods), the rate of growth for electricity declined proportionately but the growth rate of oil consumption increased.

The factors that influence the rate of consumption for different fuels in the economy could be analyzed by breaking up the data for specific fuel consump-

Table 6-3

Consumption of Commercial, Noncommercial, and Animate Energy in India, 1953-54 to 1970-71 (mtce)

	1953-54	1960-61	1965-66	1970-71
Commercial Energy	43.63	70.78	102.24	129.90
Noncommercial Energy	125.90	147.67	163.43	179.41
Animate Energy	65.15	76.00	76.90	77.81
Total	234.68	294.45	342.57	387.12

Table 6-4
Relative Share of Commercial, Noncommercial, and Animate Energy in India,
1953-54 to 1970-71 (percent)

	1953-54	1960-61	1965-66	1970-71
Commercial Energy	18.6	24.0	29.8	33.6
Noncommercial Energy	53.6	50.2	47.7	46.3
Animate Energy	27.8	25.8	22.5	20.1
Total	100.0	100.0	100.0	100.0

tion in different periods by sector. The rate of growth of total commercial energy consumption is taken as 100 and the index of growth rates for other fuels has been calculated for different subperiods and presented in Table 6-7. Details of sectoral fuel consumption for each year are given in Appendix Table 6A-3.

In the domestic sector, the share of electricity is rapidly increasing as the rate of growth is much higher for electricity consumption than for all other forms of commercial energy. Oil appears not only to be retaining its share but slowly increasing it. There appears to be a greater relationship between the use of coal and oil in the domestic sector than between electricity and other fuels.

In the agriculture sector, coal consumption has been negligible; electricity has been the major commercial energy over the two decades. The growth rate of oil during the period after 1965 shows a sudden drop. The yearly consumption of oil in agriculture reveals that oil consumption increased rapidly up to 1968-69 but declined sharply in 1969-70 and 1970-71. In the agricultural sector diesel pumps are used to lift water from wells; the need for pumped water goes up in years of monsoon failures, while it goes down sharply in years with good rainfall. The years 1969-70 and 1970-71 were years of good monsoon. No great importance can be attached, therefore, to the decline of oil consumption in agriculture during the subperiod 1965-66 to 1970-71.

In the mining and manufacturing sector, in keeping with the general trend, the importance of coal in incremental energy consumption declined gradually up to 1965 and sharply in the period 1965-66 to 1970-71.

In the transport sector, oil was the major source of rapidly increasing energy needs during all the subperiods, and the relative importance of oil in transporta-

Table 6-5
Commercial Fuel Consumption (percent)

Fuel	1953-54	1960-61	1965-66	1970-71
Coal (Direct Use)	65.8	57.1	50.7	39.5
Oil (Direct Use)	16.8	19.0	19.4	23.0
Electricity	17.4	23.9	29.9	37.5
Total	100.0	100.0	100.0	100.0

Table 6-6
Average Annual Rate of Growth of Fuel Consumption (percent/year)

Fuel	1953-54 to 1960-61	1960-61 to 1965-66	1965-66 to 1970-71	1953-54 to 1970-71
Coal	5.0	5.1	0.1	3.4
Oil	7.7	8.0	8.5	8.6
Electricity	12.0	12.5	9.7	11.5
Total Commercial Energy	7.2	7.6	4.9	6.6

tion has steadily increased; the importance of coal in the transport sector has steadily declined.

Energy GNP Relationship

During the period 1953-54 to 1970-71 the gross national product in India increased at an annual combined energy rate of 3.9 percent while commercial energy consumption increased at a rate of 6.6 percent. The intensity of energy consumption, defined as the consumption of energy (in million tons of coal equivalent) per unit of production (in billion rupees of GNP), increased significantly over this period if commercial energy alone is considered. This conclusion is emphasized in most studies. If, however, we add noncommercial energy, we find that the average increase in total energy consumption was only 3.60 percent. The intensity of total energy consumption has not increased but

Table 6-7
Index of Rate of Growth of Fuel Consumption by Sector

Sector	Period	Total Commercial Energy	Coal	Oil	Electricity
Domestic and Others	1953-60	100	46	110	153
	1960-65	100	93	94	114
	1965-70	100	-2	129	136
Agriculture	1953-60	100	–	60	169
	1960-65	100	–	69	128
	1965-70	100	–	3	150
Mining and Manufacturing	1953-60	100	74	124	155
	1960-65	100	78	24	147
	1965-70	100	14	136	194
Transport	1953-60	100	77	192	79
	1960-65	100	32	257	158
	1965-70	100	-65	336	167

has, in fact, slightly diminished. The fuel intensity of energy consumption over time is exhibited in Figure 6-1.

It would be more interesting to see how the intensity of energy use has changed in different periods within each sector. The data relating to sectoral income in different years and the consumption of commercial fuels in each sector is given in Appendix Table 6A-3. From this table the intensity of commercial energy in different sectors has been computed and is given in Table 6-8. Adding noncommercial energy and animate energy to this data provides information on intensity of all energy use by sector during selected years as given in Table 6-9.

When computed only in terms of commercial energy, the intensity of energy use appears to have increased sharply in agriculture and less in the domestic sector and the mining and manufacturing sector. In the transport sector, where fuel is a major element in the cost of transportation, improvements in efficiency may explain the tendency for the intensity of fuel use to decline. When all sources of energy supply are taken into account, we find that in all sectors the intensity of energy use has declined, probably due to the greater efficiency of

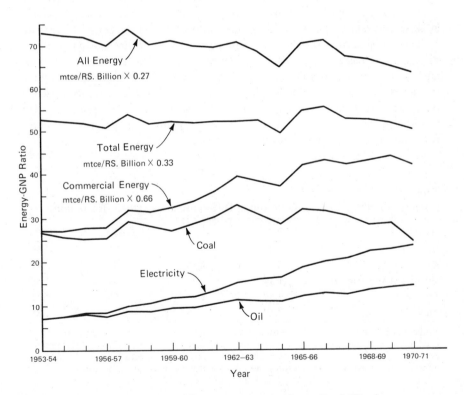

Figure 6-1. Energy-GNP Ratios in India (mtce Rs./billion).

Table 6-8

Commercial Energy Used per Unit of GNP in Different Economic Sectors in India, 1953-54 to 1970-71 (mtce/Rs. billion)

Sector	1953-54	1960-61	1965-66	1970-71
Domestic and Others	0.30	0.35	0.35	0.42
Agriculture	0.01	0.02	0.05	0.07
Mining and Manufacturing	1.14	1.21	1.34	1.39
Transport	3.56	3.22	3.02	2.76
Total	0.41	0.50	0.63	0.63

the modern (commercial) sources of energy over traditional sources of energy. In industry, increasing complexity and sophistication of products may account for the slow and steady increase in the intensity of energy use.

The intensity of commercial energy consumption by sector, fuel, and year would reveal the varying relative importance of coal, oil, and electricity in the different sectors of the economy. The results of such an analysis are given in Table 6-10. The table shows that the intensity of coal use has steadily declined in all sectors and that the rate of decline was very fast in the period 1965-66 to 1970-71 in all sectors, while in the period 1960-65, its decline was steep only in the transport sector. Intensity of oil use has increased in all sectors, but most rapidly in the transport sector. Surprisingly, the change in the intensity of oil use in mining and manufacturing has been the least. Intensity of electricity used in transport has declined over time but in all other sectors it has increased.

The major conclusions that emerge from the survey of past energy consumption data are the following:

Table 6-9

Intensity of all Energy Consumption in Different Sectors (mtce/Rs. billion)

Sector	1953-54	1960-61	1965-66	1970-71
Domestic	5.27	4.56	3.97	3.66
Agriculture	0.88	0.89	0.96	0.77
Mining and Manufacturing	1.14	1.21	1.34	1.39
Transport	6.57	5.44	4.68	4.11
All Sectors	2.19	2.09	2.11	1.88

Note: Noncommercial energy is assumed to be fully used in the domestic sector. Of the total animate energy, 20 percent is assumed to be used for transport (based on limited data available from certain farm management studies like *Farm Management Study: Ferozpur* published by Ministry of Agriculture) and 80 percent in the agricultural sector.

Table 6-10
Intensity of Commercial Fuel Consumption by Sector (mtce/Rs. billion)

Sectors	Fuels	1953-54	1960-61	1965-66	1970-71
Domestic and Others	Coal	0.11	0.10	0.10	0.08
	Oil	0.12	0.14	0.14	0.19
	Electricity	0.07	0.11	0.11	0.15
Agriculture	Coal	–	–	–	–
	Oil	0.01	0.01	0.02	0.02
	Electricity	0.003	0.01	0.03	0.05
Mining and Manufacturing	Coal	0.79	0.73	0.73	0.63
	Oil	0.06	0.08	0.06	0.07
	Electricity	0.29	0.40	0.55	0.69
Transport	Coal	2.79	2.33	1.86	1.38
	Oil	0.62	0.78	1.04	1.26
	Electricity	0.14	0.12	0.12	0.12

1. In India, commercial energy is still a minor contributor to the total energy needs of the economy. Noncommercial fuels and animal power still contribute the major share of energy needs, though their share is steadily declining.
2. With regard to animate energy, there appears to be a peak beyond which the supply cannot be increased; in India, this limit seems to have been reached in the sixties.
3. Noncommercial energy is still increasing in quantity, though its importance relative to commercial fuels is rapidly declining.
4. In India, the quantity of *all energy* used per unit increase in GNP has not changed while that of commercial energy used per unit of GNP has increased. The modern sector of the economy is still a small part of the total economy.
5. Among commercial fuels, the importance of electricity appears to increase steadily in all sectors and this increase seems to be independent of the consumption of other fuels.
6. The rates of growth of coal and oil seem to be closely linked.
7. In India, the period from 1960-61 was characterized by an increase in oil consumption at the expense of coal, and this tendency was accelerated in the period 1965-66 to 1970-71.
8. The increase in the intensity of oil consumption in the transport sector and that of electricity consumption in the agriculture sector deserve attention.

Agencies in Energy Planning and Production

In India, economic development is "planned" by the central government in consultation with the governments of the states that comprise the Indian Union.

In the Five Year Plans, the Planning Commission, after examining several possible rates and patterns of economic growth, indicates the one preferred for the plan period and sets out the policies of the government and the investment and production schedule in public sector undertakings and also the "anticipated" investment and production in the private sector. "The private sector has to function, of course, within the framework of national planning and in harmony with its overall aims and there must be continuous stress on undertakings in the private sector acting with an understanding of the obligations towards the community as a whole."[3] The Planning Commission which formulates the Five Year Plans is headed by the prime minister.

With energy being an important input in all productive activities, the plans to produce adequate energy from appropriate fuels to sustain the expected rate and pattern of growth are specified in each Five Year Plan. On the face of it, the Planning Commission appears to be the sole agency that determines the energy plan.

The views of the Planning Commission on energy production in each plan period are shaped by the interaction of various agencies concerned with the different stages of fuel production, transportation, and distribution. Besides the Planning Commission, the Ministry of Finance, which allocates foreign exchange for the import of oil, either as crude oil or oil products, plays a very important part in shaping the energy plan. The ministries of the central government that have relevance to the energy plan are the following: (1) Ministry in Charge of Coal; (2) Ministry in Charge of Petroleum; (3) Ministry in Charge of Power; (4) Ministry in Charge of Atomic Energy; and (5) Railway Ministry.[b]

[b]The subject of coal was handled by different ministries at different times. For brevity, the ministry will be referred to as a Ministry of Coal in this chapter, though the concerned ministry was:

1956 to 1962, The Ministry of Steel Mines & Fuel
1962 to 1965, Ministry of Steel Mines & Heavy Engineering
1965 to 1968, Ministry of Steel & Mines
1968 to 1971, Ministry of Petroleum & Chemicals
                 Ministry of Mines & Metals
1971 to 1974, Ministry of Steel & Mines
1974 October to date, Ministry of Energy.

The ministry in charge of petroleum has been different in different years as follows:

1963 to 1968, Ministry of Petroleum & Chemicals
1968 to 1971, Ministry of Petroleum & Chemicals
                 Ministry of Mines & Metals
1971 to date, Ministry of Petroleum & Chemicals.

The subject of power was for a long time under the Ministry of Irrigation & Power. In December 1974, a new Ministry of Energy was formed with power and coal as the subjects to be dealt with.

The Department of Atomic Energy has always been under the Office of the Prime Minister as a separate department.

The Railway Ministry is organized for operation purposes as a statutory Board called the Railway.

The ministries of the central government that influence the content of the energy plan and the manner of their interactions are represented schematically in Figure 6-2. Each ministry prepares a detailed proposal of what it considers an appropriate plan for the industry in its charge and attempts to get the other agencies to concur with it. Only the Planning Commission makes an independent study to determine an optimal plan for the sector as a whole; the ministries concern themselves with certain specific issues only. The proposals of each sector are formulated through a process of "consultations" with different agencies engaged in the development of the particular fuel resource and its utilization. To examine the process by which the proposal of each sector is formulated, we need to consider coal, oil, and electricity separately.

Before a fuel can be utilized, the resource potential for the energy form has to be explored and on the basis of knowledge obtained regarding reserves and consumer needs; plans have to be drawn up for developing the mines or projects;

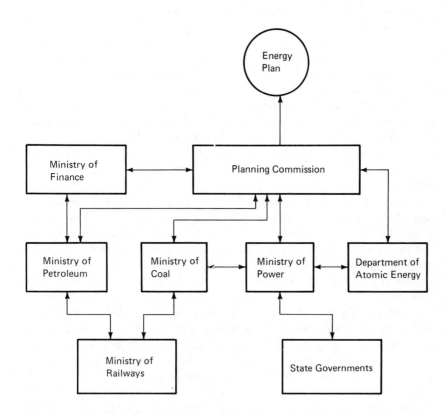

Note: For brevity, Ministry in Charge of Coal, Petroleum, and so forth are denoted as Ministry of Coal, Petroleum and so forth.

Figure 6-2. Influences in Energy Planning in India.

and the energy has to be transported to the consumer location. The activities involved in the development and distribution of fuels are:

1. Exploration and assessment;
2. Planning for production;
3. Production and refining;
4. Transport;
5. Distribution, sales, and consumption;
6. Research and development.

The agencies involved are:

1. The government at central and state levels;
2. Enterprises in the public and private sectors;
3. Interest aggregations like councils and associations;
4. Research and development agencies;
5. Consumers.

Let us take coal first. The interaction of the agencies in the different activities connected with the exploitation and utilization of coal are presented in Figure 6-3. The search for coal reserves is undertaken by the Geological Survey of India (GSI), a government agency for mineral prospecting. The official grading and assessment of coal resources is done by the Coal Controller, a government functionary endowed with certain legal powers. The findings of the GSI have to be followed up by exploratory drilling to determine the quantity of coal that could be extracted at each mine site and the likely economics of mining the deposit. This work of detailed investigation is done by the coal companies themselves. The extent of reserves proven by detailed investigations done at any point of time set the upper limit to the level of coal that could be mined. The Planning Commission computes the likely demand for coal in each plan period with reference to the levels of production anticipated in the sectors using coal and the technology adopted in such production. If the quantity required is more than the limit set by the detailed investigations or by available transportation facilities, the lower target is set as the plan target. The Ministry of Coal and the Ministry of Finance participate in the process of choosing the specific targets and the specific projects that will comprise the coal production plan. Since the steel industry, railways, and power plants are the major consumers of coal, the ministries in charge of these industries are also consulted in setting the targets and in choosing the coal projects. The major consuming industries are also directly consulted.

Prior to nationalization of the coal industry, the Ministry of Coal held formal consultations with the private coal industry periodically through the Coal Council of India. This committee consists of the representatives of private and

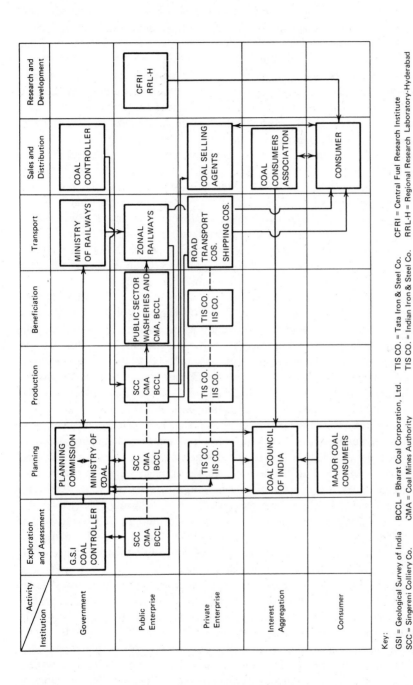

Figure 6-3. Influences in Coal Planning and Production.

Key:

GSI = Geological Survey of India   BCCL = Bharat Coal Corporation, Ltd.   TIS CO. = Tata Iron & Steel Co.   CFRI = Central Fuel Research Institute
SCC = Singereni Colliery Co.   CMA = Coal Mines Authority   TIS CO. = Indian Iron & Steel Co.   RRL-H = Regional Research Laboratory-Hyderabad

public companies, consumers, and interests as well as the representatives of all the government agencies concerned with coal production, transport, and R&D in the coal sector. The Coal Council of India was a powerful body set up by the Government of India with the main purpose of conducting reviews and studies under its supervision and guidance to plan the development, utilization, and conservation of national coal resources. To achieve this purpose the Council created four Committees: Committee on Assessment of Resources, Committee on Requirements and Utilization, Committee on Production and Preparation, and Committee on Transportation.[4]

The coal production plan formulated by such interactions specifies the incremental coal production required in the plan period, the share of the increased production expected from the private sector, and the production targets assigned to each of the public sector enterprises in the coal industry. Until 1971, there were over two hundred coal companies in the private sector operating nearly eight hundred coal mines. Over one-third of these collieries were very small mines producing 20 tons of coal per day. The oldest public sector coal company—Singereni Colliery Company (SCC)—was organized in 1948 by the princely State of Hyderabad and is now managed by the government of the State of Andhra Pradesh. In conformity with the Industrial Policy Resolution of 1956, the Second Five Year Plan stated explicitly that "it has been decided that in future the policy of retaining all new undertakings in coal in the public sector should be more strictly followed and that the additional coal production to meet the increased demand should be raised to the maximum extent from public sector."[5] In 1956, the Government of India established a new public sector coal company, the National Coal Development Corporation (NCDC). In 1971-72, the government nationalized all private sector coking coal mines, except the mines owned by the two private sector steel companies—Tata Iron & Steel Company (TISCO) and Indian Iron and Steel Company (IISCO)—and placed the nationalized mines under a new company, Bharat Coking Coal Limited (BCCL). In 1973, all the noncoking coal mines were also nationalized and placed under the control of a new company, the Coal Mines Authority (CMA), and the NCDC was merged into the new company. The whole coal industry excepting the mines of TISCO and IISCO are now under three public sector companies, GMA, BCCL, and SCC. The functions of central management and control are discharged by the Ministry of Coal, so that the importance of the Coal Council of India has been greatly diminished.

The coal industries, which are given production targets, work out detailed transportation plans with the Ministry of Railways for the movement of coal by rail and with the Ministry of Shipping for the coastal shipping of coal. Before the nationalization of coal mining, a number of private sector coal sales agents functioned as the link between the coal producers and the consumers and made all the arrangements for transportation of coal from the mines to the consumer locations. Although dwindling in numbers, these agents continue to function even after nationalization.

The principal government agencies engaged in research and development efforts in the coal sector are the Central Fuel Research Institute (CFRI) and the Regional Research Laboratories (RRL) at Hyderabad. These organizations are represented on most of the government committees concerned with the development of coal resources. CFRI has played a significant role in the popularization of low temperature carbonized coke and in highlighting the critical scarcity of primary coking coal in the country and persuading the government to undertake measures for using inferior coking coal blended with superior varieties in the steel industry. The R&D institutions give advice either directly to the industry or ministry or indirectly through the Coal Council.

From the Second Plan period until 1967, the price of coal as well as its distribution was controlled by the government. The price used to be fixed on the basis of average costs of production plus a reasonable return to the industry. In 1967, government price control was abandoned but the public sector undertakings, namely railways and electricity boards, continued to negotiate the price on the same basis, and the price settled for these customers became the guideline for the price to other consumers.

The agencies that participate in the formulation of plans for oil exploration, production, refining, and transport and the manner of their interactions are represented schematically in Figure 6-4. Exploration for oil is carried out mostly by the Oil and Natural Gas Commission (ONGC), a government agency for exploration, and Oil India, Ltd. (OIL), a Company owned 50-50 by Burmah Shell and the Government of India. Assam Oil Company explores in certain limited areas leased to it in northeastern India. These three companies are currently producing crude oil, and the relative share of their crude production in 1973 was as follows:

ONGC, 4,011 million tons

OIL, 3,102 million tons

AOC, 84 million tons

Total, 7,198 million tons

Recently some offshore areas have been leased to a few private foreign drilling companies. The scale of exploration and the resources available to exploration activity are decided by the Ministry of Petroleum on the advice of the Planning Commission and the Ministry of Finance.

In 1951, the government decided that oil produced in India should be processed completely in government-owned refineries. The Indian Oil Company, a public sector oil refinery and distribution company, was set up and has constructed refineries at suitable locations to implement this policy. In spite of the policy to accelerate oil exploration activity as much as possible, the share of indigenous crude oil in total oil consumption in India continues to be small.

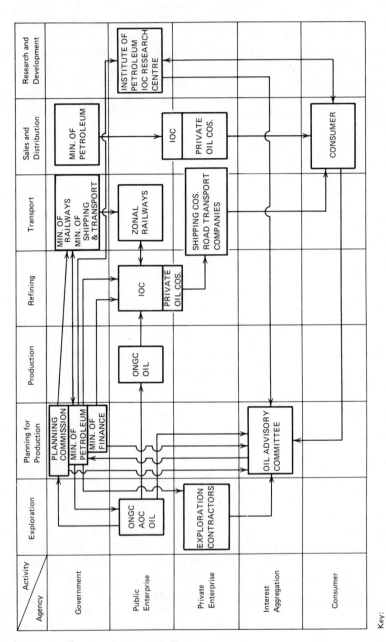

Figure 6-4. Influences in Oil Planning and Production.

Key:

ONGC = Oil & Natural Gas Commission, Oil = Oil India, Ltd.
AOC = Assam Oil Company, IOC = Indian Oil Company

Private Oil Companies: Burma Shell, Esso (now a govt. co.)
Hindustan Petrol Corporation, Caltex, Cochin Oil Refinery,
Madras Oil Refinery

The central concerns of planning in the oil sector in India have been to determine the optimum level of oil consumption in each plan period to sustain the desired rate of growth as well as the portion that could be met by refining indigenous or imported crude oil within the country and the share to be met by imported oil products. Determination of the level of oil consumption is undertaken by the Planning Commission as part of the process of formulating the developing plans. The Planning Commission consults the Ministry of Petroleum in the projection of demand and the ministry in turn consults the various consumer and producer interests. The Oil Advisory Committee, which consists of representatives of the oil companies in the public and private sectors, representatives of the major consumers, and the government agencies connected with transport and research and development, has played an important role in determining the projected oil demand.

The demand for oil products is projected by the Planning Commission on the basis of input-output models of the economy and other econometric models. As new uses of oil have been developing more rapidly than foreseen in the models, the estimates of the Planning Commission have always tended to be low compared to the projections of demand made by the Ministry of Petroleum or by the oil industry. The harmonization of the demand forecasts made by different agencies is done by iterative consultations. The Finance Ministry, which has to release the foreign exchange funds required for oil imports, has a key role in discussions regarding oil demand.

The oil plan as finally decided sets out the likely level of demand for oil products and describes how it will be supplied. The targets for refinery capacity are settled in discussions on the Five Year Plans held by the Planning Commission and the Ministry of Petroleum. In 1951 it was decided that all the crude oil produced in India would be refined in government refineries. Because production under this requirement was adequate for only part of the oil needs, new refineries had to be set up in collaboration with foreign companies that have access to crude oil. Efforts have been made to set up these additional refineries as joint sector companies with some government ownership. The refineries in India, therefore, fall into three categories: public sector (namely, IOC), joint sector projects (namely, Cochin and Madras Refineries), and private refineries (Burmah Shell, ESSO, and Caltex). In 1973, of the 20.5 million tons of crude oil refined in India, 44 percent was refined by the private sector, 34 percent by the public sector, and 22 percent by the joint sector. During 1974 the ESSO Refinery was taken over by the government and formed into a joint sector company named Hindustan Petroleum Corporation.

Even after a refinery is set up, the level of crude oil that can be imported by the private and joint sector oil companies is determined by the Ministry of Finance, which controls the release of foreign exchange to pay for oil imports. The refineries transport the product either by railway or road transport or by coastal shipping. Although the sale of products from each refinery has to be confined to a particular sales zone assigned to each company by the Ministry of Petroleum, there is very frequent product exchange among the refineries. The prices of oil products are fixed by the Ministry of Petroleum. Whenever there is scarcity of a specific oil product, distribution is controlled by the Ministry of Petroleum or by the state governments.

The Institute of Petroleum and the Indian Oil Company's Research and Development Centre are the principal R&D organizations. They are consulted to fix the specifications of products and to change the specifications so as to avoid large shortages or surpluses of refinery products. The price of oil products is based on the periodic recommendations of a price inquiry committee. On the basis of the principles suggested by the committee, the Ministry of Petroleum determines the exfactory price and the transport trade margin on oil products. The Ministry of Finance levies the duties on oil products sold in the country. The consumer price is the result of the combined decisions of the Ministry of Petroleum and the Ministry of Finance.

The formulation of the electric power plan involves a much more complex process of consultations in which the governments of the states that comprise the Indian Union participate. The agencies involved in electricity planning are represented schematically in Figure 6-5. The entire electricity industry is organized under a central statute, the Electricity Supply Act of 1948. Under this act, each state has an electricity board responsible for the generation, transmission, and distribution of electricity within the state and for the control and regulation of other supply undertakings in the private sector or those managed by local authorities like city corporations. In 1971-72, of the total power generation in the country the share of the state electricity boards was 66 percent, local bodies 13 percent, and private electricity companies 21 percent. Under the act, the state electricity boards are autonomous public corporations subject only to broad guidance on policy matters from the state governments. In practice, however, the boards are very much under the control of the state governments since they receive yearly financial assistance from the state governments who also appoint the top managers of the boards, select the investment options, and fix the rate to be charged.

Electricity is a concurrent subject under the Constitution of India, which means that the central government has the right to legislate and administer matters relating to electricity. The Electricity Supply Act of 1948 provided for broad guidance and coordination from the central government through a central authority that would be responsible for a national policy for power development. The Central Electricity Authority was finally created in 1950, but most of the functions that were to be discharged by this agency were already performed by the Central Water and Power Commission and the Ministry of Power. Periodic meetings of state government ministers in charge of power and of electricity board chairmen serve as a formal forums for mutual consultation. For nuclear power generation, the responsibility rests squarely with the Department of

223

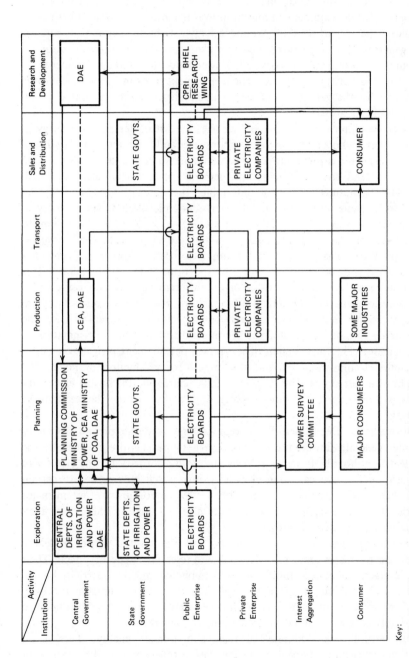

Figure 6-5. Influences in Electricity Planning and Production.

Key:

CEA = Central Electricity Authority   DAE = Department of Atomic Energy

Atomic Energy. As this department is directly under the prime minister and as the program for development of nuclear power is subject to certain larger policy constraints, the Department of Atomic Energy has been planning for nuclear power generation independently, and their plans are taken into consideration by the central government Ministry of Power and the state governments in formulating their energy programs. The Department of Atomic Energy concerns itself only with the generation of power and sells the power generated to the state electricity boards.

Power development plans depend on the forecast of demand for energy in the country as a whole and in different states separately. Since the availability of power is considered a prerequisite for rapid industrial development, all the state governments tend to overestimate the demand for energy in their respective states. The Planning Commission determines the demand for energy in the country as a whole with the help of macroeconomic models. The ministry in charge of power also makes certain forecasts. A final view of the power demand is taken after protracted consultations among these agencies. In 1962, a power survey committee was set up to make annual forecasts of power demand on a scientific basis and to indicate broadly the short-run power requirements.[6] This committee consists of representatives of the different ministries concerned with power development, the Planning Commission, the finance ministry, state electricity boards and certain research and development organizations. The power survey committee has not yet become influential in the determination of power demand. The final version of the power development plan drawn up by the Planning Commission sets out the targets for production of power and energy in different states. The state electricity boards and the private electricity companies draw up their power generation plans on the basis of these suggestions.

Although the Department of Atomic Energy and the private electricity companies generate power, the transmission network is entirely owned by the state electricity boards. Power is sold by the state electricity boards directly to consumers, or in some cases the electricity boards sell bulk power to certain private electricity companies who distribute it to the consumers. Certain major industries who have captive power plants also sell part of the power they generate to the electricity boards.

The Department of Atomic Energy and the Central Power Research Institute are the major agencies concerned with research and development. Their views are made available to the Planning Commission and the electricity boards and sometimes directly to the consumers. The electricity equipment manufacturing companies in the public sector, like the BHEL, have of late been taking a keen interest in research and development in the power sector.

With regard to noncommercial fuels and animate energy, there is no institution or agency charged with the task of forecasting likely needs or arranging for supply. Several committees that deal with problems of energy or rural development have discussed the enormity of the problem and possible solutions, but no institutional arrangements have been made so far. The Khadi and Village Industries Commission has been making feeble attempts to popularize bio-gas plants as part of their program of rural reconstruction.

Determinants of Major Shifts in Energy Plans

Having seen the process by which the energy plans are formulated and the actual trends in energy consumption, we can examine whether the patterns of energy consumption conformed to the energy plans drawn up by the concerned agencies. Since the targets for economic growth within the five-year plans were not fully realized in any plan period in India, it is not surprising that forecasts and fulfillments also differ in the fuel and power industries. We are interested in analyzing whether the deviation of fuel consumption from the plans is fully explained by the final, realized rate and pattern of growth or whether other reasons also have to be invoked to explain the divergence.

To do so, the plan targets of fuel consumption are "adjusted" to be in conformity with the realized levels of fuel consumption—that is, the "adjusted" fuel consumption levels would have been indicated in the energy plan if the planners had perfect foreknowledge of the rates of growth that were achieved in each plan period. These adjusted fuel targets are then compared with the realized consumption of energy. The details are set out in Table 6-11.

The most notable feature seen in Table 6-11 is that in each plan period oil consumption not only has exceeded the requisite level to support the realized rate of growth, but has even exceeded the original targets, even though the production of goods and services during the plan periods was below that anticipated in the plan. In the Fourth Plan, oil consumption fell below the "adjusted level" as a result of a drop in oil consumption in 1973-74 (the last year of the Fourth Plan period) as compared to the previous year 1972-73. In the case of coal and electricity, consumption has consistently been below the planned targets and adjusted targets. The deficits in the consumption of coal and electricity seem to have been made up by increased consumption of oil products.

During the Second Five Year Plan, the realized rate of growth of GNP was very close to the planned levels and the consumption of coal and electricity were also very close to the targets. Oil consumption, however, was higher than the planned level by over a third. Oil consumption in the transport sector accounts for the increase. Although the production of goods and services was close to anticipated levels, the freight moved by railways was far below the plan targets. Compared to the expectation that the total originating traffic for the railways would increase from 120 million tons to 181 million tons, the actual traffic was only 154 million tons. Much of the incremental traffic was diverted to road transport, and the consumption of gasoline and diesel oil in the transport sector

Table 6-11
Forecast and Fulfillment in Fuel Consumption

Item/Fuel	Coal (in million tons)	Oil Products (in million tons)	Electricity (in Gwh)
End of II Five-Year Plan (1960-61)			
Plan target of fuel consumption	59.77	4.30	16.60
Adjusted target	58.45	4.20	16.23
Actual consumption	55.70	5.70	16.60
End of III Five-Year Plan Period (1965-66)			
Plan target of consumption	97.00	11.72	38.70
Adjusted target	82.30	9.94	32.83
Actual consumption	66.70	12.35	30.36
End of IV Five-Year Plan (1973-74)			
Target of consumption	93.50	26.00	70.50
Adjusted target	85.00	23.63	64.10
Actual consumption	79.00	21.84	59.04

Note: These "adjustments" were made as follows: Each plan assumed that a particular rate of growth of GNP was possible during the plan period and gave the energy needs of the economy at the terminal year of the plan. We assumed that fuel (i.e., coal, oil, and electricity) consumption would be proportionate to GNP. On the basis of realized GNP, and given the anticipated GNP and fuel targets, the "adjusted targets" were calculated. The relevant rates of growth were:

		Growth of GNP/Year	
		Anticipated	Realized
II	Plan	4.5	4.1
III	Plan	6.6	2.6
IV	Plan	5.7	3.7

increased steeply. During the period 1951-1956, the refinery capacity in the country had increased from 25 million tons to 4.25 million tons. As the refinery companies, which are subsidiaries of the multinational oil companies, were skilled in developing a market for the sale of their products, the oil market increased very rapidly.

The skill with which the oil industry is able to influence the energy plan was demonstrated during the formulation and implementation of the energy plan during the Third Plan period (1960-1965). Only in the Third Plan period were some tentative approaches made towards a rational energy plan by taking into account the interdependence of various types of fuel. In 1959, in the draft Third Five Year Plan the Planning Commission set out tentative estimates of demand for fuels in 1966 as follows: coal, 100 million tons, and oil products, 9.96 million tons. In its meeting held in 1959, the Coal Council of India asserted that the "target for coal production should be nearer 110 m. tonnes than 100 m. tonnes."[7] The Oil Advisory Committee urged that the target for consumption of oil products should be 11,723 million tons.[8] During the discussions that followed, the Coal Ministry conceded that transporting such large quantities of coal over long distances by rail was likely to pose grave problems. Discussions with railways and other planning agencies resulted not only in the listing of a number of suggestions for augmenting railway capacity but also led to the position that "the feasibility of consumers in Western and South India changing over to the use of furnace oil instead of coal is also under consideration."[9] This position was effectively used by the Oil Advisory Committee, which suggested that even their forecast of demand for oil products at 11,723 million tons may have been an underestimate as "furnace oil demand will be higher, if fiscal incentives are given to encourage the industries in areas removed from coalfields to change from coal to fuel oil."[10] As a result of these discussions, in the finally approved version of the Third Plan targets for oil consumption accorded with the views of the Oil Advisory Committee, and the coal target was reduced. The resultant plan targets for coal and oil products consumption in 1966 were: coal, 97 million tons, and oil products, 11,723 million tons.

The implementation of the coal and oil plans in the Third Plan further illustrates the ability of the oil industry to shape the pattern of energy consumption. Within three years of formulating the Third Five Year Plan, in the mid-term appraisal the Oil Advisory Committee revised the estimate of demand for oil products to 16.9 million tons in 1966, and the Planning Commission accepted this by ". . . taking cognisance of the revised estimate of demand of 16.9 m. tonnes for petroleum products which has been made by the *Oil Advisory Committee*, the refinery programme has been enlarged to include certain refinery schemes to increase the refinery capacity to 17.9 m. tonnes." It also stated that "the question whether further additional refinery capacity is required to be in effective operation at the end of the III Plan is being examined."[11]

The Third Plan mid-term appraisal also led to the conclusion that the coal target for 1965-66 was not likely to be achieved. In the first two years of the plan, coal production remained unchanged at 55 million tons. The demand for steel, industrial products, and railway transport was expected to be below the original forecast. Increasing the quantity of coal moved by rail from Eastern India was proving to be difficult. Many of the private mine owners who invested in the expansion of the mines were having difficulty transporting the coal to consumers. Still, during the appraisal it was felt that the demand would be 90 million tons by 1965-66, and production would reach that level. It is obvious that the Coal Ministry as well as the planning agencies failed to recognize the implications to the coal sector of increasing production and consumption of oil.

In fact, all agencies were willing parties in encouraging the use of fuel oil in place of coal in the western and southern regions as advocated by the Oil Advisory Committee. The government, in fact, gave capital grants for conversion of equipment from coal to oil in selected industries like cement. It is interesting that while this unmerited encouragement of the use of furnace oil in place of coal was getting government support, the public sector fertilizer corporation and certain influential fertilizer technologists seriously advocated the use of coal as the feedstock for fertilizer production in order to reduce the dependence on imported feedstock. Although the quantity of the likely feedstock requirement was small compared to the available increased amount of furnace oil used in industry and power stations, this view was accepted. The government decided to set up three large (900 tons of ammonia/day) urea plants based on coal as feedstock.

With the exception of the fertilizer sector, oil use was increasing rapidly in all sectors. In a period when the oil prices in the international market were steadily declining in real terms, the Finance Ministry appears to have been unperturbed at these moves to increase the demand for oil products mostly at the cost of coal. The excellent results obtained by the ONGC and OIL in oil exploration and production from 1960 onward made the various government agencies somewhat complacent towards the increase in oil consumption. In 1961, crude oil production in India was 0.5 million tons, which increased to 1.1 million tons in 1962, 2.2 million tons in 1964, and 4.6 million tons in 1966. The convenience of importing oil enabled the oil industry to step up oil consumption without being constrained by the fact that the rate of increase in the consumption of petroleum products was faster than the rate of increase of crude oil production within the country.

In spite of the experience gained in the formulation and implementation of the Third Plan, the agencies in the coal sector repeated the same unsuccessful tactics for the Fourth Plan. Even in the last two years of the Third Plan, when coal production was stagnating around 60 million tons as against the plan target of 97 million tons, the Coal Ministry admitted that "the fall in production and dispatches has been due to slackening of demand for coal. Certain consumers have switched over to sources of energy other than coal. Examples are dieselisation by the railways and installation of oil burning equipment in cement factories." But the same ministry in consultation with the Coal Council projected demand for 1970-71 (which was to be the terminal year of the Fourth Five Year Plan) to be 125 million tons.[12] About the same time, the oil industry forecasted a requirement in 1970-71 of 25.25 million tons of oil products.[13] By then, crude oil production was increasing at a fast rate and the refinery capacity was about 16 million tons. When the Fourth Plan was finalized, the targets for consumption of coal and oil products in the terminal year of the plan (1973-74) were set at 93.5 million tons for coal and 26 million tons for oil. While the oil sector target was slightly higher than the earlier projection by the oil industry, the coal target was much lower than the earlier estimate, in fact somewhat lower than the Third Plan target.

The interplay of agencies in the formulation of coal and oil plans suggests that the coal industry, with a very large number of coal companies, was not able to make a purposeful assessment of demand and to take the necessary measures to realize the targets. In plan after plan the targets were set at high levels that were neither justified from the point of view of demand nor capable of being fulfilled by supplies. Their efforts to protect their markets were not backed by an adequate understanding of the interfuel substitution possibilities and economic logic. There were no organized sales promotion efforts in the coal sector where the middlemen sales agents functioned more or less like transport contractors. The oil sector, on the other hand, had a more sophisticated and skillful approach to demand management. Central government agencies like the Planning Commission and the Finance Ministry appear not to have functioned effectively as a central authority with a full understanding of the interrelationship of different fuels. A central agency dealing exclusively with planning and production problems in the energy sector might have achieved more desirable results.

The great dependence of the coal industry on rail transport facilities to develop its market demand dampened the enthusiasm for stepping up coal production. Between 1961 and 1965, the railway wagons allotted to coal transport increased by 4.6 percent; and between 1965 and 1970, by only 0.3 percent. Although every year the railways and the coal ministry came to an agreement on the number of wagons to be allotted for coal transport, the railways usually could not in fact provide the requisite number of wagons. Whenever there is a shortage of wagons, the available wagons are first allotted to the priority industries, namely, defense, steel, and power, and the remaining wagons, if any, are allotted to low priority uses like the domestic sector. This arrangement explains the drop in the intensity of coal use in the domestic sector in 1970-71 as compared to 1965-66. For a large section of the urban population and rural rich who use now firewood as domestic fuel, soft coke is the preferred fuel, and its consumption could have increased if facilities for transport by rail had been available.

While the inability of railways to carry the quantities of coal that might have been produced had the direct effect of reducing the level of domestic and industrial coal consumption and increasing the intensity of oil use in these sectors, the difficulties of the railways indirectly helped the increase of oil use in another way, as more and more of goods had to be transported by road. As discussed earlier, even during the Second Plan (1956-61), total originating traffic increased from 120 million tons to 154 million tons, as against the target of 181 million tons. This tendency continued throughout the sixties. The Government Committee on Transport Policy and Coordination noted in 1964 that "in particular these were pressures and bottlenecks in the movement of coal from Bengal-Bihar. . . . Difficulties were experienced in the movement of raw materials and finished products of industries. . . . Competition between the two principal forms of transport—railways and mechanised road transport—has also increased specially on long distance routes."[14] The net effect of this situation can be seen from the indices of goods transported by road and rail as shown in Table 6-12.

The rapid increase in the relative share of road transport has led to an increasing importance of oil in the transport sector and an increase in the intensity of oil use. Although plan after plan has emphasized the need for a well-coordinated transport policy that will ensure that the railways and road transport play a mutually complementary role, the lack of organizations to pursue sustained policies towards this end has led to unplanned growth of road transport and a consequent increase in oil consumption. Every effort to regulate the categories of traffic (like bulk commodities and long distance goods traffic) to be carried by road transport has been defeated by the inadequacy of the railway. The most recent case in point was the government directive issued in the wake of the oil crisis that prohibited long-distance haulage of goods by road on certain routes. This directive was withdrawn after a few months since railways could not effectively substitute for the road transport facilities.

By 1970, it was clear that a rational plan for coal development based on socioeconomic considerations and synchronized investment in coal mine development and coal transport was not possible as long as the ownership structure of coal resources continued to be as it was then (over two hundred coal companies operating over eight hundred coal mines, with widely divergent sizes and costs of production). As discussed earlier, the coal mines in India were nationalized in two stages in 1971 and 1972. Coal production, which was stagnant at around 70 million tons per year from 1967 to 1971, started picking up very fast and increased to 75.6 million tons in 1972-73, 77.9 million tons in 1973-74, and 87.5 million tons in 1974-75, and is expected to reach a level of 98 million tons in 1975-76. Organizational impediments that were partly responsible for hindering coal production in the sixties have been remedied effectively. Efforts to increase railway capacity to transport the increasing production has met with only partial success.

The use of electricity in all sectors appears to have grown independently of the growth of consumption of other fuels. The intensity of electricity use has declined in the transport sector and has increased gradually in the industrial

Table 6-12
Indices of Goods Carried by Road and Rail (1950-51 = 100)

Year	Rail	Road	Total
1950-51	100	100	100
1955-56	135	163	138
1960-61	199	316	213
1964-65	242	564	277
1970-71	288	891	355

sector and very steeply in the agriculture and the domestic sectors. In the latter two sectors, electricity is used by a very small percentage of households and farms even now; in the others, noncommercial fuels and animal power supply the remaining energy needs. State electricity boards and the state governments concerned with power production and distribution have a policy of providing electricity to all the villages as early as possible, and as provision of electricity to villages fulfills a minimum need set by the planners, a large number of villages are newly connected with the state power system every year and an increase in intensity of electricity use follows.

The relative rates of increase in the use of coal, oil, and electricity are to some extent explained by the relative price of these fuels over time. The high rate of increase in electricity consumption is to some extent due to the low price of electricity. Electricity boards, which are managed by the state governments, have to accept the pricing policies that these governments consider to be in the public interest. Because each state has felt that the availability of power at low prices would attract industry and has thus tried to keep the price for industries low, and because the agriculturists' lobby would not allow any increase in the price of power to agriculture, the net result has been that many of the electricity boards throughout the sixties, and some even now, sold power at rates that did not cover their costs. Table 6-13 sets out the indices of fuel prices.

The weighted average of the indices of oil product prices may be near those of electricity. Of the commercial fuels, electricity prices have increased the least, followed by oil and then by coal during the sixties, which is the rank order of the rate of growth of the commercial fuels. It must be noted, however, that fuel cost is only one element of the costs; equipment costs and operating costs also become relevant whenever there are technical options available for fuel substitution. But the fact that prices for electricity have remained relatively lower than for other fuels provides at least a partial explanation of the higher rate of growth in electricity consumption.

In the power sector, the one agency that is free from other pressures is the Department of Atomic Energy; in spite of this fact, the step-up in nuclear power generation has been slow. The explanation lies in the strategy for nuclear power

Table 6-13
Index Numbers of Wholesale Prices (1961-62 = 100)

Year	Coal	Kerosene	Diesel Oil	Electricity
1961-62	100.0	100.0	100.0	100.0
1965-66	121.8	146.6	110.9	124.9
1970-71	167.9	176.6	121.1	150.2
1972-73	176.8	202.9	130.5	158.9

Source: Government of India, Office of the Economic Adviser.

generation that has been adopted. As India has limited resources of uranium and very large resources of thorium, with a view to utilizing thorium, the "... nuclear power programme has to be carried out in three stages which is time consuming. The first stage will utilise natural uranium as fuel, producing power and the fissile element plutonium. The second stage will employ reactors using plutonium as fuel and thorium as fertile material, producing power and converting part of the thorium into U233. The third stage will use U233 within breeder reactors, so that while electricity is generated, more U233 is produced than is burnt up in the process."[15]

The nuclear power program was initiated in the early sixties. It was calculated that if roughly 2,700 MW of installed capacity of heavy water reactors of the first stage were established by the end of the seventies, these units operating at a 75 percent load factor would produce enough plutonium to support one new 400-500 MW fast breeder reactor during 1980s. This program was set out by DAE in its "profile for the decade of 1970-80." The DAE was also in favor of building up the indigenous capability for design and fabrication of the equipment. The slow development of these skills has led to delays in completing the projects as anticipated. But as indicated in the Report of the Fuel Policy Committee, installation of nuclear power stations will be slow up to 1983-84, by which time a total of 1,900 MW of nuclear power capacity should be set up and from then on every year nearly 1,000 MW of nuclear power capacity may be added.[16]

Alternative Patterns of Energy Consumption in the Future: Feasibility of Low-Energy Growth Profile

The survey of energy consumption in the past, GNP relationships, and the moves and countermoves of different agencies that have shaped past trends gives us some insight into the possible alternative strategies of energy management in the future. We shall first list the projections made on the basis of past trends (see Table 6-14) and then combine them with technological and macroeconomic data to determine whether the existing institutional structures would support the emergence of such a fuel-use pattern. We shall see the nature of the changes that are likely to occur if the institutional structures for energy planning and production continue unaltered. Then, we shall analyze the possibilities for reducing the intensity of energy consumption and identify the institutional factors that may favor or oppose such changes.

Demographic and macroeconomic variables relating to India and data regarding technological options likely to be available in the future are difficult to obtain for periods beyond the next ten to fifteen years. We shall, therefore, limit the horizon of the study to the year 1990. Based on the rate and pattern of economic growth anticipated by the Planning Commission of India in the draft

Table 6-14.
Forecast of Energy Demand in India to 1990-91 (Based on past trends of energy consumption; in mtce)

Fuel/Year	1970-71 (Actual)	1978-79	1983-84	1990-91
Coal (Direct Use)[a]	51.4	81.0	117.0	188.0
Oil	29.9	53.4	74.0	122.0
Electricity	48.6	97.1	163.0	315.0
Commercial Energy	129.9	231.5	354.0	625.0
Firewood	116.6	125.0	124.0	116.0
Dung Cake	26.9	26.0	26.0	21.0
Vegetable Waste	35.9	44.0	44.0	44.0
Noncommercial Energy	179.4	195.0	194.0	181.0
Total Energy	309.3	426.5	548.0	806.0

[a]Excludes the use of coal and middlings in power generation and exports.
  1970-71 = 17 mt
  1978-79 = 51 mt
  1983-84 = 78 mt
  1990-91 = 142 mt

of the Fifth Five Year Plan,[17] and The Fuel Policy Committee of India (1974),[18] the projected requirements of India up to 1990-91 are shown in Table 6-15.

Since India is well endowed with coal but has to import most of its oil, the Fuel Policy Committee examined the possibilities for greater utilization of indigenous fuels, especially in view of the oil crisis. The emphasis of the FPC's recommendations was on the substitution possibilities among commercial fuels. If the fiscal and administrative measures outlined by the FPC were adopted, reduction in the use of oil products would ensue due to (1) price elasticity of demand with respect to certain products such as gasoline, (2) increased efficiency in the utilization of oil products, and (3) the substitution of other energy forms in place of oil products. On techno-economic considerations, the FPC identified the following fuel substitutions as feasible and desirable:

1. In the domestic sector, soft coke (for cooking) and electricity (for lighting) can replace oil to a great extent.
2. In the agricultural sector, the share of irrigation pumps run on electricity rather than diesel can increase.
3. In the industrial sector, furnace oil can replace coal.
4. In the transport sector, there can be a reduction in the use of gasoline due to increased price; diesel oil used for carrying goods can be saved by use of optimal size of vehicles and their better maintenance; and the amount of

Table 6-15

Forecast of Energy Demand in India to 1990-91 (Recommended as the optimal pattern; in mtce)

Fuel	1970-71 (Actual)	1978-79	1983-84	1990-91
Coal (Direct Use)	51.4	86.6	125.4	201.9
Oil	29.9	45.4	59.8	89.2
Electricity	48.6	103.9	172.4	325.8
Commercial Energy	129.9	234.9	357.6	616.9
Noncommercial Energy	179.4	195.0	194.0	181.0
Total Energy	309.3	429.9	551.6	797.9

diesel oil used in the transport sector can also be saved by greater use of rail transport in place of increased use of road transport.

By taking the sum of all these effects, the FPC considered it possible to shift the pattern of fuel utilization as shown in Table 6-15.

The average rates of growth (in terms of coal equivalent) of commercial fuels implied in the recommended pattern of fuel usage are as follows:

1970-71 to 1978-79, coal, 6.58; oil, 5.36; electricity, 9.96

1978-79 to 1983-84, coal, 7.94; oil, 5.66; electricity, 10.66

1983-84 to 1990-91, coal, 7.04; oil, 5.88; electricity, 9.52.

The Fuel Policy Committee has recommended that the rate of increase in oil consumption should go down in the future. We have seen how the earlier plan proposals to slow down the rate of growth in oil consumption were nullified by the institutional arrangements then in existence. With the entire coal industry now under government ownership and control and with the share held by multinational corporations in oil refining and distribution diminishing, there are better chances of containing the growth of oil consumption within planned levels. The success of such regulation would, however, depend on the ability of the coal industry to produce the requisite quantities of coal and that of railways to transport the coal to the consumers.

In the post-energy crisis period, the coal industry has been able to step up production by 2.92 percent in 1973-74 and 12.34 percent in 1974-75. At the same time, the strict watch kept by the Planning Commission and Ministry of Finance on the level of oil imports has helped to maintain the level of oil consumption almost unchanged from the year 1972-73 (around 22 million tons). There were no signs of any significant shortage of oil products in the economy, except very temporary regional shortages due to transport and distribution difficulties. The oil industry, however, has argued that the lowered levels of oil consumption are the result of very tight management of oil utilization and that such management cannot be continued on a sustained basis. The brightening prospects for economic exploitation of offshore oil discovered in the Bombay High region have given rise to subtle pressures to increase the refinery capacity. Unless a well-conceived, central coordinating agency is established for the energy sector as a whole, the history of energy planning in the sixties, as discussed earlier, may be repeated in the coming years. Suitable institutional arrangements also have to be evolved for ensuring the coordination of railway development plans and coal production programs.

The FPC has taken the institutional constraints into account in arriving at the maximum possible level of interfuel substitution by 1990. The FPC did not, however, examine the possibility of changes in lifestyle that would reduce the total quantity of energy needed to sustain the desired rate of economic development. Such issues were considered beyond the scope of inquiry of this official report. It would be interesting to consider the effects of relaxing these restrictive assumptions and to examine the implications of possible changes in lifestyle on the optimal utilization of available energy resources.

The Fuel Policy Committee, as already noted, did not examine the use of animate energy. The amount of animate energy available now and likely to be available in future may be taken as limited by the maximum working bovine population that could be supported in India (i.e., 80 million). The animate power is calculated on this basis. If this estimate is added to the fuel demand based on past trends (see Table 6-3) and the intensity of all energy used in the economy is computed, we find that it is likely to be as follows: 1978-79, 1.60; 1983-84, 1.48; and 1990-91, 1.39 (in mtce/billion rupees).

This finding shows that the trend toward steadily declining intensity of energy use noticed in the fifties and sixties (see Table 6-9) will continue up to 1990-91. If the optimal pattern of fuel usage recommended by the Fuel Policy Committee (see Table 6-15) is considered along with animate energy, the intensity of energy use changes to 1.61 in 1978-79, 1.49 in 1983-84, and 1.38 in 1990-91.

We find that the intensity of energy use does not change merely by adopting the fuel substitutions considered desirable on technoeconomic grounds. These fuel shifts based on a given lifestyle and given (available) technologies are not energy saving in character. Most important is the implication of these results for low GNP countries in which noncommercial energy and animate power consti- tute a significant portion of the total energy needs. It would appear that the energy-GNP ratio is lower in the sectors and subsectors where commercial energy is used, and this results in a decrease in the overall intensity of energy use as the share of commercial energy increases in total energy consumption. If the new objective is merely to reduce the energy-GNP relationship, without foreseeing any lifestyle changes or energy-economizing technological innovations, then the objective could be realized by replacing noncommercial energy and animal power by commercial energy. This objective, surely, is no solution to the energy problem of developing countries. A proper solution to the energy problem of such countries has to be sought, not under the normal restrictive assumptions, but in the wider context of economic development as a whole based on the optimal utilization of all available resources. The desirable approach may be to take as the objective of development the poor countries as a whole and to evolve a least-cost solution to the problem of supplying the requisite energy needs. The countries that are considered poor and endowed with poor energy resources usually have forest and animal resources in significant quantities, and alternate growth strategies based on different patterns of utilization of these resources may provide energy inputs that, even if not quantitatively large in our normal scale of measurement, may be obtainable at relatively low prices and by adoption of investment programs more compatible with development objectives. In this view, it becomes more meaningful to seek what is appropriate for countries with low per capita GNP than to search for "low energy profiles" adapted to countries with high per capita GNP.

The most important objective of development planning in India is the removal of poverty. At the projected rate of growth, this goal can be achieved only if there is considerable reduction in the prevailing inequality in consumption. It is computed in the draft Fifth Five Year Plan that by 1986, 30 percent of the population, or 211 million people, will live below the poverty line (i.e., with per capita consumption below 40 rupees per month in 1972-73 prices). The composition of growth should, therefore, be such that it favors the rural and urban poor; the growth process must lead to massive employment generation and greater availability of consumer goods to the poor. Such goals have to be achieved in a setting where 80 percent of the population is rural and nearly 90 percent of rural households have land holdings of less than one hectare, and where technological innovations in the agriculture sector, (better seed and chemical fertilizer technology) have bypassed the poorer sections. We have, therefore, to seek an appropriate fuel utilization pattern that would not only provide for energy needs but would also counteract poverty. In this context, two large sources of energy—forests and animal wealth—merit careful examination. We shall consider the extent to which forests and animal wealth could be exploited as part of comprehensive development plans. The possibilities for changes in lifestyle and new innovations in technology will also be considered.

Let us first consider the option of maximizing the use of forest fuels. Forest fuels supply energy mostly to the domestic sector. The limits on the demand for forest fuels will, therefore, be set by energy needs in the domestic sector. Demographic studies show that by 1990-91, the total population will be 757 million of which 184 million will be in urban settlements.[19]

All but 20 percent of the urban population (probably the poor) will use commercial fuels in the domestic sector by 1990-91. But the rural population requires 200 million tons of coal equivalent of energy for cooking purposes only, exclusive of the lighting needs. With the addition of the needs of the urban poor, it will be 213 mtce. The vegetable waste available in the economy will be used in any case, as the private cost of this fuel is likely to be very low. In allowing for its use, the requirements amount to 173 million tons of coal equivalent, which represents the upper limit of the demand for forest fuels. In original units, this amount will be 182 million tons of firewood. India has 75 million hectares of forest, which constitutes 24 percent of the total land area. Of forested areas, about 60 million hectares are exploited and potentially exploitable. On ecological grounds, the National Forests Policy Resolution has advocated that forests should be increased to 33.3 percent of the total land area. While this increase may prove difficult in a country with mounting population pressure, it is reasonable to assume that the forested area should not be reduced. The average exploitation rate of fuel and industrial wood in forests in India has been only 0.3 tons per hectare per year. In the case of a fully productive forest of comparatively quick growing species, the rate of increment could be 11 m^3 (i.e., 8.2 tons) per hectare per annum; with other species, it might be about half this amount. While conditions in different types of forests and in different localities vary greatly, it is known that most of India's forests are in a state of serious underproductivity.[20] If proper silviculture practices were adopted and even if all the forest were to be planted with non-quick-growing species, the forest should yield about 240 million tons of wood. Planned forest development can yield more wood for fuel without denuding the area. Even on the most optimistic assumptions, the demand for wood for timber, paper, and other industrial needs would not amount to 40-50 million tons by 1990-91; 180 million tons of firewood will be available even after meeting the needs for industrial wood in 1990-91. If, however, more forest fuels are required for nonenergy purposes, 15 million acres of forest lands classified as "other forests" could be utilized. These forests, if planted with quick-growing species, could yield 90 million tons of wood.[21]

Forest lands are not evenly distributed among the states. In fact, states with high density population like Kerala have relatively less forest per capita. It would be expensive to transport forest fuels over long distances. An effort should be made to provide forest fuels from sources that are conveniently near the rural settlements. It is also necessary to keep in mind the development objective of increasing the consumption of the rural population (nearly 200 million below the poverty line) who cannot afford to purchase forest fuels and who for want of more gainful employment would be willing to collect fuel wood from the forests personally. In the olden days in India, the village community used to maintain forests near the villages where the villagers had a traditional right to collect firewood for personal consumption, usually free of cost. These village forests have gradually disappeared. The National Commission on Agriculture[22] has suggested that to supply the fuel and fodder and recreational needs of the villages, "social forests" should be set up near the villages. A village of 500 families may require 200 to 250 hectares of land for a social forest. This approach may be preferable in some areas where the existing forest land is inadequate to meet the fuel needs or where the forests are too far away from human settlements. By a proper selection of areas, it appears quite feasible to step up the firewood availability to 182 million tons of wood.

If the "forest fuel maximization" option is adopted, the pattern of energy utilization will change from the optimal pattern suggested by the Fuel Policy Committee. Forest fuel can replace the incremental use of kerosene and soft coke assumed by the Fuel Policy Committee and the new pattern could be as shown in Table 6-16.

It is also possible to reduce or eliminate the use of dung cake and replace it by 21 million tons of coal, and even then coal needs will be within the level of coal use advocated by the Fuel Policy Committee.

The investment needed to implement this option would be around 30 billion rupees. This would provide for the planned scientific exploitation of forest resources instead of their unplanned demolition and would have significant ecological benefits as well. Projects prepared recently for commercial exploitation of forests and for setting up social forests indicate that with proper organization and management, such programs can be financially viable. The constraint on the implementation of the scheme is the lack of adequate institutional arrangements and qualified technical and managerial skills to implement the program. Since there is very little information on the likely costs in different areas of the country for forest revitalization and the availability of infrastructure facilities, collection of more detailed information is an urgent necessity.

We may now examine the advantages and feasibility of optimizing the use of animal resources available in the economy. As observed earlier, the working bovine population was a little over 80 million throughout the sixties. Including milch cows and young animals, the total cattle population in different years was as follows: 203.6 million in 1956; 226.8 million in 1961; and 229.0 million in 1966.[c]

It has sometimes been suggested that this population is excessive and should be reduced. However, it has also been argued that ". . . cattle, as an economic good, plays many roles, perhaps more than any other economic good. It is a consumer good (c-good) because it is eaten; it is a machine for producing consumer goods (I-good) because it yields milk; it is an intermediate good

---

[c]Because of the unit of measurement adopted in this chapter, the substitution for oil or coal by animal power would mean a proper "replacement ratio" has to be used, and not the equivalent measures, for computing the amounts of energy replaced. This would change the total energy in equivalent measures and might give rise to confusion. We have therefore used equivalent measures as replacement measures at this stage. When the needs for oil are converted to specific units of an oil product, a proper replacement ratio has to be adopted according to the nature of work that will be done by animals in place of machines and the relative efficiencies in those operations.

Table 6-16
Alternative Patterns of Energy Consumption in India, 1990-91 (mtce)

	Based on Historical Trends	As Recommended by "FPC Coal Option"	As per "Forest Fuel" Option	As per "Animal Resource Option" Case I	As per "Animal Resource Option" Case II
Coal	188	202	165	172	172
Oil	122	89	69	70	70
Electricity	315	326	326	326	326
Firewood	116	116	173	116	25
Dung Cake	21	21	21	51	142
Vegetable Waste	44	44	44	44	44
Animal Power[a]	76	76	76	95	95
Total	882	874	874	874	874

Source: Government of India, *Indian Live Stock census 1966—Vol. I, Summary Tables*, 1971.

[a]This is not included in FPC Report.

(R-good) because it can be used for traction (apart from the manure made available as a by-product); it is also a mother machine (m-good) because cattle produce cattle."[23] The substitution of tractors for livestock would be offset by the increased demand for milch cows and beef cattle. Even if cattle were replaced by tractors in agriculture, it is unlikely that there would be a reduction in the bovine population. It is noteworthy that the number of bovine animals per 100 human population is higher in United States than in India even today.

In all forecasts of fuel demand is an implicit assumption that tractors will gradually replace animal power. Past trends that are extrapolated for forecasting demand show that during the ten-year period between 1956 and 1966, the rates of growth for cropped area, working cattle, and tractors were as follows: cropped area, 9.5 percent per year; working cattle, 1.4 percent per year; and tractors, 10.6 percent per year.

The question that merits serious consideration is whether the increase in tractors can be continued at this rate, especially at the expense of animal power. A recent study has shown that investment in tractors is not profitable for small farms using family labor.[24] In India, over 90 percent of rural households have less than one hectare of land. Private as well as social profitability of tractor use obtaining till now is the result of the existing structure of land holding. After the large farms get mechanized, the rate of tractorization may decrease. The same study has shown that while computations based on pre-oil crisis prices indicate that private and social profitability of investment in tractors did not diverge, computations using current prices show investment in farm tractors to be socially unprofitable. Farm management studies also indicate that while tractors are preferred for preparatory tilling of the soil, bullocks are preferred for intercultivation and other operations, and several large farms maintain bullocks in addition to tractors. Recent pilot plant studies done by the International Crop Research Institute for Semi-Arid Tropics (ICRISAT) in Hyderabad, India, have shown that optimum crop technology can be implemented by using animal power for all farm practices and that improved animal drawn equipment can provide the precision and uniformity required to apply optimum technology.[25] An opinion survey regarding the economy of draught animals conducted by the National Sample Survey Organisation in 1971 showed that 66 percent of rural householders had no draught animals, 17 percent had one animal only, and 17 percent one pair or more animals.[26] Of those owning one pair or more animals, over 70 percent considered that owning these animals was economical, and only 3 percent were in favor of disposing of the animals. Of those who own no animals, 25 percent were desirous of buying work animals. In sum, a vast majority of Indian farmers would like to possess more work animals or to retain those they already have. Given these facts, it would be reasonable to conclude that as a consideration of private preferences and financial and social profitability, as well as a consequence of land reforms, the population of working cattle should increase. However, there will be an upper limit to the bovine population that can be supported due to land and feed constraints. As this factor has not been examined in depth, we shall assume that the total bovine population and that the working bovine population will remain at the same level as in the sixties. This data gives the level of availability of animal resources, and the development plans, including the energy plan, should be drawn in a manner that would make optimal use of this resource.

While the stock of cattle may remain unaltered, the food grain production is expected to grow at least proportionately with the increase in population. There would be about 50 percent increase in food grain production and a proportionate increase in the quantity of roughage available for the bovine population. As most of the working cattle are maintained on this type of feed, the health and working capacity of the cattle should increase. The emaciated condition of the cattle in India has been the subject of derisive comment for a long time, but it is possible by proper management of fodder and roughage resources to improve the condition of the livestock by 1990. We will assume that when such improvement occurs, the working capacity of the cattle will increase by 25 percent, and the dung production will increase by 50 percent. The increase in the working capacity will result partly from better work performance and partly from increased days of work per year.

We can consider two possible cases of utilization of the additional animal power and dung thus generated in the economy. *Case I* assumes that there are no technological improvements but that the additional animate energy will be used in the farm sector for draught power and transport and the additional dung will be collected and used entirely for fuel purposes. *Case II* assumes that there will be technological improvements in the use of animal wastes and that the dung will be used in bio-gas plants of optimum sizes, which will lead to an increased supply of fuel for the domestic sector and nutrients to the agriculture sector.

In Case I, we get additional animate power of 19 million tons of coal equivalent and additional dung collection of 30 million tons of coal equivalent. The additional animal power will reduce the need for equivalent quantities of diesel oil; in tractors, transport trucks, and water-lifting pumps where diesel is used, dung will replace soft coke/coal.

If this option is adopted, the required energy needs in 1990-91 could be supplied as shown in Table 6-16. This option involves practically no special investments. In Case II, the cow dung available is used not as dung but as bio-gas by setting up bio-gas plants of appropriate sizes. Bio-gas plants are devices to ferment anaerobically biological and cellulosic material to produce gas with a high methane content and a sludge with 1.5 to 2.2 percent nitrogen. Animal dung by itself or along with some vegetable waste is normally used in these plants. If dung is used as dung cake only, fuel values are utilized and the nutrient is lost. If the dung is composted, compost with 0.75 to 1.0 percent nitrogen content alone is obtained and the heat value is lost. A bio-gas plant enables the heat value to be utilized while the nutrient is also "enriched." The financial and social profitability of bio-gas plants has been found to be very attractive in the Indian situation.[27] Institutional constraints, the expensive design adopted, and the problem of low fermentation in winter have hindered the adoption of bio-gas plants on a large scale in rural India. Following the oil crisis, great interest has been aroused among scientists, economists, and planners regarding bio-gas plants, and several technological improvements to reduce costs and improve fermentation efficiency have been suggested. Bio-gas plants can be of various sizes. The family size, which produces almost 60 cft of gas per day using 9.10 kg. of dry dung per day, can meet the needs of a family of five to six persons—that is, it can produce about 1.6 tce per year of energy. Families with four to five bovine animals can adopt this size plant. The community-size plant, which has a capacity of 5000 cft per day and would require about 500 kg. of dry dung, can meet the full needs of 500 to 600 people—that is, it can produce nearly as much energy as 200 tons of coal.

In India, it is reported that only 12 million rural households have four to five bovine animals. If these 12 million households use family-size bio-gas plants and if 50 percent of the dung of other animals is used in community-size plants, the gas yield, after allowing for the increased dung production, will be as follows: from family size plants, 30 mtce, and from community size plants, 112 mtce, for a total of 142 mtce. As compared to the Fuel Policy Committee's assessment that the level of consumption of dung cake will be 21 mtce, the supply could be as high as 142 mtce if Case II option is adopted. This option would lead to a decrease mainly in the use of firewood and to some extent in soft coke and kerosene. The possible energy supply situation in 1990 is presented in Table 6-16.

It should be noted that this option reduces the need for forest fuels to the minimum—that is, to the level possible from existing forests without denudation and without any investments in improving the forests. There will also be some energy saving because farm manure will replace chemical fertilizers with a consequent reduction in energy used for fertilizer production. The investment required for this option would be 66 billion rupees.[d] Although the animal resources option in Case II involves a very large investment, it has many externalities and may prove to have the highest benefit-cost ratio. However, it would call for great managerial talents to operate community-size bio-gas plants and would entail problems of organizing dung collection, valuation of dung to be bought, gas sales, and so forth.

Recent discussions on bio-gas utilization identified the concept of the Integrated Farming System (IFS), which could supply rural communities with adequate water resources, and at the same time provide for their fuel and food.[28] In this system, animal dung is digested in a suitable digester from which

[d]Computed at the rate of 2,000 rupees per family-size bio-gas plant and 80,000 rupees per community-size plant. The number of community-size plants will be 5.6 lakhs.

gas is collected separately. The slurry is washed into an algae basin (only a few inches high) where solar energy and atmospheric carbon dioxide act on it to produce algae growth (which contains 35-40 percent protein in dry condition). Algae, which floats on the surface, is "harvested" easily and the effluent from the algae basin is made to flow into deep ponds where fish and duck feed on natural planktons in the effluent. The mineral-rich effluent from the ponds is used for vegetable gardens. The major advantage claimed for IFS is that it provides a comprehensive solution to underproductivity and unemployment in rural areas. Although it is, as yet, too early to prognosticate on the extent to which IFS can be adopted in India, the system suggests one type of rural development pattern that may emerge, if resources that are now being allocated separately for irrigation, for manure production, and for fuel production are pooled and channelled towards such integrated systems.

We have looked at the domestic and agriculture sectors and the rural transport sector, where the approach was to plan for an appropriate fuel-use pattern. In industries and transport using predominantly commercial energy, it is theoretically possible to reduce the intensity of energy use by improving the efficiency of fuel utilization and by selecting more appropriate patterns of production and modes of transport. Efficiency improvements considered technically feasible have been taken note of in the "recommended fuel consumption pattern" by the Fuel Policy Committee. Increased energy and raw material prices have changed to some extent the comparative advantage of India in the international market, thereby making many activities economically less efficient. Possible rational adjustments to this situation have been briefly examined elsewhere,[29] and it was found that they are not likely to be significant unless energy-saving technologies are introduced in the near future. There are no signs of any major development in this regard, except in the energy production industries themselves. Theoretically, the transport sector provides the most economically meaningful possibilities for saving energy. Private transport is notoriously more energy intensive than public transport. Electrically run transport systems are less energy intensive than road transport but the electric systems become economically superior to road transport only when the density of traffic on particular routes is at an adequately high level. The Fuel Policy Committee has suggested the most feasible growth rates for road and rail transport in the private transport system. There are also possibilities for reducing transport needs, and hence the energy used for transport, by well-conceived urban development plans that reduce the distances from dwellings to work places. A National Policy on Urbanisation[30] is being advocated but no progress has been made. By 1991, India will have an urban population of over 180 million, and intelligent urban planning can reduce the transport needs significantly. It is difficult at this stage to estimate the costs of such policies or the amount of savings in fuel that can be achieved. These options could not be examined in detail.

Conclusions

The above discussions indicate that in India—a country with low per capita GNP—noncommercial energy and animal power are important sources of energy, and if all forms of energy are taken into account, a very slow decrease in the energy-GNP ratio is observed with commercial energy increasing in importance in the pattern of fuel usage. If rationalization of energy use is considered on restricted sectoral grounds, the possibilities for reducing energy consumption without disrupting long-term production and trade plans appear to be limited, as seen from the analysis of the Fuel Policy Committee (see Table 6-16). It is more relevant for developing countries in situations similar to India's to consider "appropriate energy profiles" that are compatible with their development goals. The Fuel Policy Committee has suggested a rationalization policy that will maximize the use of coal, an indigenously available commercial fuel. The "Coal option" has a great impact on the balance of payments. We have examined certain options that have the merit of integrating the issues of fuel supplies with the more important national development goals for reducing poverty. It is interesting to set all the options together and to examine the implications by reference to Table 6-16.

It is noteworthy that in all cases, it is possible to reduce the need for fossil fuels. Since electricity is a versatile form of energy, and in view of the production possibilities in the future from hydroelectric sources (up to a limit) and from fissile material, it is likely to be consumed according to the plans.

The presentation of the options in Table 6-16 is meant merely to indicate the limits to which each can be pushed. These are not mutually exclusive options. There is great variation in the levels of availability of different resources—of men, animals, and forests—in different regions of the country. The real solution cannot be worked out on the basis of elegant macro-models but has to be built up from micro-level studies at the regional, state, and village levels with reference to location-specific costs and relative fuel needs and resource availability.

But as we saw earlier, plans by themselves do not guarantee desired results. Institutional structures, management capabilities in each fuel industry, and the vision and efficiency of central planning agencies all have to be improved if a rational energy plan is to be implemented. In the area of forest development and animal resource development for energy purposes, there is hardly any modern management input. Existing institutional arrangements are archaic and inadequate. The task of establishing an adequate institutional infrastructure is probably the most urgent one; otherwise none of the schemes for alternate fuel supplies suggested above can be formulated and "sold" to the planners (who already have the schemes for commercial fuel production, as discussed in the second section of this chapter.

Assuming that the agencies for promoting the use of different fuels and arranging for their production will have evenly matched strengths and capabilities and that this happens very quickly, it will still be difficult to guess which direction the pattern of fuel utilization will ultimately take. Different options have varying impacts on different sections of the community; for example, the section of the rural population that will benefit most by adopting the animal resource option will be different from the sections that will derive maximum benefit from the adoption of the forest fuel option. It is, therefore, not merely the resource endowments, technical options, and managerial capabilities of the agencies involved that will determine the decisions; the ultimate decision will involve value judgments and political choices.

Notes

1. Government of India, *Report of the Fuel Policy Committee*, New Delhi, 1974, p. 4. This report is the latest official report on the Indian energy situation and includes projection of fuel demand in India up to 1990-91 and important recommendations for management of the energy sector.

2. Government of India, *Third Five Year Plan*, New Delhi, 1960, p. 194. The working bovine population has been taken from the livestock census of India for the years 1956, 1961, and 1966.

3. Government of India, *Third Five Year Plan.*

4. Government of India, *Annual Report of the Department of Coal and Mines 1957-58.*

5. Government of India, *Second Five Year Plan*, New Delhi, 1955.

6. Government of India, *Annual Report of Ministry of Power 1965-66*, p. 21.

7. Government of India, *Annual Report of Ministry of Mines and Fuel 1958-60.*

8. Government of India, *Third Five Year Plan*, p. 483.

9. Ibid., p. 525.

10. Ibid., p. 485.

11. Government of India, *Third Five Year Plan—Mid-term Appraisal*, Planning Commission, New Delhi, 1965, p. 134.

12. Government of India, *Annual Report of Ministry of Mines and Fuel, 1966-67.*

13. Government of India, *Memorandum of Fourth Five Year Plan*, Planning Commission, New Delhi, 1968.

14. Government of India, *Committee on Transport Policy and Coordination, Final Report*, Planning Commission, New Delhi, 1964.

15. Government of India, *Third Five Year Plan*, p. 397.

16. Government of India, *Report of the Fuel Policy Committee of India*, New Delhi, 1974.

17. Government of India, *Draft Fifth Five Year Plan*, Planning Commission, New Delhi, 1974, Chapter I.

18. Government of India, *Report of the Fuel Policy Committee*, Chapter III.

19. Government of India, *Draft Fifth Five Year Plan*, Chapter I, which gives anticipated population, rural and urban ratios up to 1985-86. The figures for 1990-91 were obtained by extrapolation.

20. V.P. Agarwala, "Industrial Potential of Forest Resources," *Natural Resources in the Indian Economy* (Bombay: Vadi Lal Dagli, Vora & Co., 1971), p. 52.

21. Government of India, *Report of the Fuel Policy Committee*, p. 94.

22. Government of India, *Report on Social Forestry*, National Commission on Agriculture, New Delhi, August 1973.

23. K.N. Raj, "Investment in Live Stock in Agrarian Economies: A Theoretical and Empirical Analysis," mimeo, 1967.

24. C.H. Hanumantha Rao,"Technological Change and Distribution of Gains in Agriculture," mimeo, Institute of Economic Growth, New Delhi, 1974, pp. 87-88.

25. News report published in *Hindustan Times*, Delhi, August 23, 1975.

26. NSSO, Department of Statistics Planning Commission, *The National Sample Survey—25th Round Tables with Notes on Problems and Prospects of Weaker Sections of Rural Population*, New Delhi, no date.

27. Kirit Parikh, "Benefit Cost Analysis of Biogas Plants in India," unpublished thesis, M.I.T., Cambridge, Mass., 1963.

28. Workshop on Biogas Technology & Utilisation, ESCAP, *Report of the Preparatory Mission on Biogas Technology & Utilisation*, New Delhi, July 28, 1975 to August 2, 1975.

29. T.L. Sankar, "Domestic Adjustment to Higher Raw Material & Energy Prices in Less Developed Countries," *American Journal of Agricultural Economics* (May 1975), pp. 237-46.

30. "Habitat: The U.N. Conference on Human Settlements, Regional Proparity Conference, Tehran," *Indian Reporters*, India 1975.

Appendix 6A
Statistical Data

Table 6A-1
Consumption of Energy, 1953-54 to 1970-71 (in original units)

Year	Commercial Energy			Noncommercial Energy		
	Coal (in million tons)[a]	Oil (in million tons)[b]	Electricity (in billion KWH)	Dung (in million tons)[c]	Firewood (in million tons)	Vegetable Waste (in million tons)
1953-54	28.70	3.66	7.60	46.40	86.30	26.40
1954-55	28.50	3.96	8.40	47.60	87.50	27.00
1955-56	28.80	4.66	9.40	48.80	88.80	27.70
1956-57	30.70	4.67	10.20	50.10	90.10	28.40
1957-58	34.60	5.22	11.70	51.40	91.40	29.10
1958-59	36.10	5.55	13.20	52.70	92.70	29.90
1959-60	35.70	6.16	15.40	53.30	96.30	30.20
1960-61	40.40	6.74	16.90	55.38	101.04	31.08
1961-62	44.10	7.46	19.37	56.10	102.39	31.51
1962-63	49.10	8.39	22.57	56.75	103.58	31.87
1963-64	48.60	8.65	25.21	58.57	106.88	32.89
1964-65	48.20	9.29	27.76	59.30	108.19	33.28
1965-66	51.80	9.94	30.56	61.28	111.82	34.41
1966-67	52.30	10.62	33.21	62.60	114.21	35.14
1967-68	54.50	11.28	36.76	64.07	116.92	35.97
1968-69	53.00	12.66	41.46	64.98	118.54	36.46
1969-70	56.66	13.85	45.02	65.92	120.25	37.00
1970-71	51.35	14.95	48.65	67.28	122.76	37.77

Source: For commercial energy figures: *Fuel Policy Committee Report*, 1965. For noncommercial energy: 1953-54 to 1959-60, *Energy Survey Committee Report*, 1965; 1960-61 to 1970-71, *Fuel Policy Committee Report*, 1974.

[a]Coal consumption figures exclude coal used for power generation.

[b]Oil consumption figures exclude oil used in power generation and refinery boiler-fuel.

[c]Dung weight on dry basis.

Table 6A-2
Coal Equivalent of Different Fuels

Fuels	Unit		MTCE
Coal (Coking 6640 kcal/kg: noncoking coal used in steam generation 5000 kcal/kg)	1	mt	1.0
Oil Products (10000 kcal/kg)	1	mt	2.0
Electricity	10^9	kwh	1.0
Dung (dry)	1	mt	0.4
Firewood (4750 kcal/kg)	1	mt	0.95
Vegetable Waste	1	mt	0.95

Table 6A-3
GDP and Energy Consumption in India (1953-54 to 1970-71)

Sector Year	Domestic and Others					Agriculture					Mining and Manufacturing					Transport					Total				
	GNP	TEC	Coal	Oil	Elec.	GNP	TEC	Coal	Oil	Elec.	GNP	TEC	Coal	Oil	Elec.	GNP	TEC	Coal	Oil	Elec.	GNP	TEC	Coal	Oil	Elec.
1953-54	2534	7.61	2.80	3.01	1.80	6015	0.70	–	0.50	0.20	1748	19.92	13.80	1.12	5.00	433	15.40	12.10	2.70	0.60	10730	43.63	28.70	7.33	7.60
1954-55	2658	8.24	3.00	3.24	2.00	6044	0.70	–	0.50	0.20	1897	20.70	13.80	1.30	5.60	454	15.18	11.70	2.88	0.60	11053	44.82	28.50	7.92	8.40
1955-56	2787	9.46	3.20	4.16	2.10	6054	0.83	–	0.53	0.30	2091	21.05	13.30	1.45	6.30	501	16.19	12.30	3.19	0.70	11433	47.53	28.80	9.33	9.40
1956-57	2917	9.81	3.60	3.91	2.30	6355	0.64	–	0.34	0.30	2273	21.85	13.40	1.55	6.90	521	17.94	13.70	3.54	0.70	12066	50.24	30.70	9.34	10.20
1957-58	3029	10.09	3.30	4.09	2.70	6050	1.27	–	0.67	0.60	2284	26.00	16.60	1.70	7.70	545	19.48	14.70	3.98	0.80	11908	56.84	34.60	10.44	11.80
1958-59	3156	10.91	3.70	4.21	3.00	6707	1.32	–	0.72	0.60	2421	28.23	17.60	1.83	8.80	597	19.55	14.80	4.35	0.80	12881	60.41	36.10	11.11	13.20
1959-60	3317	11.98	3.70	4.78	3.50	6613	1.49	–	0.79	0.70	2591	29.08	16.80	1.98	10.30	639	20.88	15.20	4.78	0.90	13160	63.43	35.70	12.33	15.40
1960-61	3510	12.28	3.50	5.08	3.70	7009	1.64	–	0.84	0.80	2865	34.72	20.90	2.22	11.60	687	22.14	16.00	5.34	0.80	14071	70.78	40.40	13.48	16.90
1961-62	3697	12.21	3.20	5.67	3.34	7078	1.89	–	0.90	0.99	3102	41.03	24.20	2.37	14.46	732	23.27	16.70	5.99	0.58	14609	78.40	44.10	14.93	19.37
1962-63	3914	14.00	3.70	6.23	4.07	6908	2.08	–	0.98	1.10	3378	47.37	28.00	2.87	16.50	790	25.00	17.40	6.70	0.90	14990	88.45	49.10	16.78	22.57
1963-64	4162	14.79	4.20	6.42	4.17	7108	2.21	–	1.06	1.15	3687	48.15	27.00	2.02	19.13	840	25.96	17.40	7.80	0.76	15797	91.11	49.10	17.30	25.21
1964-65	4420	15.00	3.70	6.86	4.44	7740	2.46	–	1.06	1.40	3972	50.32	27.20	2.20	20.92	881	26.86	17.40	8.46	1.00	17013	94.64	48.20	18.58	27.76
1965-66	4515	15.70	4.40	6.41	4.89	6716	3.25	–	1.36	1.89	4105	55.21	30.10	2.49	22.62	929	28.08	17.30	9.62	1.16	16265	102.24	51.80	19.88	30.56
1966-67	4661	17.07	5.00	6.62	5.45	6624	3.69	–	1.58	2.11	4258	57.57	30.40	2.79	24.38	957	28.43	16.90	10.26	1.27	16500	106.76	52.30	21.25	33.21
1967-68	4816	17.87	4.80	7.04	6.01	7696	4.20	–	1.62	2.58	4448	62.82	33.00	3.03	26.79	1014	28.94	16.70	10.86	1.38	17974	113.83	54.50	22.57	36.76
1968-69	5037	19.34	4.80	7.79	6.75	7797	5.57	–	2.11	3.46	4707	65.03	31.90	3.20	29.93	1065	29.84	16.30	12.22	1.32	18608	119.78	53.00	25.32	41.46
1969-70	5304	22.75	5.20	8.09	7.46	8277	5.17	–	1.40	3.77	4927	70.56	35.34	2.88	32.34	1122	30.91	16.12	13.34	1.45	19630	129.39	56.66	27.71	45.02
1970-71	5539	23.33	4.37	10.63	8.33	8909	5.93	–	1.39	4.54	4948	68.77	31.07	3.35	34.35	1153	31.87	15.91	14.53	1.43	20549	129.90	51.35	29.90	48.65

Sources: National Accounts Statistics, January 1975; C.S.O.; Government of India. Report of the Fuel Policy Committee, India, 1974.

Note: GDP at factor cost at 1960-61 prices, figures in Rs. 10 millions.
TEC: Total Energy Consumption (commercial).
TEC, Coal, Oil and Electricity figures in million tonnes of coal equivalent.

Appendix 6B
A Technical Note

Conversion Factors Used for Aggregation of Energy
Measures in Developed and Developing Countries

For understanding energy supply and consumption data, energy consumed in different fuel forms will have to be expressed in a common energy unit. The most commonly used measurement is the coal equivalent. The coal equivalent measure is defined as the amount of coal that would provide the quantity of energy furnished by a unit of any other energy source. For example, if petroleum products have 10 million kilocalories of energy in 1 ton and the average grade of coal in the country has 5 million kilocalories per ton, the coal equivalent of 1 ton of oil product is 2 tons of coal equivalent; in other words, 1 ton of oil equals 2 tce. Table 6B-1 sets out the gross energy in different fuels and the coal equivalent measures. For comparison, the coal replacement measures are also given in the same table.

Coal replacement measures indicate the amount of coal that would be needed to substitute for one unit of the other fuel. This measure takes note not only of the energy available in different fuels used but also of the varying efficiency of the appliances employed in using the fuels. Since the noncommercial fuels are used in the domestic sector, the coal replacement measure in all Indian studies has been obtained by first determining the efficiency of heat utilization of soft coke, a coal-derived domestic fuel. The determination of energy utilization has been made by studies in the Central Fuel Research Institute. Typical calculations by which the coal replacement measures have been derived are given below for firewood, dung cake, and vegetable waste, which are the noncommercial fuels, and also for kerosene, which is an important commercial fuel used in the domestic sector.

Table 6B-1
Gross Energy of Various Fuels and Coal Replacement Measures

Fuel	Unit	Thousand Kilocalories	Coal Equivalent	Coal Replacement
Coal	Ton	5,912	1.000	1.00
Soft Coke	Ton	5,772	0.976	1.50
Firewood	Ton	4,286	0.725	0.95
Other Vegetable Waste	Ton	3,800	0.543	0.95
Dung Cake	Ton	2,092	0.354	0.40
Kerosene	Ton	2,092	1.857	8.30
Electricity	1000 kWh	860	0.145	1.00

251

Dung Cake

Heat content of 1 ton dung cake is 2,444,000 kilocalories
Heat content of 1 ton of soft coke 5,772,000 kilocalories
Efficiency of utilization in conventional domestic oven is (a) 11.2 percent for dung cake and (b) 17.7 percent for soft coke

∴ Effective heat utilization of one ton of dung cake equals

$$\frac{11.2}{100} \times 2,444,000 = 273,728 \text{ kilocalories.}$$

If the same effective heat is to be obtained through the use of soft coke, the amount of soft coke needed will be:

$$\frac{100}{17.7} \times \frac{273,728}{5,772,000} = 0.268 \text{ ton.}$$

As per normal yield rate of soft coke the amount of raw coal that will be needed for the above is

$$\frac{1.5}{1.00} \times 0.268 = 0.40 \text{ ton.}$$

In other words, one ton of dry dung is equivalent to 0.4 ton of coal replacement.

Firewood for Heating

Heat content of 1 ton of firewood is 4,702,000 kilocalories
Efficiency of utilization is 13.7 percent

∴ Effective heat utilization of 1 ton of firewood equals

$$13.7 \times 4,702,000 = 644,000 \text{ kilocalories.}$$

If the same effective heat is to be obtained through the use of soft coke, the amount of soft coke needed will be:

$$\frac{100}{17.7} \times \frac{644,000}{5,772,000} = 0.63 \text{ ton.}$$

In terms of coal, this is equivalent to

$$\frac{1.5}{1.0} \times 0.63 = 0.95 \text{ ton.}$$

Vegetable Waste for Heating

Heat content of 1 ton of vegetable waste is about 3,800,000 kilocalories
Efficiency of utilization is 17 percent

∴ Effective heat utilization equals

$$\frac{17}{100} \times 3,800,000 = 646,000 \text{ kilocalories.}$$

If the same effective heat is to be obtained through the use of soft coke, the amount of soft coke required will be:

$$\frac{100}{17.7} \times \frac{646,000}{5,772,000} = 0.65 \text{ ton.}$$

In terms of coal, this is equivalent to

$$\frac{1.5}{1.0} \times 0.63 = 0.95 \text{ ton.}$$

Heat value and utilization efficiency of selected vegetable waste as reported by CFRI are shown in Table 6B-2.

Kerosene for Heating

Heat content of 1 ton of kerosene is 11,111,000 kilocalories
Heat content of 1 ton of soft coke is 5,772,000 kilocalories
Efficiency of utilization of kerosene for heating is 50.8 percent

Table 6B-2
Heat Value and Utilization Efficiency of Selected Vegetable Waste

Fuel	Calorific Value (kcal/kg)	Heat Utilization Efficiency
Sawdust from Salwood	4460	15.6
Paddy Husk	3440	17.0
Jute Sticks	4190	17.3
Arhar Stick	4265	19.4

Efficiency of utilization of soft coke for heating is 17.7 percent

∴ Effective utilization of 1 ton of kerosene equals

$$\frac{50.8}{100} \times 11,111,000 = 5,646,388 \text{ kilocalories.}$$

If the same effective heat is to be obtained through the use of soft coke, the amount of soft coke needed will be:

$$\frac{100}{17.7} \times \frac{5,646,388}{5,772,000} = 5.5 \text{ tons.}$$

The corresponding coal equivalent is

$$\frac{1.5}{1.0} \times 5.5 = 8.3 \text{ tons.}$$

7

Swedish Energy Policy: Technology in the Political Process

Måns Lönnroth

Introduction

This chapter aims at discussing technology as an issue in the political process. The main emphasis is on energy policy, and the discussion is very much an open-ended one. More questions are asked than answered.

The chapter was written as a part of the work in the "Energy and Society" project[1] of the Secretariat for Future Studies in Sweden.[2] It consists of two interrelated but somewhat separate parts. In the first part we discuss the decision on energy policy taken by the Swedish Parliament in May 1975, a decision that was seen by many as marking the end of one era and the beginning of another. In the second part we discuss the driving forces behind the Swedish electricity supply systems. These forces are explained here in terms of the interrelations between technical and organizational change. The two parts are tied together in the end by some notes on possible future energy policies, the introduction of new technical alternatives, and their relationships to recent and possible organizational structures. The main theme is the probability that we will not have very much choice on the technical level unless we change the division of responsibility in the energy supply system.

The Situation in 1975

The Decision of the Parliament in May 1975

The Swedish Parliament took a decision on future Swedish energy policy in May 1975. The main contents of this decision were:

An outspoken intent to decrease the historical growth rate of final energy demand to an average of 2 percent between the years 1975 and 1985, together with a commitment to try to achieve zero growth in final demand from 1990 onwards;

A series of measures to realize this goal, including a higher tax on energy, grants for retrofitting in space heating, grants for increased use of waste heat from industrial plants, and so forth, together with a large R&D program, that is divided roughly equally between supply and demand;

A series of measures on the supply side, notably a continued expansion of nuclear power;

A new decision on energy policy to be taken in 1978.

More details will be given later in this chapter. For a comprehensive summary, see the speech of the prime minister[3] and material from the Department of Industry.[4]

This decision has been regarded as the end of one era and the beginning of another. In the outgoing era, energy policy by and large was handled on the administrative level in the bureaucracy. Only rarely were fragments of energy policy discussed in the Parliament or by the government. The policy up to 1975 can be summarized as a supply-oriented policy, with the main emphasis on electricity supply. The oil supply was left to market forces. Thus it can be said that with some minor exceptions energy had not been a political issue since, roughly, the beginning of this century. We will return to this later, and only note here that at that time energy was an issue because of the intense legislative work necessary to introduce hydropower into an essentially agrarian economy.

The new era is characterized by a policy of active balancing of supply and demand with a deliberate weighting of measures to increase supply as compared to decreasing demand. This seemingly qualitative change in policy has already meant some rather marked changes in the division of responsibility between, for example, the private and the public sector, but also within different parts of the public sector.

This change occurred gradually, but two events were significant. The first one was the change in the outlook on nuclear power that took place in 1973 and the second was the oil embargo.

Nuclear Power in Sweden

Nuclear power has long been seen as the next stage in energy supply. This attitude goes back to the 1950s, when there was some worry about the rapidly increasing imports of oil, and nuclear power was seen as a method for generating space heating. More seriously it also stems from the discussion during the 1950s and 1960s on conservation of the remaining rivers in the north and the hope that nuclear power could be used to generate electricity and thus preserve parts of the wilderness.

Nuclear power was also a part of the industrial policy of the country, thereby reflecting the wish to be in the technological vanguard not only in nuclear power but also in computers, and so forth. Sweden was anxious to establish a nuclear industry of its own, and heavy commitments were made in different forms. In 1972 the Centrala Drift Ledningen (Central Operating

Management—an association of all Swedish electric power companies)[5] published a plan for building twenty-four nuclear reactors by the year 1990, which would make Sweden the most advanced nuclear power in terms of electricity generated per capita. Political agreement was unanimous.

The first nuclear plant was built by a private consortium, and the twenty-four plants were to be built by both private and public utilities. Decisions on building nuclear plants are formally taken by the government according to the law on nuclear energy. If the plants are constructed by the State Power Board, the Parliament as well has to decide upon the financing. By 1973 decisions had been taken to build a total of eleven plants, some privately and some by the State Power Board.

By now a growing uneasiness was felt, and individual members in the Parliament started asking questions about the nuclear fuel cycle among other topics. A leading person in this change of mood was Nobel Laureate Hannes Alfvén, who questioned among other things reactor safety, proliferation, waste handling, and so forth. A bill presented to the Parliament called for a halt to further expansion of nuclear power if certain requirements could not be met. The bill was rejected by the Parliament, which instead stated that "no decisions should be made on expanding nuclear power until a comprehensive study is available to the Parliament."

All that existed up to 1973 was a forecast made by CDL, which requested twenty-four plants by the year 1990. The program was specifically for generating electricity—there was no equivalent program for handling the total fuel cycle. The result was a so-called moratorium. A series of royal commissions dealing with energy forecasts, nuclear matters, and so forth were supposed to finish their inquiries during 1974, and it was concluded that a new decision should be postponed until 1975.

The resolution of the Parliament also in effect meant a change in the balance of power between the executive branch—that is, the government—and the Parliament. Without any formal changes in the laws, the Parliament made itself the final decisionmaker.

The Oil Embargo

Imports of oil expanded rapidly after 1945. Every now and then worried remarks were heard about the growing dependence on foreign energy sources, but by and large this dependence was accepted. Since the expansion was managed almost entirely by the private sector (the early attempt by the Social Democratic Government to socialize the oil industry around 1946 was never carried out), the expansion also went largely unnoticed in the official documents. The intervention of the public sector was limited to requiring certain stockpiles of reserves.

The embargo of 1973-74 changed all this. Not only did it show Sweden's vulnerability to external pressure, but it was also seen by many people as an ominous sign of structural difficulties within the industrial societies. To some, the oil crisis was taken as an excuse to try to awake the public to the fact that the capitalist economy had to change. Among others, the minister of commerce and the prime minister raised questions about the "gadget society."

The Public Debate on Energy Policy

Thus the review of nuclear power decided upon by the Parliament coincided with the oil embargo. These two events triggered a debate with two major aspects: What should the energy supply look like, and how much energy did Sweden really need?

The government decided to take the initiative in this situation and in January 1974 mounted a campaign of study groups throughout Swedish society. These study groups were organized under the aegis of the voluntary adult education associations, which in turn have strong links to different popular movements such as political parties, churches, and temperance movements. Special grants were given, and the educational associations were offered background material of different types. Most of the associations decided to write their own booklets.

The groups started in the fall of 1974, and altogether some 8,000 study groups were set up with 80,000 participants. About half of these were organized by ABF (Workers Educational Association), which is close to the Social Democratic Party and the trade unions. The other participants were divided between the Liberal and Center parties, the Conservatives, and other groups. There was also an intense discussion in the press, together with public meetings, hearings of experts, and so forth.

The debate centered around nuclear power, but it also developed into a debate on how much energy was needed, and what the relationships were between energy supply and different social goals such as high employment, welfare, environmental questions, and so forth. The debate rapidly evolved into a debate based on fundamental political views of society.

At the same time none of the political parties had any clear-cut views of future energy policy. There were of course differences—the Center party took a strong stand against nuclear power at an early stage—but by and large the programs of the political parties evolved as a result of the debate.

The government bill and the subsequent decision of the Parliament has to be seen in this light. On the most sensitive topic, nuclear power, it was decided to increase the number of nuclear plants from eleven to thirteen. This amount would secure the supply of electricity up to the year 1985.

Thus we can say that in the short run the plans of the electric power industry of 1972 were by and large continued even though the forecasts were reduced. The inertia of the factors determining demand was regarded as too large—it was not possible to change too quickly. In the short run, the viewpoint of the established energy supply system was by and large accepted. In the longer run it was not.

There is no doubt that the government and the Parliament somewhat strained the interpretation of the study groups' conclusions on how much nuclear power was acceptable. The opinion polls continue to show a strong uneasiness about nuclear power that cut across all political parties. Although all the parties have declared their views on nuclear power, it is obvious that the feelings of the public do not neatly follow the party lines. The split is much more within than between parties. In all parties, very large groups are against nuclear power, and it is much too early to declare nuclear power a nonissue. This issue apparently stirs up sentiments within the public of much greater intensity and depth than generally was foreseen.

We can thus see decision making on energy policy between 1973 and 1976 as a process where an issue that up to then had been handled by highly competent and specialized technocrats was taken out of their hands and put squarely into the range of issues that are influenced at the political level. Whether this change is temporary or not remains to be seen. No doubt the experts that hitherto had handled energy policy were severely shocked by the intensity of the debate. The established analogies, frames of reference, and paradigms were rejected. It remains to be seen what the new paradigms will look like and to whom the power to decide will be allocated.

In other words—the political debate on energy policy was very much a debate on legitimacy. The legitimacy of the established decision-making process was questioned and to some extent openly rejected. Whether it is possible or not to change the decision-making process in such a way that its outcomes are more acceptable to the public remains to be seen.

Swedish Energy Supply and Demand

The Swedish demand for energy in 1973 was roughly (in 1,000 billion watts):

Industry	154
Transportation	73
Residential and commercial	146
Total final demand	373

Today, oil accounts for over 70 percent of primary energy; hydropower, 15 percent; spent liquor, firewood, and waste, 8 percent; coal, 4 percent; and nuclear, .5 percent of the energy supply.

The Swedish energy-GNP ratio is 60 percent of the U.S. ratio. Schipper has done a detailed breakdown of the statistics and shown that this difference by and large is explained by the facts that the Swedish transportation pattern consumes much less energy than the American one and that sector by sector Swedish industry is more energy efficient.[6] The Swedish climate is on the average colder, but the homes are better insulated.

Historically, however, the Swedish situation is not as flattering. Swedish energy demand has increased 4.5 percent annually since the early 1950s. This growth is considerably faster than the GNP, and the energy-GNP ratio has increased. The Swedish economy has thus become less and less energy efficient.

A more detailed analysis shows that Swedish industry has become more and more efficient in its use of energy—that is, less and less energy is required per unit of output. All the other sectors—transportation, agriculture, commercial, and residential, and so forth—have become less energy efficient. The rise in Sweden's energy-GNP ratio is to no small degree explained by the rapid increase in household energy use: larger and warmer homes, more cars, more appliances, and so forth.

The share of energy that is supplied directly to the household has also increased over the years. It is now about two thirds of the total household energy consumption. This latter includes not only the energy needed for heating homes and driving cars, but also for building homes, producing goods, and so forth. Roughly speaking, the Swedish economy has become more and more energy efficient in *producing* goods and less and less energy efficient in *using* the same goods. Swedish energy demand to a larger and larger extent is determined by what the households do—that is, lifestyle patterns, and so forth.

But how does one analyze energy demand? The established way of describing energy use is in terms of industry, transportation, commercial, and residential sectors. Nearly all studies from different countries are made in these terms, and the latest official Swedish forecast[7] was no exception. At the same time it was obvious that the political debate very much centered around questions and topics—such as the relationship between energy and employment, standard of living, income distribution, work environment, and so forth—that simply were not possible to address through the established ways of describing energy use.

To put the case more explicitly, the established way is the way of the energy supply establishment. The breakdown into industrial, transportation, residential, and commercial use is necessary and more or less sufficient for making crude forecasts (crude since these forecasts also are invariably made without reference to the price of energy). It is a way of describing energy use that is the direct consequence of an attitude that demand shall not be influenced. Thus it is not necessary to understand energy demand or the relationship between energy use and the economy.

In order to at least approach the politically relevant questions other types of breakdowns of the statistics are necessary. One such example is shown in Table 7-1 in which the intensity of the use of primary energy for different end uses in the economy is given in terms of kWh/scr. The most obvious development is that private consumption is becoming more energy intensive. This increase is referred to above as being the result of larger homes, bigger cars, more appliances, etc.

It is also possible to relate the amount of employment—in terms of numbers of working hours—that the different end uses generate per unit. This data is shown in Table 7-2 (number of working hours/scr). The Swedish labor force has become increasingly efficient, and the fastest increase is in private consumption and export, which are both very goods-oriented sectors where it is relatively easy to substitute capital for labor.

These two tables can now be combined, and we can compute the amount of energy that is needed per unit of work for different end uses, as is shown in Figure 7-1. The most striking point is that the amount of energy needed for one hour of work for different end uses has become progressively larger over the ten-year period. Private consumption is more and more energy intensive and less and less labor intensive. The same goes for exports, while the heavily service-oriented municipal consumption has not changed at all over the years.

These figures point out where some of the main conflicts in future energy policy will be found in the following areas:

1. Between private and public consumption: Future energy demand will increase much more rapidly if we let private consumption increase quickly.

Table 7-1
Intensity of Primary Energy Use

End Use	1960	1965	1970
Private Consumption	2.13	2.62	3.06
State Consumption	1.86	1.29	1.70
Municipal Consumption	1.07	1.27	1.24
Investment Consumption	1.94	1.85	2.16
Export Consumption	3.58	3.53	4.70

Table 7-2
Employment Intensity

	1960	1965	1970
Private Consumption	62.0	46.7	26.0
State Consumption	57.6	49.0	43.7
Municipal Consumption	56.8	51.4	51.2
Investment Consumption	73.8	58.1	46.8
Export Consumption	75.8	56.5	41.1

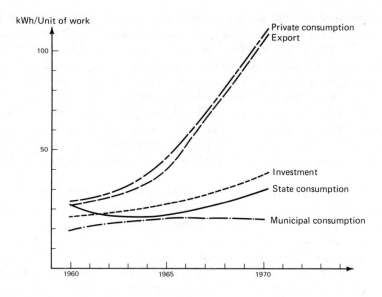

Figure 7-1. Amounts of Energy Needed for Various Units of Work.

Since the relative weight of public versus private consumption is an issue in itself in Swedish politics, energy policy is interconnected with this issue.

2. Distribution between different groups in the population: Households with high income use more energy than households with lesser income. If energy becomes scarce, the question arises how this scarce commodity should be allocated. Higher taxes on electricity and oil for heating purposes are regressive, and thus hitting lower income groups more severely. Total (= direct + indirect) household energy consumption is dominated by end-uses such as homes, transportation, food and leisure activities. Changes in consumption patterns due to energy scarcity will primarily have to effect these end-uses.

3. Between the degree of autonomy and international specialization: Swedish industry is heavily export-oriented, with a large share of the energy-consuming industries operating mainly in the export market (paper and pulp, and so forth). How large an industrial sector we will have is thus important.

Other conflict areas include environmental issues. Recently the Swedish Environmental Protection Board more or less banned increased disposal of waste hot water from nuclear reactors into the Baltic Sea. And at the same time the worry over acidification from the use of fossil fuel continues to mount. The room for maneuverability in energy supply is thus rapidly contracting, which of course increases the importance of an energy conservation policy, to which we now turn. More details on conflicts between energy policy and other policy areas can be found elsewhere.[8]

Some Aspects of an Energy Conservation Policy

The shift from a supply orientation towards a policy of deliberate management of both supply and demand in our view marks a rather fundamental change. This change is both conceptual and organizational. A supply-oriented policy is generally rather well-defined when it comes to the actors that are supposed to be influenced, controlled, and regulated. After all, there are only between ten and twenty large companies—private and public—on the total energy supply side. And the primary goal of all these actors is to produce energy of different qualities.

In contrast, the demand side consists of a very large number of decision-makers and actors. For each one, energy is not a goal in itself but one means to achieve something else, be it production of goods in an industrial plant or the self-fulfillment of an individual consumer. On the demand side, energy is usually only one part of a process designed to achieve the goals of the actors. In other words, there are reasons to believe that energy conservation policies interact in a very complex way with other policy areas, and sometimes in a rather unpredictable manner. We will give examples of this interaction later. And at the same time, since demand-side aspects of energy traditionally are nondecision areas from the point of view of the public sector, there is no administrative infrastructure through which to channel decisions on how to balance supply and demand.

An example from another policy area may be illuminating. The supply of water consists of large technical systems on either side of consumer households, industrial plants, and so forth. A fresh water supply system and a water purification system is needed, and both are very capital intensive. In many growing regions the water supply is tight, and water is taken through large tunnels from faraway areas. In southern Sweden such was the case. There was a proposal to build a huge tunnel that would cost a large amount of money. The alternative was to decrease consciously the rate of increase in water demand through water conservation policies (e.g., changing toilets, putting in new taps, etc.). It was argued that the latter approach would be much cheaper in overall cost, and certainly would strain the capital market less since the costs were more evenly spread out over time. But the decision to build the tunnel was taken. There simply did not exist any decision-making framework that was able to handle the choice in allocation of resources between building the tunnel and changing the taps and the toilets. Inertia in the existing supply-oriented structure—organizations, trade unions, construction firms, and so forth—of course pushed the same way.

This example has several characteristics that make it an interesting analogue to energy. The water system is a technically—and perhaps ecologically—very well-defined system. A number of technical components—tunnels, waterplats, plumbing systems, toilets, taps, sewage systems, pollution plats, and so forth— are all hooked together into one technical system—the water cycle—that in itself is a part of a large ecosystem. But these technically interdependent components are handled by different organizational units, which in turn are partially controlled and regulated by a large number of legal acts, statutes, rules of financing, and so forth. In other words, the organizational and institutional framework in which the technical system is embedded is a very fragmented one.

Schon suggests a relation between a technical system, the organization in which the technical system is embedded, and the theory or paradigm that the organization has as to what its roles are.[9] In the water supply case above, obviously the different actors—who all were linked together through one technical system—did not accept the idea that they could cooperate and reduce the overall demand on resources. There simply did not exist any decision-making unit that saw it as its role to look upon the technical system of water supply as its problem.

The analogies to energy are perhaps most obvious in the electricity case. Sweden has a technically continuous system with hydropower stations, national grids, transformers, distribution grids, meters in the households, and so forth, that ends in the individual refrigerator. And all these components are mutually interdependent. The organizational picture in contrast has the same fragmented outlook as in the water cycle case above. Other parts of the energy supply system have similar properties. The gas system is the most obvious one, but the oil supply system has the same type of technical interdependencies.

To our thinking, these types of interorganizational systems are very poorly understood. The technical interdependencies are matched by a system of interorganizational rules. Price mechanisms and the like are an integral part of this rule system, but by no means the only ones, or, perhaps, even the most important. Other parts of the rule system consist of rules for how costs are defined, how capital is raised, how mortgages are defined, what the technical specifications should be, and so forth. Some of these rules are decided by the Parliament, others by different bureaucratic agencies, and still others by various industrial associations.

To repeat, we think it is necessary to start analyzing the whole interorganizational rule system and not only the so-called market mechanisms. There are signs, we think, that the market mechanism is becoming less and less efficient, and not so much because of outside intervention by the national government and/or regulations but from the mere fact that energy technologies are becoming increasingly more capital intensive.

The lead times in investment decisions are growing, and thus the supply system is less and less able to respond to rapid changes in demand. Such changes in actual demand, as compared to the demand forecasts on which the investment decisions were based, can occur because of such factors as unexpected rises in capital or fuel costs that in turn require higher rates. In other words, there are risks that the suppliers may find themselves in a vicious circle of the kind shown in Figure 7-2. The main reason is that demand responds more rapidly to rate changes than supply responds to demand changes. Tendencies of this kind have been observed in the Swedish water supply system, where essentially the same cost structure exists. Kahn et al. discuss the same problem for electric utilities.[10] The net result of such a situation is that prices rise when demand falls—quite contrary to textbook economics.

A rigorous energy conservation strategy may throw the utilities into serious financial difficulties. This problem is without a doubt a serious one that greatly reduces the value of the price as a regulator. An amusing example of this type of difficulty is the problematic situation that the Swedish utilities found themselves in when the coal-wire lightbulb was replaced by the much less electricity consuming metal-wire lightbulb in the 1910s. This change also triggered a debate on how to expand the use of electricity. One issue was, e.g., whose responsibility it was to supply tenants in the cities with electric wires and so forth. When this responsibility was taken over from the tenants by the landlords installment of electric equipment was easier and thus the use of electricity stimulated. Today this division of responsibility between tenant and landlord is taken for granted, but once it was not.

Therefore it seems that as the capital intensity of the supply system grows and the leadtime of the investment decision grows, the responsiveness of the suppliers to changes in demand diminishes. Thus price as a regulator between supply and demand plays a decreasingly important role. All the changes in the rate structure of the electric utilities since the beginning of the century reflect this—the main objectives of the changes have been to stimulate demand.

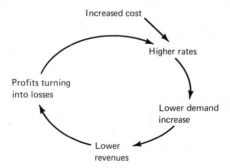

Figure 7-2. Circular Interaction of Response Factors Affecting Changes in Demand.

Summing up, there are a number of interesting aspects in an energy conservation policy. One aspect is that it is administratively complex; in other words, one might expect that the favored conservation measures are those that have rather limited side effects and require limited adjustments in other policy areas. Another aspect is that some conservation measures may create problems for the utilities. And a third aspect is that conservation technologies that do not fall neatly within the existing organizational boundaries but require new interorganizational rules are quite likely to be rejected because of the inherent complexity of the administrative situation.

Swedish energy conservation policy can be described in these terms. First of all the electricity tax was raised. The earlier tax on the cost of electricity has now been made a tax on the amount of electricity consumed. The result has been among other things that the actual development of electric resistance heating has been lower than forecast. The increased revenues of course finance parts of the conservation programs, but the money is not earmarked in any sense.

Secondly, major efforts are directed toward decreasing energy use in space heating. Retrofitting devices are encouraged and partly subsidized by public money. Stricter building codes are under way, with the aim of cutting energy use for space heating by 50 percent in new buildings.

District heating, which is an efficient way of conserving fuel as compared to individual furnaces, is promoted, but is also looked upon with some misgivings. This supply system is very capital intensive, and the financial situation of the utilities is vulnerable to the costs of retrofitting. The rate structure reflects this situation in that individual tenants pay a fixed charge and thus have very little incentive to save energy.

The transportation sector is an interesting contrast to the space heating sector. Here almost nothing has been done in terms of energy conservation. One reason is, of course, that the transportation sector only takes up about 16 percent of total energy use. Another reason is probably that improvements such as stricter mileage rules for Swedish cars doubtless would be regarded by the Common Market and others as a technical barrier to international trade. So far the action taken has been limited to pointing out that proposed changes in national transportation policy aimed at increasing the share of public transportation also have virtues in terms of resources and energy.

On the industrial side it is felt that the market mechanisms are by and large adequate. There is a possibility of financial aid for certain energy-saving investments, provided the calculated payback time is not too short. There is also a program under way for analyzing the savings potential in the steel and paper industries, which together use roughly 25 percent of the total energy in Sweden. Another program of great interest is a review of the possibilities for using industrial waste heat for district heating of residential areas. A number of projects have been discussed. Since district heating is primarily a business for the local authorities, a new type of relationship between industries and local authorities is needed, and there are a number of rather interesting conflicts coming up. Some of the projects involve combined energy systems; for example, waste heat used both for generating electricity and for hot water in district heating.

The conflicts and the number of parties involved in these very efficient energy-using plans are such that they probably cannot be solved in a decentralized way. There probably has to be a credible threat of outside intervention in order to force the parties together in an energy-efficient way. This threat by now comes from various central state agencies.

This short discussion indicates that there are numerous and interesting problems in energy conservation. Some of these problems stem from the fact that energy conservation technologies do not always fit well into the present organizational framework. We shall return to this area later.

Swedish Energy Policy in Retrospect:
Issues and Paradigms

We will now turn to a discussion of how Swedish energy policy has evolved over the years. The results are based on a rather thorough study of official documents, such as commission reports, bills, and debates in the Parliament, on energy-related matters in Sweden since the end of the last century.

We believe this time span is necessary. In fact, certain critical aspects of present Swedish energy policy—and particularly some future alternatives—can only be understood as the result of an organizational and institutional framework that has its roots in the change from coal-based electric generation to hydroelectric generation around 1900.

The most obvious observation is that Swedish energy policy as reflected in legislative action is electricity policy. In spite of the fact that electricity has only had roughly 15-20 percent of the energy market, legislative work has been almost solely directed towards electricity. The main reason is that different new technologies demand radically different institutional adjustments. For example, the switch from coal to oil and the subsequent expansion of oil use required almost no institutional change and thus went largely unnoticed in the official documents. The main exception in this case was some worried notes on dependence on foreign countries, and so forth. No action was taken, however, to reduce seriously this dependence apart from some measures on stockpiling.

Electricity, by contrast, demanded extensive legislation. The most important period was 1900-1915, when a whole series of laws made long-distance transmission economically feasible, by changes in the laws that regulated ownership of land adjacent to rivers, and so forth. Needless to say, those changes were pushed by very strong pressure groups. In one sense, the fight was between the old nonindustrialized agricultural countryside and the new industrial order. Since this breakthrough, there has been a long string of committees and the like studying different aspects of electricity supply. We think that the main lesson from these examples is the fact that different technologies demand different institutional changes and that the economic competitiveness of these technologies is to a largely unknown degree determined by the institutional aspects.

Thus, many things, like costs, that are generally regarded as solid facts, when more closely scrutinized, turn out to be concepts largely defined through a set of rules. The competitiveness, for example, of electricity from total energy plants in industries—that is, the combined generation of heat and electricity—to some extent is determined by the set of rules of the capital market, mortgage depreciation, the price of buying standby capacity from the utilities in case of a breakdown, and so forth.

This observation also holds for new technologies, such as the use of waste heat, the nuclear fuel cycle, and so forth. One example of the latter is of course the Price-Anderson Act in the United States, where the utilities only stand a limited liability in case of an accident. We have not seen any systematic studies on these types of problems, but our general impression is that the competitiveness of new technologies is determined by rules tailormade for existing technologies. The new technologies, therefore, require very strong lobby groups if they are to stand a chance of overcoming this inherent disadvantage.

The second interesting observation on energy policy is that energy as a *gestalt* is fairly new. It emerged during the 1950s. Earlier Sweden did not have an energy policy but an electricity policy, a fuels policy, and so forth. Fuel policy was to a large extent a wood policy, since wood was an important fuel. And thus fuels policy was very much a part of forest policy, which in Sweden has long traditions. Fuels policy was also to some extent peat policy, since peat was a possible fuel. In other words, the fuels policy was very much an integrated part of agricultural policy, especially since farmers in Sweden frequently owned forest land. This coupling between the fuels policy and farmers' policy changed during the 1950s, of course, when the use of oil expanded rapidly.

The rather rapid emerging of the fuel issue and the electricity issue into an energy issue during the 1950s is of course difficult to explain, but two interrelated aspects are clear. First, nuclear power emerged as a possibility for producing either hot water for district heating and/or electricity. Thus, what had been essentially two different problems—namely, how should energy consumers be supplied with space heating and how should they be supplied with electricity—now gradually merged into one problem. At the end of the 1950s, another technology stressed this merging of the two technical systems for producing electricity and space heating—namely, the possibility of oil-fired plants for the combined generation of heat and electricity. This prospect in turn, as we shall see, became a serious threat to the nuclear industry and was vigorously fought.

Second, the price of electricity gradually fell, and the use of electricity for direct resistance heating became a distinct possibility. The rate structure was changed in the beginning of the 1960s in order to promote electric space heating.

To sum up, electricity and fuel became one energy issue because of technological change that held out the possibility of merging two hitherto separate technical supply systems and that made electricity economically competitive with fuel for space heating.

The third observation we would like to make is that the outlines of an energy conservation policy were clearly visible in the early 1950s. At that time an official study on fuel was published, where the concerns of the mid-1970s were clearly foreseen. A strong case was made for saving energy, investing in house insulation rather than oil, developing heat pumps, and so forth. Six years later the same commission published a second report, in which the pattern was back to normal again. The main emphasis was on energy supply, and the main emphasis within this area was on nuclear power.[11]

The reason given for the proposed conservation policy in the first study was mainly foreign policy—that is, the dependence on imported oil had expanded rapidly. This dependence was, however, by and large accepted as normal five years later. It is not inconceivable that a contributing reason for this policy was that a major conservation policy would have been very complicated administratively. To increase energy supply through nuclear power certainly looked much easier. The 1950s in Sweden marked a surge in the belief in the market mechanism as regulator between supply and demand. This surge was, on one hand, a reaction to the austere administrative system that was necessary in order to allocate the scarce resources during the Second World War, but on the other hand, the very fast increase in GNP and welfare during the 1950s led many to believe that essentially all problems could be solved through market mechanisms. The interrelations between policies and business cycles can easily be seen in transportation policy.[12]

What about future changes in paradigms of energy policy? For obvious reasons these are difficult to conceptualize, but some hints can be drawn from the discussion above. First, to a large extent the changes in policy patterns during the 1950s seem to be related to technological change. Secondly, the present paradigm is based largely on the implicit assumption that energy is sold on the market in what the thermodynamicists call high-quality form,[13] either as fossil fuel—oil, coal, gas—or as electricity produced by fossil fuel or hydroelectric or nuclear stations. Low-quality energy—waste heat—is frequently not sold at all on the market but dumped.

This paradigm is consistent with a concept of efficiency that is based on the first law of thermodynamics. This law says that energy is conserved—that is, cannot be destroyed or consumed, but can be saved. And the energy conservation policies of probably all countries are based on the assumption that energy should be saved—in *quantitative* terms.

Therefore, a possible new paradigm evolves as a consequence of basing energy policy on the second law of thermodynamics, which says that while energy *is conserved in quantitative terms* energy process also means a *degrading of energy in qualitative* terms. Such a paradigm would recognize that energy is abundant, but that high-quality energy is a scarce resource. And what should be conserved is therefore not energy but what the thermodynamicists call *free energy*. Weinberg and Goeller have some interesting footnotes on the fact that the materials policy of the future is critically dependent on the scarcity of free energy.[14] If free energy is not a scarce resource, then materials, metals, and so forth are not scarce either. But if free energy is scarce, then (new) materials will become scarce.

High-quality energy is necessary mainly for process heat—for example, making steel out of iron ore, for transportation, for some electrical machinery, and so forth. Low-quality energy is sufficient for uses such as space heating. The argument can be carried further, and it seems that a society where high-quality energy is scarce but low-quality energy is abundant will look quite different from a society where high-quality energy is also abundant.

Summing up, it seems that a shift from an efficiency concept based on the first law of thermodynamics to an efficiency concept based on the second law should have some important technical and thus institutional consequences. We will touch on this problem again in the last section.

Swedish Electricity Policy

Swedish electricity policy has been based on water power since the beginning of this century. By the end of the 1950s, the end of the expansion of hydroelectric power could be seen, however, and gradually nuclear power came to be an alternative. By now it is fair to say that Swedish electricity policy depends to a very large extent on how large a role nuclear power can play. We shall deal with these topics in this section.

Nuclear power could conceivably expand in Sweden if the present feelings about safety, etc. are reduced. Sweden has a large portion of the uranium resources of the Western world. With present reactor technologies (LWR) the Swedish uranium reserve could sustain a reactor program of roughly 50-60 LWRs producing a total of 9,000 TWh, which should be compared to the annual energy consumption in Sweden of roughly 400 TWh.

The electricity industry (both producers of electricity and the industries producing equipment related to electricity production and consumption) has maintained that the existence of Swedish uranium is reason enough for a strong commitment to continued expansion of nuclear power. However, recently some doubts have been heard. Global uranium reserves may be severely strained during the next twenty-five years, and since Sweden's economy is a very open one, it is conceivable that Sweden will be forced into exporting some uranium.

Therefore it is not easy to evaluate the benefits and the costs of Sweden's having a large uranium reserve. The mining of this low-grade ore is highly controversial from an environmental standpoint. The Swedish uranium shales are situated in southern Sweden, in an area that for ages has been inhabited and that has a very strong agricultural tradition. Furthermore, the main reserves are situated in a unique mountain that is widely renowned for its beauty. The whole issue, from the decision-making point of view, is complicated by the fact that the local authorities (probably) have the right to veto any exploitation that they do not like. Under the present laws of physical planning, it is not clear whether the government has the right to overrule the local authorities.

The issue of Swedish uranium is therefore interconnected with issues of environmental policy, the relations between central and local governments, and the openness of the (Swedish) nuclear fuel cycle and the Swedish economy in particular. There are obvious possibilities for deadlocks in the decision processes.

This situation is by no means unique to Sweden. In fact, it seems that the major obstacle towards continuing growth in the use of natural resources is not so much the physical or geological limits as the social impact of very large-scale operations. Such conflict between local interests and the national interest is clearly visible not only in the United States, when it comes to issues such as strip mining, but on an international scale. The position of Norway vis-à-vis the production of North Sea oil is a good example. Why should country X disrupt part of its social system just to satisfy country Y's demand for raw materials? One can see conflicts coming up within and between the rich countries—conflicts of the same type as have been the rule rather than the exception between the poor and rich countries.

The development of the breeder reactor has to be seen against this general background. The breeder is thrifty with scarce resources like uranium but lavish with other resources like capital, skilled manpower, ability to organize large-scale technological projects, and so forth. At the same time, it is obvious that an energy supply system based on breeder reactors and a full-scale plutonium fuel cycle has a large number of problems of its own.

We can thus summarize the situation right now in the following way. The Swedish authorities have accepted the step from hydroelectric to nuclear power. The logical next step is the breeder economy. At the same time, it is obvious that such an economy has some not entirely positive features. It is therefore necessary to understand how technical options are created and foreclosed in a decision-making process. Only through such knowledge will we be able to create an alternative to the breeder.

For all these reasons we think it necessary to understand the forces that introduce new technology into the electricity system. We have therefore started a rather deep retrospective study of Swedish electricity.

The definition of technology is not very clear and differs with different authors. We will try to distinguish between machine technology—designing of tools and technical systems—and social technology—the organizational structure in which the machine technologies are always embedded. Obviously machine and social technology interact. Certain types of technical solutions require certain types of organizations, and a given type of organization will choose new technologies according to certain patterns.[15] Thus, it seems that technical change requires organizational continuity and that organizational changes most frequently occur along "technical continuities"—that is, upstream and downstream.[16] This interaction was already obvious in the very first phase of electricity. Electricity for light was first introduced by those towns and cities that already had a network for the production and distribution of gas. There are obvious similarities between electricity and gas from an administrative point of view. Moreover, the input was the same (coal).

We will go back to the end of the nineteenth century. This time period is important because the organizational structure of the 1970s is largely the result of overlapping organizational structures reflecting two types of electricity production technology.[17] The development will be described in three rough historical phases and then possible evolutions in the future will be discussed.

Phase I: Limits in Transmission Technologies

Transmission technologies were a limiting factor until the turn of the century. Production was close to the consumers, and coal-fired plants were used. The producers used DC (direct current) since DC transmission was simpler and thus developed earlier. The high transmission costs of DC also created local monopolies. The situation is described in Figure 7-3, which shows that the distributor and the producer of electricity in cities belonged to the same organizational unit.

The first important change was in transmission technology. When long-distance transmission based on AC (alternating current) was feasible, hydropower became available. The industries that first used this conversion process

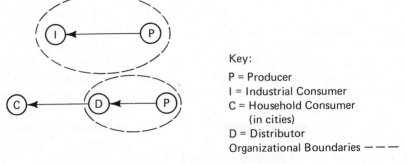

Key:

P = Producer
I = Industrial Consumer
C = Household Consumer
   (in cities)
D = Distributor
Organizational Boundaries – – –

Figure 7-3. Early Organizational Model for the Production and Distribution of Electricity in Sweden.

were the paper and pulp and steel industries. The reason was simple: They were huge fuel consumers and had thus acquired large forests. In some cases they owned both banks of a river, and according to the law of that time, they therefore had the right to use the river for hydropower.

Long-distance transmission of AC and the subsequent possibility for using hydropower was an attractive prospect for the emerging industrial order. However, the legal framework was an obstacle that by and large reflected the order of an agrarian and self-sustaining economy. Negotiations on hydropower where there were several owners of the river banks were extremely complicated under the law of the time. Consequently, the advocates of the industrial and market economy attacked. In spite of resistance, the laws regulating waterflows and so forth were changed in order to increase the use of hydropower, irrigation schemes, and the like. The emerging capitalist class had a highly pragmatic attitude towards the concept of to whom private property was private.

When the older order finally was defeated, a new conflict emerged. Who should control the natural resources—private owners or the nation as a whole (i.e., the state)? It is interesting to note that the Conservatives at the time were split on the role of private ownership. Some of the Conservatives reflected the views of the old aristocracy that was firmly bound to the concept of a strong nation-state. Others were more oriented towards the capitalist class.

The government became involved in 1909. The first object was the electrification of the railway between Kiruna and Narvick, which was used for iron ore exports, as was typical of the period. Hydropower expanded through direct user intervention: The earliest hydropower stations were built by the consumers themselves (mainly industry). The largest project was the hydropower station of Trollhättan, which was built by a public utility that later evolved into the State Power Board. Conversely, the State Power Board can only be understood in terms of its role as a builder.

The role of the consumers of electricity is interesting during this period, especially in the diffusion of electricity into the rural areas, which was frequently financed cooperatively by the consumers. At the same time, electricity use in the cities and towns expanded through local, frequently public, utilities that were often coal based. The net result was that the distribution of electricity was separated from the production of electricity. This situation had important consequences for the future that can be seen as the result of the changeover from coal to hydroelectric power in the cities and the problem of raising capital and hooking up consumers in the rural areas.

Phase II: The Producer's Phase

Changes in the water law up to 1918 made expansion of hydropower possible, and during the 1920s the prospective rivers were divided between the private producers and the state. The private producing companies were in turn owned by the big consumers of electricity—the big industries and also some big cities.

The organizational pattern in the beginning of this phase was very fragmented. Local producers sold more or less directly to local consumers, and producers tried to create local monopolies by choosing different voltages, frequencies, and so forth. The process of standardization of technical norms for voltage, frequency, stability, and the like is on the surface a process for increased efficiency but can also be seen as a prerequisite for concentration of power and the domination of the large and few over the small and many. These aspects seem to be poorly understood but are clearly visible even now on the international scale.

Gradually the Swedish system was organized in regional blocks, and cooperation between different producers began, as shown in Figure 7-4.

The large distances between the north of Sweden, where the hydropower originated, and the big consumer areas in the south stimulated technical development. Through cooperation between producers (e.g., ASEA) and users (e.g., the State Power Board), Sweden developed a unique skill in long-distance transmission of electricity. But the heavy investments necessary for the long-distance grid between northern and southern Sweden also raised the question of what the necessary organization should look like. A new and very important function emerged: the long-distance transportation of electric power.

Figure 7-5 is meant to show that after a period of regional cooperation Sweden finally got a national "multiorganization."[18] The birth of this national system was not painless. On the contrary, there was a fierce struggle over the rights to build long-distance transmission lines. This struggle was brought to a head in 1936 and was not resolved until 1946, when the government reserved the building rights to the State Power Board. One of the reasons for the conflict was the fear that the organization that controlled the big lines *and* the transformers at the end of the lines also to some extent controlled the other producers.

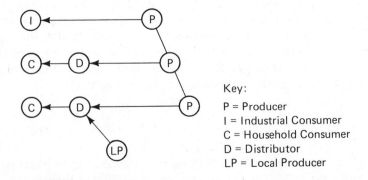

Key:

P = Producer
I = Industrial Consumer
C = Household Consumer
D = Distributor
LP = Local Producer

Figure 7-4. Regional Cooperation Model for the Production and Distribution of Electricity in Sweden.

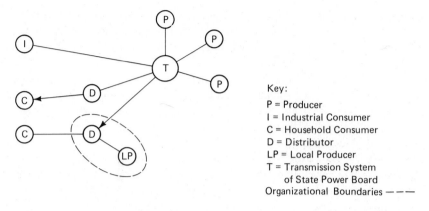

Figure 7-5. "Multiorganizational" Model for the Production and Distribution of Electricity in Sweden.

The mechanism for this control is in itself worth mentioning. Under the existing laws, it was (and is) possible for two producers to compete for the same customer. If one of the producers has a contract with a customer and thus has the transmission line to the customer, the other producer can offer to build its own line and, perhaps, charge lower rates. When the State Power Board controlled the transformer stations from which the main producers had their regional lines, the State Power Board thus was able to raise a silent threat to build a line of its own to the customers of the producers. In other words, the rate structure of the private electricity producers was partly controlled by the State Power Board, and some of the producers existed almost at the mercy of the State Power Board. No wonder there were ill feelings.

This example is typical of the struggle for strategic control. Gradually the transportation system made a central board dispatching system look efficient and thus possible. The net result was a series of very complex deals between the different producers and a gradual socialization not of the ownership but the management decisions. The bitterness of the private producers did not ebb out until the late 1950s, when other struggles began.

The national grid and the system of rules around it was perhaps the major factor in giving the State Power Board strategic control over electricity production. This phase between the 1920s and the late 1950s can be characterized as the *period of the producers*. Technical and geographic reasons led to a centralized multiorganization dominated by the State Power Board.

*Phase III: The Beginning of the Merging of the Fuel
and the Electricity Systems*

Until the 1950s the fuel supply system in Sweden existed side by side with and independently of the electricity system. In the cities there had been an early change from individually heated apartments to central heating using hot water. The hot water was generated first by coal-fired furnaces and later by oil. (The switch to oil was nearly completed during the 1960s). The landlords were the driving force behind these changes.

The next step was taken in 1950, when district heating was introduced by the cities (i.e., the same organizational body as the electricity distributor and sometimes producer). The 1950s also marked a surge of urbanization in Sweden, during which the cities grew rapidly, housing was scarce, and new housing was controlled by the cities.

Figure 7-6 shows the situation that most commonly emerged. The big cities expanded more and more into different aspects of the energy scene—gas, heating, electricity, and so forth. District heating schemes take a long time to build and consequently the change was gradual. But the rate of change was fast at roughly 20 percent increase per year.

At about the same time nuclear energy became a possible future alternative. The earliest discussion on nuclear energy was almost exclusively focused on district heating. Nuclear energy was thus seen as an alternative to imported oil. Somewhat later, cogeneration—that is, combined production of hot water and electricity—became an interesting prospect for nuclear energy.

The first plant discussed was such a combined plant. It would have been placed in the city of Västerås, which also happened to be the home town of ASEA, a company that was already interested in nuclear power as a future market. The plant would have been a joint venture between the city of Västerås and the State Power Board.

At the end of the 1950s oil became gradually cheaper. At the same time, the complexities of nuclear power began to surface. Since most of the rivers had been used for hydropower, the end of the hydropower era was clearly seen. This fact was also stressed by the growing environmental groups. Resistance to further expansion of hydropower grew during the 1950s and 1960s, and the private and public electricity producers laid aside their quarrels in the face of the

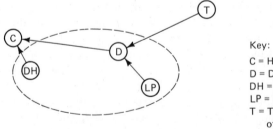

Figure 7-6. Organizational Model for the Production and Distribution of Electricity in Swedish Cities.

new enemy. It was necessary to conceive of a different way to produce electricity.

Essentially two alternatives existed. One was steam plants that used either fossil fuel or nuclear power, and the other was combined generation of steam and electricity. The first was an extension of the electricity production of the past; the second was a radical break. The system would have been as shown in Figure 7-7 in the cities with a growing district heating system. Combined generation (CG) means not only that the local producers could have produced for local distribution and bought the rest from the national producer, but also that they could have started to sell electricity to the national producer. This changing situation involved the national producing systems as well, and a rather fierce struggle started. The fight to some extent was over the rate of expansion of electricity production. Combined generation by the cities and distributors was a threat to the expansion of electricity generated by the block of producers. It was to be stressed that this struggle was the result of technical change that allowed a new actor, the electricity distributor; to enter the battlefield. The main point here is that the distributor has several roles at the same time—that is, the Swedish cities are also in charge of district heating, water supply, roads, streets, and so forth.

To some extent district heating schemes also were foreclosed by the cities themselves—large suburban areas of single family dwellings are more expensive to heat through district heating than multiple family dwellings. In other words, much the same reasons that during the 1950s foreclosed public transportation as a viable option also made district heating a limited choice.

When the first nuclear plant planned for Västerås was cancelled, the city decided to build a combined oil-fired plant of its own. There was also a strong movement to organize a number of other cities in central Sweden in a block to counteract the dominant State Power Board.

It seems that an electricity system based on a combination of hydropower and combined generation would have had a rather different organizational

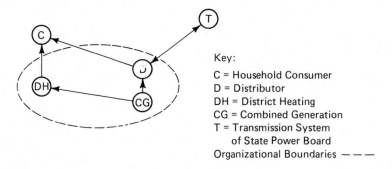

Key:

C = Household Consumer
D = Distributor
DH = District Heating
CG = Combined Generation
T = Transmission System
    of State Power Board
Organizational Boundaries — — —

Figure 7-7. Organizational Model for the Production and Distribution of Electricity in Sweden in the Period of Emerging Nuclear Power.

structure from a system based on simple electricity production. In the former the electricity production of the combined plants would have been largely controlled by the market for hot water, and the hydropower stations used for "evening out" the load. In other words, the electricity system would have been much more restricted.

The fight over combined generation raged through the 1960s. A large number of cities wanted to build CG plants during the 1960s, and the State Power Board responded by lowering prices so as to make the plants of the cities uneconomic. At the same time electric resistance heating was extensively promoted. The distributor's cartel was crushed but the combined generation was accepted by the State Power Board which also controlled the conditions for its use. Nuclear power was thus drawn into the system both through expanding the market for electricity and through keeping alternative means for producing electricity outside. What on the surface looked like a discussion of different technical options showed itself to be a struggle for domination of the total electricity system.

Phase IV: Some Future Complications

The gradual merging of the fuel and electricity systems will accelerate as a result of the 1975 energy policy decision. The most probable outcome is increasing conflict, both among different producers of energy and between producers and consumers. New technical options, such as the use of waste industrial heat to produce electricity and hot water for district heating of homes, will inevitably confuse the hitherto well-defined roles of producers and consumers. Increased use of energy supply systems that are more capital intensive and thus have small variable costs will inevitably increase the conflict between producers and users. Retrofitting of homes heated by district heating will reduce revenues to the producers and will thus be seen as threatening. The same goes, of course, for electrically heated homes, but here the producers can defend themselves to some extent by expanding the market.

Among other aspects of the energy policy, the State Power Board has responded to the increased use of combined generation with contracts by which the plants are run on the terms of the electricity system, rather than on the terms of the heating market. One result is of course that attempts to organize cities as a "countervailing power" are made much more difficult.

It is probably a fair summary to say that there are a large number of new technical options for an energy conservation policy. However, a number of these options create serious problems for existing organizations and are hindered and hampered by rules, laws, rate structures, and so forth. Consequently, the first obstacle in the way of a resource-conserving energy policy is not technical but institutional. It remains to be seen how far-reaching the institutional changes have to be, but they cannot be limited to the demand side. In other words, actions that promote conservation of energy have to be implemented by actions that change the incentive system of the energy producers in a direction that makes them less apt to solve problems through expansion of demand. How this is to be done is obviously not clear, but one of several ways probably involves rather deep changes in the whole financial structure of the system. Another way is probably to strengthen groups, such as local and regional authorities, whose interests are at least not entirely parallel. It is on these levels that many of the technical options for conserving energy have to be implemented, and it is on these levels that conflicts between both private and public interests—for example, over the use of waste heat from industries—and between national and local public interests have to be solved.

Some of these ideas will be elaborated in the last section, where we hint at two different strategies for the future.

Two Possible Future Strategies for the Swedish Energy Supply System

The main theme of this chapter has been to stress the interrelationship between technical and organizational systems and also to point out the importance of what could be called the "interorganizational rule system"—that is, the set of rules that decide legitimacy, division of responsibility, specialization, and the role of coordination between different organizations. In the concept of organizations we include informal ones like households, groups of households in the same geographical area, and so forth.

Now it is possible to use these admittedly vague ideas to speculate on the type of institutional environment or milieu that different technical options on the energy supply side have. In order to do this we have to recall the discussion on thermodynamics. Energy occurs in different forms, very roughly described as high-quality and low-quality forms. High-quality forms can be used to perform mechanical work, drive electrical systems, or produce the high temperatures needed for melting ores, producing metals, and so forth. Examples of high-quality forms are fossil fuels, methanol, and high voltage electricity. Low-quality forms are essentially heat with a small difference of temperature between the hot body and the environment.

With some stretching of the concepts, we can describe possible supply alternatives in the same terms—high and low grade. Low-grade sources are then waste heat, solar heat, wind power, and other sources of low-quality and/or reliability. High-grade sources are fuels like oil, methanol, and electricity with high reliability.

We can also describe energy use in terms of high and low quality. But here low-quality energy use refers to the form of energy that is sufficient in the process in question, not the actual form used. Waste heat or solar heat is sufficient for space heating, even if electricity is more frequently used. In other words, energy use can be described in terms of whether high- or low-quality energy is necessary or sufficient for the process. We can thus make a simple matrix, as shown in Figure 7-8.

The energy supply system today is almost entirely based on high-quality energy (i.e., boxes 1 and 2 in the figure). Whether or not low-quality energy is sufficient for a given process obviously depends not only on the type of process but also on the technical system in question. In other words, to change the user's system from box 2 to 4 may demand substantial investments in new equipment, and so forth.

From this perspective, we have two possible principles for the future. The first principle is the continuation of the present one—extensive electrification, synthetic fuels, and so forth and possibly centralized conversion of low-quality energy into high quality through solar towers, wind driven hydrogen production, and so forth. Such a principle is very flexible for the energy user, and can thus be called a *strategy of flexibility*. In the matrix above, the principle is based on boxes 1 and 2.

The second principle is based on boxes 1 and 4. Low-grade sources are used where these are sufficient, and high-grade sources are used where necessary. Such a principle calls for closely matching the thermodynamic characteristics of possible supply alternatives and the user's process. An appropriate name is therefore a *principle of matching*. This seems to be the only principle through which the supply system can be based entirely on renewable resources.

These two principles, which admittedly are extremes and obviously can be mixed to some extent, have obvious differences. The flexibility principle is bound to be more and more capital intensive on the supply side. Demand will

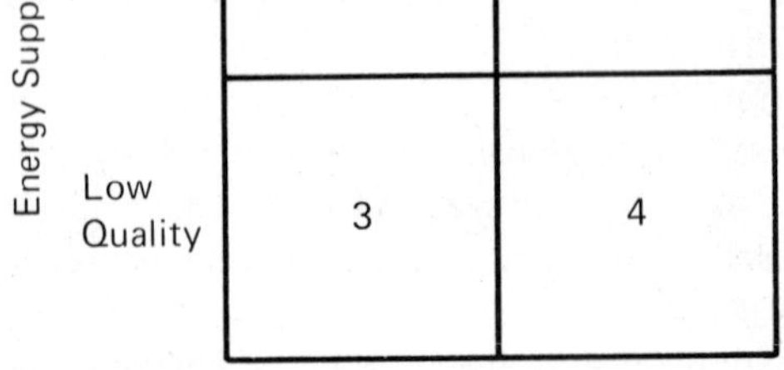

Figure 7-8. Quality of Energy Matrix.

have to be predictable and free of surprises; otherwise the profitability of the supply sector will be in jeopardy. This principle is open to vicious circles of the type described in the section on Swedish Energy in Retrospect, and one can foresee that this principle will be stabilized through a system of rules—in particular a rate structure—that minimizes the risk of fluctuating demand. This principle also calls for institutions capable of generating not only large amounts but also large chunks of capital. The most typical technical component in this principle is the breeder and its fuel cycle, which is a technical system of such size and complexity that the ensuing institutions will have to transcend national boundaries.

Another interesting property of this principle is that in all probability it will lead to an increased role for central governments as opposed to local authorities. The type of stalemate between local veto power and national interests that is possible within the present legal system in many countries will have to go.

The matching principle, on the other hand, has to be aimed at adapting to local situations. It will in all probability be very capital intensive, perhaps more so than the first strategy. But the institutions necessary for allocating the capital will be different. Large amounts of capital will have to be disseminated to a very large number of energy users, such as individual households, blocks, cities, and so forth. This principle will also need a centralized energy supply system, partly for the high-grade use and partly for backing up the low-grade systems.

Another interesting difference between these two principles is the demand for professionals. The matching principle calls for a large number of persons skilled in adapting to local situations and in bringing together consumers and suppliers. The flexibility principle calls for persons skilled in handling large centralized supply systems based on high technology. These differences obviously have organizational consequences. A decentralized approach based on cooperation between local initiative and central knowledge is necessary in the matching case, whereas the central production of energy is the single most necessary component in the flexibility case.

What about abundance and cost of energy? Most likely energy would be more plentiful and perhaps cheaper in the first principle than in the second. In all probability the first principle will give a higher standard of living, measured as it is today in terms of GNP.

Therefore, the choice between the two principles involves not only how much energy we want; it is probably a choice between two different societies with different institutions and different ways of deciding what is good and bad. This does not make the choice easier.

Post-election Epilogue

In September 1976 the Social Democratic Government was voted out of office by a small margin. It is difficult to say what role nuclear power played in the

282

outcome—both parties that rejected nuclear power lost votes compared to the 1973 election. But both the outgoing Prime Minister Olof Palme and the incoming Thorbjörn Fälldin declared that nuclear power tipped the balance.

The new Government is a coalition between three parties of which two by and large share the view of the Social Democrats on nuclear power. The third party, the Center Party, is the largest Party in the Government and consequently its leader, Thorbjörn Fälldin, is Prime Minister.

Nuclear power was not an issue in the campaign until during the last two weeks, when Thorbjörn Fälldin made some very strong commitments against letting reactors under construction get on-line.

Nuclear power seems to be the single most complicated issue in the Government. The Center Party backed down on its earlier commitments and accepted the starting up of the next reactor to get on-line, subject to the condition that the utility had signed a contract on reprocessing. Negotiations on reprocessing are under way with United Reprocessors. For subsequent reactors, starting up will be accepted only if reprocessing and a safe scheme for waste disposal can be demonstrated. The parties in the Government seem very much split on the problem of whether the proposed schemes for reprocessing and waste disposal are safe enough.

The coalition parties have declared that they will propose a referendum if they cannot come to an agreement on nuclear power. Undoubtedly the uncertainty about nuclear power has increased and this has, in turn, generated shock waves of uneasiness through the utilities, capital market, trade unions, and so forth.

Notes

1. Secretariat for Future Studies. "Energy and Society: Conceptual outline introducing a future study." Stockholm, December 15, 1975.

2. Secretariat for Future Studies. *Programme for Future Studies in Sweden.* Stockholm, November 1975.

3. The Prime Minister. "Address to the meeting of the Executive Committee of the Social Democratic Labour Party." Sundsvall, Sweden, February 1, 1975.

4. The Ministry of Industry. *Energy Planning in Sweden.* Stockholm, 1975.

5. Centrala Drift Ledningen. (Central Operating Management). *Sveriges Elkonsumtion, 1975-1990.* Stockholm, 1972.

6. L. Schipper and A.J. Lichtenberg, *Efficient Energy Use and Well Being: The Swedish Example.* Energy and Environment Division, Lawrence Berkeley Laboratory, University of California, April 1976.

7. Energi Prognos Kommitéen, *Energi 1985-2000*. Ministry of Industry. Two volumes. Stockholm, 1974.

8. Secretariat for Future Studies. "A Progress Report from the Future Study 'Energy and Society' ". Stockholm, February 19, 1976.

9. Donald Schon, *Beyond the Stable State*. (London: Temple Smith, 1971.)

10. Edward Kahn, Mark Davidson, Arjun Makhijani, Philip Caesar and S.M. Berman, *Investment Planning in the Energy Sector*. Energy and Environment Division, Lawrence Berkeley Laboratory, Berkeley, California. LBL-4474.

11. Department of Commerce, *Fakta om olja*, SOU 1953:12, Stockholm, 1975; and *Bränsleförsörjningen i atomåldern*, Del I-II. Del I SOU 1956:46, Del II SOU 1956:58. Stockholm, 1956.

12. Lars Anell, Anna Hedborg, Måns Lönnroth, and Lars Ingelstam, *Skall vi asfaltera Sverige?* (Stockholm: Pan & Nordstedts, 1971.)

13. "Efficient Use of Energy: A Physics Perspective." The American Physical Society, January, 1975. (Reprinted in ERDA Authorization Hearings— Part I, House Committee on Science & Technology, February 18, 1975.)

14. H.E. Goeller and Alvin M. Weinberg, "The Age of Substitutability or What Do We Do When The Mercury Runs Out?" Institute for Energy Analysis, Oak Ridge, Tennessee. Paper presented at a symposium on "A Strategy for Resources," Eindhoven, The Netherlands, September 18, 1975.

15. Donald A. Schon, *Technology and Change: The New Heraclitus*. (New York: A Delta Book, 1967), and Bo Persson and Pierre Guillet de Monthoux, "Filters: Limits to Technological Choice." Eco Research Institute, Linköping, Sweden, January 25, 1976.

16. J.D. Thompson, *Organizations in Action*. (New York: McGraw-Hill, Inc., 1967.)

17. Sheldon Novick, "The Electric Power Industry," *Environment*, Volume 17, Number 8 (November 1975).

18. Hans Esping and Måns Lönnroth, "Strategisk planering och den offentliga sektorns struktur." Stockholm, June 4, 1974.

8

Energy Policy Planning in the United States: Ideological BTU's

I.C. Bupp

Mobilizing for Energy Independence

The American state no longer seems to have any real choice between planning and not planning. It will either choose to plan well and comprehensively, or badly and haphazardly. If the second, there is likely to be chaos, resulting inevitably in more crisis, which in turn will cause an inexorable demand for more planning plus more coercion.

—George C. Lodge[1]

Among the Americans there is a general statement, shared by both political parties, of the natural predominance of private enterprise in the economic sphere and of the subordinate role of public initiative in any situation other than a manifest national emergency. The Western Europeans, who have no such assumption . . . have in consequence been spared the awful doctrinal wrestling, in which Americans tend to engage whenever any bit of the economic field has to be divided afresh between the public and private sector.

—Andrew Shonfield[2]

One of Richard Nixon's many unprecedented acts as President of the United States was to send Congress the first message on national energy policy ever submitted by an American president. Mr. Nixon's June 4, 1971, message set the frame of reference within which energy policy has been debated in the United States in the ensuing four and a half years.[3] The basic theme, as the title suggests, was that the nation's energy supply system was inadequate to the job that would be required of it in the coming years. Two factors—"growing demand for energy and growing emphasis on cleaner fuels" were going to "create an extraordinary pressure on our fuel supplies. . . . That is why our efforts to expand the supply of clean energy in America must be immediately stepped up." Specifically, ". . . the time [had] now come for government and industry to commit themselves to a joint effort to achieve commercial scale demonstrations in the most crucial and most promising clean energy development areas—the fast breeder reactor, sulfur oxide control technology and coal gasification."[4] Because of its persistence in ensuing statements, the underlying imagery is worth emphasis. The "demand" for BTUs of energy is seen as something akin to a military commander's demand for ammunition: "I'm going to need a zillion, but I've only got umpty-seven." Just as a sufficient supply of bullets is necessary to

285

win a battle, "... a sufficient supply of clean energy is essential if we are to sustain healthy economic growth and improve the quality of national life."[5]

Some seventeen months later, the Arab oil embargo caused an escalation of presidential rhetoric, but no modification of the dominant metaphor. "We must therefore face up to a very stark fact. We are heading toward the most acute shortages of energy since World War II." The impending supply deficit could now be quantified: "Our supply of petroleum this winter will be at least 10% short of our anticipated demands, and it could fall short of as much as 17%."[6]

Given this conception of the nature of the problem, it was obvious that mobilization was the appropriate response:

In World War II, America was faced with the necessity of rapidly developing an atomic capability. The circumstances were grave. Responding to that challenge, this Nation brought together its finest scientific skills and its finest administrative skills in what was known as the Manhattan Project. With all the needed resources at its command, with the highest priority assigned to its efforts, the Manhattan Project gave us the atomic capacity that helped to end the war in the Pacific and to bring peace to the world.

Twenty years later, responding to a different challenge, we focused our scientific and technological genius on the frontiers of space. ... The lessons of the Apollo Project, and of the earlier Manhattan Project, are the same lessons that are taught of the whole of American history: Whenever the American people are faced with a clear goal and they are challenged to meet it, we can do extraordinary things.

Today the challenge is to gain the strength that we had earlier in this century, the strength of self-sufficiency. Pure ability to meet our own energy needs is directly limited to our continued ability to act decisively and independently at home and abroad in the service of peace. ...

Let us unite in committing the resources of the Nation to a major new endeavor ... "Project Independence." Let us set as our national goal, in the spirit of Apollo, with the determination of the Manhattan Project, that by the end of this decade we will have developed the potential to meet our own energy needs without depending on any foreign energy sources.[7]

"Project Independence" was the centerpiece of the legislative program that Mr. Nixon subsequently submitted to Congress. It was seen as entailing three concurrent tasks:

The first task is to rapidly increase energy supplies—maximizing the production of our oil, gas, coal and shale reserves by using existing technologies and accelerating the introduction of nuclear power. These important efforts should begin to pay off in the next 2 to 3 years. They will provide the major fraction of the increased supplies needed to achieve energy self-sufficiency.

The second task is to conserve energy. We must reduce demand by eliminating nonessential energy use and improving the efficiency of energy utilization. This must be a continuing commitment in the years ahead.

The third task is to develop new technologies through a massive new energy research and development program that will enable us to remain self-sufficient for years to come.[8]

One year later, a new president issued another Presidential Energy Message, but with the same imagery:

I believe in America's capabilities. Within the next ten years, my program envisions:

200 major nuclear power plants,

250 major new coal mines,

150 major coal-fired power plants,

30 major new oil refineries,

20 major new synthetic fuel plants,

the drilling of many thousands of new oil wells,

the insulation of 18 million houses, and

construction of millions of new automobiles, trucks and buses that use much less fuel.

We can do it. In another crisis—the one in 1942—President Franklin D. Roosevelt said this country would build 60,000 aircraft. By 1943, production had reached 125,000 aircraft annually.[9]

Professional economists have tended to treat the Nixon-Ford Project Independence theme with varying degrees of scorn. To them, it is "Hamlet without the Prince" in that it more or less ignores the principle that the amount of energy "needed" or "demanded" at any time is a function of the price of energy at that time. In fact, the executive branch has and continues to be highly ambivalent about the relationships among the supply of and demand for energy and its price. Presidents Nixon and Ford have repeatedly noted with approval the principal that the supply of energy is elastic with respect to price, and they have sought to base their mobilization programs, in part, upon it. Thus, in March 1974, Nixon vetoed a bill that would have "rolled back" the price of certain domestically produced crude oil:

If we are to achieve energy independence, hundreds of billions of private dollars will have to be invested. . . . This money will not be invested if investors do not have reasonable assurance of being able to earn a return in the marketplace.[10]

Similar forthrightness about the demand side has been rare. In November 1973, Mr. Nixon did admit that: "Market forces are also at work allocating fuel. Due primarily to huge increases in prices for foreign oil, the price of gasoline has risen . . . [and] this obviously discourages the consumption of gasoline." But, "there is a limit . . . to the amount of market allocation through higher prices which we will allow. We will not have consumers paying a dollar per gallon for gasoline."[11]

For the most part, however, the executive branch's perception of the relationship between price and demand has been overshadowed by devout adherence to the proposition that copious supplies of cheap energy are causally linked to economic growth. There may be lower demand at higher prices, but the cure is worse than the disease. For, while supplies may then in the economists' narrow sense be "sufficient," the nation as a whole will be manifestly worse off. Energy supplies that may be sufficient to clear the market may not be sufficient to meet other national policy goals, such as a growing GNP, an aggressive foreign policy, and so forth.

The economists have not been especially helpful in sorting this situation out. They have repeatedly pointed out that the only *evidence* for a linkage between cheap energy and economic health is cross-sectional correlations, which may well be spurious. However, what the critics of the administration themselves conceive the nature of the true causal linkage to be remains unclear. The administration's position, whatever its ultimate validity, retains the enormous advantage of being simultaneously straightforward and intuitively compelling.

Moreover, almost no one aside from a relative handful of professional academics considers that the price elasticity of demand for energy is pertinent to the problem. No public agency with responsibility for energy policy formulation or execution in the United States has seriously argued that reliance on the market clearing action of price increases is an appropriate response to the nation's energy problem. Two basic arguments appear to underlie the virtually universal rejection of a "neoclassical" solution.

First, it has been argued that because consumers in all sectors are constrained by the energy consumption characteristics of an existing stock of capital goods, the short-term elasticity of demand may effectively be zero. Until this stock of goods is replaced, further price increases for energy will be only inflationary. There have been numerous reports that this argument has been taken seriously even within the Ford Administration.

A more important reason for the rejection of the neoclassical solution is ideological. The leaders of the Democrats in Congress, and especially Senator Jackson, are convinced that energy price increases are regressive. To allow price increases to bring supply and demand into balance is to force the poor and disadvantaged to pay while the rich and the powerful benefit. In basing their own energy policies on this belief, Senator Jackson and his Democratic colleagues appear to have broad support in American society. The effects of energy price increases are very widely regarded as grossly inequitable.[a] A variety of forces are at work in American society to reinforce this consensus: pervasive images of profligate Arab princes; sensational revelations of payoffs, kickbacks,

---

[a]In a national public opinion survey conducted by the author in September 1975, less than twenty-five percent of the respondents were willing to have their gasoline and electricity bills double "if they were convinced this would solve the energy crisis."

bribes, and general moral tawdriness at high corporate levels; and, perhaps most significantly, a high sensitivity to all price increases.[b]

The chief preoccupation of the constituents of congressional Democrats is balancing the family checking account. The representatives of these citizens in Congress, and most especially in the House of Representatives, are persuaded that the surest way to become dis-elected in 1976 is to become identified as part of the cause rather than the solution to that problem. The consensus of professional politicians in the United States is that inflation will be the single most sensitive political issue in coming years. For the foreseeable future, this sensitivity is certain to be reflected in a profound reluctance on the part of Congress to accept price increases as a mechanism for expanding United States domestic energy supplies.

While congressional Democratic leaders have rejected the price increase elements of recent executive branch energy policy proposals, they have nonetheless warmly embraced the imagery of mobilization. Agreement on the relevance of atom bomb and moon-landing projects to the energy problem is the common ground between the Ford Administration and its corporate constituency on the one hand and Congress and its inflation-obsessed constituency on the other. There are two elements to this consensus. The first is a direct and simple faith that technology must be able to increase supplies of energy while it simultaneously reduces—or at least holding constant—its real cost. The second is a more subtle but not less profound belief that we know how to proceed in order to realize these benefits—that is, by "massive" (an extremely popular adjective) funding of research and development. Presumably, the relevant constraints are merely fiscal. Given adequate (i.e., "massive") funding, the organizational and management lessons of the Manhattan Project, Apollo, and the Atomic Energy Commission's light water reactor R&D program are more or less certain to succeed in providing society with new, cheap methods of extracting, capturing, converting, and using energy. The mobilization metaphor is central to these related beliefs and the consensus that they support.

In February 1975, Senator Jackson introduced legislation that would establish a National Energy Production Board to achieve ". . . the rapid mobilization of the materials, manpower, and financial resources needed to accelerate on an urgent basis the exploration, development and production of the vast coal, oil and gas reserves that underlie our public lands. . . ."[12]

Senator Jackson picked up the themes set out by Presidents Nixon and Ford: "No nation on earth responds to a critical challenge like the United States. When the chips are down, we have on many occasions demonstrated the capacity

---

[b]In the same national survey, the respondents, by a two-thirds majority, ranked inflation as more important than either the energy crisis or unemployment—by two independent measures.

to establish priorities and organize for action. Our wartime mobilization under the leadership of the War Production Board is one example. The Apollo program in the 1960's is another."[13] New governmental machinery was needed. "The plain inescapable fact is that the present federal bureaucracy is ill-equipped to mount the kind of all-out national effort we need to accelerate domestic energy production and achieve energy self-sufficiency. We need a single specialized, mission-oriented action agency empowered to overcome bottlenecks, and marshall government-wide resources. . . ."[14]

Significantly, the first witness at the hearings was a former director of the Office of Defense Mobilization (a Korean War agency) and prior to that, a high official in the World War II War Production Board. Mr. Henry Fowler recalled that:

This country was able within 3 or 4 years to create and complete the Manhattan project for the manufacture of the components needed to make the first atom bomb; to construct a brand-new synthetic rubber industry to replace the raw rubber supplies that had been cut off; to construct the Alcan Highway to Alaska; to complete both the Big Inch and the Little Inch oil pipelines; to produce unprecedented numbers of warplanes, ships, tanks, guns, munitions, and communications equipment and to greatly expand the availability of the supplies of key materials, plants and facilities necessary to war production and the maintenance of essential civilian supply.[15]

In fact, the roots of Senator Jackson's proposed National Energy Production Board go deeper than the World War II mobilization effort. They derive from a view of the proper nature of the relationship between government and industry that was first clearly articulated in the United States during the debate over the New Deal's National Recovery Association (NRA). The "Blue Eagles" proponents espoused what one observer has termed a "corporatist" vision of government and business collaborating in the pursuit of agreed economic objectives.[16] Senator Jackson shares with the intellectuals of the New Deal the belief that the principle of uncoordinated competitive enterprise in pursuit of maximum profits and/or growth is obsolete. His proposed National Energy Production Board, like the NRA, would be an instrument for bringing together under coordinated control the activities of disparate governmental agencies and competing industrial groups.

Mr. Fowler noted with some understatement the political difficulty of gaining acceptance for such an instrument: "There may be those who would have a vague fear that this type of affirmative government action would lead to nationalization or socialization."[17] Nor was Senator Jackson, himself, wholly oblivious to the problem: "Those that talk socialization and [sic] going to nationalize everything, the fear mongers, really do not have the vision as I see it. They can't dream the big things that we can do, and the things we need to do."[18]

As it developed, very few had the vision. The NEPB proposal quickly got into substantial difficulty in spite of a widespread feeling in Congress that "something" had to be done to push domestic energy development. The trouble, in the words of one close observer, was "the idea's enormous cross-section for flak from the major industrial actors and the environmentalists at the same time."[19] Both groups have responded to the proposal as a threat to their own perceptions of the public interest and have criticized or even ridiculed it as either fascist or socialist. There appears to be essentially no realistic prospect that a mobilization instrument of the sort envisaged by Senator Jackson's legislation can be approved for the foreseeable future.

The *Energy Independence Authority* is the Ford Administration's alternative to the Jackson mobilization strategy. In early October President Ford submitted legislation to Congress to create a government corporation to provide loans, loan guarantees, price guarantees, or other financial assistance to private sector energy projects. The EIA would have a limited life (ten years); its financial outlays and commitments were intended to be recovered by the government and would be used in conjunction with private sector financing "to the maximum extent possible." The EIA would not have authority, except for very limited periods, to own operating facilities related to energy production, transportation, or transmission. The Administration proposed that the EIA be given financial resources of $100 billion.[20]

Like the NEPB, the EIA is a direct descendant of a New Deal agency: in this case, the Reconstruction Finance Corporation (RFC). Generally considered to have been a far more successful institutional innovation than the NRA, the RFC was conceptually an instrument for planning the allocation of available capital resources. It seems that Mr. Ford, too, had a vision: "My vision is of dramatic action to produce oil and gas from coal, safe and clean nuclear and coal generated electric power, harness the energy of the sun and the natural heat within the earth and build numerous other energy facilities."[21]

And like the attempt of Democratic rivals to build upon New Deal experience, the administration proposal instantly became the object of ridicule from both ends of the ideological spectrum. Liberals and environmentalists were outraged at "a giveaway to the big oil companies," while the presumptive recipients of the largess denounced the proposal because it would force them to compete for government grants and loan guarantees by fitting their R&D programs to "bureaucratic" or "political" energy supply whims and fancies.

The Wall Street Journal blasted the proposal in a lead editorial:

It rests on the magnificent assumption that if the government would only spend $100 billion on urban renewal, it could build a Great Society; that if it only spent $100 billion on poor people it could eliminate poverty; and that if it only spent $100 billion on energy research, the United States will have energy independence. . . . How did the President make such a horrendous mistake. . . . In one swoop he's embraced the principle of government preemption of the private sector, credit allocation, fiscal gimmickry, bigger bureaucracies and multi-billion dollar subsidies.[22]

Subsequent press reports suggested that in fact, Mr. Ford's vision notwithstanding, the EIA had an effective constituency of one: Vice President Rockefeller.[23] Officials high within the administration—Treasury Secretary Simon, Commerce Secretary Lynn, the chairman of the Council of Economic Advisers—were widely reported as objecting on philosophical grounds to the notion of "government meddling in the marketplace." It was argued that this would damage other sectors of the economy by diverting capital and would merely create another bureaucracy to subsidize investments that would be made in any event.

In our judgment, George Lodge is correct in arguing that the essential problem here is ideological:

We now find ourselves confronted with newer, more complex, and more intense versions of the same difficulties the New Deal planners sought to solve in the thirties. The past thirty-five or forty years have been a strange ideological interlude during which we have been able to avoid the divisive issues raised by . . . Berle, Means, Tugwell, and Dewey. Our ideological conscience during this time has been distracted by the unifying presence of 'enemies' abroad. . . . Viet Nam marked the traumatic end of that era.[24]

Behind the criticism of both Senator Jackson's NEPB and Mr. Rockefeller's EIA is a combination of fear and pessimism about the ability of government to shape events. These fears are shared equally by the left and the right. It is neither an accident nor a mistake in terminology that the NEPB and the EIA have been denounced as "fascist" by the left as they were simultaneously being attacked as "socialist" by the right. Clearly, what both sets of critics saw were potentially powerful organizations that lacked authority. Where such authority might come from is a question that has not been seriously addressed—or perhaps even articulated—by the businessmen, academics, and politicians who have defined the U.S. energy problems as primarily a problem of mobilization.

An Alternative Model: Supervision Instead of Collaboration

Shonfield observes that among the variety of political impulses that shaped the reforms of the New Deal, there was a rival to the "corporatist" vision of a new type of collaboration between business and government. This alternative view emphasized supervision rather than collaboration. The supervision was of an essentially judicial character. In Shonfield's opinion, this "judicial rot" represented "the principle of anti-planning deliberately elevated to a way of life."[25] It is supervision, rather than collaboration, that has nonetheless emerged as the dominant element of the public policy response to the U.S. energy problem. The effect has been to prevent the mobilization that a broad spectrum of American business and government leadership believes to be acutely required.

The situation with respect to the substitution of coal for oil as fuel for fossil-fired steam-electric plants is typical. Electric utilities in the United States are now all subject to air quality requirements mandated by both state and federal law. In accordance with the specific mandate of the 1970 Clean Air Act, the federal Environmental Protection Agency (EPA) has promulgated national ambient air quality standards for six pollutants, among which is sulfur dioxide (SO_2). The 1970 legislation also required each state to develop a "state implementation plan" (SIP) to enforce compliance with these ambient standards. Each SIP was required to include "emission limitations, schedules, and timetables for compliance with such limitations and such other measures as may be necessary to insure attainment and maintenance of ambient air quality standards" (Sec. 110). All of the coal available as fuel for electric power plants in the United States contains sulfur in varying amounts from about 1 percent (by mass) to several percent. In principle, three options are available for preventing air pollution by the sulfur compounds produced as a byproduct of combustion while at the same time permitting the use of high sulfur content coal. First, the coal can be processed before it is burned to remove some or all of the sulfur. Second, equipment can be installed as part of the exhaust stage of the conversion process to remove pollutants from the flue gas before it enters the atmosphere. Finally, steps can be taken to release the pollutants into the environment in a way that minimizes or even eliminates hazards to health or property.

Technology for processing pollutants out of coal prior to combustion is not yet commercially available or economically feasible. A process was developed in Germany during World War II to transform coal into sulfur-free gas. It is, however, cumbersome and expensive. A number of alternate schemes are in various stages of research and development, but the timing of their commercial availability is uncertain.

Against this background, an acrimonious debate has developed in the United States over the relative merits of the two remaining choices. The federal Environmental Protection Agency requires as a matter of policy a commitment on the part of an electric utility to install "continuous emission reduction systems" as a condition for permission to burn high sulfur content coal. Virtually the entire U.S. utility industry—with the support of various other agencies of the federal government—has challenged this policy. In the industry's view, flue gas desulfurization (FGD) systems—commonly referred to as "stackgas scrubbers"—are unreliable, uneconomic, and unnecessary.

The industry position is that no vendor in the United States has a completely functional scrubber system that has been sufficiently tested to prove reliability at the same level as present boiler reliability. Hence, the industry argues, scrubber failure could impair the operation of generating units. Second, FGD backfit costs could be in the range of 15-20 percent of the capital cost of fossil-fired power plants, exclusive of penalties associated with an estimated 2-6 percent loss in output capability. Moreover, FGD operating costs, including the completely unresolved problem of waste disposal, could further increase electricity operating costs by yet another 15 percent.

Finally, the utilities claim it to be significant that the 1970 Clean Air Act explicitly provided for emission limitations as a means to an end—that is, "the attainment and maintenance" of ambient air quality standards—not as ends in themselves. In many state implementation plans, emission limitations were set at levels that are admitted to be more stringent than required to meet the EPA's national ambient air quality standards. This "overkill" was due to the fact that the states were given only nine months to prepare their implementation plans and therefore had to take shortcuts. One popular shortcut was to set emission limitations based on the capabilities of available control technology rather than on what was really required to meet ambient standards. Another was to apply limitations developed for an already "polluted" area to other regions, many of which already met the standards.

The Clean Air Act also required EPA to approve state emission limitations. EPA has almost always disapproved control strategies other than continuous emission controls (low sulfur fuel or scrubbers). The agency has interpreted the phrase "emission limitations" to mean a congressional intent to require continuous controls. This interpretation has, to date, been sustained by the courts. In fact, the courts have even gone beyond EPA policy and appear to have established the case law precedents for a doctrine of "nondegradation" of the air in regions that have not yet reached the federal ambient air quality standards.

In *Sierra Club* v. *Ruckelshaus*,[26] an environmentalist organization asked the court to enjoin the EPA from approving portions of state implementation plans that would have allowed deterioration of existing clean air regions up to the national ambient standards. The court agreed with the Sierra Club. This decision has been reaffirmed several times by other courts. It is important to note that "nondegradation" is a common-law development of the courts and hence cannot be changed by administrative or executive action. Only the U.S. Congress can reverse it by amending the Clean Air Act. Thus, federal common law as it now appears to stand prohibits degradation of air beyond its present quality, a policy which in many regions of the United States constitutes an absolute legal prohibition on burning coal without highly effective and reliable continuous emission control equipment.

Following eight months of debate, Congress enacted the Energy Supply and Environmental Coordination Act (ESECA) on June 22, 1974.[27] A principal objective of this legislation was to encourage the conversion of oil-fired steam-electric plants to coal. ESECA required the Federal Energy Administration (FEA) to prohibit power plants from burning natural gas or petroleum upon an FEA determination that a facility meets defined criteria regarding equipment, coal supply, and reliability of service, and on the condition that the EPA agrees that the facility in question will be able to burn coal without violating air quality standards. EPA was, however, given authority to suspend both state and federal emission controls up to June 30, 1975.[28] Contrary to the expectations of the utility industry, Congress allowed the June 30, 1975, expiration date to pass without taking any action to extend this provision. As a consequence, companies that had converted all or part of their generating equipment to a dual fuel capability found themselves with no legal authority to burn high sulfur coal—the only coal available east of the Appalachians—and with little realistic possibility that such authority could again be obtained under existing state and federal law.

The legal and political situation is further confused by the fact that the executive branch of the federal government has by no means spoken with one voice on these matters. At one time or another, the Federal Power Commission (FPC), the Commerce Department, the Interior Department, the Federal Energy Agency, and the Office of Management and Budget have publicly expressed doubts about the wisdom of a full-scale commitment to scrubbers as the solution to sulfur oxide pollution. Even the Council on Environmental Quality has on occasion been less than enthusiastic. The principal source of opposition against EPA policy has, however, been the FPC.

Under the 1935 Federal Power Act, the FPC has a mandate to ensure an abundant and reliable supply of electricity. This responsibility has placed the FPC in direct conflict with the EPA on a variety of issues since the latter agency was created in 1970. The two bureaucracies have collided head-on over scrubbers. The FPC concurs with the utility industry about the high cost and unreliability of scrubbers. As an alternative, the FPC, like the utilities, prefers development of coal desulfurization technology. Until suitable liquefaction or gasification techniques have been demonstrated on a commercial basis, the FPC believes that utilities should be allowed to use tall stacks and intermittent controls to meet clean air standards.

Other government agencies with a stake in the scrubber issue (including the White House) have been reluctant to become involved in the technical debate about the reliability of the technology. Various White House staff members have been quoted to the effect that the technical feasibility issue is something on which the White House cannot take a public position due to lack of technical expertise. Both the Nixon and the Ford Administrations have, nonetheless, supported amendments to existing environmental legislation that would authorize the intermittent control strategy favored by the utilities.[29]

The Council on Environmental Quality, usually an ally of EPA, also believes that utilities should have the option of using intermittent controls, but that there should not be a final commitment to any single strategy until more scientific information is available on the health hazards of sulfur oxides and until scrubbers have definitely proven their reliability.

The opposition to scrubbers as the best technology to control pollution goes deeper than the argument over whether some particular machinery can be made to work reliably and cheaply. It also involves some basic questions about what constitutes "pollution" and how to measure it, as well as controversy over what constitutes "safe" or "hazardous" levels.

Since the EPA established the national primary standards in terms of SO_2 concentration at ground level, considerable research has been done upon the health effects of SO_2.[30] In general, this research has failed to turn up any evidence of health hazards directly and unambiguously linked to SO_2. It has, moreover, become clear that quantitative assessment of the health effects of varying SO_2 concentration levels will be far more difficult than had been assumed when the national primary standards were promulgated. Establishing the precise nature of the linkage between SO_2 emissions and the presence in the environment of SO_4 in its various forms has developed into an intricate technical problem. Contrary to expectations, SO_4 concentrations in the atmosphere have remained constant even though SO_2 levels have dropped sharply. The electric utilities have begun to argue that SO_2 was never really the problem; the real "air pollution" problem is SO_4. This situation would be very troublesome if true because the catalytic converter now required to be installed on new automobiles could well be a large producer of SO_4.

In summary, it has become at least arguable that national air quality policy—together with implementing and enforcing plans—was drawn up before all the scientific answers were in. Industry has taken the position that adherence to these plans could very likely result in some costly mistakes. Specifically, pending resolution of the nature of the SO_2-SO_4 linkage, the electric utility and paper industries have increased the pressure for an amendment of the Clean Air Act that would permit tall stacks of intermittent control systems as a strategy for meeting ambient standards. Environmentalists strongly oppose such an amendment. It is their position that the available scientific evidence (conceded to be meager) is compatible with the proposition that even existing SO_2 ambient standards do not adequately protect public health from sulfate particles. Preliminary studies could in the environmentalists' view imply that emissions should be reduced as much as is technologically feasible, *as an end in itself.* Tall stacks and intermittent control standards do not, of course, reduce emissions but rather use the dispersion characteristics of the atmosphere to attain ambient SO_2 standards. Conceivably, such a system might not be effective in attaining an ambient sulfate particle standard. However, no such standard yet exists; nor has the effectiveness of dispersion techniques for attaining one been tested.

Hence, means to ends have become symbolic issues to the competing constituencies of a variety of public and private agencies. This has happened at the same time that fundamental questions have surfaced about the relative value of alternative and partially conflicting ends and even about how to measure progress toward those ends. The legal situation is, if anything, more tangled.

Resolution of the multitude of conflicting laws and regulations requires cooperation and coordination among state governments, the agencies and branches of the federal government and between the courts and the executive branch of both state and federal governments. To be blunt, the authority necessary to bring about such cooperation and coordination is not present in any existing American political or economic institution.

Nuclear Power: Promise vs. Performance

Nuclear power was a major element of the energy mobilization plans formulated in the wake of the 1974 OPEC price increases and embargo. A number of official and private studies have urged growth of the nuclear power sector in the United States from less than 50 GWe in 1974 (about 6 percent of total electricity production capacity) to more than 800 GWe by 2000, by which time nuclear power would contribute more than 40 percent of national electricity capacity. (For example, the FEA's November 1974 *Project Independence Report*, argued, as part of an "accelerated development strategy," for 93 gigawatts of installed nuclear capacity by 1980 and 240 gigawatts by 1985.[31]) These same plans have also projected a leveling off of the price increases that plagued nuclear power during the first fifteen years of its "commercial reality" in the United States. In addition, most official statements argued that for the foreseeable future nuclear power would "remain" the cheapest of all realistic alternatives to oil for the generation of electricity.

Two years after these plans were announced both predictions seemed to be highly dubious. In the United States at the end of 1975, cheap electricity from light water reactors (LWRs) remained a hope rather than an accomplishment. Between 1965 and 1973, cost increases for nuclear plants consistently exceeded overall inflation rates. Contrary to both official and private statements in support of Project Independence, there was no evidence by the end of 1975 that the real (i.e., constant dollar) costs of nuclear power plants had begun to stabilize. Indeed all available evidence pointed to quite the opposite; the capital costs of LWRs in the United States were continuing the decade-long trend of exceeding the overall rate of monetary inflation.[32] As usual, there were many confident explanations for the unexpected cost increases of nuclear plants. Contrary, however, to what one might infer from the literature on nuclear power economics, the precise nature as well as the relative importance of these forces remained unclear.[c]

In spite of the official optimism in the aftermath of the OPEC embargo,

---

[c]One important complicating factor was the way the electric utility industry handles the problem of inflation in estimating the cost of a power plant that will require many years to design and build. For more detail on this technical problem, see I.C. Bupp and R. Treitel, "The Economics of Nuclear Power: De Omnibus Dubitundum," working paper, M.I.T. Center for Policy Alternatives, Cambridge, Mass., February 1976.

forecasts for nuclear power in the United States have actually been considerably and continuously revised downward since 1970 (see Table 8-1). In fact, ERDA has recently become even more pessimistic than Table 8-1 suggests. The 82 GWe and 205 GWe of installed capacity projected for 1980 and 1985 respectively were actually a "moderate-high" growth case (see Table 8-2).

A case-by-case review (Table 8-3) of the status of nuclear plants either under construction or on order as of December 1975 suggests that by 1985 it is likely, but by no means certain, that the existing 53 GWe of nuclear capacity will be supplemented by an additional 60 GWe. Hence, something on the order of 100 GWe of generating capacity would appear to be a realistic "base case" for the anticipated contribution of nuclear power to the U.S. national energy supply system by 1985. Now, with somewhat higher uncertainty assume that essentially all of the additional plants "on order" are completed by 1985, or alternatively that some of them (say, 10 percent) are delayed or cancelled but that the capacity they represent is replaced by new orders in the 1976 to 1978 period, and that all of this is complete by 1985. This assumption would give a 1985 U.S. nuclear economy of something like 200 GWe. Against this background, the ERDA "high" case (Table 8-2) looks very optimistic since it implies either something like fifteen orders per year in the 1976 to 1978 period or a considerable shortening of the commitment to completion period.

Speculation about developments beyond 1985 are extremely risky, but as a simple organizing device, let us propose three scenarios:

1. A moratorium (de facto or de jure) on nuclear plant construction beginning in 1976-1978 and leaving the United States with a "base case" of 100 GWe of installed capacity through the rest of the century;

Table 8-1
Comparison of USAEC Nuclear Power Forecasts, 1962-1975

AEC Forecast Made in Year	Installed Nuclear Power at End of Calendar Year (GWe)		
	1975	1980	1985
1962	16	40	—
1964	29	75	—
1966	40	95	—
1967	61	145	255
1969	62	149	277
1970	59	150	300
1972	54	132	280
1973	47	102	255
1975	40	82	205

Source: The Atlantic Council of the U.S., *Nuclear Fuels Policy*, Report of the Atlantic Council's Nuclear Fuels Policy Working Group, Washington, D.C. 1976, p. 65.

Table 8-2
ERDA 1975 Electricity Generating Capacity Projections

| | Actual 1975 | GWe Installed at End of CY | | |
		1980	1985	1990
Low:				
Total	492	604	785	980
Nuclear	38	70	160	285
Nuclear % of Total	8%	12%	20%	29%
Medium Low:				
Total	496	620	800	1,040
Nuclear	39	76	185	340
Nuclear % of Total	8%	12%	23%	33%
Medium High:				
Total	500	630	820	1,075
Nuclear	41	82	205	375
Nuclear % of Total	8%	13%	25%	36%
High:				
Total	505	654	875	1,180
Nuclear	43	92	245	470
Nuclear % of Total	9%	14%	28%	40%

Source: The Atlantic Council of the U.S., *Nuclear Fuels Policy.*

2. "Modest" growth involving completion of the additional 100 GWe now "on order" plus an average of ten new orders per year during the twenty-year 1980-2000 period for a total installed capacity on the order of 400 GWe by the beginning of the twenty-first century;

3. "Strong" growth of an average of twenty new orders per year until the end of the century for a 600 GWe nuclear economy by 2000.

These numbers are not meant to be projections or predictions, but merely pigeonholes to organize thought. The crucial point here is that all present trends point unambiguously to the prospect that the future of the nuclear industry in the United States is much more likely to be at the low, rather than the high, end of this range. Three interrelated circumstances are producing this outcome. First, there are the capital cost problems to which we have already referred. Although it is true that the costs of electricity from coal are also growing at alarming rates, it appears to be the case that with some regional exceptions (notably the Northeast), the competitive posture of the nuclear power is worsening. Second, there is no evidence that intervention by nuclear critics in power plant construction programs will either decrease or be less successful in the foreseeable future than it was in the past. Third, a new and highly acute set of problems has arisen with respect to the light water reactor fuel cycle in the United States. Some additional detail will be helpful on each of these matters.

Table 8-3
Status of Nuclear Power in the United States, December 1975

Status of Plants	Number	Aggregate Capacity (MWe)
Complete[a]	54	36,766
Plants under Construction		
90% complete	9	8,738
50-90% complete	12	12,010
25-50% complete	11	11,384
25% complete	28	29,418
	60	61,550
Plants "On Order" but Not Yet under Construction	86	97,712
	200	196,028

[a]Includes all of the plants ordered before 1966 (18 altogether). No plants ordered after 1968 were yet ready for operation. In 1966, orders for 21 plants were announced. Of these, 18 were complete. In 1967, orders for 27 plants were announced; 15 were complete. In 1968, orders for 14 plants were announced; only 3 had been completed by the end of 1975.

Nuclear Economics: Persistent Bad News

There is widespread agreement that on the average nuclear plants in the United States that are complete or nearly complete have cost on the order of twice as much, in real (constant) dollars, to build as was estimated at the time they were ordered.

There are considerable differences of opinion, however, about what this development implies for the future. Generally, the position of the reactor manufacturers and many electric utility companies is that the real costs of nuclear power are now known with a far greater degree of confidence that was possible at the time of the original plant orders; the only problem is to take account of the effects of monetary inflation. Today, in the view of many advocates of nuclear power, the only significant source of uncertainty in predicting the cost of a plant ordered now for operation in the early 1980s is how to correct today's engineering estimates for tomorrow's inflation. The absolute difference in current dollars can easily be substantial. For example, the current dollar value of $450 1975 dollars escalated for ten years at an average annual rate of 7 percent is $885; at an average annual rate of 8 percent, it is $972.

A less optimistic view of the status of nuclear power economics admits that large uncertainties remain with respect to the real as distinct from the current dollar costs of nuclear plants, but contends that the same is true for coal-fired plants.

With respect to the first of these positions, in the fall of 1974, the FEA's Project Independence estimated the cost of a reactor ordered in 1974 for

1982-83 operation to be \$455/kw in 1974 dollars.[33] More recently, a major architect-engineer firm has reportedly been quoting prospective nuclear plant customers a price of \$450-\$500/kw for a plant "started today-finished today." A capital cost in the range of \$450/kw (1975 dollars) is, *we agree*, about what presently complete or nearly complete plants have on the average cost. However, to predict that this will turn out to be the real cost of new plants ordered today is to assume that the forces that in the past have caused errors in such engineering estimates no longer exist. This is a heroic assumption.

The more optimistic predictions about the future costs of nuclear power are based on the assumption that the costs of any future safety-related modification to present nuclear plant designs will be relatively minor *and* the belief that future licensing-related delays in the construction process will not greatly increase the time between application for a construction permit and fuel loading over that experienced in the past. Both of these beliefs rest upon an assessment of the status of the controversy over reactor safety, which may turn out to be correct, but which is not supported by any empirical evidence. This contention— or hope—implies that "the worst is over" and that there is "light at the end of the tunnel."[d] The principal difficulty with this assessment of the nuclear safety controversy in the United States is that it ignores the extent to which the administrative and judicial processes for licensing power plant favor the intervenors.

Regulatory Processes

The Federal Administration Procedure Act of 1946 sets the ground rules governing the procedures by which utilities relate to government agencies. Central to this legislation are the notions of procedural and substantive "due process."

Procedural due process requires that adequate notice be given to all interested parties that at a certain time, date, and place a specified matter involving a regulated company will be the subject of a public hearing to be held by the pertinent regulatory agency, for the purpose of presenting evidence relevant to the matter at issue. The fundamental constitutional purpose of procedural due process is to guarantee that all parties affected by the administrative powers of government have a means of knowing what their rights are and how they may be protected. The principal means to this end is a public hearing for the purpose of presenting and rebutting evidence through discovery and cross-examination.

---

[d]The temptation to press the analogy between the nuclear industry's struggle with its critics and the American war with the Viet Cong is strong. Let us merely suggest that electric utility executives with major commitments to nuclear power might well regard the image as something less than a source of comfort.

Substantive due process requires that decisions issued by government regulatory agencies must accord with constitutional guarantees against confiscation of property. The rights to both procedural and substantive due process are enforced and protected by a further right, that of judicial review, which permits the appeal of regulatory decisions to the courts.

Formal cases, decided by either state or federal regulatory bodies, are of two types: those initiated for a purpose of "rule making" and those that require a decision on a contested issue (adjudication).

Rule Making. Rule making is legislation by the administrative branch of government. When properly made, such rules have the force of law. Enabling statutes have typically conferred upon independent agencies the authority to adopt rules and regulations within standards set by the statutes. At the federal level, the statutory provisions setting the standards to be met by administrative rule making have generally been very broad. Regulatory agencies have typically been granted the authority to mandate rules governed only by very broad legislative statements of purpose. The underlying assumption was that the legislature was in no position to specify the details of complex technical matters.

Recent environmental legislation (e.g., the 1970 Clean Air Act and the pending strip mine control legislation) represents a dramatic break with this pattern. Much of this new body of law represents an attempt by Congress to specify the technical standards that in the past were usually left to the discretion of administrative agencies. It is a response to the common complaint that under the old pattern the administrative agencies were simply given the authority to work out the details of regulation effectively "in cahoots" with their regulatees.

The procedure by which rules are adopted varies in different statutes. A given commission may or may not be required to hold a public hearing before it adopts a rule. Even when not required to do so, commissions considering the adoption or amendment of a rule may (a) inform interested parties of the matter under consideration, (b) invite the filling of written comments, and (c) provide for a public hearing. Although not specifically required to do so by the Atomic Energy Act of 1954 (as amended) the USAEC and the new Nuclear Regulatory Commission (NRC) have customarily followed all of these practices in issuing rules relating to the operation of nuclear plants.

Adjudication of Contested Cases. A formal case for adjudication may be instituted by a utility, by one or more of its customers, or by a regulatory commission acting on its own motion. Hearings may take place before the commissioners themselves. However, the more common practice is for cases to be heard by a "hearing examiner," an appointed official whose function and responsibilities are similar to those of the trial judge. The hearing examiner serves as a representative of the commission and as its agent. Ordinarily, he is empowered to make an initial decision on the case, which he then passes on to the commissioners themselves for final decision. Hearing examiners serving in federal commissions are, by law, independent of agency control so far as decision making is concerned. In state commissions, examiners are not always independent to the same degree.

It has often been asserted that testimony presented during commission hearings is not bound by the same strict rules of evidence that prevail in courts of law. The consensus among lawyers, however, seems to be that as a practical matter, there is little if any difference between the courts and the regulatory commissions in this regard. Commission decisions, once made, may be the subject of an application for a rehearing. If such an application is rejected, the aggrieved party may appeal the matter through the courts under his right of judicial review.

The fundamental constitutional purpose of this apparatus should be emphasized. It is designed to protect the rights of the individual from arbitrary acts by the government. The key postulate is that guarantees of such protection are worth the risk of substantial incremental monetary costs and/or delays.

Judicial Review. Regulatory statutes almost always designate the court to which appeals from agency decisions may be taken. The decisions of the federal commissions may be reviewed initially in the U.S. Court of Appeals. The decisions of the state commissions are reviewed in the state court systems, with the possibility of ultimate appeal to the U.S. Supreme Court if constitutional issues are raised.

Regulatory commission decisions and the orders implementing them may be appealed to the courts on a number of grounds: (1) that the statute relied upon by the commission was unconstitutional; (2) that the commission exceeded its statutory authority or jurisdiction; (3) that the commissions' order was not supported by findings; (4) that the findings were not supported by substantial evidence; (5) that the order violated specific constitutional guarantees; (6) that the order resulted from unlawful procedure or some other error of law; or (7) that the order was based upon a misinterpretation of the law.

The courts have usually accepted commissions' findings of fact as conclusive if based upon substantial evidence. This procedure is known as the Substantial Evidence Rule, which was established by the Supreme Court early in the history of the Interstate Commerce Commission.[e] Hence, as a practical matter, judicial review of administrative decisions ordinarily relates to legal and constitutional issues.

---

[e]"Once a fair hearing has been given, proper findings made, and other statutory requirements satisfied, the courts cannot intervene in the absence of a clear showing that the limits of due process have been overstepped. If the Commission's order, as applied to the facts before it, and viewed in its entirety, produces no arbitrary result, our inquiry is at an end." See *FPC* vs. *Natural Gas Pipeline Co.*, 62 Supreme Court 736, 742 (1942).

The Regulatory Program of the U.S. Atomic Energy
Commission and Its Successor, the Nuclear
Regulatory Commission

The principal regulatory powers of the NRC derive from the Atomic Energy Act of 1954 (as amended). As presently constituted, this regulatory program consists of several sequential and conceptually distinct functions: the establishment (by rule making) of radiation protection standards; the licensing of facilities and materials; inspection to assure compliance with licenses; and sanctions to achieve such compliance when necessary. A.E.C.'s historic lack of willingness to use aggressively the very harsh sanctions available to it has been the subject of continuing controversy. The NRC is under considerable pressure to reverse this pattern.

One aspect of the internal organization of the nuclear licensing process that is unique is the so-called separated staff. A "separated staff" is established within the commission for each case that goes to a public hearing. The purpose is to prevent those presenting the NRC staff position in a hearing from discussing a case, except on the record, with the hearing examiner or members of the commission. The effect is a more or less complete separation of the staff from the NRC in formal cases, often to the extent of leaving the commissioners without technical assistance in making their own decisions.

Applications to construct and operate nuclear power plants are reviewed through a five-stage regulatory process. (NRC procedures for licensing the use of nuclear materials are somewhat simpler.)

Applications Submittal. Initially, the applicant is required to submit a detailed description of the proposed facility and a study of every possible risk in its operation. This submittal is known as the Preliminary Safety Analysis Report. Since 1971, an accumulating body of new federal case law has had the effect of substantially broadening the scope of NRC regulatory review of license applications. Under this new law, applicants are required to submit comprehensive environmental impact analyses (including cost-benefit studies) of any installation requiring an AEC construction and/or operating license. These environmental analyses receive the same detailed review as the nuclear safety analyses. They may be the subject of separate adjudicatory hearings and/or judicial review.

NRC Staff Review. In this phase, the application is evaluated by the technical staff of the NRC, assisted by technical personnel at the "National Laboratories" at Oak Ridge, Tennessee; Hanford, Washington; and Argonne, Illinois. It is not uncommon for important differences of opinion on matters of technical fact to develop between the NRC staff in Washington and laboratory scientists. In the past, such differences have been a major source of licensing delays, particularly with respect to the environmental analyses.

The Advisory Committee on Reactor Safeguards. A part-time advisory committee made up of nationally recognized experts works with the NRC staff in undertaking an independent and exhaustive study of reactor applications. The report of the ACRS is submitted to the NRC chairman and thereafter made public. Although the ACRS makes recommendations rather than formal decisions, its recommendations, especially if adverse, may govern the final decision. There have been several instances of differing recommendations by the staff and the ACRS. As a practical matter, an adverse report by the ACRS has meant either cancellation or drastic modification of an application.

Hearings. A formal hearing before a hearing examiner provides the applicant, NRC staff, and intervenors with an opportunity to present testimony. Intervenors are granted full rights of discovery and cross-examination, as provided by the procedural due process requirements of the 1946 Administrative Procedure Act. The hearing examiner issues an initial decision following these hearings.

Final Action. The initial decision of the hearing examiner becomes final unless one of the parties files an exception. However, if no exception is filed, the commission, as a matter of policy, institutes a review of the initial decision on its own motion. In preparing its final decision, the commission has substantial legal assistance but little technical help since it is precluded from consulting experts on reactor safety in the regulatory staff. The commission has rarely overturned a hearing examiner decision.

Historically, the chronic problem with the internal AEC review process has been independent technical expertise. In many cases neither the commission *nor the staff* has been in a position seriously to challenge either the laboratories (whose scientists are *not* government employees) or the prestigious ACRS. It is generally conceded that the ACRS was the real strength of the system during the early years of reactor commercialization when only a few applications needed to be processed per year. As the number of applications snowballed in the late 1960s and early 1970s and as environmental legislation, in effect, doubled the workload per application, the entire system often came close to complete collapse. The degree to which these problems have come under control since the separation of NRC from the AEC is not at all clear.

To understand the present situation, it is helpful to distinguish between the pre-construction permit (CP) issuance phase of the plant licensing and construction process and the post-CP phase. For the nuclear plants licensed to operate in the United States in 1974-75 (14 plants), the average time between CP issuance and operating license (OL) issuance was 5.5 years, with a minimum of 3.75 years and a maximum of a little more than 7 years.[34] However, the CPs for all of these plants were issued prior to March 1972. At that time nuclear plant applications were permitted by AEC regulations to conduct site exploration; site excavation including the driving of piles; and the construction of roadways, railroad spurs, and transmission lines; as well as construction of non-nuclear facilities. Moreover, prior to March 1972, the AEC liberally granted exemptions that often allowed much work on nuclear facilities up to grade level. Many utilities were thus able to accomplish one to two years of construction prior to CP issuance. Under present Nuclear Regulatory Commission rules this will not be possible for companies which have applied for CPs subsequent to March 1972.

This change in federal regulatory practice alone could, therefore, lengthen the time between CP issuance and fuel loading by many months. A critical question, of course, is whether this new delay will be compensated by an equivalent shortening of the pre-CP licensing phase. We know of no evidence that this is happening and indeed are inclined to infer from press reports and (admittedly limited) personal observation that quite the opposite is true. There appears to be a proliferation rather than a consolidation of review authority at the state and local level often in series with, rather than parallel to, federal procedure. At the federal regulatory level—the NRC—the historic tendency of lists of safety analysis questions to become lists of lists of questions continues. Moreover, there has been no observable decline in either the desire or the ability of antinuclear power intervenors to use these administrative and judicial processes to impede the construction of plants.

Many in the nuclear power and/or electric utility industries now concede the high probability of further increases in the real absolute costs of nuclear power but insist that the comparative economics of the technology are not likely to deteriorate relative to those of coal, which is the only realistic alternative. This view, in their opinion, is critical because the future of nuclear power *depends* on developments in the coal industry where it appears that the same general forces that caused unanticipated increases in the costs of nuclear power are now operating to bring about the same result with respect to coal.

The first point we would make is that there are obvious limits to the pertinence of the comparative economic situation. If nuclear plants ordered in 1974-75 require fifteen years to enter service and cost more than $1 billion 1975 (i.e., not escalated) dollars, the prospects for nuclear power in the United States are poor, regardless of what happens to the costs of coal plants. Having said this, we would concur that all the evidence available to us points unambiguously to substantial increases in the absolute cost of coal-fired power.

Unfortunately, there is really very little more that we can say quantitatively. All that is really clear is that the construction of a nuclear plant has in the past been a qualitatively different enterprise from construction of a coal plant. The issue is whether this will continue to be the case. At present, quantitative information is not available to answer this question.

In 1974, my colleagues and I wrote:

If things continue as they have in the recent past, coal delivered to a plant at 58¢/million BTU will be competitive in 1975. Coal delivered at 89¢/million BTU will be competitive with nuclear power by 1980 . . . it is a reasonably safe guess that coal delivered at $1.00/million BTU should be competitive with nuclear power any place in the country by the early 1980s if present trends continue.[35]

The critical question, two years later, is obviously whether it is still reasonable to predict the "break-even price" of coal in the United States to continue to increase. On balance, I believe it is reasonable to make such a prediction. But it is an extremely chancey business about which honest men can obviously differ. What I am far more confident about is that the only way to make a determinate case about the comparative economic status of nuclear power in the years ahead is to pick a set of best-case assumptions for reactors and simultaneously a set of worst-case assumptions for coal.

The LWR Fuel Cycle: New Problems for the
U.S. Nuclear Industry

In the past several months, major new uncertainties have arisen in connection with the LWR fuel cycle in the United States.

To understand the dimensions of this extremely serious problem, some further detail on the various stages of the fuel cycle will be helpful.[36]

An LWR of the size now being delivered in the United States (about 1,000 megawatts) requires approximately 35,000 kilograms of enriched uranium annually during the life of the plant. This amount is roughly equivalent to a lifetime demand for natural uranium of about 6,000 short tons (one million pounds for the initial core plus an annual makeup of about 400,000 pounds). Uranium is a relatively abundant mineral found in a wide variety of forms in the earth's crust. Typically, however, the quantities of uranium per unit ore are not great. Concentrations of oxide on the order of a few pounds per ton are common in presently commercial ore grades. Concentration in the range of 50 pounds per ton are quite rare and have been considered extremely rich.[f]

Once mined, uranium ore must be processed in a mill to separate the uranium from the host rock and other minerals. The product of the milling operation (known as "yellowcake") is a salt containing between 70 percent and 80 percent U_3O_8.

To utilize uranium efficiently in LWRs, the concentration of the isotope

---

[f]Deposits of uranium are graded by industry and government in terms of percent U308 in the mine or mineable ore. Historically, concentrations of 0.1 percent to 0.3 percent have been considered of commercial value. The lowest grades in the government's "$15 per pound" category contain on the average about 0.1 percent U308. Some exceptionally rich deposits in the United States contain as much as 0.5 percent U_3O_8. For comparative purposes, uranium contained in Tennessee shale varies between .006 percent and .008 percent U_3O_8

U235 must be increased.[g] The process by which this is done makes use of the differences in the rate at which gases of varying molecular weight diffuse through a porous barrier. Hence, to provide "feed" for the enriching process, "yellowcake" is converted to UF_6 as the third stage of the LWR fuel cycle.

In enriching uranium, it is common practice to express the amount of work involved in the process in terms of a measure called simply "separate work units" (SWUs). A crucial fact about the enrichment process is that the amount of separate work required per unit output of enriched product is not a constant, but is a relatively strong function of both of the other two parameters—the amount of feed and level to which the waste stream, or "tails," are depleted. In general, more enriched product can be produced per unit of separative work by raising the U235 concentration in the waste stream. This, however, increases the amount of feed material needed per unit output. Since separative work capacity is fixed for a given plant, the output of enriched uranium can, in effect, be enhanced by operating the plant "inefficiently"—that is, by raising the "tails assay" and hence demand for feed.[h]

The fact that there is a strong interdependent relationship among feed requirements, separative work requirements, and "tails assay" has important commercial significance. It has been the policy of the government to operate its enrichment facilities in order to conserve separative work units at the expense of feed requirements by raising "tails assay." The net effect, of course, is to increase demand for uranium ore. All other things being equal, increasing the "tails assay" from 0.2 percent to 0.3 percent U235 also increases the demand for feed by 20 percent.

The final step at the "front end" of the fuel cycle is fabrication of the enriched product of the diffusion plant into small ceramic pellets of uranium dioxide (UO_2). These pellets are clad in stainless steel and assembled into bundles for insertion into the core of the reactor.

Three important physical processes take place during the production of electricity from uranium fuel: spontaneous fission of the U235, the capture of neutrons by U238, and the creation of a variety of "fission products." The capture of neutrons by U238 without the occurrence of fission results in the production of plutonium, which in principle can be used as a complementary

[g]Uranium as found in nature consists of several isotopes. The principal ones are U235 and U238; of these, U235 is the lighter, comprising 0.7 percent of the mass of naturally occurring uranium; that is readily fissile.

[h]For reference purposes, it is helpful to remember that three separative work units are required to produce one kilogram of 3 percent enriched product from six kilograms of natural uranium feed if the remaining five kilograms of waste or "tails" are depleted to 0.3 percent U235 by mass. What happened here is that 0.0280 kilogram of the 0.0427 kilogram U235 that was originally present in the six kilograms of feed has been concentrated in one kilogram of product. The remaining U235 is discharged in five kilograms of 0.3 percent tails. For more detail, see The Atlantic Council of the U.S., *Nuclear Fuels Policy: Report of The Atlantic Council's Nuclear Fuels Policy Working Group*, Washington, D.C., 1976, p. 111.

fuel after extraction from the spent fuel elements and reblending with additional U235 into a "mixed oxide" fuel.[i]

After a bundle of fuel rods has been irradiated and can no longer be effectively used for power generation, it must be removed from the core of the reactor and stored for several months in a water pool adjacent to the plant for cooling.

As a practical matter, the LWR fuel cycle in the United States stops at this point. There are no operable facilities to reprocess the irradiated fuel to recover uranium and byproduct plutonium. Moreover, several operating nuclear power plants have virtually exhausted their "interim" cooling space. Others will exhaust such space within the minimum time now required for completion and licensing of new facilities. If the electric utilities that own these plants are to avoid sharp reductions in power or outright shutdown, only three options exist. First, the effective storage capacity of in-place interim cooling facilities can be increased by rearranging the physical configuration of the spent fuel. Several U.S. utilities have plans under way to do this. The problem is that such an arrangement requires federal license, the application and review of which is subject to the administrative and judicial delays inherent in any action with nuclear safety implications. Second, new on-site storage facilities could be built at relatively modest expense. Again, however, this requires a license. Finally, spent fuel from a number of reactors could, in principle, be transported to a central repository. No such facility now exists or is under construction. A central storage facility with capacity to support ten plants is estimated to cost $50 million and to require four years to build independent of any licensing delays.

The gravity of these problems has not been widely recognized. The fact is that the operation of any reprocessing capability in the United States is further away than one would infer from public literature. The problem is not technical. Reprocessing on an industrial scale began some thirty years ago in the United States. The problem is political: What specific configuration of physical processes will be judged acceptable for licensing? By mid-1976, there was no clear answer to this question; nor was there a realistic prospect that there would be such an answer until at least mid-1977.

Because of this uncertainty, it is extremely difficult to assess the prospective economics of a complete LWR fuel cycle in the United States. The potential economic advantages of reprocessing spent fuel are straightforward enough. First, natural uranium feed requirements are reduced by 15-20 percent through

---

[i]When a fuel element is ready for discharge after irradiation, the initial enrichment of 2.8 percent U235 will have been reduced to approximately equal the U235 content of natural uranium (i.e., about 0.7 percent). But the irradiated fuel will also contain about five grams of fissile plutonium per kilogram uranium. It will also contain about 25 grams of other nonfissile but highly radioactive products per kilogram uranium. It is these products that during reprocessing must be separated from the still useful uranium and the byproduct plutonium for permanent storage.

the recycling of recovered uranium. The use of byproduct plutonium in "mixed-oxide" fuel results in an *additional* 15-20 percent savings in natural uranium requirements. Moreover, while uranium recycle causes no significant decrease in demand for separative work, the recycle of plutonium also produces a 20 percent savings in separative work requirements.

However, while savings in feed and separative work requirements as a result of recycle are easily calculated, the economic incentive to reprocess is not nearly so clear. In principle, it is obvious that the fundamental question is simple enough: Is the value of the recovered uranium and plutonium greater than, or at least equal to, the cost of reprocessing?

Since the value of the recovered uranium is just as obviously dependent upon the cost of ore and the cost of enriching, both of which are highly likely to increase, the economic case for reprocessing should look good. The problem is that the value of plutonium—whether it has a positive or negative value—is completely uncertain. Without plutonium recycle, the economics of reprocessing are acutely sensitive to the price of uranium ore. In mid-1976 it was judgment of the U.S. nuclear industry that without plutonium recycle, reprocessing economics are too risky to justify further capital investments.[j]

The NRC has announced its intention to decide whether plutonium cycle will be permitted by mid-1977, which is a very optimistic time schedule. It seems far more likely that no decision will be made until late-1977, at the earliest.

This hiatus is the controlling item in closing the fuel cycle in the United States. A new reprocessing plant in South Carolina is currently complete in the sense that it could begin operation in a matter of months with three output streams: uranium in liquid nitrate form; plutonium, also as a liquid nitrate; and waste product liquids. The Barnwell plant was originally designed to ship recovered uranium and plutonium as nitrates, an arrangement with some technical advantages to fuel fabricators. It seems likely, however, that even if plutonium recycle is permitted, the NRC will require that uranium and plutonium be shipped as solid oxides rather than as liquid nitrates. An additional investment of $100 million and a two- to three-year construction period would be required to add a suitable nitrate to oxide conversion facility to the Barnwell plant. The industrial consortium that built the Barnwell plant has taken the position that it cannot consider making this investment until the NRC has approved plutonium recycle. The second problem at Barnwell is waste packaging. The NRC is likely to license Barnwell (independent of the plutonium issue) only if the owners agree to add facilities to convert liquid radioactive wastes into an insoluble nonleachable solid. This requirement represents an

[j]The governments "forward costs" are costs of production incurred after geological investigation, land acquisition, and exploration are complete. Moreover, no allowance is made for profit. Division into $8, $10, and $15 classes are indicative only of relative costs of recovering ore from these different reserve classes. They indicate that other things being equal, $15 reserves cost on the order of twice as much in mine and mill as $8 reserves.

additional $300 million investment. (Again, there is no technical problem since the required process has long been well known.) However, the present position of the owners of Barnwell is that waste solidification and management is a responsibility of the federal government.

What all of this means is that there is no realistic prospect of Barnwell operating on a commercial basis until *at least* the early 1980s. Accordingly, there is no realistic prospect for the fuel cycle to be fully "closed" in the sense of an in-place operating plant sufficient to support even the "base-case" 200 GWe nuclear economy burning recycled uranium and plutonium, until at least the mid-1980s. And this is very optimistic.

It is clear that all of this adds up to considerable pressure on the price of uranium ore, at least for the next ten to fifteen years.

In fact, by combining the estimates in Table 8-4 with the possibility of further government actions to conserve separative work at the expense of the feed requirements, it seems reasonable to suppose that the actual demand for uranium ore could well be on the order of 50 percent to 100 percent greater for any given number of operating plants than it would have been if the fuel cycle had been fully closed.

Partly because of this very real prospect, U.S. utilities have precipitated a near-panic search for uranium to fuel the nuclear plants already built or nearly built. As a result, the average price of milled uranium rose from about $7 per pound in early 1974 to about $40 per pound by early 1976. To make matters even worse, the economic picture is further clouded by the fact that public data about uranium prices in the United States is virtually without commercial meaning. Historic prices as well as all available government estimates about future prices reflect little more than historic variable costs of production.[k] Even setting aside the fact that the government's "forward costs" ignore both exploration and development costs and return on investment, it is quite probable that new environmental restrictions on mining and milling activities will shortly make historic costs worthless as guides to the future. Although it has not been widely noted, uranium mining and milling is the most capital-intensive part of the entire LWR fuel cycle. To meet even modest growth—the 400 GWe case—a new investment of at least $1 billion per year in uranium mining, exploration, development, and mill expansion will be required during the next ten to fifteen years. Like virtually every other aspect of nuclear power, the uranium business

[k]For example, uranium ore in the American western states has often been found beneath the water table. This means that mines must constantly be pumped out, discharging large amounts of water-bearing radium, heavy metals and suspended solids. It is virtually certain that such discharges from new or even existing mines will be required to meet far more stringent and, hence, costly standards.

During the milling process, it has hitherto been standard commercial practice to put the waste material, from which yellowcake has been extracted, in large, unprotected piles. The result was vast mounds of low-level radioactive material that is subject to wind and water erosion. Pending regulations at both the federal and state level, again, impose far more rigid standards.

Table 8-4
Incremental Cumulative Increase in Demand: No PU and V Cycle

By	U_3O_8 Demand	SWV Requirements
1985	+ 9%	+ 4%
1990	+14%	+ 7%
1995	+24%	+13%
2000	+27%	+13%

Source: Calculated by the author from data in The Atlantic Council of the U.S., *Nuclear Fuels Policy.*

makes inordinant cash demands. Moreover, the risk—reward ratio for uranium is not especially attractive from an investment standpoint. The value of a minimum-size deposit compares poorly with that of other minerals, such as copper. The profit per pound may be higher for uranium, but uranium ore bodies tend to be relatively small and expensive to mine. Uranium has not proven to be a financially attractive commodity. Hence, it is by no means clear that the investments needed to sustain the "front end" of the LWR fuel cycle can be counted on, even in the absence of pressure from the failure to "close" the cycle.

Although the absolute dollar amounts are substantial (Table 8-5), the total fuel cycle investment required to support the nuclear power plant is only on the order of 7 percent to 10 percent of the capital cost of the plant itself. It has been widely assumed that because this is a relatively small fraction of the total, the fuel-cycle investment would somehow automatically be made if the investment and power production facilities were assured. It is now evident that this assumption was invalid.

The uncertainties and risks of the two investments are quite different. Uranium mining and milling in the best of circumstances is a high-risk venture. Enrichment and reprocessing, because of their capital-intensive nature and large facility size requirements, involve considerable risks associated with down-time. But ironically perhaps, most important, uncertainty about the future of the nuclear industry had, itself, become a major element in the fuel-cycle cost and investment outlook. Uncertainty in the mining and milling industry, for example, feeds on the uncertainty in the utility industry and vice versa.

The mining industry is understandably hesitant to commit capital to exploration and development in the face of a declining market for reactors. This hesitation, in turn, arouses doubts in the power industry about the availability of adequate supplies of fuel. Utilities must consider the future of uranium supply very seriously before ordering plants, for they face the possibility of intervention on this issue. The critics of nuclear power have proven adept at exploiting, for their own ends, situations for which they are in part responsible. The same nuclear critics, who have partly caused both the capital and fuel-cycle problems

Table 8-5
Estimated Capital Investment Requirements to "Close the Fuel Cycle" for a 200 Reactor Economy ($ billions 1975)

	With PU & V Recycle	Without PU & V Recycle
Mining and Milling	$ 2.20	$3.00-$4.00[a]
Conversion	0.20	0.30
Enrichment	5.60	7.50
Fabrication		
U	0.40	0.50
MOX	0.25	–
Reprocessing	2.80	–
Waste Solidification	0.40	–
Waste Storage	0.15	–
Interim Spend Fuel Storage	0.20	1.00
	$12.2	$12.3

Source: Calculated by the author from The Atlantic Council of the U.S., *Nuclear Fuels Policy*.

[a]Depending upon government tails assay policy.

of nuclear power have not been in the least reluctant to cite these very problems as justification for challenging nuclear power plant license applications. The effect is multiplying uncertainty. Delays in the commitment of new plants increase the reluctance of the mining industry to explore the new ore deposits, and so on. These lead times are, of course, not sequential but they are highly interactive. Investment in some plants and facilities will be completed on time.

The point is that reliable and efficient production of electric power and nuclear fission requires the operation of a complex and entirely interactive set of processes and services. This system does not exist in the United States today. In the best of circumstances—that is, with the cooperation of all the affected parties and interests—it would, in our judgment, require a minimum of another ten years to establish such a system. The fact is, of course, that the affected parties and interests are not cooperating; indeed, they are openly antagonistic. It has become commonplace to see admissions in nuclear industry trade journals that the industry has problems. So did the captain and crew of the *Titanic*.

LWR Development: A Model for New Energy
Supply Technologies?

The state of the nuclear power business in the United States is troublesome enough in its own right. It is even more disturbing in light of the widely shared belief that the joint government-industry research and development program on LWRs is a model that can be imitated in launching new mobilization plans for other energy supply and/or conservation technologies. In retrospect, many of the present problems of nuclear power had their roots in errors made by industry and government during both the conception and execution of LWR development.

The USAEC reactor development program was a novelty in U.S. industrial experience. For the first time, the federal government assumed responsibility for planning and directing the development of a new civilian technology from its conception to its commercial introduction and acceptance. The significance of this precedent was noted several years ago: "It raises the possibility that future developments, such as achieving controlled thermonuclear power, shall be treated in the same way."[37] Several important characteristics of the AEC program have not, however, heretofore been widely noted.

In 1947, the AEC's General Advisory Committee (GAC) stated that "the fact of supreme importance" with respect to power reactor development was "the shortage of fissionable material." In the committee's view, "the only hope for power reactors lay in those which would breed more fissionable material than they consumed."[38] This report was the GAC's first on the government's nuclear R&D program. The emphasis on efficient fuel utilization, however, became a persistent and ultimately dominant element in the AEC's development efforts. Between the mid-1950s and the mid-1960s, the AEC provided varying degrees of financial assistance for R&D and in some cases for the construction of prototypes of different reactor concepts. The principal objective was to promote the development of a sequence of designs that would culminate in a breeder reactor, where the basic criterion of "progress" was enhanced efficiency in the consumption of fissionable uranium. Throughout the entire period, the whole idea of "reactor development" was seen in terms of a single dimension with inefficient light water technology of the Shippingport type at one end and the breeder at the other. The purpose of AEC financial assistance to industry was to promote movement away from primitive light water cooled and moderated technology toward the "true breeder."

In retrospect the reasons for this virtual obsession with a single parameter of a complex system are clear enough. As the early GAC report suggests, they follow directly from the government's overall nuclear priorities in the postwar years. By far the most important of these priorities was the production and conservation of an extremely scarce and precious substance: fissionable material. At the time of the first GAC report, plutonium production had dropped to a fraction of its wartime rate and further declines were in prospect. Sustained operation of the three plutonium-producing reactors at Hanford had caused expansion of the graphite moderating material. The Army had been forced to shut down the oldest reactor in 1946, and the two remaining plants were operating at greatly reduced power to conserve their lives.[39]

In the first two years of its existence, the AEC did not manage to put together much in the way of a coherent reactor development program in spite of periodic prodding by the GAC.[40] By the summer of 1949, there were four loosely related projects underway: the Navy's submarine propulsion program, a "materials testing reactor," an experimental breeder reactor at the Argonne National Laboratory, and an "intermediate breeder" at General Electric's Knolls Atomic Power Laboratory.

The USSR's first atomic bomb detonation in August 1949 caused the AEC's four reactor projects to be increasingly oriented toward military needs. By the spring of 1950, essentially all of the efforts of the AEC's national laboratories on reactor development were geared to military projects.[41] The submarine propulsion reactor had become the focus of Argonne's work, and Westinghouse was building new facilities to expand the program. Oak Ridge was told to give top priority to the materials testing reactor—a facility that would neither produce plutonium nor propel ships, both of which would have sped up the development of reactors of either type.

Only GE at Knolls remained heavily committed to a strictly civilian project with its intermediate breeder. Serious technical problems had, however, arisen with this project. In order to keep alive any hope for breeding fissionable material, GE scientists had been forced to move to higher neutron energies. But at such energies, the reactor would not be a good power producer. The goal of a single plant that would both generate electric power and replenish its own fuel supply looked increasingly difficult to achieve.[42]

The following two years saw a steady growth of activity on military reactors, first for submarine propulsion and then for aircraft. Highest priority, though, was given to increasing the supply of fissionable materials for weapons and military propulsion. In early 1952, the national laboratories' chief mandate was to develop improved designs for new plutonium production reactors; next was a plutonium production reactor capable of economic power generation.[43] Meanwhile, the laboratories and industrial contractors had been making progress in reactor construction: The experimental breeder at Argonne operated at design power for an extended period in 1952; the materials testing reactors went critical on March 31, 1952; by November the first submarine prototype was essentially complete and a second was well under way. At the same time there was not a single AEC-supported project whose purpose was to achieve a reactor directly advancing commercial nuclear power. In the face of growing technical problems and persistent pressure from the AEC, GE had canceled the intermediate breeder project in the spring of 1950 in favor of work on the submarine reactor. In April 1951, the AEC's Director of Reactor Development observed that "the cost of construction of a nuclear power plant is still essentially unknown. We have never designed, much less built and operated, a reactor intended to deliver significant amounts of power economically."[44]

In January 1951, the AEC had received proposals from several industrial groups expressing willingness to bring their technical resources into the atomic energy program. Very little came of this beyond some joint government-industry studies of the practicability of private industry's building additional reactors for the production of weapons material.

At the beginning of the Eisenhower Administration, no major project had been undertaken by either government or industry to develop a reactor technology with the primary objective of producing electrical energy. The first Eisenhower budget eliminated an AEC request for funds to instruct a pilot power plant. At the urging of the Joint Committee on Atomic Energy (JCAE), however, the House Appropriations Committee restored the money. Shortly thereafter, the AEC announced that Westinghouse and Duquesne Light Company would build and partially finance a power plant in Shippingport, Pennsylvania, based upon the "pressurized water reactor" technology (PWR) developed by the former under the naval nuclear propulsion program. Shippingport essentially would be a "scaled-up" version of the reactor designed for the canceled nuclear aircraft carrier. The JCAE later claimed full credit as originators of what they then saw, and what has since generally been conceded to have been the first major step toward commercial nuclear power in the United States.[45]

In 1954, the JCAE completely rewrote the original 1946 atomic energy legislation. The revised statute allowed private ownership of reactors under AEC licenses. Under the leadership of Lewis Strauss, the AEC chose to interpret the new legislation as a mandate to rely principally on private industry to develop a commercially viable power reactor technology. This interpretation was a source of chronic distress to the Democrats on the JCAE who used a variety of arguments to prod the AEC into a more aggressive program.

In January 1955, the AEC announced a new "Power Demonstration Reactor Program" (PDRP) and offered to review on a competitive basis proposals for government assistance for privately financed reactor projects. The AEC would, for acceptable proposals, waive all charges for the use of fissionable materials, would undertake certain mutually agreeable basic research in the national laboratories at government expense, and would enter into fixed-sum R&D contracts for procuring technical and economic data from the applicants. The fixed-sum commitment placed a ceiling on AEC participation, so that the economic risks of the project would be borne by the applicants. The JCAE Democrats did not regard the terms of this program as generous; nor was industry especially enthusiastic. The AEC received only four proposals. There was, moreover, a great hue and cry from public power advocates that municipally owned utilities and rural electric cooperatives were effectively barred from sharing in the bounties of nuclear power because they lacked access to the substantial risk capital required by the PRDP's terms. The AEC finally responded to JCAE prodding by issuing a "second round" PRDP invitation in September 1955. This time the AEC would consider requests for financing reactors in whole or in substantial part, but would retain title to the portion that was financed. Seven proposals were submitted under the second round.[1]

The JCAE was not mollified. By early 1956, the senior Democrats were enraged by what they considered to be the glacial pace of the AEC's reactor development program. The United Kingdom was widely cited as having already far outstripped the United States because of Strauss' misguided policies. In January 1956, a panel of businessmen and academics appointed a year earlier by Senator Anderson published a report which among other things recommended that the AEC expand its program to the extent of constructing a full-scale prototype plant for each major reactor type.[46] AEC Commissioner Murray, a Democrat holdover from the pre-Strauss commission, publically called for a $1 billion government financed reactor construction program.

Strauss remained adamant. In his view all that was needed was the removal of certain roadblocks in the path of private development of nuclear power, such as the possibility that a combination of utilities working cooperatively on a reactor project might be considered a violation of the Public Utility Holding Company Act. Another roadblock was the need to protect industry against the financial liability that a serious nuclear accident would entail. Legislation to eliminate these difficulties was soon passed. Meanwhile, the Democrat's dissatisfaction crystallized into legislation jointly sponsored by Senator Albert Gore and Representative Chet Holifield. The "Gore-Holifield" bill would have directed the AEC to construct six full-scale prototype nuclear plants wholly at governmental expense. After a long and acrimonious debate, the bill was reported out by the JCAE in a substantially weakened version. An even more watered-down version passed the Senate but was killed by the House.

Although the battle over reactor development policy saw further periodic skirmishes throughout President Eisenhower's second term, "Gore-Holifield" was the highwater mark of the Democrats' assault upon Strauss' policy. The Democrats on the JCAE never effectively challenged the central premise of the Strauss policy that the government should restrict its activities to exploring "advanced" reactor concepts (i.e., more efficient consumers of uranium) on a pilot scale—that is, to building small experimental plants. The AEC under Strauss never accepted the responsibility for building large reactors. In 1957, a "third round" of PRDP invitations was issued, but once again the terms precluded any direct government financial assistance toward the construction costs of a power plant.

The business community remained deeply divided on the issue of a large government-financed reactor construction program. Some private interests op-

---

[1]It is difficult to overemphasize the impact of the intense and highly ideological contemporary debate over public power production on the content and scope of reactor development in the United States. At first approximation it was the dominant structural influence. See Philip Mullenbach, *Civilian Nuclear Power: Economic Issues and Policy Formation*, (New York: The Twentieth Century Fund, 1963), Chapter 1 and passim.

posed such a program and viewed private investment in reactor projects as insurance against the entry of the federal government into their business. Many utility executives believed that if the government began to construct full-scale reactors, then the government would be in the power business, and investor-owned companies would be squeezed out by "massive atomic TVAs."

The AEC's conception of reactor development was shared by agencies in other countries with similar responsibilities. In France, for example, it was only the relatively limited amount of available money that restricted the same proliferation of pilot and prototype plants of different reactor concepts. The same was roughly true in Great Britain and, later, in Germany. In all of these countries, it was believed that the appropriate answer to the difficulties of early nuclear plants in competing economically with declining fossil fuel costs was the development of more efficient reactor concepts. It was the common belief in the United States and Europe in the 1960s, as well as the 1950s, that in order to improve the economic performance of nuclear power plants, it was sufficient to concentrate on improving the physical performance of the reactor cores. This peculiarly *scientific* definition of the problem caused a diversion of attention from a variety of circumstances that were at least as important in the short term and that would ultimately prove to be far more critical in achieving a power plant technology that really was commercially viable.

In the United States, the institutional arrangements through which the AEC reactor development program was managed reinforced the way the problem was defined. The principal frame of reference was competition among AEC laboratories and potential equipment manufacturers for the limited funds available to pursue alternative "promising" concepts through prototype construction. Each laboratory had a favored concept, such as molten salt at Oak Ridge, as did each potential competitor to Westinghouse. The object of the game was to persuade, *on the basis of scientific argument*, the AEC, together with an electric utility partner (in the case of the manufacturers), that one's own particular gimmick offered the best chance of economically competitive power. Each of these "sales pitches" was couched in terms of the particular concept's potential comparative advantages on a number of physical dimensions. It was everywhere assumed that the relationship between progress along these dimensions and improvement of the relative economic status of nuclear power was both simple and direct.

In retrospect this conception of the nature of the linkage between improving the physical performance of the reactor core and improving the commercial status of nuclear power was inadequate on two counts. First, the design of more advanced concepts led in many cases to unforeseen and highly difficult engineering problems. The British experience with the "advanced gas" concept was the most dramatic illustration. Second, while it may have seemed scientifically rational to explore alternative design concepts before choosing the "best" machine, this completely overlooked the realities of the market for the technology. Reactor manufacturers, especially in the United States, were not interested in waiting for the results of lengthy experimental programs and prototype construction efforts in order to choose the optimally efficient concept. Rather, the manufacturers were under strong commercial pressure to turn the know-how gained in operating AEC contracts into a profitable business.

In these circumstances, most of the AEC efforts to promote the development of alternative concepts was effectively a waste of money. Moreover, it is now clear that "development" entails a great deal more than proving the scientific or even the engineering viability of alternative design concepts through the construction of prototypes. Even the highly successful operation of a prototype plant is by no means a sufficient condition to establish the commercial viability of a reactor concept. One of the principal lessons of the past thirty years of nuclear development is that the major difficulties of putting a new technology on sound commercial footing remains to be faced *after* the successful operation of the first prototype. This lesson has never been clearly perceived by the government agencies that have supported reactor development and may partly explain the long succession of enthusiasm followed by disillusionment that has characterized the programs of these agencies.

In summary, then, in the United States the government's "in-house" reactor R&D program primarily reflected the interests of one of the AEC's principle constituencies: the scientists and engineers employed at the national laboratories. From their perspective, the development of an efficient core design was the most interesting and important problem. It was also the problem to which their own skills were pertinent. This definition of the problem fit nicely with the AEC's overriding concern with conserving fissionable uranium. Second, the Eisenhower Administration, partly for political reasons, chose to define the public sector's responsibility in reactor development in very limited terms. As a matter of public policy, the Strauss-headed AEC adopted and maintained a fundamentally passive role in relating to both buyers and sellers of nuclear power plants. The result was a program that left to the private sector essentially total responsibility for the fulfillment of a number of conditions that today can be seen to be necessary, if not sufficient, for the successful integration of nuclear power into an energy supply system.

Like any high technology product, the operation of a nuclear power plant requires the support of a variety of ancillary services and industrial processes. The best TV receiver is worthless without a source of electrical power, or the most advanced aircraft useless without landing facilities. The most efficient nuclear steam supply system is similarly dependent on such support services. The unfortunate consequence of the way reactor development was managed in the United States is that in many cases such services either do not yet exist at all—waste disposal—or have serious unresolved problems—spent fuel reprocessing. The mistake of the AEC's reactor development program was to assume that the uncoordinated actions of private companies would guarantee that all necessary support services would somehow become automatically available as soon as an effective reactor had been designed. In effect, random attention was given to different components of the nuclear power system, depending only on whether some company happened to perceive, either correctly or incorrectly, the possibility of profit. This led to a highly uneven development of the components of what is in fact an extremely interdependent system. It is important to emphasize that the problem was not merely a few errors of omission such as the well-recognized failure to develop an acceptable waste disposal technology. The problem was that no single institution was paying attention to, much less in a position to assume responsibility for, the need to coordinate the development of the entire system. There was, in short, no planning. One consequence is the near shambles of the LWR fuel cycle in the United States.

Conclusion

It is tempting, therefore, to simply accept the history of LWR commercialization as an object lesson on the need for strong central planning in the research development and demonstration phases of introducing new energy technology. To some, the matter is not quite so clear-cut. It has, for example, recently been argued that the dominant characteristic of the U.S. energy supply system remains the fact that it is a market system.[47] The government's major responsibility is to correct failures in the operation of the market mechanism. The government should restrict itself to identifying actions or inactions that cause nonoptimal allocation of resources from the point of view of society as a whole. In general, only three broad categories of market failure affecting the technological innovation process justify government intervention.

1. *Externalities:* situations where the relevant decision-making unit is unable fully to perceive or to capture all of the costs or benefits associated with its activities;
2. *Indivisibilities:* cases in which all the benefits and costs are fully perceived and appropriable by the relevant decision-making unit, but where the costs of carrying out specific research, development, or demonstration tasks would be significantly lowered if supported by government on a nationwide basis (the reason for government support is that the economics of scale are so large that the federal government may be the most efficient body to undertake the work);
3. *Public goods:* products from whose benefits it is impossible or impractical to exclude any citizen regardless of how much (or how little) he may desire them (e.g., lighthouses, an army).

According to this line of argument, it is only on grounds of safety and/or security that the government has any legitimate role in nuclear reactor development at all. If nuclear material did not represent a potential hazard to health and if it were not a potential weapon, there would be no need for any governmental reactor program. Hollomon specifically rejects several popular justifications for federal support of R&D: long development lead times (the appropriate government activity is to influence the private discount rate); balance-of-payments considerations (investments in energy R&D must be compared with all other possible investments that would increase exports or reduce imports); the need to conserve energy (higher prices reflect the changing value of energy relative to other goods and services); and the perception that certain research "ought" to be done.

The mere fact that not all perceived needs in the economy are being met is *not* a sign that irrational allocation decisions are being made, or that government intervention is called for. On the contrary, it is the function of prices to allocate limited resources among unlimited needs. . . . the market may be working perfectly, the only problem being that certain groups in society do not like the consequences and wish to alter them by political action.[48]

In my view, Hollomon's analysis is less helpful as prescription than as diagnosis. It is perfectly true that the problem of energy policy formulation in the United States is that different groups in the society do not like the consequences of certain policies and are committed to political action to prevent them. But the apparent disagreement between Hollomon's neoclassicism on one hand and Jackson-Rockefeller corporatism on the other should not be allowed to obscure a fundamental area of agreement. Both remain committed to an essentially liberal and unplanned economy. The calls for mobilization and the various implementation schemes to deal with the energy problem are a *tactical concession* to what are perceived to be the exigencies of a specific set of circumstances.

These circumstances and the remedy they require are believed to be sharply limited in scope as well as duration. No sane commander of the allied armies would have relied upon the uncoordinated decisions and actions of brigade, regimental, and battalion leaders to carry out the Normandy invasion. Likewise, cooperation, communication, and mutual assistance are necessary to an all-out mobilization to produce and conserve energy in the name of more jobs, continued economic growth, and of course, national security. If this means greater government intervention in the market, so be it. That is the unfortunate price we must pay, in the view of most American businessmen and many political leaders, because a capricious diety put all that oil under Kuwait instead of Kansas. Hollomon, too, readily concedes that if mobilization is necessary, then "planning follows as the night follows day." What he does not concede is that the specific characteristics of the energy problem in the United States require such drastic measures. The basic point for our purposes is that the debate at this level is merely a tactical disagreement about the appropriate response to a relatively limited set of circumstances about whose precise consequences and costs reasonable men disagree.

The ideological debate in the United States is between those who represent the framework of American authority and substance—New Dealers as well as neoclassicists—and the groups and individuals who support supervision of industry as an alternative to collaboration—that is, cooperative programs between government and business. The increasingly powerful movement to regulate industry in the United States reflects a different set of values. It is a call to restrain economic growth in the name of environmental protection and enhanced social equity. If that means changing lifestyles, reducing or eliminating private profits, and restricting the freedom of business activity, so be it. The salient point about this debate, as George Lodge vividly demonstrates, is that neither side has the authority to make its proposals, decisions, or actions legitimate in the eyes of the other.

Therefore, in the United States, there is simultaneously a tactical debate within the centers of power and influence and a deeply ideological debate between that establishment and a set of outside forces with a fundamentally different set of aims.[m] This situation is responsible for the contradictions of present energy policy in the United States: grandiose proposals and immobilism.

Notes

1. George C. Lodge, *The New American Ideology* (New York: Knopf, 1975).

2. Andrew Shonfield, *Modern Capitalism: The Changing Balance of Public and Private Power* (Oxford: Oxford University Press, 1965).

3. "Message to the Congress on a Program to Insure an Adequate Supply of Clean Energy in the Future," June 4, 1971, reprinted in U.S. Congress, Senate, Committee on Interior and Insular Affairs, *Executive Energy Messages* (Washington, D.C.: GPO, 1975), pp. 1-12.

4. Ibid., p. 3.

5. Ibid., p. 1.

6. Richard M. Nixon, "Address on the Energy Emergency," November 7, 1973, reprinted in *Executive Energy Messages*, pp. 81-87.

7. Ibid., pp. 85-86.

8. Richard M. Nixon, "Proposals to Deal with the Energy Crisis," January 23, 1974, reprinted in *Executive Energy Messages*, pp. 114-40.

mThe situation is further complicated by varying levels of concern about income distribution that cut across these two debates. Senator Jackson is profoundly concerned about the regressive effects of energy price increases. Meanwhile many of the "no-growth" interests are manifestly guilty of environmental elitism.

9. The President's 1975 State of the Union Message including Economy and Energy," reprinted in *Executive Energy Messages*, pp. 175-247.

10. Richard M. Nixon, "Veto of the Energy Emergency Act," March 6, 1974, reprinted in *Executive Energy Measures*, pp. 143-46.

11. Richard M. Nixon, "Address on the Energy Emergency," November 7, 1973, reprinted in *Executive Energy Measures*, pp. 81-86.

12. U.S. Congress, Senate, Hearings before the Committee on Interior and Insular Affairs, *National Energy Production Board*, 94th Congress, 1st Session, Washington, D.C., March, 1975.

13. Ibid., p. 1.

14. Ibid., p. 142.

15. Ibid., p. 49.

16. Shonfield, *Modern Capitalism*, p. 309.

17. *National Energy Production Board*, p. 53.

18. Ibid., p. 117.

19. Personal communication with a staff member of the Senate Interior Committee.

20. The White House, *Energy Independence Authority Fact Sheet*, Office of the Press Secretary, October 10, 1975.

21. Quoted by *The Wall Street Journal*, September 25, 1975 p. 20.

22. Ibid.

23. For example, Dennis Farney, "Mr. Ford's $100 Billion Elephant," *The Wall Street Journal*, September 30, 1975.

24. Lodge, *The New American Ideology*, pp. 268-69.

25. Shonfield, *Modern Capitalism*, p. 322.

26. 344 F. Supp. 253 (DDC, 1972).

27. Public Law 93-319.

28. U.S. Congress, Senate, Committee on Interior and Insular Affairs, *Factors Affecting Coal Substitution for Other Fossil Fuels in Electric Power Production and Industrial Uses*, a background paper prepared by the Congressional Research Service, (Washington, D.C.: GPO, 1975), pp. 27-28.

29. Based on interviews with numerous executive branch officials and congressional staff members.

30. The following is based largely on information contained in the U.S. Congress, Senate, Committee on Public Works, *Air Quality and Stationary Source Emission Controls*, a report by the Committee on Natural Resources of the National Academy of Sciences, the National Academy of Engineering, and the National Research Council, 94th Congress, 1st Session, Washington, D.C., March 1975.

31. U.S. Federal Energy Administration, *Project Independence Report* (Washington, D.C.: GPO, 1974), p. 113.

32. See, for example, "Power Plant Economics," H.F. Brush, Bechtel Power Corporation, testimony given before the Connecticut Public Utilities Control Authority, January 21, 1976.

33. U.S. Federal Energy Administration, *Project Independence Report*, p. 286.

34. Nuclear Regulatory Commission, Division of Reactor Licensing, *Analysis of the Potential for 200 Nuclear Power Plants To Be in Operation by 1985*, Washington, D.C., October 28, 1975.

35. I.C. Bupp and R. Trietel, "The Economics of Nuclear Power: De Omnibus Dibitudum," working paper, M.I.T. Center for Policy Alternatives, Cambridge, Mass., February 1976. The data set was assembled in the summer of 1974 and includes cost records of 35 complete or nearly complete nuclear plants and 46 coal plants. None of the coal plants included flue gas desulfurization equipment.

36. The following draws heavily upon The Atlantic Council of the U.S., *Nuclear Fuels Policy: Report of The Atlantic Council's Nuclear Fuels Policy Working Group*, Washington, D.C., 1976, Appendix B.

37. G. Eads and R. Nelson, "Governmental Support of Advanced Civilian Technology: Power Reactors and the Supersonic Transport," *Public Policy*, vol. XIX, no. 3 (Summer 1971), p. 421.

38. Richard G. Hewlett and Francis Duncan, *Atomic Shield: A History of The USAEC*, vol. 2, Wash 1215 (Washington, D.C.: GPO, 1969), p. 29.

39. Ibid., p. 40.

40. Ibid., p. 115.

41. Ibid., p. 417.

42. Ibid., pp. 421-22.

43. Ibid., pp. 514-15.

44. L.R. Hafstad in *Scientific American* (April 1951), quoted by Hewlett and Duncan, *Atomic Shield*.

45. Harold P. Green and Alan Rosenthal, *Government of the Atom* (New York: Atherton Press, 1963), pp. 253-54. The following account draws heavily upon the Rosenthal and Green analysis of the politics of reactor development in the United States during the 1950s.

46. U.S. Congress, Joint Committee on Atomic Energy, *Review of the International Atomic Policies and Programs of the United States*, 86th Congress, 2nd Session (Washington, D.C.: GPO, 1960), 6 vols.

47. J. Herbert Hollomon et al., *Energy Research and Development* (Cambridge, Mass.: Ballinger Publishing Company, 1975).

48. Ibid., pp. 21-22.

Comparing Energy Policies: Political Constraints and the Energy Syndrome

Leon N. Lindberg

Dimensions of Comparison

The purpose of these two concluding chapters is to tie together the seven case studies and to relate them to the analytical and policy concerns presented in Chapter 1. My treatment must then be selective and will leave aside many interesting dimensions of comparison. National energy policies share three common characteristics when examined over the thirty-year postwar period and in political economy terms:

1. The evolution in energy consumption and supply in the post World War II period was essentially identical in all seven nations. The dominant trends producing a steadily increasing demand for energy that had been established by the early 1970s have *not* substantially changed as a consequence of the price shocks and supply uncertainties introduced after 1973.

2. Although there are important differences in formal institutional structures and political processes, energy policy making is still dominated by three characteristics inherited from the 1950s and 1960s: Decision rules or criteria are almost exclusively supply oriented; supply strategies are committed to highly complex and capital intensive technologies based on nonrenewable resources; and a closed decision process is dominated by energy producers and distributors and is not readily accessible to other groups and other perspectives.

3. These striking similarities seem to reflect the influence of the same general factors: certain dynamics common to complex bureaucracies, the roles and value orientations of an industrial technocracy, and the political and ideological hegemony of dominant industrializing elites. These factors take different forms and interact in different ways in each nation, but they constitute roughly comparable political and organizational obstacles to effecting any substantial change in established consumption trends or in the substance of energy policy.

These three characteristics—continued increases in energy consumption, public policies that focus almost exclusively on the supply side, and institutional and structural obstacles to the adoption of alternative policies—make up a *syndrome*, that is, a group of symptoms that occur together and that describe a pathology or a system malfunction. The rest of this chapter will be devoted to a detailed analysis of this energy syndrome.

In the final chapter, I will turn to the question of how the syndrome might be "treated," that is, what policy implications flow from a comparison of these seven cases. Two broad conclusions will stand out: 1. Conservation, demand limitation, and greater emphasis on technologies making lesser demands on national control capacities may be the only ways to avoid polarization, political stalemate and increasingly dangerous policy drift in energy. 2. Even though no nation has so far succeeded in overcoming the various obstacles to adopting such policies, there are significant differences in the extent to which alternative policy criteria have penetrated the policy debate, mass publics have been mobilized and made aware of the larger stakes, and the decision-making process made more "permeable" to contending views. Such steps seem prerequisite to policy change, and an examination of the several partially deviant cases does point to a number of proposals and hypotheses for overcoming obstacles to policy change.

The Evolution of Energy Consumption and Supply

The broad similarity in the pattern of outcomes in the period 1945-1976 is most striking. These outcomes are not substantially different for Hungary or the United Kingdom, Canada or India, France, Sweden, or the United States. Whether capitalist or communist, centrally planned or market-oriented, indicative planning or authoritative planning economies, the similarities prevail and the differences are only marginal. The story of these thirty years can be summarized as follows:

1. An immediate postwar period of energy shortages and preoccupations with the security of supply was followed by an unprecedented period in which prices fell and supplies were plentiful. All seven nations experienced rapid increases in energy consumption that began in the 1950s and strongly intensified in the 1960s.

2. This growth was accompanied by a declining reliance on domestic coal and the rapidly increasing importance of petroleum and natural gas. To some extent, this dependence weakened government controls over energy supply and demand, since coal was generally nationalized and the oil industry was in private hands and organized internationally.

3. For most nations, there was a concomitant move from relative self-sufficiency in energy supply to reliance on imported energy. This shift was perhaps most striking in France, which produced 70 percent of its energy needs from domestic sources in 1950 and only 24 percent in 1972.

4. Nowhere were these developments anticipated or forecast accurately, even where extensive government planning was firmly institutionalized. But policymakers by and large were not overly concerned because uncertainties as to supply were simply displaced to the oil import sector. They assumed that cheap oil would be a permanent fixture of the economic scene. They did not question that the goal of energy policy was *to meet demand*. Indeed, national policymakers typically collaborated with energy corporations to stimulate demand.

Policy and planning in energy were then equated with developing the "necessary supply."

5. All these developments seem to have come about less as conscious policy than as an uncoordinated reaction to various changes taking place at the time: aspirations for rapid industrial development and a *style* of development geared to capital intensive GNP growth that maximized short-term quantitative output over considerations of long-term resource utilization; increases in living standards, the huge expansion in the use of the private automobile, and the seduction of the "American model"; pressures from businessmen and government planners alike for cheap energy to improve competitive positions in an increasingly internationalized global economy; changes in the structure of production toward energy-intensive industries like plastics and petrochemicals, and toward the mechanization of agriculture; and the policies and promotional activities of multinational oil companies or nationalized energy industries.

6. The costs and vulnerabilities of increased dependence on foreign supplies were not considered highly salient, even where they were carefully evaluated. Other factors, such as international competitiveness or rapid growth weighed heavily in the balance. The possibility of an oil boycott by OPEC was discounted by almost everyone; nor were serious questions raised about policies that left basic decisions about the price and supply of a vital national resource in the hands of a few powerful private firms. Even where a national oil company was created, as in France, it tended to take signals from the "majors" and to operate according to identical commercial criteria.

7. The trend toward increased intensiveness of energy use and increased consumption of petroleum was an important stimulant to economic growth, which involved important changes in the structure of the economy and in the consumption habits and expectations of publics and elites alike. Not the least important of these has been a marked tendency toward greater vertical and horizontal concentration in energy industries and a reinforcement of their channels of access to government policy making.

8. Although the efficiency of energy use for a given level of GNP varies substantially from one nation to another, the recent historic trend had generally been toward greater efficiency. But beginning in the mid-1960s, this relationship began to reverse itself in most of our countries (Hungary seems to be an exception). By the early 1970s, more energy was required each year to maintain any given level of GNP. One factor in this development was probably the marked trend toward increased reliance on electric power, on more centralized distribution grids, and on larger and larger production units.

9. With the exception of Sweden, conservation has generally been neglected save for symbolic and largely rhetorical appeals. European governments did raise taxes, principally on gasoline, but the United States has taken virtually no action whatsoever. The slight decline in energy consumption in 1974-75 was due mainly to the mild winter or to the economic recession, or to once-for-all

measures like switching from oil to coal in power stations and consumption rates rose again in 1976 (by 12 percent in the first half) along with economic recovery.[1] Government policy continues to stress the supply side. Projections of demand, and the increasing growth rate of demand, are still treated essentially as the *givens* of policy, not as objects of policy. Government measures to authorize increases in overall energy prices are designed and debated in the West and in the East in terms of providing incentives and capital for a massive effort to increase supply rather than as a spur to conservation. Little serious attention has been given to economic incentives or to research and development allocations directed at gross energy waste in industrial production, households, and transportation.

10. As far as alternatives to petroleum are concerned, nuclear energy and coal are stressed by most developed countries. They receive the lion's share of research and development funds, both governmental and private. In the United States, ERDA's 1976 and 1977 budgets allocate 77.6 percent and 78.2 percent respectively of available funds to various aspects of the nuclear program, with coal receiving a poor second at 7.2 percent and 7.7 percent. There has been, practically speaking, no serious effort in the areas of solar energy or other nondepletable or "income" sources except as long-range future possibilities (1.8 percent in both years in the ERDA budget). Energy-poor developing countries like India have much clearer incentives to develop such technologies in the short run (e.g., bio-gas), but have had no option except to replace now ruinously expensive oil imports by burning firewood and dung. This practice may contribute to meeting the immediate energy deficit but has such disastrous consequences for agricultural production as erosion, declining soil quality, and so forth. As Eckholm has pointed out:

The development and dissemination of renewable, decentralized, and low-cost energy sources for the half of mankind now burning wood, crop residues, or dung for fuel figures centrally in the amelioration of global environmental stress. Current energy research and investment patterns, in the poor as well as rich countries, betray a heavy preoccupation with new fuels for industry and the machines of the rich, while the pressing energy crisis of the masses in the poor countries is given short shrift.[2]

11. The full development of nuclear and coal resources and technology, as well as the discovery and exploitation of new petroleum deposits (and such sources as oil shale, tar sands, methane, and so forth), seems to require that petroleum prices remain at least as high as they are at present and that other energy prices increase substantially, regardless of the fate of OPEC. This situation is equally the case in the capitalist world and within COMECON. Indeed, because presently favored alternative sources of energy are very expensive and require massive investments and long lead times, it would be disastrous for at least the United States, the United Kingdom, and Canada if oil prices were to fall substantially. This conclusion stands in sharp contrast to the

rhetoric of U.S. policy and to its preoccupation with ways to undermine OPEC unity.

12. A trend toward higher energy prices may be absorbable for some time in the rich industrialized countries without a disruptive impact on the overall economy, but it is producing "chronic depression conditions for the share of humankind, perhaps a fourth, that might be termed economically and politically marginal."[3] Indeed, the predominant impact (however unintended) of post-1973 government policies in the capitalist and communist world alike has been to worsen the situation in the resource-poor developing countries. Further, little real progress has been made toward a system of international mechanisms, such as recycling "petrodollars," that might substantially improve their lot. By the end of 1976, the external debt of the developing countries had soared to $170 billion, and doubts were multiplying that such a debt could be managed. Even in the developed countries, the impact of the price shock began to seem more permanent than temporary as the 1976 recovery faltered, and some economists spoke of a permanent lowering of achievable growth rates.

13. Notwithstanding the rapidly escalating prices of coal and nuclear energy, and the massive resources being devoted to each, there is little prospect of either making much of an impact on the overall energy supply situation before the year 2000. Petroleum will continue to occupy the central position at least until then. Nuclear reactors involve problems of safety and waste storage, as well as political problems, and are experiencing rapidly escalating capital costs. The breeder reactor will not make a significant contribution before the twenty-first century, even if political controversies and cost considerations do not delay it further or eliminate it totally as a viable alternative. Coal has many shortcomings as a substitute for oil, and technologies for conversion of coal to liquid or gas are relatively underdeveloped and quite costly.[4] A radically increased consumption of coal will require massive infrastructure developments and capital infusions and will also raise serious questions about environmental and health effects that seem likely to slow down and ultimately limit its development.

14. There would seem, therefore, to be no chance whatsoever that the basic facts of petroleum interdependence and vulnerability will be substantially altered over the next fifteen to twenty years. Indeed, the trend in the United States was toward increased dependence on imports of petroleum even during the 1974-1976 recession, and by 1976 the United States was importing over 40 percent of its oil. Studies released in 1976 by OECD's International Energy Agency foresaw a rise in imports by industrialized countries of from 23 percent to 48 percent by 1985.[5] And it is not unlikely that Eastern Europe and even the USSR will also be forced to step up their petroleum imports from the Middle East.[6]

15. In spite of mounting political, technological, and environmental problems and controversies, nuclear energy—conventional reactors, then the breeder, and then the fusion reactor[7]—remains the leading candidate of most official

energy policy as a successor to oil and natural gas. The chapters on France and the United States show the power of the political and bureaucratic forces, in addition to the foreign policy ambitions, that impel countries in this direction. These have been able so far to effectively exclude alternative policy strategies directed toward conservation or nondepletable sources like solar energy.

16. Additional incentives for pushing nuclear development include the calculation that in a global nuclear economy the United States, USSR, West Germany, France, and other countries with a developed nuclear industry will be in a dominant pivotal position quite analogous to that enjoyed by OPEC. Asymmetries in technology will overshadow asymmetries in access to natural resources.[8] In the short run, there are obvious strategic and balance-of-payments advantages for oil-dependent countries with advanced nuclear technology to develop and expand as rapidly as possible the export market for nuclear reactors and nuclear fuels. It is ironic that the escalation of reactor and fuel costs, to which the domestic political controversies over nuclear power have contributed, create further incentives for emphasizing exports.

17. International oil companies continue to dominate the petroleum market and to extend their interests in coal and uranium.[9] The initiative for any greater supervision or control of their actions would have to come from the United States, but this type of policy would go against the American political and ideological grain, as Bupp's chapter makes clear.

18. Energy autonomy dominates the rhetoric of energy policy, and its principal short-term manifestation has been support for U.S. initiatives in the OECD-based International Energy Agency and in broader international gatherings. The main thrust of U.S. policy has been to emphasize the common interests of the advanced capitalist states (United States, Western Europe, and Japan) as distinct from and perhaps antagonistic to those of the socialist bloc, the oil-producing countries, and the resource-poor developing world. U.S. policymakers have shown little enthusiasm for the negotiation of substantively new interdependence rules and regimes beyond those that will more or less maintain existing hegemonic relationships. It does not seem too strong to say that the United States has sought to use energy policy as part of its general foreign policy effort at a reassertion of leadership and policy dominance vis-à-vis Western Europe and Japan.[10] U.S. policy toward the oil-producing countries has relied heavily on the twin strategies of propping up those leaders with a vested interest in sharing in and stabilizing the political economies of the rich countries and of relying on massive arms shipments to offset balance-of-payments deficits. Other than that, the U.S. preference has been for a confrontational posture toward the more radical members of OPEC and, at best, a muted enthusiasm for discussions of a new world economic order.

19. Paradoxically, perhaps the most active process of international cooperation and medium- to long-term accommodation of interests in the energy field are occurring within the nascent Nuclear Suppliers' Group, which began secret

331

meetings in the summer of 1975.[11] The participating countries—United States, USSR, West Germany, France, Canada, United Kingdom, Japan, Sweden, Belgium, the Netherlands, Italy, E. Germany, and Poland—find themselves competing for what is expected to be a rapidly expanding export market for nuclear reactors and nuclear fuels.[a] On the other hand, they appear to share an interest in limiting the perils of nuclear proliferation. But it could well be that the upshot of their activities will be to water down existing International Atomic Energy Agency regulations and safeguards and totally overwhelm its already weak regulatory capacities. It is notable that the IAEA has been shifting, in the words of *The Economist*, from a regulatory agency to "an open partisan of the greater use of nuclear power in poor countries"; fully two-thirds of the IAEA budget now goes to information, technological advice, and energy audits heavily weighted towards the international promotion of nuclear energy.[12]

20. The chief conclusion to be drawn about the international dimension of national energy policies is that they are generally nationalist and neomercantilist in tone and content. A *sauve qui peut* mentality reigns and has already increased the disintegrative tempo within the European Community[13] and strained COMECON relations as well. Nor do the prospects for cooperation among consuming countries in the IEA seem bright. U.S. and West European policy-makers have very different energy options and perceptions of their long-term interests.[14] They have clashed repeatedly on what position to take toward both the oil-producing states and the oil-poor developing countries. Some net consuming countries may conclude bilateral agreements with producer countries in which guaranteed supplies of oil are exchanged for stable long-range investment opportunities, industrial goods, market access, and technical aid. But these will likely be at the expense of a broader approach that might take the interests and needs of the oil-poor developing countries into account.

Central Actors, Dominant Policy Criteria, and Supply Strategies

The foregoing descriptive summary clearly supports the overall conclusion that national policies toward energy are fixed in much the same trajectory as before the 1973-74 crisis. That stimulus has not yet brought about any substantial change in policy. Oil-importing countries are as exposed to future supply and price uncertainties in 1977 as they were in 1973. Policy change has occurred largely at a symbolic level—a "politics of reassurance"—in the form of "Projects

---

[a]Recent studies by the International Atomic Energy Agency and a U.S. Senate Subcommittee predict the installation of over 350 nuclear generating plants in the Third World by 1990. Furthermore, France and Germany have announced plans to export nuclear reprocessing plants—facilities that produce suitable materials for atomic bombs as well as reactor fuel. *The New York Times*, November 2, 1975; *The Washington Post*, January 17, 1976; and *Newsweek*, March 8, 1976.

Independence." In fact, the changed circumstances of energy price and supply seem to have stimulated essentially perverse responses, especially when policies are evaluated on the basis of the broad political economy criteria we proposed in Chapter 1. Thus, our apprehension presented there in the form of a "worst-case" scenario: We confront a period of sharpening domestic economic and political instability and intensified insecurity and conflict in international relations.

Why has there been so little policy adaptation in the face of major changes in the situation? Two kinds of answers are most typically offered by students of public policy. Those who operate out of a pluralist mode of analysis tend to see politics as the consequence of struggle and bargaining among representatives of competing interests within and outside government. Because there are many actors and interests, the policy outcome is "rarely intended and rarely preferred by any one of the actors individually."[15] None of the actors can or really try to determine the means and ends appropriate for society as a whole. Policy changes only incrementally. Policy outcomes are increasingly unsatisfactory because more and more groups are making demands on government and expecting ever-higher levels of performance. Excessive expectations produce "overloaded governments." Demands exceed available resources, and there are too many values to balance, and too much uncertainty and conflict, to sustain the "shared appreciations" upon which policy must rest. Policy failures result not from the inability to acquire or process information "but from our difficulty in finding those shared appreciations which our common life requires."[16]

Other analysts emphasize the extent to which the agenda of politics—the determination of what will become an issue—is controlled by the elites of complex bureaucratic organizations, each of which is based upon a separate institutional sector.[17] By virtue of their expertise, hierarchical control, and ability to mobilize resources, interorganizational coalitions of such elites generally dominate policy outcomes and are only occasionally constrained by their political base or by the processes of pluralistic politics. Their goals are to increase their individual and collective resources, to eliminate conflict and competition by controlling the agenda and excluding other actors, and thus to maintain their control over what the state does and does not do. There is no monolithic structure of such elites dominating all areas of policy at all times. Rather, there are many, partially overlapping and often competing, vertical policy networks seeking to manage the flow of public policy in their particular sphere of interest, be it transportation, public health, or energy. Typically, these networks actively resist horizontal coordination, control, or intersectoral planning, and this accounts for the rigidity of policy even as the boundaries of policy problems expand.

Which interpretation seems to be borne out by the foregoing case studies? Many of the chapters, notably on Canada, the United States, Britain, and Sweden, are rich in their depiction of the pluralist arena of energy policy: the multiple, contending actors, their strategies of mobilization and bargaining, the specific issues over which they struggle, the discrete decisions that are made or not made. These processes constitute the dramatic micro-detail of energy politics, and here national differences are perhaps more important than similarities. But one critical advantage of looking at a broad policy area in many different countries over an extended period of time is that it forces the analyst to lift his eyes from the infinitely varied micro-details to the broad pattern of institutional interactions and policy outcomes. At this level, the chapters seem to me to converge on two specific conclusions: First, most energy policy systems have been and continue to be dominated by a relatively small, stable, and closed circle of organizational elites, and second, energy policy making is "incoherent" and "sectoral," uncoordinated and reactive, fragmented and "immobilist." At first glance these characterizations may seem contradictory; if policy making is fragmented and immobilist, how can it also be effectively dominated by a relatively small group? An elite analysis would argue, however, that they are simply opposite sides of the same coin.

Elite Control in Energy Policy

To speak of "energy policy" in the 1945-1975 period is almost a misnomer. Energy considerations have been subordinated to other policy goals—primarily to maintaining economic output and national power. By and large, energy policy has only very recently emerged as a distinct area of concern in its own right. What has passed for energy policy is a collection of decisions and nondecisions that have had their genesis in efforts of public officials and private actors to cope with other policy concerns that inevitably have energy implications. Decisions have been taken in other spheres on the basis of criteria internal to them, and the energy consequences toted up afterward. Neither capitalist nor communist nations have developed criteria for energy policy per se, apart from the supply imperatives of the energy production industries or the vulnerability concerns of national security.

Government policies have as a consequence been short run and reactive: Expand supplies to meet demand, socialize risks that the private sector is unwilling or unable to assume, nationalize or regulate to facilitate the efficient production and transmission of energy, externalize adjustment problems to other nations or to the oil import sector where possible. Energy producers—whether private corporations, multinational oil companies, nationalized coal industries, privately owned public utilities, or central electricity boards—have developed natural symbiotic relationships with government officials, regulatory boards, and other parts of the executive and legislative branches. They have enjoyed privileged access to policy making, directly by means of elaborate structures of cooptation and consultation and indirectly by virtue of the fact that policymakers have had a general propensity to identify the efforts of producers to increase supply with the national interest itself.

In capitalist and communist nations alike the general rule has been a "symmetry of objectives" between fuel industries and governments. Capitalist governments are described by several of our authors as having been disinclined to intervene in the "laws of the market," which is obviously so in the case of petroleum, but also even with regard to the criteria of performance set for nationalized coal industries, and so forth. The optimization models used by Hungarian planners also assumed that energy demands had to be met. The development targets and system of information in socialist central planning gave rise to patterns of influence favoring the assumptions and priorities of the energy production sector, much as did the play of market forces on the efforts of "indicative" planners in the West.

A principal legacy of the period of rapid growth and low or falling energy prices was this close symbiosis between energy industries and government agencies. These early policies have had a lasting impact on the structure of government and on the pattern of government-industry relations such that active response to the rising prices and potential shortages has proven very difficult. The central actors in energy-related decision processes have by and large remained the same, as have decision criteria and preferences as to supply strategies. Coal ministries were superceded by fuel or power ministries, and these have given way to energy agencies, administrations or ministries, but these latter still group much the same cohorts of elites and technical experts and continue to reflect the structure of the energy industries and their relative bargaining power. Energy decision making still tends to be restricted to "a very limited set of actors dominated by a small technocracy." The technical content of the area has limited access to it and has determined the professional origins of the staff and their patterns of recruitment, as well as their relationships with industrial and professional constituencies. Policymakers have been petroleum, or coal, or oil, or nuclear men. And those within the government tend to share basic orientations with colleagues in industry and the universities. All have a strong supply orientation, a common faith in technology, and "an engineering mentality."

As the boundaries of energy policy have expanded, new groups and interests have been mobilized and have claimed representation in the decision process. When these interests have become politically visible, specialized agencies have been established to represent them, or direct consultative arrangements have been created where the interest claiming representation is sufficiently narrowly defined and well organized. But this process leaves the relationships of "traditional" energy agencies to their clienteles more or less undisturbed. Networks linking energy supply agencies and producers and distributors of energy are everywhere much more highly organized than are proponents of new or alternative technologies, such as solar, or interest groups, such as consumers, workers, or local communities. Agencies assigned tasks of energy conservation are particularly isolated and politically vulnerable; there are no organized interests with a powerful stake in limiting energy consumption, and thus the task is not legitimated in the "preservation values" of the policymaker.

A common conclusion in the foregoing chapters is that energy policy systems are very resistant to change in spite of abundant information that suggests existing policies are inadequate or counterproductive. They uniformly resist forces for the consideration of alternative technologies or other economic development options. The "supply orientation" combined with a pervasive faith in technology produce organizational routines that the British chapter characterized as a "selective misperception of uncertainty." Established relationships with "producer groups" are also an important device for handling uncertainty and are themselves powerful forces for inertia. The tradition of closed incremental and technocratic decision making obscures broad policy. The use of mathematical models emphasizes the role of the established expert and disqualifies the outsider. The preferred practice of regulatory agencies is, case by case, rooted in precedent and favors the proven over the novel.

Fragmented and Incoherent Policy Making

The case studies emphasize the great difficulty that governments have experienced in coordinating the contradictory roles thrust upon them in the course of the evolution of the energy problem. To the historically primary function as producer and promoter of energy production have been added the roles of regulator, consumer, and agent for less powerful interests, regimes, or provinces. But chapter after chapter has emphasized that new competing values have *not* been balanced or integrated, that alternative outcomes seem not to have been systematically evaluated to take account of uncertainty, and that new information relevant to the underlying definition of the problem has not been integrated adequately into explicit causal inferences that might become the basis of policy change. Rather, complex decisions are fragmented into simpler components and treated separately, outcomes are loosely integrated, payoffs are specific and short run, and outcomes oscillate over time as policymakers respond to one or another aspect of the problem. Our authors would implicitly concur with Steinbrunner that

[I]f there are substantial interactions between the separate components of a problem, one would expect this to go unresolved. One would expect further that the system would be prone to gradually evolving crisis in the problem areas.[18]

Bupp's characterization of the United States is perhaps the most stark. He describes federal energy policy as a picture of "immobilism"—a combination of grandiose proposals backed by establishment rhetoric of mobilization metaphors recalling the Manhattan and Apollo projects—persistently cancelled out by "antiplanning" in the form of supervisory or regulatory policies. But all our authors point to evidence of inertia, conflict, and confusion in national policy, to difficulties the governments have encountered faced with the necessity of expanding the definition of energy policy to "adjacent sectors," and to the absence of overall coherence in energy and economic development policies. Governments are described as overwhelmed by the rapidity with which decisions have had to be taken and by the magnitude of their implications for society.

Those who propose to reform energy policies by resort to nationalization of the oil companies or the energy sector generally, or by introducing more "planning," will have found little reassurance in these case studies. Nationalized energy corporations have not behaved substantially differently from privately controlled ones, at least in the past. The existence of an elaborate state planning apparatus in France and a long tradition of state tutelage, coordination, and resource allocation did not save the French from following essentially the same policy trajectory as did the United States, where public planning is anathema and where the dominance of private power in the evolution of energy policy is most obvious. Indeed, the most elaborately state-planned systems—France and Hungary—are in many ways the most firmly launched on the policy trajectory we have described. Surely there has been less public controversy there (e.g., over nuclear energy) than elsewhere, and neither faces the deep policy reevaluation that an extended period of political debate and policy stalemate may bring about in such countries as the United States, Canada, and Sweden.

The above remarks should not be taken as a brief for capitalism, or the "liberal state," or the self-equilibrating virtues of the market. Indeed, the chapters on Sweden and the United States seem to show persuasively that reliance on the price mechanism cannot manage the problems raised by energy policy (particularly on the demand side). What I do mean to suggest is that since almost all of the politico-economic systems we have examined have managed the energy problem badly, we must go beyond superficial system-level attributes in our effort to understand what determines policy content and how to change it.

The fragmentation and incoherence of energy policy became apparent with the transition from an era of cheap and plentiful energy to one in which considerations of cost and the prospect of resource depletion must be seriously taken into account. This shift has put considerable strain on the closed energy system described above. The type of strain, and its extent, varies from nation to nation, but once again the pattern is similar. First, the expansion of energy policy boundaries has brought into the system (if only peripherally) new organizational actors (new governmental agencies and new elites) with somewhat different perceptions of the problem and responsibilities. More and more sectors of industry and more and more public agencies are involved and the problems of interorganizational management referred to, notably in the Swedish chapter, become more pressing. And since energy involves complex international interdependencies, the policymakers of many other nations become de facto participants in any nation's energy policy system. Second, the environmental, employment, health, and safety consequences of one or another proposed energy technologies and the foreign and security policy implication of import dependency have in the liberal democracies mobilized a variety of "outside" groups and previously inattentive publics. For the first time, perhaps, the circle of energy policy making has been pushed outward and in varying degrees has become subject to the open political conflict and adversary politics stressed by pluralist theories of policy. Ad hoc advocacy groups multiply; royal commissions and legislative commissions are established; antinuclear initiatives are placed on the ballot; court cases are filed; energy policy issues become subsumed to political party rhetoric or to deep-seated ideological divisions in society. Bupp's chapter on the United States spells out how this political polarization has produced stalemate or "immobilism" in policy. Sweden may also be a case in point in view of the apparently important role of the nuclear issue in precipitating the defeat of Prime Minister Palme and the Social Democrats in the September 1976 elections.[19]

The potentiality for policy stalemate and immobilism as the number of actors and concerned publics multiplies, and as alternative policy criteria are advanced with more or less political force behind them, should not be underestimated. On the other hand, we should not lose sight of three related points. First, the multiplication of actors and effervescence at the level of pluralist conflict and debate may obscure from view the domination of policy by the same "elite cartels" and policy criteria simply because only marginal, incremental changes can be made from the established trajectory. Second, fragmented decision networks can also serve to insulate decisionmakers from the electorate and from pluralist politics, by virtue of the information and organizational costs imposed on contenders by the existence of many dispersed decision sites.[20] And third, in the absence of action by governmental authorities, energy outcomes may be controlled by the private sector organized along national or international lines, by virtue of the influence they have in so many countries over the determination of both energy demand and energy supply. It is considerations like these that suggest that elite control and public policy fragmentation and incoherence may be opposite sides of the same coin.

A contending view would hold that what we have termed fragmentation, conflict, and incoherence in policy should be interpreted as the beginning of an active "search phase" in policy development. The inner circle of actors is being challenged by outsiders, established criteria are being widely criticized, and a new policy consensus may be emerging. All of this takes time, and given the complexities and uncertainties of energy policy, it is much too early to reach any firm conclusions as to the responsiveness or nonresponsiveness of policy. New vested interests may well develop around newly created institutions and alternative technologies, thus gradually attenuating the pattern of elite control. Even if the elite structure does not change, the perceptions of their long-term interests may change or at least become more ambivalent. This is likely to be the case increasingly as the logic of international interdependence imposes itself, and will likely force national elites into more cooperative behaviors.

It is not possible to reject flatly this interpretation, nor would we want to do so. Indeed, the record does suggest some support for such a position: The Swedes have opened a full-scale debate over energy options; solar energy proponents seem to be making some headway in the United States and France; and nuclear power has become increasingly controversial in many nations, most recently in the United Kingdom. Orders for new fission reactors fell off drastically in 1976 in the United States as the economic viability of nuclear energy was increasingly questioned. The French and West German governments have begun to modify their positions on the export of nuclear reactors, reflecting a growing concern for proliferation and a responsiveness to United States diplomatic initiatives.

I fear, however, that these are unlikely to amount to more than incremental modifications of present policies. I reach this conclusion because the energy consumption patterns and governmental policies that have supported them seem to me to conform closely to the long-term interest perceptions and survival imperatives of some of the most decisive social groupings in advanced industrial societies. And these are not readily subject to change because they are embedded in deeply seated organizational, cultural, and political/ideological factors that interact with and reinforce the pluralist and elitist constraints on policy adaptation discussed above.

In the absence of a sharper break with the past, the imperatives of a "hard energy path" are likely to become more and more dominant, mandating rapid increases in supplies of energy that will be available only through the fission program and crash development of coal, and requiring strenuous efforts to overcome domestic opposition and to guarantee the security of access to overseas supplies. Such a policy path will increasingly reinforce the very characteristics our authors have singled out for criticism: the closed, overly-centralized, technocratic, and nationalistic nature of energy policy systems.

Obstacles to Policy Change

In spite of a general suspicion of so-called convergence theories, I find it impossible to avoid the conclusion that the energy policy experience we have reviewed points to the existence of three common structural or systemic characteristics that sharply constrain efforts to change present policy and that may in some sense inhere in the "logic" of industrialism and modernism, as these are presently understood and practiced in East and West, North and South. The complex array of forces associated with industrialization and technological change have produced, or are producing, mass societies in which men and women's roles are defined by association with economic organization or activity; consumption values are shaped by a largely manipulated culture; the political environment is dominated by the centralization of political and economic activity and by a symbiotic relationship between government and industry; and elites and publics have a common orientation toward resource intensive economic expansion in which the multiplication of the application of energy is taken to be synonymous with modernity.[21]

The political structure of growth- and consumption-oriented industrializing societies is dominated by three closely interrelated social institutions (or formations or classes) with characteristic organizational natures, survival needs, and motivating ethos.

1. All such systems develop complex bureaucracies as public authorities intervene on an ever-widening scale in economic and social activities. Such bureaucracies seem prone to certain behavioral patterns in decision making that theorists have alternatively dubbed "dynamically conservative," "cybernetic," or "sectoral." Such patterns respond to their own organizational and political imperatives, but constrain the search for alternative policies toward energy and development.

2. Closely linked to or interpenetrating with these bureaucratic organizations is an "industrial technocracy," which I would identify as a cadre of professionals, management and efficiency experts, natural scientists, and engineers and economists, in government, corporations, universities, factories, and so forth. Their skills are vital to the progress of industrialization, to the power of organizational elites, and to the "reproduction" of the basic structures of control in industrial society. They are also the preeminent carriers of a cultural orientation that embodies a manipulative and anthropocentric attitude toward man and nature (and natural resources), the elevation of efficiency and productivity as prime values, and an uncritical faith in the technological fix as the solvent of all problems. Their influence in the development of the current trajectory of energy policies has been amply documented in this volume.

3. Overarching these levels of the political system or types of politics (i.e., government bureaucracy, industrial technocracy, as well as myriad formal institutions and processes, competing groups, and elites in other sectors (industry, agriculture, labor, military)) is a level of control that Marxian analysis names "class." Here is determined the "framework of economic appropriation" and "cultural hegemony" that defines the basic structure of society, the disproportionate allocation of the social product (e.g., as between consumption and investment), objective class relations, the "dominant social logic," and the rules defining the permissible range of pluralistic or elite competition.[22] This is, naturally enough, an elusive level of analysis, if only because the exercise of power in such contexts seldom involves overt political participation. Nor are the dynamic interrelationships over time and across policy arenas between this level and elite and pluralist spheres of influence or control clearly demarcated or constant. Nevertheless, difficult as it may be to pin down, I think the Marxian insight is real. But there is no reason to limit its application to capitalist society. The energy policy record we have reviewed does suggest the existence of

modernizing or industrializing "classes" or "social formations" whose ethos, power, and political-cultural hegemony may be at stake in the debates over energy policy.

In what follows, I will try to suggest why and in what ways these purported common structural or systemic characteristics of industrial society seem to me to obstruct an alternative energy policy. No conspiracy theory is intended. The system, as I see it, can be very loosely articulated (policy really *is* incoherent, inconsistent, fragmented, and so forth), though this obviously varies substantially from one nation to another. Contradictory forces are clearly at play. But the short- and medium-term resolution of these contradictions may require increasing both energy consumption and production as rapidly as possible, whatever the consequences.

Sectoral Outcomes and the Dynamic Conservatism of Bureaucracy

A growing body of literature suggests that there are strong conservative forces operating in the ways individuals in complex bureaucracies deal with the challenges presented by rapidly changing, complex, and interactive problems. These forces tend to reinforce a disaggregated, incremental, and sectoral approach to policy that implicitly advantages established groups and assumptions about policy and militates against "societally optimal" decisions or "higher level" value integration. John Steinbrunner has summarized this literature in his *A Cybernetic Theory of Decision*. The following propositions based on his treatment seem particularly suggestive.[23]

1. *The decisionmaker confronted with policy interdependence and sharp value tradeoffs typically seeks to deny the tradeoffs unless a highly structured external situation compels him to recognize them.* The decisionmaker is guided by "minimally articulated, preservative values" that do not "yield a coherent preference ordering for alternative states of the world under tradeoff conditions" (p. 86). His values are based on holding a small number of critical variables (rooted in past experience) within tolerable limits, and in order to accomplish this, he examines alternatives sequentially. His essential purpose is personal and organizational survival and not the achievement of some optimal outcome. The separate values of a complex problem will normally not be related to each other but rather be *decomposed* and assigned separately to different organizational subunits, each of which is conceptualized in terms of one problem with a single value (p. 108).

One of the most general conclusions reached by our authors about national energy policies is that they tend to be developed sectorally and therefore are "uncoordinated and reactive," "patchworks of partial solutions" developed in isolation from each other. As the problem has expanded to encompass new values, interdependencies, and tradeoffs, the complexity of public administration has expanded too, but in a way that has preserved the earlier agency lines of functional jurisdiction more or less intact. Agencies originated according to the source and form of the energy supply. Successive reorganizations generally maintain these industry demarcations intact as they do the relative bargaining power of different energy industries in the public administration.

This conclusion provides one further explanation for the persistence of a sectoral pattern of decision making that avoids confronting tradeoffs and fails to develop a common "value metric" by means of which policy options can be compared and evaluated. Confronting value tradeoffs is painful and is bound to affront some important interests within the administration or outside. Administrators normally have no notion of a higher utility measure that subsumes all dimensions of value and provides the basis for relative assessments of concrete choices, nor have they been able to call upon technological expertise regarding the interrelationships and interdependencies among policy sectors. The "critical variables" that govern the evaluation of options are still those that assure supply and maximize growth.

2. *The decisionmaker will seek to control uncertainty and "preserve internal simplicity" by screening out information that his organization's established repertory or response pattern is not programmed to accept.* Selective feedback and the "recipe" or standard operating procedures will govern the processing of information. "Favorable outcomes will be inferred for preferred alternatives and . . . unfavorable outcomes will be projected for alternatives the decision maker intends to reject" (p. 123). Serious calculations of alternatives are thus avoided. Wishful thinking and other "mechanisms for the subjective resolution of uncertainty will prevail" (pp. 112-22). Established feedback channels will limit the scope of new information to that derivable from predetermined definitions of system performance. If policies seem unable to meet these criteria, the search for alternatives will be highly constrained and change will be slow and incremental. Complex organizations have a limited set of responses, and they proceed with these until forced out of them by performance failures. Under conditions of rapid change this failure to evolve higher and more general conceptions of decision objectives classically results in "low-level suboptimizations." This outcome is further encouraged by another standard mechanism for handling complexity, namely, the creation of more complex organizations by fragmenting problems into a larger number of specific problems and multiplying the number of decisionmakers.

3. *In situations of sharp conflict among multiple actors and organizational subunits, the most likely outcomes are the dominance of private or sectoral goals and/or an oscillation over time between competing policy goals* (p. 130). We should not expect a collective decision process in which multiple actors consensually work toward an explicit shared analysis; nor will political leadership provide value integration. It is more typical of high-level leaders or managers to focus *sequentially* on the decision issues raised by individual actors or by

separate organizational subunits. They will not generally integrate across values or contenders in their deliberations. The coordination that does take place is guided by selective feedback and organizational routines described earlier. There is a tendency in such a system for private or sectoral values to prevail over or to constrain general or public values. Private or sectoral payoffs are simpler, narrower in scope, and more immediate. Higher level payoffs to "society" involve complicated social effects hard to predict, explain, or even observe" (p. 146). Such factors clearly weigh in favor of a policy geared to assuring national energy supply and against conservation, demand limitation, or international cooperation.

If conflict among the contending actors and value positions is especially intense, the most likely response will be "... at different times to adopt *different* belief patterns for the same decision problem. Since his own experience does not commit him to a particular belief pattern, [the high-level policymaker] will adopt several competing patterns, not at once, but in sequence" (p. 129). The sectoral decomposition of complex problems and the selective processing of information that characterizes lower and middle levels of the organizational hierarchy will thus normally not be corrected at the higher levels. This will have uniquely severe consequences in a field like energy where capital requirements for supply alternatives are so high as to mandate clear choices among competing technologies and where lead times are such as to require a sustained commitment to one or another option. The net effect in several of our countries (most notably the United States) seems to have been to delay full-scale development of any coherent energy policy. The paradoxical result is that demand continues to go up, and imports must be relied upon to fill the widening gap between demand and domestic energy supplies.

4. *Cybernetic decision processes and their characteristic policy outcomes will be especially prevalent, and resistant to change, in an organizational setting in which well-established subunits have been assigned highly technical tasks and are staffed by individuals with strong, well-anchored beliefs rooted in extensive professional training.* A central analytical issue with regard to cybernetic processes is how the basic structure for dealing with complexity and uncertainty was established and how it is sustained. What is the origin of organizational routines and recipes, the response repertory of decisionmakers, or the "acceptable level objectives," by which organizations measure performance and which determine the "selective monitoring of feedback channels"? Steinbrunner suggests the answer lies in "stable features of the mind" encountering "stable features of organizational decision processes," both of which act across the idiosyncracies of men and cultures (p. 124). Three such features can be distinguished. They operate to constrain either structural or policy change "short of substantial changes in personnel" (p. 137). Each seems to play an important role in energy policy making.

First, organizations that have been in existence over a relatively long period of time and that have been conceded competence over a highly specialized range of tasks are particularly prone to develop firm organizational routines that specify these tasks and the expertise necessary for them and that insulate the organization and the policymaker from outside challenge. Second, such organizations are most likely to have institutionalized close and lasting relationships or alliances with outside groups for the exchange of information and mutual support. Such clientele relationships serve to further insulate and protect the task definition and to structure the kind of information or expertise deemed relevant to its performance. Third, the decisionmaker who has experienced "highly structured professional training (such as engineering or theoretical economics)" (p. 134) may be typically "committed to one alternative which he invests with substantial significance in terms of very general values" (p. 131). Steinbrunner refers to this type of individual as a "theoretical thinker."

With his beliefs established in a long-range framework and well anchored, his inference management mechanisms are able to handle the pressure of inconsistency in any short-term situation. Inferences of transformation and impossibility, the selective use of information, and other inconsistency management mechanisms are brought to bear for this purpose. Since the theoretical thought process is strongly deductive and thus relatively less dependent upon incoming information in order to *establish* coherent beliefs, incoming information can be molded and even ignored or denied with greater ease than is the case with other thought patterns. The theoretical thinker thus can act quickly and with great confidence in those fluid, chaotic situations of short duration which cause a great deal of distress to others operating in different modes of thought.[24]

The Industrial Technocracy and Paradigms of Energy Policy

The importance of "theoretical thinking" and the cognitive orientations of those involved at critical junctures of the policy process brings us to the role of the industrial technocracy and to what Lönnroth calls "paradigms of energy policy." Without getting into all the issues raised by the relationship between politics and technology, three aspects of the role and values of expert advisors do stand out in the policy record we have reviewed: first, the specific makeup of the reigning community of scientific experts; second, the substantive impact these people seem to have had on energy policy; and third, the general view of politics and conflict that seems to be implied by policy systems in which technical and scientific expertise plays increasingly important roles.

1. The foregoing chapters have highlighted the importance of certain kinds of technical training (engineering, coal and petroleum geology, nuclear physics, systems analysis, cost-benefit analysis) for people recruited to play energy policy roles in public bureaucracies. They have also pointed to the importance of relatively closed communities of expertise that tie such policymakers and

advisors to similarly trained people in industry and the universities. By virtue of their professional socialization and common experiences in the postwar evolution of energy policies that emerged from a symbiotic government-industry system, a common perception of the problem and of how it was to be resolved quite naturally emerged. Political decisionmakers—cabinet members, undersecretaries, or legislators—have not generally been in the position to (or inclined to) challenge these basic presumptions. The range of energy policy options has thus been rather narrowly constrained over most of this period. This constraining or structuring role of experts seems particularly powerful where government is called on to undertake new "entrepreneurial" programs that are initially seen as largely technological, that provide growing benefits to outside groups who then become advocates of the program, and that do not challenge any strongly established interests.[25] Such "communities of expertise" can thus become quite entrenched and self-perpetuating. The roles played by nuclear engineers and nuclear physicists in and out of government and in combination with electric utilities and the nuclear industry seems a particularly striking and apt example.[26]

2. What have been the substantive implications for policy? The answer includes: an overweening faith in progress and a technological optimism that admits of few limitations to the ability of scientific knowledge to solve problems if sufficiently massive investments of capital and manpower are made; a commitment to very large, increasingly sophisticated and complex projects requiring considerable administrative coordination and centralization; insensitivity to social or political byproducts or externalities of technology; a preoccupation with resource and capital intensive technologies and a trained incapacity to think in terms of labor-intensive technology or resource limits; methodological commitments that disaggregate and subdivide problems; and a trained incapacity to see that energy, ecology, and economics form a single, unified system.[27] Economists in particular have been criticized for neglecting the exhaustibility of natural resources as a variable and for grossly overestimating the self-equilibrating, self-healing capacities of market economies and the ability of technology to meet any resource challenge by devising improved extraction processes.[28]

3. Straussman has described technocratic values as incorporating efficiency and rationality as behavioral norms; a view of history as one of inevitable progress; a view of society that minimizes conflict and sees it as a corollary of ignorance; and a faith that the application of knowledge will reduce conflict and that depoliticization is both desirable and inevitable.[29]

A number of problems arise when such an ethos comes to suffuse the analysis of public policy problems, and these are especially intense in the energy field where technological uncertainties and conflicting expert testimony is so prevalent. The technocratic "ethos" assumes the desirability of separating scientific questions from political and social value questions, assumes further that the scientific and technical questions are the more decisive and that they can be resolved on scientific grounds apart from ethical considerations, and finally, by perpetuating the notion that scientific expertise is the main requirement for making reasoned choice among technological alternatives, restricts participation in such decisions and frustrates democratic control of technology. Established interests and long-standing alliances among government bureaucrats, industry technocrats and managers, and their legislative patrons are the usual beneficiaries.

An interesting case in point is provided by the proposal made in 1975 to establish in the U.S. a "science court" as an integral part of the White House science advisory machinery.[30] The proposal stems from an expressed dissatisfaction with the way scientists have contributed to recent public debates, notable examples are nuclear power, the SST, the ABM. The science court would restrict itself to identifying the significant questions of science and technology raised in a policy debate and would organize adversary proceedings presided over by panels of "impartial scientific judges." The judges would then issue their judgment as to the facts pertaining to the dispute, and these would be made public.

Critics of the proposal have noted that the proposal comes from sources close to the executive branch, which would presumably organize the process, and that the felt need for such a court seems to have coincided with the politicization of technological issues and with the increase in outside challenges to the corps of government-industry experts. Casper argues that separating scientific and value questions is the reverse of what is needed:

For major public policy issues with technical facets, the political and social value questions are almost invariably far more significant than those relating to science and technology. If the science and technology questions are isolated for separate consideration by a science court, they are likely to acquire a greater political impact than they deserve.[31]

According to Casper, it is this overemphasis on technical matters that has contributed to "the current syndrome of crisis reaction, narrow technical debate, and piecemeal 'technical fixes' which fail to address basic long-range problems" (p. 30). He denies the premise that politicians and citizens are unable to weigh the claims of experts and proposes the establishment of "public adversary forums" that are much more open and where the only judges will be "the American people and their elected representatives" (p. 33).

The science court and other proposed adversary processes are directed explicitly at improving the quality of information available to the public. But public awareness and discussion tend to occur, if at all, well after the fact of important decisions. This is evidenced today by the nuclear power debate; it may be evidenced a few years hence in public concern about the proliferation implications of a then-developed laser enrichment technology. A serious effort to bring about more democratic control of technology will have to go beyond mechanisms to promote public understanding; it will have to deal directly with the nature of the decision-making process per se, in particular with the influence of the technology policy alliances.[32]

The point is not that there is no difference between a technical and a value question, or that technocrats are simply politicians under another name. Rather it is to draw attention to some of the political implications of arrangements that insulate technical from value concerns in public policy. This is especially important as we try to explore the subtle relationships between the industrial technocracy and the values it embodies, and established structures of power in industrial societies. This is directly relevant to the question of the relevance of the foregoing analysis for future policy. We may grant that in the past technocrats constrained choice on energy policy-making without being convinced that there is any necessary reason to assume they will continue to do so. Some bureaucratic, self-interest, and cognitive reasons have been noted above. To these should be added two lines of argument about the relationship of technocrats and technocratic counsel to the exercise of political power. The first of these holds that "the primary social role of experts is to legitimize policy decisions made by the real holders of power."[33] According to this view, all policy alternatives pose inherently conflictual value choices. Choice symbolizes the victory of a particular structure of power since value disparities reflect the balance of power. Once decisions are made, technical explanations and justifications are used to diffuse conflict and legitimize deicsions. Experts can also be useful scapegoats if policies fail. A second argument is that technocratic culture and policy making support the status quo by effectively insulating dominant elites from challenge by making efficiency and productivity into primary values and by inculcating a culture of passivity or alienation. "Scientific and technical rationality and manipulation are welded together into new forms of social control."[34]

[B]y virtue of the crucial role assigned to the scientifically trained, self-selecting elite positivists tend toward a presumed benevolent authoritarianism which, in the more democratic societies of North America and northern Europe, is usually implicit rather than overt.[35]

Such formulations are probably too sweeping. There can be no doubt that scientific expertise must continue to play a central role in the evolution of energy policies. After all, much of the criticism of present policies comes from the scientific community. Furthermore, any search for alternatives such as are implied by a so-called soft energy path will depend critically on technological or factual arguments as well as on making these technological perspectives more politically visible and influential. Nevertheless, we should not underestimate the extent to which existing energy policy systems continue to institutionalize a technology-policy relationship that obscures and militates against alternative conceptions of energy policy.

Dominant Classes and Economic Growth

Implicit in an effort to analyze how dominant classes or social formations can be said to shape or constrain policy is the assumption that we can identify fundamental social rules and ideologies that, while seldom if ever explicitly contested, structure and limit pluralist competition and the decision range of organizational elites. Can we pinpoint an ultimate consensus or ideological hegemony that conditions people's conception of what is possible and desirable and that determines which elites and organizations will exist and how the basic resources of labor, energy, raw materials, and capital will be allocated? Kelly et al. in their study of environmental policy in the United States, USSR, and Japan conclude that the key factor creating ecological damage and obstructing policies and programs designed to safeguard the environment in all three nations is a common commitment to national power and resource and capital-intensive economic growth measured in GNP terms. These overarching goals are more important than differences in political system, economic structures, and other cultural values, and they account in all three nations for the "marked dissoci-ation between what is said and what is done" and "the virtual absence of a *public interest* frame of reference."[36] The operational meaning of the public interest "has come to be dictated by dominant political and industrial forces."[37] A similar emphasis on the role of dominant forces and ideologies can be seen in the literature on the history of industrialization. The rhythm of industrialization depends on the rate of gross capital formation, and Marx, Keynes, and many others have pointed out the coercive social arrangements and institutional transformations necessary to bring about and sustain high levels of capital accumulation.[38] In the words of Dean Burnham:

The take-off phase of industrialization has been a brutal and exploitative process everywhere, whether managed by capitalists or commissars. A vital functional political need during this phase is to provide adequate insulation of the industrializing elites from mass pressures, and to prevent their displacement by a coalition of those damaged by the processes of capital accumulation.[39]

Such "insulation" can be provided by a totalitarian monopoly of power, feudal patterns of deference, restrictions on the right to vote to middle and upper classes, or political arrangements that fragment power and result in low electoral mobilization and loose partisan linkages between the electorate and elected officials. Under the conditions of modern mass societies all of these are buttressed by myths and ideologies enshrining consumption and growth and by some sort of commitment to guaranteed minimum levels of income, economic security, and other welfare services and benefits.

How do these themes apply to the energy policy record we have reviewed? Energy policies are supply oriented and dominated by producers' interests; other groups and other criteria challenge them in various ways, but with little impact on actual outcomes; governmental bureaucracies are dynamically conservative; and technocratic values increasingly suffuse policy formulation. All of these are consistent with a view of the larger picture in which dominant industrializing elites or social forces in communist and capitalist, developed and developing nations alike struggle to maintain the existing pattern of production, social priorities, and economic expansion, in spite of resource and energy supply constraints in the form of depletion, price increases, or import dependency. This view seems to offer us a higher level explanation of why it is that none of our nations can address the demand side, in spite of conservation rhetoric, and why none can exercise effective control over the social costs of large-scale, centralized, capital-intensive supply technologies, in spite of known technological and organizational alternatives.

The Swedish chapter in particular has pointed out that conservation and alternative technologies are extremely difficult to implement precisely because they call into question those values or myths that have provided limited policy coherence or political legitimacy in the past—in both capitalist and noncapitalist systems. Capitalist market-oriented systems must confront issues of publicly determining what is produced, and what is to be the composition of final demand and production, rather than leaving it to the market or to powerful groups with dominant control over the market. It will be difficult to avoid explicit attention to what is a societally optimal allocation of investment and to the political institutions appropriate to such a task. Further, a demand-side policy makes much more complex demands on "liberal" governments in that it involves alterations in individual behavior and consumption habits, not to mention regulation and control of the activities of powerful corporations and semi-autonomous agencies. If economic growth cannot be relied on to guarantee full employment and a reduction of income and wealth inequalities, how can governments avoid much more extensive intervention in the labor and capital markets? How can demands for critical services be met without more government intervention in income distribution and in the determination of the balance between public and private consumption? If the transition to a service economy must be accelerated, how can this be accomplished short of a dramatic expansion of the size of the public sector—as employer and as provider of vital services that will not be supplied by the market? Policy challenges of this character pose enormously difficult problems for liberal capitalist societies by calling into question not only the position of dominant elites but also the overall ideological legitimacy of the system. They seem to require a role for public authority and a degree of planning that is, for the United States at least, as Bupp reminds us, totally unacceptable to "those who represent the framework of American authority and substance." Other capitalist countries do not share this intense ideological aversion to expanding the scope of public planning, but few have addressed the complexities and value uncertainties of demand-side strategies.

The Eastern European centrally planned, or command, political economies may have an easier time imposing demand limitation and conservation strategies, if only because their relative isolation from the world market in the 1950s and 1960s delayed and attenuated the impact of cheap energy on economic structures and consumption habits. There is some evidence of this in the Hungarian chapter but available materials on the Soviet Union and the rest of Eastern Europe suggest that such strategies are unlikely to go much beyond limitations on private consumption. And this course must eventually meet resistance from the public even in these societies where the promise of increased living standards and consumption have also been important in assuring public quiescence. Rapid industrial growth and materials-intensive development remain the primary policy goals especially in the Soviet Union and the more developed East European countries. Increases in energy production and consumption—especially electrification—have an ideologically privileged position. (Lenin's slogan: Communism is Soviet power plus electrification.) Technological optimism and "cornucopianism" have a persuasiveness that has faded somewhat in the West. These may suffice to provide a limited short-term value consensus on the basis of industrial development, but they imply heavy costs to alternative values such as environmental quality, long-term resource utilization, national autonomy, decentralization, economic flexibility, and individual lifestyle choices.

In short, dominant forces based on an industry-state symbiosis and pursuing mercantilist, growth-as-usual policies *cannot develop an elite coalition or attract popular support for a development policy based on energy conservation and demand reduction.* There is no incentive to do so, and no rationalizing ideology and political legitimacy such as would be necessary to confront the implications of resource depletion and the imperatives of an international management of scarce resources.

Måns Lönnroth has dramatized the basic choices in energy-cum-development policy as a centralized "flexibility" strategy that is capital intensive on the supply side (and which most governments have embraced) and a more nuanced, partly decentralized "matching" strategy that is capital intensive on the demand side. He does not minimize the costs of the latter in terms of prices, employment, and the balance between private and public consumption. The interesting issue raised by the total set of case studies and by the analysis of obstacles to policy change is *whether and under what circumstances any nation can consistently and effectively pursue either strategy.*

The political problem seems to be the following. The changing situation of industrial (and industrializing) societies—rising input prices for energy and materials, impending depletion, and declining marginal efficiencies of capital and energy—seems to create a uniform need to increase investment at the expense of consumption if economic growth and employment and the existing pattern of production and consumption are to be sustained. In Marxian terminology, this is a "reproductive imperative" for both communist and capitalist dominant elites. In short, all industrial societies face a return to the accumulation problems that characterized earlier stages of industrialization. The questions are: How can the transfer from consumption to investment be brought about under modern conditions, and who will bear the burden of adjustment?

With the policy trajectory that presently characterizes most countries the answer to who will bear the burden seems fairly clear: Individual consumers will pay higher prices for energy and other goods; welfare programs will be eroded and tax policies will be manipulated to provide direct and indirect subsidies to increase energy production; utilities and energy producers will resolve their uncertainties by increasing demand for energy; industry and agribusiness will maintain energy intensive production patterns and will not be required to make real energy conservation efforts; inflationary forces will be controlled by deflating the economy and accepting higher rates of unemployment (or lower wages); and strong countries will shift the burden to the weaker ones and to the underdeveloped periphery. Whether the domestic and international political conditions for such a pattern of capital accumulation exist is much less clear. At a domestic level, the differential abilities of dominant groups to insulate themselves from pluralist pressures and from organizational demands will be important determinants of the relative success such strategies can expect to have.[40]

To argue that there are dominant classes and an hegemonic ideology is not to ignore that the new situation contains contradictions that threaten that dominance by making uncertain that the desired set of policies can be obtained. The effervescence of the pluralist political arena, the ability of large organizations to defend their interests, and the fragmentation of decision making may block the needed capital accumulation, at least on the above distributive terms. International developments—new OPECs, wars, boycotts, terrorism, monetary and inflationary crises—may have similar consequences, and some nations will be more vulnerable to them than others.

Some would argue that in the United States the democratic constraints on capital formation at the expense of consumption are less strong than in Britain or some Continental nations where governments are more centralized, electoral participation more ideologically coherent and extensive, and trade unions more politically effective.[41] The economic difficulties of Britain, France, and Italy may be cases in point. On the other hand, Bupp's analysis of the United States suggests an alternative interpretation. The government-business symbiosis in the

United States is not as firmly established or legitimate in the eyes of either party[42] or in the public ideology. The market cannot provide the coordination necessary for the long-range investments and complex interactions involved in technologies like nuclear power. And the ideological opposition (or ambivalence) to planning on any systematic basis, combined with the highly fragmented decision structure that has given environmentalists and nuclear opponents so many points of entry may continue to produce the present disarray in which neither a coherent supply nor a coherent demand policy can be developed.[b]

Such an outcome seems less likely in France where the industry-government symbiosis is long established and was never *really* made subject to challenge from democratic politics and where planning is widely accepted and highly centralized decision processes are fully institutionalized. Saumon and Puiseux' analysis suggests that so far it has been relatively easy in France to bring about the consumption-to-capital accumulation shift required for a supply strategy. Prices have been allowed to rise (notably for gasoline); subsidies are available; the nuclear commitment was made without specific considerations of cost and capital implications; and adversary groups have played a much lesser role. Elites in Hungary seem to be in an even stronger position in these regards, whereas Britain and Canada and India seem to lie somewhere between France and the United States. Sweden may be one country in which something approximating a demand-oriented "matching" strategy may be emerging. It is also the nation in which democratic electoral processes, trade union power, and elite values most clearly constrain a capital-accumulation process that would increase inequalities of income and wealth. On the other hand, Swedish policymakers will not be able to escape the imperative to increase savings and reduce individual consumption. A demand side strategy seems likely to be as capital intensive, at least in the short run. Whether this can be made politically acceptable and under what terms remains to be seen.

The foregoing discussion has tried to do two things: first, to pinpoint those constraints on energy policy that can be fruitfully analyzed at the level of class or dominant social forces (resource intensive growth as a societal goal and the modalities of capital accumulation): and second, to indicate in what ways class control over policy outcomes may be coming under challenge in some nations. National differences on these several dimensions will be an important starting point for the policy implication discussion that follows. But one final comment is in order. To argue that dominant elites in a country like the United States (or perhaps Canada or Britain or even France) may not be able to assure ready translation of their preferences into policy does not deny that they can probably prevent an alternative policy from emerging. The chief result of such a stalemate will of course be rising oil imports and the host of international consequences described in detail in our worst-case scenario and resumed early in this chapter.

[b]Note the mounting business community criticisms of energy policy; for example, "GM Hits U.S. Energy Policy," *The Washington Post*, September 30, 1976.

Summary

It is widely believed that uncertainty, complexity, misguided government pricing policies, and short-run struggles for advantage among competing groups, elites and publics, are the chief obstacles to the development of energy policies that would be more responsive to the changed conditions of the late 1970s. If that were so, we might expect that advances in knowledge, the elaboration of more comprehensive macro-analytic techniques, and the rationalizing adjustments that are compelled by the logic of the market and of incremental pluralist politics could be relied upon to bring about an eventual return to some kind of equilibrium in which the consumption of energy reflected price, supply vulnerability, long-run exhaustion of resources, ecological and environmental externalities, and the claims of other countries.

The analysis presented here suggests that although such adjustment processes may well be set in motion, they are likely to be severely constrained by an interacting set of institutional and structural obstacles. In other words, there are important lags and rigidities that hinder the rationalizing capacities of economic and political "markets." Unless these obstacles are better understood and unless they can be removed or attenuated, the momentum of past policies seems likely to prevail with consequences resembling those sketched out in the worst case scenario of Chapter One.

Table 9-1 summarizes this analysis of constraints on change in energy policy. Across the top of the table are arrayed eight distinctive characteristics of national energy policy systems that emerged from our comparisons. Along the left-hand side are listed five different levels of the political system, or types of politics. In the policy analysis literature these are usually treated as competing explanations of particular policy or structural outcomes. I have viewed them as *a hierarchy of partially overlapping and mutually reinforcing constraints on policy and policy change.* That is to say, I have argued for a complex pattern of interdependencies among these different levels or types of politics, the broad outlines of which are suggested by the order in which they are listed in Table 9-1, i.e., from the least constraining at the top to the most constraining at the bottom.[c] The ordering of constraints is not necessarily rigid across time or policy areas, and some interesting variations exist from one country to another. Nevertheless, it does seem to be an accurate representation of what has happened to date in national energy policies.

The pattern of interaction is extremely complex and most of the cells in the matrix could probably be given some kind of "score" for any particular nation. This has not been attempted here because the range of nations under study and the evidence at hand does not permit such precision. What I have done is to

[c]The most questionable entry in my opinion is the placement of "bureaucratic conservatism." Viewed as "bureaucratic politics" it belongs adjacent to "group struggle," but viewed as an aspect of the "autonomy of the state" it belongs more or less where we have placed it.

Table 9-1
Institutional and Structural Obstacles to Change in Energy Policy

Types of Politics or Levels of the Political System	Distinctive Characteristics of the Energy Policy System							
	Closed Circle of deciders	Resistance to the representation of other actors	Supply-oriented and technological fix policy criteria	Resistance to alternative criteria: demand, resource conservation, new economic order	Inadequate or limited public discussion of technological choices	Sectoral, and incremental decision-making and sub-optimization	No capacity to coordinate the system (fragmentation and oscillation)	No effort to seek new bases of higher level value integration
Group struggles for power and shares national income and competitive bidding for votes by politicians interested in short run and reelection.			X			X	XX	
Power of a network of vertically stratified organizational elites to control options and the policy agenda.	XX	X	XX			X	XX	
Bureaucratic conservatism and cybernetic processes in decision making.	X			X				
The policy role of technocrats and the technocratic culture of industrialism.	X	X	XX	X	XX	XX	X	X
Class reproduction requiring resource intensive growth and non-egalitarian capital accumulation.	X	X	X	XX	X			XX

identify with *x* and *xx* those interactions I feel have been generally "important" or "very important" in energy policy. This analysis suggests that substantive change in energy policies involves reforming the energy policy system, and that the key to the reform of an energy policy system lies in finding ways and means for countering or overcoming particular negative characteristics by means of political action focused on the corresponding political system level(s) or centered in a particular type(s) of politics. What this implies for policy will be developed in the next chapter.

Notes

1. *The Economist*, April 10, 1976 October 2, 1976, and December 11, 1976.

2. Eckholm, *Losing Ground: Environmental Stress and World Food Prospects* (New York: M.W. Norton and Co., 1976), pp. 183-84.

3. Ibid., p. 187.

4. See two articles by Allen L. Hammond, "Coal Research (II): Gasification Faces an Uncertain Future," *Science*, vol. 193 (August 27, 1976), pp. 750-53; and "Coal Research (III): Liquefaction Has Far to Go," *Science*, vol. 193, (September 3, 1976), pp. 873-75.

5. *The Economist*, April 10, 1976, p. 107.

6. Arnold L. Horelick, "The Soviet Union, the Middle East, and the Developing World Energy Situation," *Policy Sciences*, vol. 6, no. 1 (March 1975), pp. 42-43; John A. Berry, "Oil and Soviet Policy in the Middle East," *The Middle East Journal* (Spring 1972), p. 151; and "Middle East Development Needs Outgrow Soviet Scope," *Middle East Digest*, vol. 19, 31 (August 1, 1973).

7. See for example William D. Metz, "Fusion Research (I): What Is the Program Buying the Country?" *Science*, vol. 192 (June 25, 1976), pp. 1320-24.

8. Nazli Choucri, *International Politics of Energy Interdependence: The Case of Petroleum* (Lexington, Mass.: Lexington Books, 1976), Chapter 9, "Structures of Interdependence for Alternative Sources of Energy."

9. See Horst Menderstrausen, *Coping with the Oil Crisis: French and German Experiences* (Baltimore: Johns Hopkins University Press, 1976), pp. 6-8 and 44-64.

10. Lawrence Scheinman, "United States International Leadership," in J.C. Hurwitz (ed.), *Oil, The Arab-Israeli Dispute and the Industrial World: Horizons of Crisis* (Boulder, Colo.: Westview Press, 1976), Chapter 1.

11. Walter C. Patterson, "Exporting Armageddon," *The New Statesman*, August 27, 1976, pp. 264-66.

12. *The Economist*, February 28, 1976, p. 74. For a recent and balanced

statement on the IAEA system see Lawrence Scheinman, Statement before the Senate Committee on Government Operations, Washington, D.C., mimeo, January 19, 1976.

13. See Mendershausen, *Coping with the Oil Crisis*, pp. 98-99. Also *The Economist*, October 2, 1976.

14. Scheinman, "United States International Leadership."

15. John Steinbrunner, *The Cybernetic Theory of Decisions* (Princeton, N.J.: Princeton University Press, 1974), p. 141.

16. Hugh Heclo, "Conclusion: Policy Dynamics" in Richard Rose (ed.), *The Dynamics of Public Policy* (London and Beverly Hills: Sage Publications, 1976), p. 257.

17. For a statement of the elite paradigm and a systematic comparison with pluralist and class approaches, see Robert Alford, "Paradigms of Relations Between State and Society," in Leon N. Lindberg et al. (eds.) *Stress and Contradiction in Modern Capitalism: Public Policy and the Theory of the State* (Lexington, Mass.: Lexington Books, 1975), pp. 145-60.

18. Steinbrunner, *The Cybernetic Theory of Decisions*, p. 85.

19. *Business Week*, September 27, 1976; *The Washington Post*, September 19 and 20, 1976.

20. For further discussion of the relationship between elite control and decentralization and fragmentation in decision-making, see Alford, "Paradigms of Relations," p. 156, and his *Health Care Politics: Ideological and Interest Group Barriers to Reform* (Chicago: Chicago University Press, 1975).

21. Donald R. Kelley, Kenneth R. Stunkel, and Richard R. Wescott, *The Economic Superpowers and the Environment* (San Francisco: W.H. Freeman & Co., 1976), pp. 285-86.

22. Alford, "Paradigms of Relations," pp. 147-48, 151, and 157-58. See also his "Participation and Public Policy: Paradigms of Power," paper delivered at the 1976 Annual Meeting of the American Political Science Association, Chicago, September 2-5, 1976.

23. Steinbrunner, *The Cybernetic Theory of Decisions*. Specific page references are in the text.

24. Ibid., p. 132.

25. D. Schooler, Jr., *Science, Scientists and Public Policy*, (New York: Free Press, 1971).

26. John S. Steinhart, "The Impact of Technical Advice on the Choice for Nuclear Power," in Lon C. Reudisili and Morris F. Firebaugh, *Perspectives on Energy* (New York: Oxford University Press, 1975), pp. 504-13.

27. See Howard T. Odum, "Energy, Ecology and Economics," *Ambio*, vol. 2, no. 6 (1973), pp. 1-8; and Barry Commoner, *The Poverty of Power* (New York: Alfred A. Knofp, 1976), especially Chapters 1 and 2.

28. "Nicholas Georgescu-Roegen. Entropy and the Measure of Economic Man," *Science*, vol. 190 (October 31, 1975), pp. 447-49; Alan G. Chynoweth, "Materials Conservation—A Technologist's Viewpoint," *Challenge*, January-February 1976, pp. 34-36; M. King Hubbert, "Survey of World Energy Resources," in Reudisili and Firebaugh, *Perspectives on Energy*, pp. 118-21; and Nicholas Georgescu-Roegen, *The Entropy Law and the Economic Process* (Cambridge, Mass.: Harvard University Press, 1971).

29. Jeffrey D. Straussman, "Technocratic Counsel and Societal Guidance," in Leon N. Lindberg (ed.), *Politics and the Future of Industrial Society* (New York: McKay, 1976), pp. 153-54.

30. Arthur Kantrowitz, "Controlling Technology Democratically," *American Scientist*, 63 (1975), p. 505. For a proposed set of guidelines for the court, see Task Force of the Presidential Advisory Group on Anticipated Advances in Science and Technology, *Science*, vol. 193 (1976), p. 653.

31. Barry M. Casper, "Technology Policy and Democracy," *Science*, vol. 194 (October 1, 1976), p. 30. Copyright 1976 by the American Association for the Advancement of Science.

32. Ibid., p. 35.

33. Straussman, *The Cybernetic Theory of Decisions*, pp. 151-52.

34. Herbert Marcuse, *One Dimensional Man*, as cited by Straussman, ibid., p. 158.

35. Theodore Geiger, *Fortunes of the West*, as cited by Straussman, ibid.

36. Kelley et al., *The Economic Superpowers*, pp. 288-89.

37. Ibid., pp. 289-90.

38. See Andrew Martin, "The Politics of Economic Development in Advanced Industrial Societies," in Ronald Inglehart (ed.), "Problems of Advanced Industrial Society," a Special Issue of *Comparative Political Studies* (forthcoming, October 1977).

39. Dean Burnham, "The Changing Shape of the American Political Universe," *American Political Science Review*, vol. LIX, no. 1 (March 1965), p. 24.

40. Martin, "The Politics of Economic Development."

41. Ibid., and Burnham, "The Changing Shape of the American Political Universe."

42. See David Vogel, "Why Businessmen Mistrust Their State: The Political Consciousness of American Corporate Executives," paper delivered at the 1976 Annual Meeting of the American Political Science Association, Chicago, September 2-5, 1976.

10

Comparing Energy Policies: Policy Implications

Leon N. Lindberg

Policy Relevance

Alvin Weinberg, nuclear bomb project physicist, long-time advisor to United States governments, and presently director of the Institute for Energy Analysis at Oak Ridge has been a vigorous proponent of nuclear power, referring to the choice as an essentially unavoidable "Faustian bargain." This now familiar phrase was doubtless meant to underscore that that course would not be without risks and disadvantages. More recently he and a co-author have reiterated their optimism on the technological side, referring to themselves as "cornucopians" to distinguish their views from so-called "neo-Malthusians."[1] They acknowledge that there will be an "imperative need for steadily increasing energy supplies," but deny that depletion of existing energy and other material resources will "create catastrophe," "provided man finds an inexhaustible, non-polluting source of energy" (p. 688). Moreover, the price of prime energy must be kept as low as possible since "[e]nergy is the ultimate raw material," and "living standards will almost surely depend primarily on the cost of prime energy" (p. 689). The problems will not be technological, but *political* and *institutional*, and on this score, they seem to admit to mounting concern, if not rank pessimism. Weinberg and Goeller wonder whether we will be able to make the transition to these new energy sources "without incurring drastic social instabilities." They find that at present the "capacity and foresight to plan and execute the transition" is lacking in both marketplace and public institutions, and conclude by urging "attention to those institutional deficiencies that now prevent us from passing through [this transition] ... without causing the boat to capsize" (p. 689).

The foregoing analysis of the roots of policy rigidity and fragmentation and the constraints on policy change should be seen as an effort to specify what these institutional deficiencies are, how they emerged, how they interact with each other and with structural characteristics of industrial society, and how these combine to fix the energy policies of most nations in a trajectory that seems neither viable nor desirable. It would be a distinct understatement to say that I conclude that Goeller and Weinberg's concerns are well founded! Admittedly my analysis may be controversial and in the nature of the case, can only be based on partial evidence and a short reaction time over which to observe government policy under real strain. Further research along these lines is clearly called for. But even if the reader is skeptical about some parts of the analysis, he or she cannot help but be impressed by the complexity of energy choices and by how deeply they challenge governments and established assumptions about policy at the levels of ideology, consensus, authority and legitimacy, bureaucratic organization, and national sovereignty. I have not attempted to underestimate the sheer complexity of the energy problem, nor have I sought to portray the state (or government) or the political process as subject to any kind of conspiracy or coherent control by any small group. But I have tried to go beyond the most visible level of energy policy conflict involving individuals and groups in pluralist arenas and elites in structured, organizational arenas to deeper but more elusive factors involving bureaucratic decision processes, the cultural roles of technocratic expertise, and the overarching structures of political and ideological hegemony.

The reader may well ask how such an approach can be made policy relevant short of utopian assumptions about man and society and/or comprehensive and substantially revolutionary economic and political change. My own answer is that to be policy relevant requires avoiding both the *cynicism* (or hopelessness) of assuming only a total system change will help and the *irrelevance* that follows from a failure to identify the real roots of the problem. Only a multidimensional analysis such as has been attempted here can set the stage for a properly focused discussion of "what is to be done" about energy. In this chapter I will try to identify what general implications for the substance of energy policies might be extracted from a comparison of the policy experiences described in our seven case studies. These policy implications are of three different orders. One set is founded directly on *the empirically based analysis we have made of the nature of policy making in energy* and of the factors that constrain the ability of energy policy systems to adapt to changing conditions. The volatile and turbulent interactions between technology and politics and among energy, economic development, security, health and safety, and the distribution and stability of political and economic power counsel three risk-minimization maxims that I believe any reasonably prudent policymaker should keep constantly in mind and that can be implemented in the short run. These maxims may asuage the worst symptoms of the energy syndrome but will not deal with its causes.

The second set of policy implications is founded on my *evaluation of the outcomes of present policies*, that is to say, on the analysis presented in Chapter 1 of the multiple, long-run consequences a continuation of present patterns of energy consumption are likely to have. In Chapter 1, I stated that all the authors represented in this book shared the view that energy policy criteria needed to be broadened radically if nations are to achieve politically viable or desirable long-term policies. The relationship (or the distinction) between concepts of the viability and the desirability of policy is a tricky subject. Both raise questions of "from whose standpoint," in terms of what values or preferences," "in what time frame?" The scenario presented there shows clearly our conviction that the only viable energy policy in the long run would be based on values that might be termed egalitarian, internationalist, and conservationist. Present policies are a long way from embodying such values and the obstacles to them have been our main preoccupation. I therefore propose some alternative principles that I believe should guide change in energy policies and will have more desirable long-run consequences. These principles are the beginnings of a strategy for treating the causes of the energy syndrome.

This second set of proposals is avowedly contingent on more or less far-reaching institutional or structural reforms, whereas the first set seems to me to be in principle less so. This is not to suggest, however, that either the risk-minimization maxims or the alternative policy principles will be perceived as "realistic" from the perspective of those who participate in the policy-making process. And this for at least three reasons. First, and most important, my purpose here is not to address any particular policymaker, and not even primarily policymakers in general. We have sought above all to ask radical questions, in the sense of those that get to the root of things. And one of our principal findings is that energy policymakers, their criteria of choice, and the institutional systems in which they are embedded are *part of the problem*. It follows that the purpose of policy recommendation will be to highlight that fact and to illuminate the consequences that flow from it. The goal is to challenge perceived notions of what is "practical" or realistic and to avoid being prematurely constrained by the momentum of the past. The second reason flows from the first; the maxims and principles may not seem "realistic" because they are stated categorically (i.e., without regard to costs or tradeoffs) and at a very general level. Their applicability to any particular nation depends on its particular circumstances, energy resources, import dependency, economic structure, and the specific interplay of institutions and groups that condition the capacity or will of governing elites to offend some well-established interests. Finally, it can be persuasively argued that the maxims will not be perceived as "realistic" because their implementation will entail consequences that could only be counteracted if one also moved actively towards goals the present system seems to exclude—that is, energy conservation, emphasis on renewable resources and progress towards some kind of new world economic order.

The third group of policy implications addresses the issue of the institutional and structural reforms that seem necessary in order to reorient basic energy policies, that is, to break through the energy syndrome. Here the starting point of the analysis will be *differences in policy response* among our countries, and the analysis will involve looking for political correlates of a variable capacity to counteract common challenges that inhere in the nature of complex problems and the structure of the industrial state. The evidential basis for such an analysis draws heavily on a contrast between the Swedish case and the others, and is admittedly slender. My purpose is to present an agenda for future inquiry rather than a set of firm conclusions.

Technology-Politics Interactions

One starting point for a discussion of policy relevance is to go back to Goeller and Weinberg's familiar dichotomization of the "technological" and the "political." The data from our case studies and the comparative analysis and interpretation of them would seem to affirm that technology and politics are not divisible. At least four points seem important here.

1. The deep faith in technology as a solvent for all problems on the part of technologists *and policymakers* has not only been misplaced (the history of nuclear and coal research demonstrates that research and development expenditures do not automatically and predictably produce breakthroughs), but is itself to some extent politically and institutionally based. It may also be a source of policy error and organizational complexity.[2]

2. A capital-intensive supply strategy relying on complex technologies like fission, coal conversion, and fusion (paid for by the public through reduced public services, higher taxes, prices, and unemployment rates and uncertainties about health, safety, and the environment) is itself a principal cause of political instability, polarization, and policy stalemate. Bupp's characterization of the United States may well have much wider applicability. Controversies over energy policy, especially nuclear power, may increasingly precipitate a situation of immobilism in which "neither side has the authority to make its proposals, decisions, or actions legitimate in the eyes of the other" and where "the authority necessary to coordinate the system" does not exist. A striking if indirect confirmation of this thesis was given by Eric Reichl, president of Continental Oil's coal development company in discussing the prospects for the production of oil and gas from coal. Reichl observed that "technology is not the key to success in coal conversion: politics is."[3] He went on to contrast the "national commitment" to develop synthetic fuels made by Germany in the 1930s to the present lack of a political consensus on this subject in the United States. One finds similar admiring references in the business press to the forcefulness and single-mindedness with which the Soviets are pursuing their fission and breeder programs. The price to be paid for such a "consensus" and "national commitment" will be judged by some others as too high!

3. On the international level as well, technology will not "solve" the politically infused conflicts that underlie the complex system of petroleum interdependence and the emerging system of nuclear interdependence. These conflicts involve simultaneously policy issues, world order issues, value controversies, and political loyalty conflicts, not to mention the development prospects of one-half to two-thirds of the world's population. Peter Odell notes that there is a "technocratic tradition" that predominates in Western establishmentarian analyses of the energy crisis. It implies that "nothing the rest of the world tries to do in its own interest need produce more than an appropriate logistical sort of response to ensure that our own standards are not undermined."[4] But the

fundamental change in the world economic order signalled by the OPEC actions of 1973 and 1974 pose much "more than econometrically determined adjustment problems."[5] What is involved is the evolution and establishment of new norms, rules, and institutions for managing international resources. How sanguine shall we be at this level if individual nations cannot develop consensually based energy policies?

4. Recently we have been deluged with energy policy analyses that are very heavily oriented to relatively short-term, single-point forecasts about demand, supply, conversion, and transmission efficiencies, demand-supply balances, or long-range resource estimates of how much of what is in the ground and retrievable at what price. I would never argue that such work is unimportant, nor deny that the energy crisis is ultimately to be defined in terms of demand-supply ratios. Nevertheless, as the authors of the British chapter observe, there is a tendency for such technocratic forecasts to "merely serve to obscure the uncertainties and the scope for policy choices." More useful—and relatively undersupplied in the literature—are studies that focus systematically on the medium term, on the interaction between technological and political issues, and on potential turning points and observable constraints and that "identify courses of action which may be needed if blatantly undesirable outcomes are to be avoided."

Risk-Minimizing Maxims

How should the prudent policymaker deal with such volatile and potentially destabilizing interactions between politics and technology? Are there feasible strategies that might be adopted within the framework of existing policy criteria, and the multiple constraints I have described? What can be done without questioning existing institutional practices, operative rules of the pluralist game, and the power of established elites or the ideological and class structure of societies?

The three risk-minimizing maxims proposed below seem to me to speak to presently dominant elites, classes, and nations who would seem to have an enlightened self-interest in avoiding immobilism in energy policy, in preserving minimal internal political consensus based on sustainable growth, and a relatively stable international system. Because the risks that are to be avoided will have undesirable and possibly irreversible consequences for everyone, and not only for the presently powerful, these risk-minimizing strategies seem to me generally desirable and probably prerequisite to any more extensive policy or structural changes.

1. *Avoid reliance on policies and technologies that threaten to overload the decision making and control capacities of the society.* There is great political and economic risk and uncertainty inherent in exclusive commitment to complex

systems based on unproved potentials of future resources and/or requiring future scientific or engineering breakthroughs. This is especially true where important structural side effects on the political economy and negative externalities are involved. Political interactions can be highly volatile, as the U.S. experience with nuclear energy has proven, and as the proposed crash programs for increased coal production may show again.[6] Bupp notes that "reliable and efficient production of electrical power from nuclear fission requires the operation of a complex and entirely interactive set of processes and services." This network extends beyond national boundaries, for the nuclear fuel cycle is already international in scope. Bupp concludes that the necessary infrastructure does not exist in the United States and would take ten years to put into place even if political controversy, legal challenges, and governmental wavering over policy were suddenly to disappear. But such controversy is not abating and shows signs of spreading and of straining political consensus in even the most stable nations.[7] In addition to the polarization of decision processes and the risk of stalemate, there is the even more serious longer-run implication of a nuclear economy in the form of ". . . a highly centralised society . . . with an elite guarding and making decisions" and foreclosing any society's "desire for a decentralized society, with more local decision making and autonomy."[8] The introduction of large-scale nuclear fission energy production will impose an irreversible burden "of continuous monitoring and sophisticated management of a dangerous material, essentially forever."[9] It would assume degrees and durations of domestic political stability and police control that are neither possible nor desirable. The minimally prudent policy-maker should abandon the breeder reactor and phase out the present generation of nuclear reactors as rapidly as possible.

2. *Avoid reliance on policies and technologies that seem likely to foreclose or severely limit future technological options, either because they dominate scarce resources and/or create political vested interests too powerful to be overcome.* Our analyses offer firm empirical support for Amory Lovins' assertion that a hard energy path and a soft energy path may be mutually exclusive.[10] The energy policy system whose rigidities and malfunctions I have detailed is a *product of past policies that were "hard,"* in that they emphasized energy supply, symbiotic relationships between public policymakers and energy producers, large-scale centralized facilities and electricity grids, and so forth. A future policy that is predominantly oriented toward rapidly increasing energy supplies, and that gives the lion's share of current research and development aid, tax and expenditure subsidies, and political support to high technologies such as nuclear fission or fusion and coal gasification or liquefaction, and that implies increasing levels of international vulnerability and conflict, shows every promise of intensifying those characteristics of energy policy systems that we have strongly criticized. Such a policy will also reinforce the very political and institutional factors that have constrained policy innovation in the past.

Once massive commitments of capital, human, and physical resources to high technology and centralized supply technologies have been made, they will be very difficult to reverse for reasons amply discussed in Chapter 9. The necessary infrastructures, the security requirements, and the supporting values and social structures seem likely to create an even more closed network of bureaucratic-technocratic-dominant class power than exists at present. Conservation and renewable resource policies will be all but excluded. A predominantly hard policy "depends on difficult, large-scale projects requiring a major social commitment under centralized management." It requires "compulsory diversion" from those priorities preferred by politically weaker constituencies, and threatens to create a "world of subsidies, $100-billion bailouts, oligopolies, regulations, nationalization, eminent domain, corporate statism." It renders a policy of conservation and decentralized renewable resources prohibitively difficult because it starves "its components into garbled and incoherent fragments," and because it changes "social structures and values in a way that makes the innovations of a soft path more painful to envisage and to achieve."[11]

Since it is impossible to be certain about the long-run technical or economic viability of such technologies as the breeder reactor, nuclear fission, or coal conversion (not to mention their political or environmental viability), it would seem quite imprudent for a policymaker to run the risk that short- and long-term alternatives will be effectively excluded by the unanticipated political, bureaucratic, and cultural consequences of an unbalanced energy policy.

3. *Avoid reliance on policies and technologies that promise to make the international environment more volatile and conflict prone.* In view of the rigidities and pathologies of national energy policies, it would be imprudent and shortsighted indeed, even from a narrow national or elite interest point of view, to allow dependence on oil imports to continue to grow, or to continue to promote the exportation of nuclear reactors and fuels. Reliance on oil imports substitutes more and more for policy. It sustains uncertainty and vulnerability and has a high potential for eventually creating conditions in which military interventions may well be impossible to avoid. It can be viable only if the nations involved are able to negotiate comprehensive, long-term, probably bilateral, reciprocal development and trade agreements. Whatever short-run advantages nuclear exports may hold as a "bail-out" for domestic nuclear industries, for political leverage, or for the balance of payments, these will be outweighed by the many dangers inherent in nuclear proliferation. There seems at present very little realistic prospect of evolving lasting international rules and institutions to manage the degree of interdependence and mutual vulnerability both these trends imply. This lack is particularly the case in the nuclear field and is an additional reason why the prudent policymaker should move rapidly to halt nuclear proliferation. This latter is something that can in all likelihood only be accomplished if the nuclear powers—or most of them—themselves renounce nuclear energy or explicitly schedule its phasing out.

Principles for a Long-Range Energy Policy

The three risk-minimizing maxims proposed above do not constitute an energy policy or a set of positive principles upon which a desirable policy might be based. Governments could take these steps and still pursue narrowly nationalist, environmentally destructive policies that centralize political power and worsen the distribution of income and amenities. The proposed maxims would only accommodate to the most immediately dangerous interactions among political systems, technological options, and the energy problem. Several positive principles do, I think, emerge from our analyses, from our concern for long-run political viability, for broadening energy policy criteria, and from our expressed value preferences. But these would clearly imply varying degrees of system change.

Policy Principle I: *Energy conservation and a phased transition toward a more labor-intensive economy should become primary goals of national energy policy*. This transition is in all likelihood unavoidable and will come about as a result of prolonged economic recession and instability unless public policy measures are taken to ease the change. Such an economy probably implies "lifestyles of elegant frugality,"[12] a more egalitarian distribution of benefits and burdens, societal control (or ownership) of energy and other resources, and some degree of regulation of the composition of production and consumption. Some general policy implications of such a primary orientation might include:

1. Substantial price increases will be necessary in order to encourage energy conservation. But these increases should be brought about and managed in such a way that large industrial consumers of fuel stock or of final energy (especially electricity), and individual consumers of energy will bear proportionately more of the burden than small businesses and individual households. Flat rate or inverted utility pricing schemes and "life-line" proposals that guarantee low prices to small consumers would be steps in this direction.[13] So would BTU or energy resource taxes geared to income levels.

2. Industry and agriculture should not be permitted simply to pass on higher fuel and energy costs to the individual consumer or freely to commit the economy to energy intensive products. Rather they should be induced to shift to less energy-intensive and more labor-intensive processes and products. Corporations should no longer be able to determine the demand curve for energy on the basis of their own short or long term interests.[14]

3. A BTU tax or energy resource tax with proceeds going to fund public programs in support of conservation, research and development of solar, wind and other renewable resources,[15] or "to reward those who reduced their energy use or those who were severely disadvantaged,"[16] is much to be preferred to allowing energy prices to rise in response to market demand. The market distributes the proceeds to energy producers (oil companies, uranium producers, public utilities) whose economic interest is to *increase* or at least maintain existing levels of demand and to promote nuclear energy and coal conversion.

4. Conservation policies will reduce capital needs and diminish the severe uncertainties in the energy supply sector, but transfers from consumption to investment will still be necessary to meet mounting capital requirements on both the demand and supply sides. But these should not take the form of public subsidies at the expense of reductions in minimum public services or disproportionately increase the relative tax burden of low- to medium-income families; nor should privately owned utilities be permitted to use "forward pricing" strategies as ways of building capital for plant expansion. There might be greater resort to floating stocks and bonds. Otherwise consumers both pay higher prices and contribute to private equity capital.

5. A more energy efficient economy implies replacing energy with labor and thus lower labor productivities and probably reductions in real wages.[17] Active public intervention will be necessary to induce changes in the technology of production if large increases in unemployment are to be avoided. Compensatory public welfare programs and measures of progressive tax reform are important parts of a package that could make such consumption and income losses acceptable.

Policy Principle II: *The development of renewable, nonpolluting, relatively low-technology, and decentralized sources of energy supply should receive priority over fossil fuels and nuclear fusion.* This does not deny that most economies will continue to depend heavily on fossil fuels over the next twenty years, but implies that these sources should be seen as stop-gaps and support for them should not be permitted to drive out research funds for the alternative fuels or to block regulatory and tax incentives needed to make noncommercial sources economically viable.

1. The public sector must take the initiative here since initial costs are high and studies show that private corporations lack the interest or incentives to invest in alternative technologies. In the United States, for example, almost all research on solar, wind, ocean thermal, and industrial waste heat is dependent on federal funding.[18]

2. Policymakers should take into account that public utilities (whether privately or publically owned) seem most likely to resist commercialization of solar technologies as well as the production of power by private industry from steam now used solely in industrial processes.

3. Private capital markets are unlikely to be a promising source of funding for alternative energy technologies, chiefly because large lenders seem overwhelmingly committed to nuclear and fossil fuel power. There are also "technical problems with utility ownership of solar equipment which are considered major risks by financial institutions."[19]

4. Renewable energy sources are much less likely to involve excessive centralization or monopolization of control because such resources are more equitably distributed over the globe and the equipment involved is designed on a different scale.[20]

5. The costs of energy from renewable or continuous sources can probably

be kept relatively constant, thus easing the economic transition to a less energy-intensive society.

6. A mixed strategy involving much greater use and a more rapid introduction of renewable sources of energy will facilitate a system in which the quality of an energy resource can be matched to the work to be done—that is, diffuse, low-grade solar for space heating, electricity from burning coal or uranium for operating machinery, running trains, and so forth.[21]

Policy Principle III; *The transition to an energy-efficient economy based on renewable resources will require that the industrial nations develop a positive unexploitative international strategy.* Such a strategy would ideally imply:

1. The negotiation of a new regime for the multilateral management of remaining reserves of petroleum. There can be no denying that the world must continue to rely primarily on petroleum for at least the rest of the twentieth century. This can be an advantage rather than a source of mounting instability. Petroleum has many obvious advantages as a fuel, and existing reserves in the Middle East can supply world needs for many years at very low capital costs. Capital could be freed meanwhile for investment in conservation and alternative sources.

2. Such a regime could not be nonexploitative unless it were based on: energy conservation and demand restraint in the developed countries to lower their oil import requirements and allow access to these resources by developing countries; stable prices and guaranteed supplies by producer countries in exchange for development aid and/or solar energy investments to assure these countries energy self-sufficiency in the future and perhaps a continued role as energy producers after their petroleum is exhausted; mechanisms for the recycling of oil revenues and development aid to energy and resource-poor Third World nations that do not increase their dependence on multinational firms or on centers of financial power in the major industrial countries.

3. Low technology and decentralized sources of supply—in contrast to nuclear and fossil fuel options—are additionally desirable because they will not perpetuate or intensify asymmetrical international dependencies or vulnerabilities. Indeed, solar conversion technologies make use of a plentiful source available everywhere (if unequally) that can be used in particular by poor countries to reduce their technological dependency on the advanced countries.[22]

Variations in System Response and Avenues for Reform

System response to the energy crisis can be conceptualized and measured in terms of changes or continuities in three components: *energy policies* (from supply to demand orientation, nonrenewable to renewable resources, and so forth), *the outcomes of policy* (patterns of consumption, production, import dependency, degrees of and trends in energy intensity, and so forth), and *the structure and behavior of the energy policy system* (dominant actors and policy criteria). I have suggested that these three are causally related to each other in complex and interactive ways, the broad outlines of which are described in the previous chapter. Falling prices and rising supplies of energy brought about changes in aspirations, economic structure, and growth and development policies. These in turn produced structured energy policy systems that stimulated demand, heightened aspirations, and further affected economic structure and policy. When prices began to spurt and resource depletion appeared as a real threat, past outcomes and an established policy system both (and in interaction) have served as constraints upon policy changes that might bring about a new pattern of consumption-production outcomes. We have labelled this characteristic set of responses *the energy syndrome.*

Three ways in which this syndrome *might* be broken are suggested in our array of case studies, though in none of our countries has this yet occurred. India might represent a situation in which the *external crisis* will become so severe that the "internal" constraints will be overcome. Policies, outcomes, and the energy system will change because the needed supplies of energy are simply not available. The United States, on the other hand, could prefigure a process in which *an internal crisis of policy immobilism* rooted in the social side effects and distributive implications of energy policy choices eventually precipitates a crisis of escalating instabilities in the energy demand-supply relationship that changes the system. Finally, Sweden suggests a sequence in which *deliberate efforts are undertaken to change policy and to reorganize and redirect the energy policy system* in order to bring about changes in consumption and production.

It may well be that external or internal crises will be the most likely avenues to change, that the situation will have to get much worse than it is in order to overcome obstacles to change.[a] But the costs will undoubtedly be very high and the outcomes unpredictable.[b] It is therefore eminently worthwhile to examine in some detail the one case in which positive policy action to break out of the syndrome seems to be occurring and to learn what is involved, what made the effort possible, and upon what its success seems to depend.

[a]Sir Geoffrey Vickers argues that "increasingly dramatic disasters" will constitute the "shared experiences" necessary to induce the kinds of policy change appropriate to today's challenges. "We are creatures ill equipped to respond to what is only anticipated. Some trigger is needed to convince the busy cushioned, comfortable West of the instabilities which are visible enough to the destitute, the impotent, the disillusioned and the desperate, even in their own countries." See his *Freedom in a Rocking Boat: Changing Values in an Unstable Society* (Harmondsworth: Penguin Books, 1972), p. 21.

[b]Heilbronner (and many others) see authoritarian governments as a most likely outcome. See his *An Inquiry into the Human Prospect* (New York: Norton, 1974). In the short run there is no reason to assume system and policy change would be in an energy-resource conserving direction. Crisis can as well strengthen existing individual elites. For a similar argument, see Bertram Gross, "Planning in an Era of Social Revolution," *Public Administration Review* (May-June 1971), pp. 259-96.

This method, of course, raises the issue of the extent to which factors that seem to influence policy outcomes in one political system can be useful for the analysis and evaluation of policy and institutions in another nation. This can be understood at several different levels. Most simply (and most superficially) it can be a problem of *transferability*. Can lessons be learned in Nation A that will lead to feasible reforms in Nation B so that B will achieve policy successes enjoyed by A? The answer most often given by policy analysts is negative, but I doubt that the topic has been sufficiently studied to permit a categorical response. A second exercise is the search for *functional equivalents*. Even if specific factors that seemed critical in Country A cannot be found in or transplanted to Country B, an understanding of *why* that factor plays the role it does in B may suggest how similar results might be achieved within the unique sociopolitical and cultural contexts of A. A third analytical level is that of *normative criticism*. Policy comparisons can illuminate the extent to which the ways in which policy options and the agenda formation process are constrained or conditioned in different nations by institutional, structural, or ideological factors—that is, it may suggest that certain problems will not be satisfactorily resolved in Country B because of the way in which power is concentrated, decision sites dispersed, or false consciousness is propagated by a hegemonic ideology. Examples of all three types of "cross-polity learning" will be found in what follows.

Until the fall of 1973, Sweden was as firmly set on an energy-intensive and import-dependent growth path as any country. Energy consumption had grown at an average annual rate of 4.5 percent over the postwar years and by the 1970s Sweden's energy consumption was one of the highest in the world. Imported oil accounted for a full 71 percent of the total energy supply. Swedish authorities were predicting energy consumption would double by 1985 and triple by 2000. In order to meet the anticipated future demand and diminish dependence on imports, the Swedes embarked on an ambitious nuclear program calling for the construction of twenty-four generating stations. The technology was of Swedish design and manufacture and large reserves of uranium exist in the country. By 2000 Sweden would have been the world's leading producer and consumer of nuclear power as measured by percent of total energy needs supplied. Thus Sweden was more vulnerable to the oil boycott and price increases than any other country, with the possible exception of Japan. Yet the response to the boycott and price rise was quite distinctive. The oil price increase was absorbed without allowing unemployment rates to rise above 2 percent or the growth rate to suffer materially.[23] And a public debate stimulated by these events led to a shift in energy policies that, even if it was not decisive, has no real analogue elsewhere. At least a start was made toward the risk minimization and positive policy principles outlined in the previous sections.

The outlines of the debate between opponents and proponents of nuclear power and of supply versus conservation strategies took much the same form in Sweden as in other countries. But the outcome was different. In the Spring of

1973 the Parliament had voted a one-year moratorium on the construction of new nuclear plants. A vigorous public discussion with enormous media coverage ensued. In 1974 energy study circles involving 80,000 Swedes (1 percent of the population) vigorously discussed the issues.[24] The question of nuclear power became quite polarized, with several established political parties taking positions opposing its further development. Early in 1975 Prime Minister Palme announced a new position for the ruling Social Democratic party in which the number of new nuclear plants to be built would be cut and specific targets would be set for a reduction in the growth of energy consumption from 4.5 percent annually to 2 percent in the early 1980s and 0 percent in 1990. An energy tax was to be imposed to stimulate conservation and industrial innovation, and substantial research and development allocations were made for research on alternate sources of energy and conservation. According to Palmgren, half the Swedish energy research and development budget is allocated to conservation and a quarter to new energy sources.[25]

Nevertheless, the Swedish bureaucracy and the Social Democratic party remained committed to a limited nuclear energy policy and invoked the need to reduce dependency on imported oil as the main justification. (They also actively pursued negotiations for direct long-term government-to-government contracts with oil-producing countries.) But the issue of nuclear power became a major point of difference between Prime Minister Palme and Thorbjörn Fälldin, the Center party leader of the opposition "bourgeois coalition" in the election of September 1976. Fälldin proposed not only to cancel the scaled-down nuclear program that Palme would have implemented, but to dismantle the nuclear plants already operating. According to press reports, the nuclear issue dominated the closing stages of the campaign, seemed to have an impact on younger voters, and upset the momentum of the Social Democratic strategy.[26] What the response of the new government will be is far from certain, however, since Fälldin's position is not shared by the other two opposition parties.

It is also much too early to judge to what extent the efforts to limit energy consumption will in fact succeed. Statistics available in the fall of 1976 indicated that in spite of the measures taken, and in spite of the economic situation, energy consumption had increased by 4.8 percent and 2.7 percent, respectively, in the two latest budget years.[27]

Many of the constraining factors delineated earlier are evidently at work in the Swedish case as well, though Lönnroth's analysis suggests they may be somewhat attenuated. On the other hand, the decisions taken to date by the government do not indicate a clear departure from a conservative search for acceptable rather than optimal solutions and a trend toward policy oscillation rather than decisive choices.[28] Some have argued that the preeminence of the goals of full employment and equality of condition and of maintaining high rates of growth and competitiveness in export markets will make it harder rather than easier for Sweden to confront the nascent tradeoffs between economic growth and energy consumption.[29] In any case, while it is premature to consider Sweden to be a model in the development of an alternative approach to energy policy, a comparison of the Swedish case with the others is suggestive because the Swedes have been able to organize a more open search process than goes on elsewhere and to erode somewhat the institutional and structural obstacles that I have stressed. The probabilities of subsequent policy and outcome changes are thus higher, but nothing can be guaranteed. Policy immobilism á l'Américaine is another possibility. It may not be possible for the Swedes to carry policy and institutional change far enough. Or perhaps the obstacles and tradeoffs inherent in the energy problem itself preclude a reasoned response by democratic procedures. If so, we are left with the two alternatives of external and internal "forcing" as paths to change.

What we must promote is a reorientation of national energy policies toward a search for *transitional strategies* in which there is an active search for the political, social, economic, and technological keys to lower energy futures, even though most nations will have, in the short to medium term, little alternative to reliance on coal, imported oil, and, probably, fission reactors. The danger we have stressed is that existing energy policy systems are actively and passively obstructing such a search. Therefore, altering these systems is imperative if we are to expand the choices available to us.

Overcoming Obstacles in the Policy System

The behavior of the Swedish energy policy system in response to the events of 1973-74 is distinctive in the following ways: Alternative policy criteria penetrated policy debate at the highest political levels; the mass public has been mobilized and made aware of the larger stakes of energy policy; and decision making at the bureaucratic-technocratic levels has been made permeable to new actors and new perceptions of the problem. What accounts for these differences between the Swedish response and that of other countries? Several factors can be excluded at the start. There is no reason to suppose that the Swedes are better at thinking of solutions or at analyzing problems. Swedish public debate and research in the area draws heavily on what goes on in the United States and elsewhere. Similarly, intrinsic features of energy policy—complex tradeoffs, uncertainty, too many actors, foreigners intruding upon decision space, technological obstacles—seem to be more or less the same for all countries (though some do have fewer real supply options than others). They cannot explain the different institutional response (though they could explain why, ultimately, institutional change may not be enough). And much the same is true with regard to systemic characteristics that the Swedes share (more or less) with the other countries or upon which they are not distinctive. This includes political characteristics such as a highly centralized governmental apparatus with strong regulatory powers, the number of political parties, the degree to which nationalization is an important policy instrument, practices of central planning, existence of plural interest groups capable of defending their partial interests, a public accustomed to full employment and high levels of consumption. The list of excluded factors also includes economic characteristics such as GNP per capita, GNP-energy ratio, energy import dependency, energy endowments, and the relative importance of primary, secondary, and tertiary sectors. I am not arguing that these political and economic variables are not involved, but that the significance they have (or can have) as obstacles to (or facilitators of) institutional and structural change will depend on other intervening factors.

A number of avenues of reform as suggested by the Swedish case are listed below. These are arranged vertically according to a hierarchy of constraints or obstacles derived from the analysis in Chapter 9 as summarized in Table 9-1. The entries in the righthand portion of the page show the nature of the policy problem posed at each level by the corresponding constraint, as well as the intervention or action that seems to be indicated or appropriate and the system characteristics or political factors I take to be decisive as political conditions for overcoming obstacles to policy change at each level. Although interdependencies exist among the levels it is impossible to say in advance what concrete form these will take in any nation. A clear implication, however, is that even though limits to reform are set by how far down the matrix you can go, policies and policy systems can be improved even if it proves possible to intervene on only a few levels of the system.

Constraints or Obstacles to Policy Change

Policy Problem, Appropriate Action or Intervention and Political Conditions

Interest group struggle and short-term electoral strategies preclude policy coordination and more than incremental change.

Make groups and the public aware of the long-term consequences of present policies and outcomes in order to alter perceptions and definitions of self-interest and to encourage equal sharing of burdens of adjustment. Strongly articulated (quasicorporatist) systems of interest representation encourage recognition of the interdependence of claims; past policies emphasizing welfare, full employment, and reduction of inequalities of income and wealth encourage solidaristic over competitive norms.

Dominant elites and organizations in the energy supply sector seek to limit participation, restrict policy criteria, and defend their sectoral interests.

Regulate the energy sector to separate production from distribution, to eliminate vertical and horizontal concentration in the energy industry, and to encourage decentralization and regional/local control over demand; increase the resources and access of agencies and groups

| *Constraints or Obstacles to Policy Change* | *Policy Problem, Appropriate Action or Intervention and Political Conditions* |

with interests in alternative sources and conservation, and incorporate them into the policy system; reorganize the "interorganizational rule system" to permit alternative technologies to become viable; remove direct and indirect subsidies that make energy intensive production cost-effective; supplement market criteria in large-scale, capital-intensive interorganizational resource allocations. A strongly organized public sector with established public confidence and which is perceived as independent of control of any partial interest; quasicorporatist interest representation; national energy companies to compete with private sector and assure access to information.

Dynamically conservative bureaucracies act to retard information feedback (and therefore change in effective loci of decision or criteria) and reinforce sectoral decision making.

Formal institutional provisions for regular external policy review by special commissions or ad hoc task forces whose recommendations have privileged access to higher policymakers. Encourage interchanges among bureaucratic, political, and central-local personnel. Build contingency, experimentation, and advocacy of competing designs into policy formulation and planning processes. Institutionalized roles for royal commissions and other special inquiries that are autonomous of legislative or executive branches; local/regional autonomy; coordination among levels and integration across values must be done outside bureaucracy, probably by political parties.

The policy role of technological expertise and technocratic culture retards change in the locus of decision and policy criteria and makes public participation in technological decisions more difficult.

Create specific procedures to assure democratic control of technological choices before massive investments and essentially irreversible decisions are made; do not separate technical from ethical dimensions of decision; balance physical sciences-engineering-economics with biological sciences-ecologists-social scientists in the political advisory system. Political parties are most effective agency for mobilizing and informing

Constraints or Obstacles to Policy Change	*Policy Problem, Appropriate Action or Intervention and Political Conditions*
	publics and for balancing the industrial technocracy that all industrial states require; adversary interest groups may play analogous—if less effective—roles.
Dominant "class" interests in rapid growth and capital accumulation encourages resistance to changing deciders, or criteria, to public debate and prevents consideration of alternative development and growth strategies.	Seek to forge a stable symbiosis between elite and pluralist politics that can reduce class politics to a minimum; basis for such a symbiosis might be a labor-intensive, human services economy of stocks in which individual consumption, growth, profit maximization/capital accumulation are superceded as the chief standards by which performance and welfare are measured. Political parties can act as "brokers" between levels of the system only if they take explicit programmatic stands and rely on mass mobilization (maximum discussion of alternatives, high visibility for contending views, high electoral participation) as a means of political competition; quasicorporatist interest representation.

The formulations are tentative and exploratory. They raise far more questions than they answer. Each entry leads into a host of classical issues in a variety of fields: public administration, organizational theories of innovation, interest-group and party theory, theories of economic regulation, theories of "consociational democracy" and "neocorporatism," democratic theory, and philosophies of equity and justice. My purpose here is to set them forth as a set of interrelated hypotheses for further development and empirical investigation. What I hope I have shown is that policy-relevant hypotheses can be derived from a systematic analysis of intersystem differences in policy response.

Each entry will recall—but leave unresolved—the questions posed earlier as to the usefulness of crossnational comparisons for policy design: transferability versus functional equivalents, versus normative criticism. Nevertheless, a brief discussion of the aspects of the Swedish political system that seem to me to have been decisive as variables intervening between a capacity for changing the energy policy system, on the one hand, and other system characteristics and the intrinsic nature of the energy macroproblem on the other will indicate some specific directions future research might take.

1. *Systems of Interest Representation.* The "quasi-corporatist" involvement of interest-group representatives at all stages of policy formulation and across

the gamut of policy fields is an especially distinctive feature of Swedish politics.[30] The blue-collar workers federation (LO), white-collar and professional associations, and the employers' association are the most important, but the network of organized groups is extensive and dense. Much of the credit for the success of Swedish stabilization policies (very low unemployment, moderate inflation) has been attributed to informal wage and price restraint and agreements hammered out between employers and employees.[31] These so-called central organizations are represented on royal commissions, regulatory and planning agencies at national, regional, and local levels, and apparently played an important part in promoting and organizing the 1973-74 public debates and energy study circles that initiated the reassessment of Swedish energy policy.

Many theorists[32] (recalling earlier debates in the interwar period and even earlier[33]) have begun to argue that thus incorporating the major "social partners" in the decision process encourages restraint in the pressing of particularistic demands and discourages defensive veto group actions on behalf of vested interests. Such a recognition of the "interdependence of claims" seems integral to any significant approach to the issues raised by energy conservation, demand limitation, and transitions to lifestyles of "elegant frugality." The policy effects of such systems can be various, however. Social conservatives and proponents of "industrial growth as usual" also call for "self-restraint" on the part of workers and "sacrifice" by consumers, and they often propose corporatistic arrangements.[34] The difference in the Swedish case seems to be that the trade unions play a pivotal role not only in the interest group system, but have very close ties to the political party that has governed Sweden for most of the past forty years.

In other words, while quasicorporatist (or tripartite) arrangements can be used to forge an intergroup consensus on how to distribute benefits and burdens, they may also serve as mechanisms for an engineered acceptance of continued inequalities and political hegemony. Nevertheless, even in national settings in which interest groups are much less tightly organized and "solidaristic" than they are in Sweden, a consideration of how to instrument some sort of more meaningful formal involvement of major interested groups in energy policy systems ought to be high on the agenda of those who wish to change energy policies.

2. *The General Pattern of Economic and Welfare Policies.* Swedish economic and social policy has emphasized high employment, income transfers, and the provision of growing levels of human services. The distribution of income and wealth, of access to public services and amenities, of exposure to economic or environmental risk is among the most egalitarian in the world. Such an approach to an "equality of condition" may be a prerequisite for individual and group willingness to accept voluntary restraints in the pressing of claims, to make sacrifices in "the general interest" and to develop a capacity to confront the distributional consequences of resource depletion and the prospects of a

transition to a more labor-intensive economy. This is borne out, at least impressionistically, by what we know about the nature and circumstances of the Swedish energy debate, especially when we contrast those discussions with the manifest unwillingness (fear) of analysts and governing elites in other countries explicitly to confront the distributional issues. Two related considerations are the extent to which the public perception of the energy problem—most strikingly in the United States—is colored by an abiding suspicion that the "crisis" is/was manufactured by the oil companies or energy combines (in league with the government) for their own interests, and by the reluctance of governments—again most notably the United States—to act as if a long-term problem really existed.

The greater the inequalities of opportunity and condition are, the more pervasive is the perception that policy is really dominated by powerful industrial interests; and the more persistent the suspicion that government serves these interests, the more difficult it will be to "tame" the group struggle or to modify "competitive consumerism" at the individual level.

3. *Public Authorities with Strong Regulatory Powers.* Earlier I rejected this variable as necessarily associated with a capacity to change energy policies or the energy policy system. Regulatory power can be used, and in our cases usually is, to maintain or reinforce the existing closed circle of deciders and the patterns of elite and class control and, thus, more strongly to perpetuate the policy trajectory (Hungary and France). On the other hand, United States, British, and Canadian experience—in energy and in other spheres such as growth and stabilization policies—points to the importance of a strong regulatory capacity on the part of public authorities as a prerequisite to dealing with issues like conservation and demand limitation. The formation in Canada and Britain of national oil companies attests to a growing realization that new instruments of economic intervention are required.

In the case of Sweden, the facts of trade union power and Social Democratic control of the government have produced a pattern of intervention *on behalf of majority interests (workers and consumers) in which political power could be used to counterbalance the economic power of business.*[36] The Swedish labor market policy (a keystone in stabilization policy) relies heavily on regulation and incentives to force industry to adopt rationalization and effi- ciency measures and thus to be able to pay high, standardized wages.[37] This experience created the instruments necessary for the adoption of energy conservation measures and underlies the confidence that zero energy growth can be made an explicit goal of policy.

Any action to change the energy production system, to recast the network of "interorganizational rules" that determines the viability or profitability of alternative energy technologies, or to induce energy producers and consumers to change their priorities, presupposes a regulatory authority independent of the energy industry.

4. *Formal Administrative Arrangements.* Another distinctive feature of the Swedish system of government is a set of formal arrangements for assuring regular "external" policy review of the administration. These include royal commissions, the antisecrecy legislation, the *remiss* system of interest group consultation, and of course, the ombudsman.[38] Students of Swedish public administration also stress the organizational division of responsibility between small ministries with major responsibility for policy initiation, and large boards that implement policy.[39] Major changes in policy frequently are initiated by royal commissions or other ad hoc inquiries, and this seems to be the case in energy as well. Devices of this kind seemed to have opened up the bureaucratic-technocratic decision system that had been set on a high energy growth-nuclear trajectory and to have led to the incorporation of new policy criteria. The personal role of Palme and a Delegation on Energy Policy originally attached to the prime minister's office were especially important.

The usefulness of such devices to counteract bureaucratic conservativism in order to penetrate closed decision systems, and to break out of the constraints of incremental policy change have long been promoted by planners and by students of public administration and organizational theory. But experience suggests that the effectiveness of such arrangements depends heavily on other factors: Can such policy reviews be kept free from capture by the groups with the largest stakes in the outcome? What assurance can there be that bureaucrats or top policymakers will pay any attention to their findings?

5. *Local-Regional Autonomy.* The Swedish chapter placed special emphasis on the relationship between the local authorities in towns and cities and such central bodies as the State Electricity Board. Lönnroth pointed out that "we will not have much choice on the technical level unless we change the division of responsibility in the energy supply system." Local authorities may see an interest in schemes for decentralized energy production (e.g., wind, solar, and as byproducts of industrial production) and in small-scale generating installations in which waste heat can be used for space heating that central electricity boards or electrical utilities will not share. It may well be that the importance of local control (or ownership) of public utilities may not be cost considerations at all, but rather the possibilities provided for energy-efficient, decentralized planning. Such arrangements might also facilitate the dissemination of capital to individuals, blocks, or cities, thus breaking through the formidable obstacles constituted by the close relationships among banks and other lending agencies, energy generating utilities, and oil, coal, and uranium producers.

While such decentralization of the energy supply system may be a prerequisite for conservation or for the exploitation of nonrenewable energy resources, there seems no guarantee that decentralization *will* have these effects. The experience of many federal systems (United States and Canada) is that local political control often means *less public participation and more control by local or nationally organized economic power.* Patterns of local citizen mobilization, the regulatory powers of local governments, and their access to capital or influence over capital markets all enter as critical variables. And decentralized planning and innovation in the end require some kind of aggregation, coordination, or overall "rule setting" or "rule maintenance." In the Swedish case these seem to be provided by the central government and by the political party system.

6. *Systems of Political Party Competition.* One of our principal conclusions has been that immobilism, stalemate, and "irrational" policy debates are serious problems in policy fields where volatile politics-technology interactions are involved and where social and political side effects are massive and long lasting. The question of how to bring about some sort of democratic control of technology is also long standing. How can policy debates be expanded to include those who are likely to be affected by such political and economic implications of technological choices in energy as the concentration of market power in energy-industry-banking complexes, health-safety-environmental concerns, fiscal strains on budget and on welfare services, and the perils of an international plutonium economy? And how can we adopt organizational measures to build checks on experts and on the role of technical advice, or to introduce decentralization in the energy supply system, without exacerbating the already marked fragmentation and incoherence of policy?

In the Swedish case, citizen mobilization and system coordination are provided by a party system wherein competing parties rely on explicit programmatic stands and maximum voter mobilization to compete for public support. The parties played an important role in the original nuclear debate in 1973, in the preparation of materials for the citizen study circles, and in articulating the issues in the 1976 parliamentary elections. In other countries, such as the United States, ad hoc citizens groups have been functionally equivalent, at least at the level of advocacy and voter mobilization. But such groups would seem to have a limited capacity for positive policy making and none at all for system coordination; nor are they likely to have resources to match those of the energy industry-government agency establishment.

7. *Elite Values and Ideologies.* A key factor in explaining the pattern of Swedish economic policy since the 1930s and its innovativeness at the substantive and institutional levels, has been the political influence and control exercised by the coalition between the Social Democratic Party and the trade unions. Economic growth and price stability are important policy goals, but full employment and equality have been more important. The employment problems attendant to increased rates of labor participation, the inflationary pressures that may arise as an increasing share of expenditure is accounted for by the public sector, and the capital accumulation problems that have emerged with reversed trends in materials prices are all being addressed in the context of these values.[40] If equality of the distribution of income and wealth and high rates of employment are policy imperatives, it may be easier to build an elite-mass

coalition in favor of less materials-intensive growth, lower growth rates, more or less stable shares to profits and to wages, and lower levels of personal consumption as against public consumption.[41]

Robert Alford, in a discussion of the relationships among pluralist, elitist, and class politics emphasizes the fluidity of these relationships and stresses the role that "power brokers" may play in straddling the divisions among interest groups, state agencies, and different levels of government. He holds open the possibility that such brokers might be able to "link together the historical sequence of processes which, in a stable symbiosis of elite and pluralist politics, reduces the possibilities of class politics to a minimum."[42] The Swedish Social Democratic party seems to see itself as such a broker and to have played policy roles consistent with such a function.

Conclusions

Research into social, economic, political, and organizational obstacles to change in energy policies and energy policy systems and how they might be overcome will be a complex and subtle task. The argument from Swedish experience was intended neither to glorify that case (there is a danger of overestimating its degree of success) nor to suggest that there is a single necessary path that nations must follow if they wish to reorganize their energy policy systems and launch a search for viable *transitional strategies*. The purpose was to isolate some of the main variables that help explain Swedish "exceptionalism" and to explore their relationship to each other and to those aspects of the energy policy system that our authors found constrained policy change. I hope that the analysis will have convinced the reader of the urgency of inquiring further into these matters and will have indicated some fruitful and provocative points of departure.

The Swedish pattern of response is, broadly speaking, a democratic socialist one. Societies in which egalitarian and participatory values are less highly salient, and/or where a strong regulatory role for the state is rejected in favor of "market mechanisms," may well prefer, or have no alternative to, policy strategies that put much more emphasis on price policy or on adversary regulatory politics and the mobilization of ad hoc groups to limit central governmental authority, or on anti-trust and anti-monopoly legislation. In other words, there are doubtless other strategies for dealing with the lags and rigidities I have identified. How effective they will be is a question that cannot be addressed here, but should clearly become a prime focus of energy policy research. But the lessons derived from the Swedish case do suggest at least three principal challenges for Neo-Liberal or Neo-Conservative reform strategies: On what bases can the real income reductions and life-style changes that seem inevitable (at least for the developed world) as a consequence of the rising prices and long-term availability limits of energy, be made acceptable to the members of ever more tightly interconnected and interdependent societies—national and global? Can political coalitions in favor of reform be forged and held together in the absence of mass political consensus on the goals to be achieved? How will it be possible to implement and enforce the market mechanism, or to regulate or control private concentrations of economic and political power without a strong and independent state?

Notes

1. H.E. Goeller and A.M. Weinberg, "The Age of Substitutability," *Science*, vol. 191 (February 20, 1976), pp. 683-89.

2. See C.J. Abrams and Todd LaPorte in Leon N. Lindberg (ed.), *Politics and the Future of Industrial Society* (New York: David McKay, 1976), especially pp. 25-40.

3. In Allen L. Hammond, "Coal Research (II): Gasification Faces an Uncertain Future," *Science*, vol. 193 (August 27, 1976).

4. Peter Odell in a book review of three books on energy in *Challenge* (September-October, 1976), pp. 55-56.

5. Ibid.

6. For example, see Alexander Cockburn and James Ridgeway, "Energy and the Politicians," *New York Review of Books*, April 15, 1976, pp. 19-25; see also Hammond, "Coal Research (II)."

7. "European Doubts About Nuclear Power," *Science*, vol. 194 (October 1976), p. 164; "British Body Sees Danger in Fast Breeder Reactors," *The Washington Post*, September 23, 1976; and Uno Svedin, "Sweden's Energy Debate," *Energy Policy*, September 1975, pp. 258-61.

8. Jeremy Bugler, "Countdown to the 'Breeder'," *New Statesman*, July 2, 1976, p. 13.

9. Allen V. Kneese, "The Faustian Bargain," *Resources*, Resources for the Future, Washington, D.C., September 1973, pp. 1-5.

10. Amory B. Lovins, "Energy Strategy: The Road Not Taken?" *Foreign Affairs*, vol. 55, no. 1 (October 1976), pp. 65-96.

11. All quotations in this paragraph are from Lovins, Ibid., pp. 91, 92, and 96.

12. Bruce Hannon, "Energy Conservation and the Consumer," *Science*, vol. 189 (July 11, 1975), pp. 95-102.

13. For an account of efforts to introduce such measures by initiative, see "Massachusetts Electricity Rates Are on the Ballot," *The Washington Post*, September 26, 1976.

14. On how U.S. urban transport systems were dismembered by General

Motors, Standard Oil of California, and Firestone Tire Co., see Barry Commoner, *The Poverty of Power*, pp. 188-91; Bradford C. Snell, "American Ground Transportation: A Proposal for Restructuring the Automobile, Truck, Bus, and Rail Industries," Subcommittee on Antitrust and Monopoly of the Committee of the Judiciary, U.S. Congress, Senate, Industrial Reorganization Act, Appendix to Part 4, Washington, D.C., 1974; Emma Rothschild, *Paradise Lost* (New York: Vintage, 1973).

15. See Luther J. Carter, "Energy Policy: Interdependence by 1985 May be Unreachable without BTU Tax," *Science*, vol. 191 (February 13, 1976), pp. 546-48. See also interview with Denis Hayes, "The Case for Conservation," ibid., p. 546.

16. Hannon, "Energy Conservation and the Consumer," p. 101.

17. See ibid, for a full discussion.

18. "Survey Finds Companies Hindered in Energy Plans," *The New York Times*, July 4, 1976, Reports findings of a study of 140 U.S. corporations carried out by Stewart W. Herman, James C. Cannon, and Alfred J. Malefatto.

19. Mark Northcross, "Who Will Own the Sun?" *The Progressive*, April 1976, p. 16.

20. Bent Sørensen, "Energy and Resources," *Science*, vol. 189, July 25, 1975, p. 256.

21. For a full discussion, see Commoner, *The Poverty of Power*, pp. 7-32.

22. Carol Steinhart and John Steinhart, *Energy: Sources, Use, and Role in Human Affairs* (North Scituate, Mass.: Duxbury Press, 1974), p. 316.

23. Hans Brems, "Swedish Fine Tuning," *Challenge*, March/April, 1976, pp. 39-42.

24. For accounts, see Tage Levin, "The Swedish Bill on Energy Policy," Appendix 1. "Local Discussion Groups—A case study of individual influence on the political decision-making process," Prime Minister's Office, Stockholm, June 26, 1975; also Ruth Link, "Skimp or Squander," *Sweden Now*, no. 1 (1975), pp. 22-26.

25. Leif Palmgren, "A Brief Discussion of Swedish Energy Policy," *Current Sweden*, no. 94 (October 1975), 5 pp.

26. "Sweden's Ruling Socialists Face Close Race in Election," *The Washington Post*, September 19, 1976.

27. Nu slösar vi med el igen," *Från Riksday och Department*, vol. 1, no. 26 (August 26, 1976).

28. See Jerome H. Garris, "The Atomic Energy Debate in Sweden and the U.S.," paper delivered at the Annual Conference of the Society for the Advancement of Scandinavian Studies, Madison, Wisc., May 2, 1975.

29. Robert C. Sahr, "Energy and Economic Growth Policy and Environmental Constraints: An Analysis of the Swedish Case," unpublished manuscript.

30. For a general discussion, see M. Donald Hancock, *Sweden: The Politics of Postindustrial Change* (Hinsdale, Ill.: The Dryden Press, 1972), Chapter 6.

31. Ibid., pp. 160-63; Uno Svedin, "Sweden's Energy Debate," pp. 258-61; and Hans Wachholz, "Nuclear Power—For and Against," *Current Sweden*, no. 94 (October 1975), 5 pp.

32. For a general discussion, see Leo Panitch, "The Development of Corporatism in Liberal Democracies," paper delivered at the 1976 Annual Meeting of the American Political Science Association, Chicago, September 2-5, 1976. See also Philippe Schmitter, "Still the Century of Corporatism," *The Review of Politics*, vol. 36, no. 1 (January 1974), pp. 85-131; and his "Modes of Interest Intermediation and Models of Societal Change in Western Europe," paper presented at the Congress of the International Political Science Association, Edinburgh, Scotland, August 15-20, 1976.

33. See especially Charles S. Maier, *Recasting Bourgeois Europe* (Princeton, N.J.: Princeton University Press, 1975).

34. For details, see ibid., and Schmitter, "Still the Century of Corporatism," passim.

35. See for example, Andrew Shonfield, *Modern Capitalism* (London: Oxford University Press, 1965), especially the chapters on the United Kingdom and United States.

36. Andrew Martin, "Is Democratic Control of Capitalism Possible" in Leon N. Lindberg et al. (eds.), *Stress and Contradiction in Modern Capitalism* (Lexington, Mass.: Lexington Books, 1975), pp. 13-56.

37. See Assar Lindbeck, *Swedish Economic Policy* (Berkeley: University of California Press, 1974); and Gunnar Eliasson, *Investment Funds in Operation*, Occasional Paper 2, National Institute of Economic Research, Stockholm, 1965.

38. Hancock, *Sweden: The Politics of Postindustrial Change*, pp. 156-60.

39. Ibid., pp. 205-05; Nils Andrén, *Modern Swedish Government* (Stockholm: Almquist & Wiksell, 1961); and Brian Chapman, *British Government Observed* (London: George Allen & Unwin, Ltd., 1963).

40. On the discussion of employment and rising public expenditures, see the statement by LO official Rudolf Meidner, "The Trade Union Movement and the Public Sector," speech delivered at the 20th Convention of Public Services International, New York, October 10, 1973. On the capital formation debate, see Andrew Martin, "Capital Formation Issues in the United States and Sweden," unpublished manuscript, and his "The Politics of Economic Development in Advanced Industrial Societies" in Ronald Inglehart (ed.), "Problems of Advanced Industrial Society," a special issue of *Comparative Political Studies* (forthcoming, October 1977).

41. For an argument in favor of such an approach to economic policy based on a U.S.-West German comparison, see Burkhard Strumpel, "The Changing

Face of Advanced Industrial Economies," to appear in Ronald Inglehart (ed.), ibid.

42. Alford, "Participation and Public Policy: Paradigms of Power," paper delivered at the 1976 Annual Meeting of the American Political Science Association, Chicago, September 2-5, 1976, p. 14.

List of Contributors

I.C. Bupp
Harvard Business School, Cambridge, Mass.

J.H. Chesshire
Science Policy Research Unit, University of Sussex, England

István Dobozi
Institute for World Economics, The Hungarian Academy of Sciences, Budapest

David W. Fisher
Department of Man-Environment Studies, University of Waterloo, Waterloo, Ontario

J.K. Friend
Institute for Operational Research, London and Coventry

Robert F. Keith
Department of Man-Environment Studies, University of Waterloo, Waterloo, Ontario

Måns Lönnroth
Delegation on Energy Policy, Secretariat of Future Studies, Stockholm

J. de B. Pollard
Institute for Operational Research, London and Coventry

Louis Puiseux
Direction générale des Etudes, Electricité de France, Paris

T.L. Sankar
Planning Commission, New Delhi

Dominique Saumon
Department of Energy Systems, Electricité de France, Paris

J. Stringer
Australian Graduate School of Management, University of New South Wales, Sydney

A.J. Surrey
Science Policy Research Unit, University of Sussex, England

About the Editor

Leon N. Lindberg is professor of political science and environmental studies at the University of Wisconsin-Madison. He has held research appointments at the Brookings Institution, the Carnegie Endowment for International Peace (Geneva), the Center for International Affairs, Harvard University, and The Center for Advanced Study in the Behavioral Science, Stanford, and has been a visiting professor at the University of Geneva and at the Institut Universitaire de hautes études internationales. During 1971-1972 and 1974-1976 he was chairman of the Council for European Studies. His publications include *The Political Economy of Energy Policy: A Projection for Capitalist Society* (1976, coeditor and coauthor), *Politics and The Future of Industrial Society* (1976, editor and coauthor), *Stress and Contradiction in Modern Capitalism: Public Policy and the Theory of the State* (1975, general editor and coauthor), *Regional Integration: Theory and Research* (1971, coeditor and coauthor), *Europe's Would-Be Polity* (1970, coauthor), and *The Political Dynamics of European Economic Integration* (1963). A book entitled *System Change and Policy Response in Advanced Capitalist Nations* is forthcoming. He is currently directing a research project for the Brookings Institution on the politics of global inflation.